Making Early Medieval Societies

Making Early Medieval Societies explores a fundamental question: what held the small- and large-scale communities of the late Roman and early medieval West together, at a time when the world seemed to be falling apart? Historians and anthropologists have traditionally asked parallel questions about the rise and fall of empires and how societies create a sense of belonging and social order in the absence of strong governmental institutions. This book draws on classic and more recent anthropologists' work to consider dispute settlement and conflict management during and after the end of the Roman Empire. Contributions range across the internecine rivalries of late Roman bishops, the marital disputes of warrior kings, and the tension between religious leaders and the unruly crowds in Western Europe after the first millennium – all considering the mechanisms through which conflict could be harnessed as a force for social stability or an engine for social change.

KATE COOPER is Professor of Ancient History at the University of Manchester. Her most recent book is *Band of Angels: The Forgotten World of Early Christian Women* (2013). Other publications include *The Fall of the Roman Household* (Cambridge, 2007) and the collection of essays, co-edited with Julia Hillner, *Religion, Dynasty and Patronage in Early Christian Rome* (Cambridge, 2007).

CONRAD LEYSER is Fellow and Tutor in History at Worcester College, University of Oxford. He is the author of *Authority and Asceticism from Augustine to Gregory the Great* (2000). Other publications include the collection of essays, co-edited with Lesley Smith, *Motherhood, Religion, and Society in Medieval Europe, 400–1400* (2011).

Making Early Medieval Societies

Conflict and Belonging in the Latin West, 300–1200

Edited by

Kate Cooper

University of Manchester

and

Conrad Leyser

University of Oxford

CAMBRIDGE
UNIVERSITY PRESS

CAMBRIDGE
UNIVERSITY PRESS

University Printing House, Cambridge CB2 8BS, United Kingdom

Cambridge University Press is part of the University of Cambridge.

It furthers the University's mission by disseminating knowledge in the pursuit of education, learning and research at the highest international levels of excellence.

www.cambridge.org
Information on this title: www.cambridge.org/9781107138803

First published 2016

Printed in the United States of America by Sheridan Books, Inc.

A catalogue record for this publication is available from the British Library

Library of Congress Cataloguing in Publication data
Cooper, Kate, 1960– editor. | Leyser, Conrad, editor.
Making early medieval societies : conflict and belonging in the Latin West, 300–1200 / edited by Kate Cooper and Conrad Leyser.
LCCN 2015032436| ISBN 9781107138803 (hardback) | ISBN 9781316503607 (paperback)
LCSH: Civilization, Medieval. | Church history – Middle Ages, 600–1500. | Social structure – Europe – History – To 1500. | Conflict management – Europe – History – To 1500.
LCC CB351 .M234 2016 | DDC 909.07–dc23
LC record available at http://lccn.loc.gov/2015032436

ISBN 978-1-107-13880-3 Hardback
ISBN 978-1-316-50360-7 Paperback

In Memoriam Mary Douglas

Contents

Preface and acknowledgements

This volume traces its roots to a conference held in 2005 at the University of Manchester, 'The Peace in the Feud: History and Anthropology 1955–2005'. We met to celebrate a fiftieth anniversary. In the spring of 1955, the Professor of Social Anthropology at Manchester, Max Gluckman, delivered a series of lectures on BBC Radio's Third Programme, entitled 'Custom and Conflict in Africa', exploring how the tensions endemic in a number of African traditional societies were held in check by the power of tradition. Gluckman's book by the same name came out later in the year. His aim, he averred, was to study 'how men quarrel in terms of certain customary allegiances but are restrained from violence through other conflicting allegiances which are also enjoined on them by custom. The result is that conflicts in one set of relationships, over a wider range of society or through a longer period of time, lead to the reestablishment of social cohesion.'[1] There was a paradoxical 'peace in the feud', Gluckman argued: while the forces of vengeance and violence were perhaps intrinsically destructive, they could be harnessed to socially constructive purpose.

Gluckman explicitly sought to attract the attention of historians of medieval Europe, and his challenge was met with a ready response from his Manchester colleague, Michael Wallace-Hadrill. In 1959, the *Bulletin of the John Rylands Library* carried an article by Wallace-Hadrill, 'The Blood-Feud of the Franks', which offered a re-interpretation of revenge violence in Merovingian Gaul precisely along the lines suggested by Gluckman. The nature of Wallace-Hadrill's collegial contact with Gluckman has not been documented, and it has yet to be established whether we are to imagine sustained face-to-face conversations in a Manchester common room or a more intermittent exchange conducted largely via print and broadcast.

Whatever its medium or extent, the Gluckman/Wallace-Hadrill encounter at Manchester remains one of the more influential moments

[1] M. Gluckman, *Custom and Conflict in Africa* (Oxford, 1955), p. 2.

of mid-twentieth-century intellectual history, for it gave new life to the close relationship that had persisted between anthropologists and medieval historians in the English-speaking world in the early days of anthropology as a free-standing discipline. Many pioneering anthropologists, such as E. E. Evans-Pritchard, had taken their first degrees in History at a time when the study of medieval charters was seen as the foundation of any historian's training.

As a result of the 2005 conference, an increasingly hardy band of colleagues began to meet and to exchange drafts. Our attention was drawn back to Gluckman's central questions: how does a social order hold together when centralized structures of authority are weak, or absent altogether? How do societies harness conflict to reinforce social order? We hope our readers will agree that the conversation between historians and anthropologists is still very much alive.

We remain grateful to the several sponsors of the original Conference, 'The Peace in the Feud', held under the auspices of the Manchester Centre for Late Antiquity. At the University of Manchester, these were: the Centre for Inter-disciplinary Research in the Arts, the School of Arts, Languages, and Cultures, the Faculty of Humanities, the School of Social Sciences, the Wellcome Trust Unit, and the Manchester Museum, which hosted the Conference Dinner in the shadow of a large dinosaur skeleton. Sponsorship came also from Jean Monnet Centre, and from Blackwells, who published Gluckman's *Custom and Conflict*. Our abiding thanks to the conference speakers whose contributions are not represented in the pages which follow: Philippe Buc, Stuart Carroll, Guy Halsall, John Hudson, Maia Green, the late J. D. Y. Peel, David Pratten, the late Terence Ranger, Richard Rathbone, Lyn Schumaker, Chris Wickham, and Ian Wood. Further thanks are due to Philippe Buc, Maia Green, and to Stephen D. White, who led postgraduate workshops, as did Richard Rathbone, whose conversations with the editors at Cumberland Lodge in the mid-1990s were a lasting source of inspiration.

In the making of the volume, we have had support from the John Fell Fund at Oxford University and the Lightbody Fund at Worcester College, which enabled us to meet to discuss drafts. We are beholden to Hannah Williams, for unstinting and indispensable editorial support, extending over many years. Our thanks also to successive editorial teams at Cambridge University Press, latterly under the genial guidance of Elizabeth Friend-Smith. Finally, we wish to thank the volume's contributors for exceeding our most ambitious hopes of scholarly collaboration, and for having the patience, grace, and sheer staying power to wrestle the intensity and excitement of face-to-face discussion into print.

All of those who were present at the Conference will remember the closing remarks of Mary Douglas. Her own contribution to the conversation between History and Anthropology needs no introduction. It is to her memory that we dedicate this volume.

KATE COOPER AND CONRAD LEYSER

Contributors

RICCARDO BOF, University of Manchester

KATE COOPER, University of Manchester

MARIOS COSTAMBEYS, University of Liverpool

PAUL FOURACRE, University of Manchester

CONRAD LEYSER, Worcester College, University of Oxford

R. I. MOORE, Newcastle University

DAVID NATAL, Österreichische Akademie der Wissenschaften

HELMUT REIMITZ, Princeton University

MARTIN J. RYAN, Brighton

STEPHEN D. WHITE, Emory University

JAMIE WOOD, University of Lincoln

Introduction: making early medieval societies

Conrad Leyser

As a title, 'Making early medieval societies' is, at best, oxymoronic: to many, it will just seem like wishful thinking. In the default view, 'the Middle Ages' is when societies fell apart (at least in the Latin West, which is the focus of this book). Medieval times begin with the fall of Rome; they end with the chaos of the Italian Wars, or, more locally, the Wars of the Roses. In between, order is occasionally and temporarily restored, as in the Empire of Charlemagne – but disintegration is never far away. The Carolingian Empire collapsed after three generations, and, according to a highly influential school of thought, civil society was cut back to the bone at the hands of feuding warlords. Seen in this light, the whole medieval period stands introduced by Augustine, bishop of Hippo, who died in 430 with barbarians at the gates of his city. In the *City of God*, Augustine cast an apparently bleak eye on what held the social order together. Two people who did not speak the same language had less in common with each other, he opined than a man and his dog: only through the massive exercise of force had the Roman Empire been able to bring 'peace' to the world. The State, Augustine famously asserted, was robbery on a grand scale.[1] What price, then, 'making early medieval societies'?

While most twenty-first century medievalists would object loudly to this stereotyped view of their period, tacitly, we consent. Of course we know that the very idea of the 'Middle Ages' is no more than a messy set of polemical claims disseminated by various interest groups in Western Europe from the self-styled 'Renaissance' onwards;[2] and that the standard periodization of European history (ancient-medieval-early modern) has been disrupted by the emergence of 'Late Antiquity' in the second half of the twentieth

[1] Augustine, *De civitate Dei* XIX. 7 on peace; IV. 4 on the State as robbery. My thanks to the contributors for their several suggestions; none of them should be held responsible for the shortcomings of what follows.

[2] See P. Burke, *The Renaissance Sense of the Past* (London, 1969); and now I. Wood, *The Modern Origins of the Early Middle Ages* (Oxford, 2013).

century.[3] The rise of global history may help us to see still more clearly the parochialism of the whole schema.[4] For all that, 'medievalism' is still pervasive, and nowhere more so than where the early Middle Ages are concerned. Few historians celebrate their arrival. Indeed, the past ten years have witnessed a pulse of energy in asserting that the end of the ancient world was a violent catastrophe.[5] Those who dissent cast the process in terms of 'downsizing' or 'abatement' – but even this more neutral language colludes in the notion that the Middle Ages were in some way second best. In the absence of the State (whether Roman or Carolingian), early medieval societies in the West are seen to have coped more or less well. 'Degradations' from imperial order might even be 'possibilities', but that is about as far as most early medievalists are prepared to go.[6] The mood here is post-imperial, perhaps in Britain especially: we are after empire, so were they.[7]

The problem is, we have not weaned ourselves away from a conception of history where the State is central, the source of all meaning and goodness. In the nineteenth century, when medievalists pioneered the establishment of History as a discipline for the training of citizens, this worked to the advantage of the Middle Ages. The fall of ancient Rome was seen in terms of progress towards the modern nation-state. However rough and ready, the barbarian kingdoms were seen as an advance on imperial tyranny. It was not long, however, before traditional prejudices reasserted themselves. In most conventional histories of the State, the Middle Ages

[3] See M. Vessey, 'The Demise of the Christian Writer and the Remaking of "Late Antiquity": From H.-I. Marrou's St Augustine (1938) to Peter Brown's Holy Man (1983)', *Journal of Early Christian Studies*, 6 (1998), pp. 377–41; cf. also the hostile discussion of A. Giardina, 'Esplosione di tardoantico', *Studi Storici*, 40 (1999), 157–80; the (less hostile) A. Cameron, 'The "Long" Late Antiquity: a Late Twentieth-Century Model', in T. P. Wiseman (ed.), *Classics in Progress: Essays on Ancient Greece and Rome* (Oxford, 2002), pp. 165–91; and W. Liebeschuetz, 'The Birth of Late Antiquity', *Antiquité Tardive*, 12 (2004), 253–61.

[4] A new periodization is proposed by G. Fowden, *Before and After Muhammad: the First Millennium Refocussed* (Princeton, NJ, 2014). R. I. Moore, 'Medieval Europe in World History', in C. Lansing and E. English (eds.), *A Companion to the Medieval World* (Chichester, 2009), pp. 563–80 argues for the utility of the Middle Ages on a world history scale. Both agree that the eleventh century is a turning point.

[5] See in particular P. Heather, *The Fall of Rome: A New History of Rome and the Barbarians* (London, 2005), and B. Ward-Perkins, *The Fall of Rome and the End of Civilization* (Oxford, 2005).

[6] C. J. Wickham, 'The Other Transition: From the Ancient World to Feudalism', *Past & Present*, 103 (1984), 3–36, at 36.

[7] As a glance at the titles of recent British discussions might suggest: J. Smith, *Europe After Rome: A New Cultural History, 500–1000* (Oxford, 2005); C.J. Wickham, *The Inheritance of Rome: A New History of Europe 400–1000* (London, 2009); P. Booth, *Crisis of Empire: Doctrine and Dissent at the End of Late Antiquity* (Berkeley, CA, 2014). On 'optimistic' American functionalism, see Stephen. D. White in this volume, below pp. 226–7.

come off badly: the epoch is defined as the period in which public justice falls into private hands. 'Feudal anarchy' reigns, as predatory lords roam the continent. This story of the privatization of justice shores up, in a very basic way, our sense of modernity.

The fable of privatization, if we may call it that, can be invoked whenever one chooses to initiate 'a medieval period'. Two junctures are most commonplace: the fifth century, after the fall of Rome, and the tenth century, after the end of the Carolingians.[8] Fashion veers one way, then the other, as to which juncture is more popular. In the past generation or so, scholars have run from one side of the boat to the other, as it were. The renewed vigour of the 'Fall of Rome' debate coincides precisely with the draining away of energy from the debate over the 'Feudal Mutation' around the Year 1000. Holding both periods in the same field of vision, so as to compare the plausibility of the privatization fable, seems to be beyond us: the attempt to do so is one of the key impulses behind this book.[9]

To query this fable is not to pretend that imperial and post-imperial Europe were the same as each other – but it is to insist that the State, whether Roman or Carolingian, looked a lot bigger when it was no longer there. The whole notion of a 'medieval privatization of power', whenever it is deployed, trades on a fantastical image of imperial public majesty, a fantasy that took hold *after* the formal collapse of empire, and that has lasted ever since.[10]

We should adjust for this distortion in any discussion of public and private spheres. In the ancient and medieval world, after all, the sphere of 'the private' was greater than even the wildest contemporary right-wing scenario. Thus family, economic, and religious life were 'private' enterprises. They fell into the domain of the household. 'The public' was strictly and narrowly defined as that which pertained to official business of State. Government in this period was a crude, lean mechanism

[8] For critique of the privatization model for the Year 1000, see Stephen D. White, 'Tenth Century Courts at Mâcon and the Perils of Structuralist History: Re-reading Burgundian Judicial Institutions', in W. C. Brown and P. Górecki (eds.), *Conflict in Medieval Europe: Changing Perspectives on Society and Culture* (Aldershot, 2003), pp. 37–68 and F. L. Cheyette, 'Some Reflections on Violence, Reconciliation, and the "Feudal Revolution"', in the same volume, pp. 243–64. See also T. Reuter's contribution to 'Debate: the "Feudal Revolution"', *Past & Present*, 155 (1997), 176–95.

[9] See, for example, Cheyette, 'Some Reflections'; and M. Innes, *State and Society in the Early Middle Ages: the Middle Rhine Valley, 400–1000* (Cambridge, 2000). Both offer a critique of the Year 1000 debate, but in both accounts, 'privatization' in the earlier period is taken as unproblematic: 'medieval society' is seen to take shape in the sixth and seventh centuries, after the fall of Rome and with the seizure of public power by incoming Germanic elites.

[10] See, for example, J. L. Nelson, Review of *The Peace of God: Social Violence and Religious Response in France Around the Year 1000*, ed. T. Head, R. Landes (Ithaca, NY, 1992), *Speculum*, 60 (1994), 163–9.

designed to maximize the benefits of surplus extraction, and to minimize the amount of 'governing' involved. When the Roman State in the West ceased to function, it makes little sense to describe this as a 'privatization' of power, because most power in this world was already 'private': the Roman father's word was absolute.[11]

In this book, then, our starting point is not governmental power, but the prior and basic question of social order. What was it that held societies together? How did these social bonds change? To ask and to answer these basic questions, we turn for inspiration to social anthropology; that said, readers should be warned at once that we are working with a minimally theorized notion of 'the social'. We are more interested in the language of our sources than in constructing our own taxonomies, and accordingly have taken a broad, unfussy view as to what constitutes a 'social bond'. As one similarly minded scholar puts it, 'Between coercion and chance lie the associations that are to some extent chosen'.[12] These do include family relations, to the making and remaking of which people in this period devoted much of their energies; these also, emphatically, include religious ties. Indeed, given the etymology of *religio*, the element of 'bonding' in religious association would have been obvious to Latinate contemporaries, in a way that modern audiences still struggle to recapture.

All of this lands us necessarily squarely in the domain of 'the private' as defined before the eighteenth century. We do not, however, look entirely to collapse 'the public' or 'the institutional' as categories into a notional pre-modern world of exclusively personal conflicts and exchanges.[13] Both the family and religion had coercive, public, and hence political and institutional dimensions. The State, necessarily, enters into the discussion. What we need to make possible is a history where the rise and fall of systems of government is the symptom, not the cause of wider shifts in social order.

Is this to reinvent the wheel? At least two kinds of account have long put the social order ahead of the State: one, the weaker version, comes broadly speaking out of varieties of social and economic history, the

[11] See K. Cooper, 'Closely Watched Households: Visibility, Exposure and Private Power in the Roman *Domus*', *Past & Present*, 197 (2007), 3–33; and below in this volume. Work in progress by Hannah Probert (Sheffield) will follow the development of *pater potestas* into the early Middle Ages.

[12] R. Mottahedeh, *Loyalty and Leadership in an Early Islamic Society* (rev. edn., London, 2001), p. 5.

[13] See W. Pohl, 'Staat und Herrschaft im Frühmittelalter: Überlegungen zum Forschungstand', in S. Airlie, W. Pohl, and H. Reimitz (eds.), *Staat im frühen Mittelalter* (Vienna, 2006), pp. 9–38, esp. 13–15. A warning is here issued about the dangers of 'primitivizing' medieval forms of political association – aimed in part at Anglo-American admirers of the work of Otto Brunner (on whom, see Stephen D. White's contribution, below pp. 231–8).

other stronger version out of cultural history. In the weaker version of the story, what happens in our period is that the State withers away, while the ruling elite continue, their pattern of life largely uninterrupted. This view can take different forms. A classic version is the Pirenne thesis, which views the fall of the Roman State in the fifth and sixth centuries as a non-event. Ancient networks of exchange across the Mediterranean, Pirenne insisted, were not disrupted by the political changes in the western half of the Empire.[14]

A different application of the same basic idea is to be found in close studies of elites. John Matthews' *Western Aristocracies and Imperial Court*, for example, in particular as read by one medievalist, conjured a view of aristocratic power stretching back to the Roman Republic and forward into the medieval centuries.[15] On this account, the real motor of history is not political power, but the social, cultural, and economic power of what may be a very ancient regime.

Pirenne and Matthews share the conviction that late ancient/early medieval society is impervious to the epiphenomenon of political change: thus the weaker version. The stronger view is that the creation of different forms of social relationship actually overpowers the State. The classic example of this is Edward Gibbon's *History of the Decline and Fall of the Roman Empire*. Gibbon, notoriously, went so far as to argue that Christian superstition – a form of fanaticism or hypocrisy – corroded the entire fabric of the Roman social order, so that the State in the West stood no chance of surviving.

The great modern exponent of this tradition is Peter Brown. In his first collection of essays composed in the 1960s, *Religion and Society in the Age of St Augustine*, Brown looks to render vivid to readers '[t]he sudden flooding of the inner life into social forms'. 'This', he continues, 'is what distinguishes the Late Antique period, of the third century onwards, from the classical world'.[16] Christianity here does not consume the Empire: where Gibbon decries superstitious otherworldliness, Brown sees 'the holy', a force strong enough to supplement, or indeed create, institutions

[14] H. Pirenne, *Mohammed and Charlemagne*, tr. B. Miall (New York, 1939); Pirenne of course also argued that the Carolingian Empire made little difference to the social order of the Latin West: only the rise of towns after the first millennium created a new network of exchange. See his *Medieval Cities: Their Origins and the Revival of Trade*, tr. F. D. Halsey (Princeton, 1925); and for comment, J. Dhondt, 'Henri Pirenne: historien des institutions urbaines', *Annali della fondazione italiana per la storia amministrativa* 3 (1966), 81–129.

[15] J. Matthews, *Western Aristocracies and Imperial Court, 360–425* (Oxford, 1975); reviewed by P. Wormald, *Journal of Roman Studies*, 66 (1976), 217–26.

[16] P. R. L. Brown, *Religion and Society in the Age of St Augustine* (London, 1972), p. 13.

in this world.[17] But Brown shares absolutely with Gibbon the determination that religion is a social phenomenon, independent of the State.

These are all highly familiar directions of travel – and yet medievalists have not followed them through. Our suspicion is that an overturning of basic assumptions is within reach. Stereotypically, the Middle Ages witnessed a contraction of the social, a move away from a cosmopolitan world of strangers into the 'face-to-face' association of people who know each other. We ask whether the picture can be inverted. Throwing off the Roman State, new forms of association, newly extended trans-regional bonds, flourished in the Latin West. The same may be true in the post-Carolingian context. As a student of upper Lotharingia and Champagne has recently remarked, the end of empire 'was more likely to be a consequence not a cause' of changes in the nature of social relations on the ground.[18] With a degree of reluctance, we offer the slogan, 'The Middle Ages: Thin State – Big Society'.[19]

Conflict, cohesion, and the anthropological turn

'Big Society' in our period was replete with conflict. We make no attempt to efface this. On the contrary, our focus is on the function of conflict in the forging of new social bonds. This a fundamental feature of modern sociological discussion. Georg Simmel argued consistently that society depended for its existence on conflict.[20] We take our own cue from Max

[17] P. R. L. Brown, 'The Rise and Function of the Holy Man in Late Antiquity', *Journal of Roman Studies*, 61 (1971), 80–101; a theme developed in his *The Cult of Saints: Its Rise and Function in Late Antiquity* (London, 1982), and subsequently *The Rise of Western Christendom: Triumph and Diversity, 200–1000* (2nd edn. Oxford, 2002; rev. edn 2013).

[18] C. West, *Reframing the Feudal Revolution: Political and Social Transformation Between Marne and Moselle, c.800-c.1100* (Cambridge, 2013), p. 168.

[19] For the benefit of some possibly bewildered readers: 'Big Society' was an election slogan of the Conservative Party in the UK elections of 2010. On the one hand it signalled a retreat from the extreme position of Mrs Thatcher that 'There is no such thing as Society'. On the other, it served to rebrand the familiar Conservative nostrum that the State should scale back in the provision of public services. 'Big Society' was thus a euphemism for 'privatization'. The phrase went on to acquire a degree of academic notoriety, as the UK Arts and Humanities Research Council was seen to have encouraged research into 'Big Society'. See www.thebigsociety.co.uk; and www.opendemocracy.net/ourkingdom/bob-brecher/ahrc-and-big-society-reflections-on-neo-liberal-takeover-of-academy. My thanks to Caroline Humfress and Tom Lambert for helpful discussions here.

[20] G. Simmel, 'The Sociology of Conflict: I', *American Journal of Sociology*, 9 (1903), 490–515. Cited by, for example, P. J. Geary in 'Vivre en conflit dans une France sans état: typologie des méchanismes de règlement des conflits, 1050–1200', *Annales E.S.C.* (1986), pp. 1107–33, trans. and repr. as 'Living with Conflicts in Stateless France: a Typology of Conflict Management Mechanisms, 1050–1200', in Geary, *Living with the Dead in the Middle Ages* (Ithaca, NY, 1994), 116–24, with the discussion in Brown and Górecki, *Conflict in Medieval Europe*, at pp. 17–18.

Gluckman's classic study, 'The Peace in the Feud', published in the opening issue of *Past & Present*, and then again the same year in Gluckman's *Custom and Conflict in Africa*.[21] Gluckman's message, which drew on the research of Evans Pritchard, was one of reassurance. African 'tribal society' might seem to be riven with conflict and liable to self-destruction in an endless cycle of violence between feuding families. Such conflicts, Gluckman showed, far from being random or relentless, had their own carefully modulated rhythm: custom ensured that conflicts were self-limiting, and even generative of social cohesion.

Gluckman's insights, and those of the 'Manchester School', have themselves been generative of a half century of discussion by students of the early medieval feud and of violence in general (as Stephen D. White surveys with brio below). In 1959, his colleague in History at Manchester, Michael Wallace-Hadrill, published a study, 'The Blood-Feud of the Franks', in which he adduced Gluckman's study to argue that there was an element of restraint in the apparently untrammelled savagery of the Merovingians, as narrated by Gregory of Tours.[22] The extent to which Wallace-Hadrill actually drew inspiration from direct collegial contact with Gluckman is debated.[23] Two things are clear, however. First, Gluckman actively hoped that medievalists, with whom he will have studied prior to becoming an Africanist, would take notice of his observations;[24] and second that Wallace-Hadrill's essay, however casually, did just that. Medievalists went on to produce specific studies of feud among the peoples of early medieval Europe;[25] more broadly in the 1980s, they took a now well-observed anthropological turn, in landmark volumes on dispute settlement and on community formation.[26]

[21] M. Gluckman, 'The Peace in the Feud', *Past & Present*, 8 (1955), 1–14; Gluckman, 'The Peace in the Feud', in Gluckman, *Custom and Conflict in Africa* (Oxford, 1955), chap. 1 (pp. 1–26).

[22] J. M. Wallace-Hadrill, 'The Blood-Feud of the Franks', *Bulletin of the John Rylands Library, Manchester*, 41 (1958–9), 459–87; repr. in Wallace-Hadrill, *The Long-Haired Kings and Other Studies in Frankish History* (London, 1962), pp. 121–47.

[23] I. Wood, '"The Blood-Feud of the Franks": A Historiographical Legend', *Early Medieval Europe*, 12 (2006), 489–504. See also B. Rosenwein, 'Francia and Polynesia: Rethinking Anthropological Approaches', in G. Algazi, V. Groebner, and B. Jussen (eds.), *Negotiating the Gift: Pre-modern Figurations of Exchange* (Göttingen, 1991), pp. 361–79.

[24] Gluckman, *Custom and Conflict in Africa*, p. 4.

[25] See, for example, K. Leyser, *Rule and Conflict in an Early Medieval Society: Ottonian Saxony* (London, 1979), esp. p. 102.

[26] S. Reynolds, *Kingdoms and Communities in Western Europe, 900–1300* (Oxford, 1984); W. Davies and P. Fouracre (eds.), *The Settlement of Disputes in Early Medieval Europe* (Cambridge, 1986); followed by the same editors', *Property and Power in Early Medieval Europe* (Cambridge, 1996); and *The Languages of Gift in the Early Middle Ages* (Cambridge, 2010), in which J. L. Nelson's 'Introduction' reflects on the group's engagement with anthropology (pp. 1–17).

Charting the whole relationship between History and Social Anthropology in the past two or three generations is beyond our remit.[27] A synoptic view would be that we have been through at least two stages of the romance comedy plot: the couple meet, there are complications ... While we await the resolution, we can spell out some of the costs and the benefits of a social anthropological approach as we see them.

A first danger is that the anthropological turn will serve only to reinforce stereotypes of the Middle Ages by lending an exotic primitivism to the period. We may appeal to, say, the Nuer of the Sudan to help us imagine medieval Europe as an alien social world, but when we posit that medieval allegiances were 'tribal', all we have done is to create an inverted image of what we perceive modern society to be. There is an ideological investment here of which we should beware, and medievalists have been highly alert to this.[28]

Some scholars, indeed, have gone further in identifying a full circularity of argument in the use by medievalists of social anthropology. In one view, anthropological theories of ritual are derived, ultimately, from the ritual specialists of the medieval Church: these 'theories' can never attain analytical perspective on the period from which they descend.[29] Sometimes the circularity is patent. Anthropologists (especially, it seems, of Africa) come to their material with an explicit sense of medieval Europe as a useful point of reference for understanding their material.[30] This exported European cultural baggage is then re-imported by medievalists as a form of 'external' perspective. What Richard Rathbone has called 'The Analogy' between tribal Africa and medieval Europe can be an object lesson in false glamour.[31]

A third, perennial, danger is that historians in the thrall of anthropology lose track of time. In our envy of the anthropologist's participant observer status, our 'ethnographies' of medieval societies, while 'richly textured',

[27] For the United States, see further Brown and Górecki, *Conflict in Medieval Europe*, pp. 6–10.

[28] See Pohl, 'Staat und Herrschaft'; Davies and Fouracre (eds.), *The Languages of Gift*, pp. 259–60. On the same tendency within anthropology, see A. Kuper, *The Invention of Primitive Society: Transformations of an Illusion* (London, 1988).

[29] P. Buc, *The Dangers of Ritual: Between Early Medieval Texts and Social Scientific Theory* (Princeton, NJ, 2001).

[30] Gluckman, *Custom and Conflict*, p. 45. Also J.-L. Amselle, *Mestizo Logics: Anthropology of Identity in Africa and Elsewhere* (Stanford, CA, 1998), p. 74, appealing to Jacques Le Goff, *L'Imaginaire medieval* (Paris, 1985), p. 341. Amselle is in turn invoked in Airlie, Pohl, and Reimitz (eds.), *Staat im frühen Mittelalter*, p. 197. See also P. Geary, 'Gift Exchange and Social Science Modelling: the Limitations of a Construct', in Algazi et al. (eds.), *Negotiating the Gift*, pp. 129–40.

[31] Richard Rathbone, in discussion at 'The Peace in the Feud: History and Anthropology, 1955–2005', Conference at the University of Manchester, 2005.

can fail to include any account of change, or indeed any analytical component. Ironically, the most stringent warning here has been issued by an anthropologist. Empirical observation, Paul Dresch cautions, avails us nothing unless we also notice the cultural frames that give meaning to any of the social dramas we see unfolding. Dresch takes medievalists to task for their fascination both with Gluckman, and with Pierre Bourdieu. Gluckman, in his view, was driven by an unexamined set of 'common sense' assumptions; by contrast, Bourdieu, while methodologically more articulate, nonetheless sustains an equally unreflective account of humans as self-interested strategists. This view of agency leaches culturally and historically specific content when it is applied.[32]

All of that said, there are some real benefits to the History–Anthropology encounter (as Dresch would not dispute). Social anthropology decentres the State, and refocuses attention on the family and religion. These were topics expressly excluded from the purview of History at the moment of its professional inception in the nineteenth century – not coincidentally, the zenith of the European nation-state across the world. By contrast, the disciplinary origins of Anthropology reside in the era of imperial 'abatement' in the mid- twentieth century.[33] In Britain, the first Departments of Anthropology were established after the Second World War, when the failings of the European nation- state were all too clear, not least to governments themselves. Max Gluckman and his colleagues had the explicit brief from the British government to answer the question, whether it was safe to move to 'indirect rule' of the colonies. This required the applied study of kinship groups in segmented warrior societies. 'There is no such thing as the power of the State', Radcliffe-Brown announced, as his colleagues set about devising a new typology of political life.[34]

Meanwhile, French ethnographers, above all Claude Levi-Strauss, also started with kinship, albeit from a different perspective. The French tradition focussed on exchange rather than conflict. 'Society' for

[32] P. Dresch, 'Legalism, Anthropology, and History: a View from Part of Anthropology', in Dresch and H. Skoda (eds.), *Legalism:Anthropology and History* (Oxford, 2012), pp. 1–39, esp. pp. 5–15. For a sympathetic anthropology of Bourdieu and his work, see T. Jenkins, *The Life of Property: House, Family, and Inheritance in Béarn, South-West France* (New York, 2010), esp. pp. 81–2 (on strategy), and pp. 129–58. On strategy, see also Brown and Górecki, *Conflict*, ix–x.

[33] See A. Kuper, *Anthropology and Anthropologists: the Modern British School* (3rd edn. London, 1996); J. Goody, *The Expansive Moment: the Rise of Social Anthropology in Britain and Africa, 1918–1970* (Cambridge, 1995).

[34] M. Fortes and E. E. Evans Pritchard (eds.), *African Political Systems* (Oxford, 1940) signals in their Editor's Note (p. vii): 'We hope this book will be of interest and use to those who have the task of administering African peoples'. There follows A. R. Radcliffe Brown's preface, with its refusal of State power as a useful category (p. xxiii).

Levi-Strauss began with the incest taboo.[35] The prohibition on marriage within kin groups led to the exchange of women between different families. 'Social', as opposed to 'natural', relations developed from here. This distinction between nature and culture of course had its problems. Notoriously, two different schools for the anthropology of kinship developed: while the French approach remained centred on alliances between families, the English anthropology of kinship insisted that the family line and its maintenance was the key locus of meaning.[36] In the event, after a generation of intensive discussion, anthropologists abandoned 'kinship' as a useful category of analysis: it was no longer seen to hold the key to social organization. Only recently, with fieldwork conducted not only in former colonies, but in IVF clinics in Britain and the United States, has kinship returned to the anthropological table.[37] Historians have been slow to respond to these vicissitudes – but any discussion of kinship has the enduring merit of taking us into the tissue of social relations, and away from the State as the starting point.[38]

Engagement with anthropology has also lent energy to the history of religion. Before the era of professionalization, historians had discussed religion as a matter of course – witness, however hostile, Edward Gibbon – but a consequence of History's conscription by the nation-state was to inhibit this. Religion fell foul of 'the omission [from historical study] of those parts of human experience which are not related to public affairs', and this was still an issue at the turn of the 1960s.[39] Victorian History's loss was Anthropology's gain: since the late nineteenth century, the study of religion had been integral to the analysis of the social organization of 'primitive' peoples. This was expressly theorized in the French tradition founded by Emile Durkheim, and even the more pragmatic Anglo-Saxon tradition did not beg to differ. Thus Gluckman's *Custom and Conflict in Africa* led readers from Evans Pritchard's work on feud

[35] C. Lévi-Strauss, *Les structures élémentaires de la parenté* (Paris, 1949).

[36] For a survey, see Kuper, *Anthropology and Anthropologists*, pp. 159–75. R. Fox, *Kinship and Marriage: An Anthropological Perspective* (Cambridge, 1967) sought to resolve the 'descent' vs 'alliance' approaches.

[37] Recent work departs from M. Strathern, *Reproducing the Future: Essays on Anthropology, Kinship, and the New Reproductive Technologies* (Manchester, 1992); and C. Thompson, *Making Parents: the Ontological Choreography of Reproductive Technologies* (Cambridge, MA, 2005). J. Carsten, *After Kinship* (Cambridge, 2004) is a helpful overview.

[38] See, for example, R. le Jan, *Famille et pouvoir dans le monde franc (viie-xe siècle). Essai d'anthropologie sociale* (2003); or the refreshingly ambitious D. W. Sabean, S. Teuscher, J. Mathieu (eds.), *Kinship in Europe: Approaches to Long-Term Development (1300–1900)* (New York, 2007); neither refers to current anthropology of kinship.

[39] R. W. Southern, 'The Shape and Substance of Academic History: An Inaugural Lecture delivered before the University of Oxford, 2 November 1961', in R. Bartlett (ed.), *History and Historians: the Selected Papers of R. W. Southern* (Oxford, 2004), pp. 87–119, at p. 99.

among the Nuer, towards his work on witchcraft among the Azande. Historians took slightly longer to respond here than to the 'Peace in the Feud' – but in 1968, to celebrate the thirtieth anniversary of the publication of Evans Pritchard's *Witchcraft, Oracles, and Magic Among the Azande*, his pupil Mary Douglas convened an interdisciplinary conference in London. Among those who spoke were Keith Thomas and Peter Brown. Three years later appeared the former's *Religion and the Decline of Magic*, which brought Azande villagers into dialogue with their Essex counterparts in early modern England, and the latter's article on the rise and function of the Holy Man in Late Antiquity.[40]

Waxing nostalgic about such 'first contact' moments between History and Anthropology should not make us forget that there is a great deal of work still to do. The anthropological turn is not finished: in fact, it may not have properly begun. Wallace-Hadrill's uptake of Gluckman on feud on the one hand, and on the other Brown's uptake of Douglas are too easily taken to represent two different initiatives, the one focussed on the study of power in medieval Western Europe, the other attuned to 'the holy' in the eastern Mediterranean. This is in fact a mischaracterization, certainly of Brown's intentions, which were precisely to contribute to a discussion of the settlement of disputes in the later Roman Empire.[41] Now nearly sixty years on from Gluckman's article, for all that we are further forward, we lack a sustained history of 'informal' power and social order from Marcus Aurelius to Mohammed and beyond.[42] Our histories of exchange in this period do not include the exchange of women – according to Levi-Strauss, the most basic of all social transactions.[43] If the anthropological turn allows us to develop this, we should steer into the skid.

We could also do worse than turn back to Augustine. Seen as a theorist of the State, he is a glass-half-empty pessimist: as a theorist of society, however, Augustine can be stunningly upbeat. Full peace on earth may be beyond us, but we are never without some peace.[44] A wife who has given away her child's inheritance without consent from her husband is recalled

[40] P. R. L. Brown, 'The Rise and Function of the Holy Man in Late Antiquity', *Journal of Roman Studies* 61 (1971), 80–101, repr. in his *Society and the Holy in Late Antiquity* (1982). Brown's retrospective 'The Rise and Function of the Holy Man in Late Antiquity, 1971–1997', *Journal of Early Christian Studies*, 6.3 (1998), 353–76 recalls tea in 1967 with Mary Douglas.

[41] See Brown, 'The Rise and Function of the Holy Man in Late Antiquity, 1971–1997'.

[42] Cf. P. R. L. Brown, *The World of Late Antiquity, AD 150–750: From Marcus Aurelius to Mohammed* (London, 1971).

[43] An omission noted in Davies and Fouracre (eds.), *The Languages of Gift*, pp. 6–7.

[44] See Davies and Fouracre (eds.), *Settlement of Disputes*, p. 233 on the 'contentious' peace of early medieval societies.

to 'the trustful partnership' (*tam fida societas*) of her marriage. Even robbers, in their scheming together, have a kind of peace between them.[45]

Making early medieval societies

We begin in the later Roman Empire, or more precisely in the late Roman household. Kate Cooper explores what an account both of the Roman State and of the Christian Church would look like if we start from the household. In this 'minimalist' perspective, governors and magistrates, bishops and abbots come across not as corporate men, but as Roman *patres*. Their power as decision-makers could be uplifting and terrifying in equal measure, precisely because it was personal, intimate, and not always predictable. One upshot of this approach is that Gibbon's insistence that the rise of the Church led to disintegration of the State might turn out to be true – but this would be because Christian leaders are creative of social fabric, not destructive.

We take soundings of episcopal performance as impresarios of conflict and of loyalty in the two studies following. David Natal and Jamie Wood land us straight into the thick of church politics in the later fourth century. In studying two relatively obscure arenas of conflict in northern Spain and southern France, Natal and Wood show how bishops actually started to cut their teeth – to convert social capital as local 'big men' into something we might start to call institutional power.

Helmut Reimitz's study of Gregory of Tours reads his *Ten Books of Histories* as an attempt to resist what he (Gregory) took to be a malign trend in the making of social order, namely 'the ethnic turn'. In this reconstruction, Gregory could see the writing on the wall: that a key element in the post-Roman dispensation would be 'Frankishness'. Here a bishop strives to prevent the formation of social bonds whose grounds he mistrusts. In the manner of Augustine, Gregory sought to flatten the claims of earthly potentates and earthly schemes of value in the name of otherworldly standards and currencies.

Next, Martin Ryan looks afresh at Bede as a social thinker. In the past generation, Bede has lost all credibility as a 'cloistered monk': capturing the momentum of revisionist scholarship, Ryan maps out Bede's vision of the social order and of social change. In the present context, his essay contributes to a wider discussion among early medievalists about

[45] See Augustine *Ep* 262.5 to Ecdicia, discussed in K. Cooper, 'Insinuations of Womanly Influence: An Aspect of the Christianization of the Roman Aristocracy', *Journal of Roman Studies*, 82 (1990), 150–64, at 158–60 For the peace of thieves, see Augustine, *Civ. Dei* XIX. 12.

ecclesiastical 'reform' as a discourse of social transformation.[46] This has centred on the writings of Carolingian churchmen. One implication of Ryan's chapter is that this reform programme did not depend on the Empire for its genealogy: its outlines can be found earlier, in the court monastery of Monkwearmouth-Jarrow.

Riccardo Bof and Conrad Leyser head into the confrontation between religious specialists and lay potentates. They track Christian teaching about marriage and divorce, following the convoluted development of tradition from late Roman North Africa to Carolingian West Francia. On the one hand, they find a new understanding of marriage as a divinely sanctioned social bond; on the other, they show that dogmatic intransigence was less quick to take hold than we might think. The goal of churchmen was ultimately to keep the peace.

Identifying the moment at which the Church began to conceive itself autonomously, without the awning of Empire, is the goal of Conrad Leyser's essay. He argues that the two or three generations after the death of Charles the Fat, the last legitimate Carolingian, are decisive here. It was at this juncture that bishops and their canonists, especially in northern Italy, took cognizance of themselves as belonging to an institution that could function independently of imperial protection. To do so, they summoned the resources of the past. Cultural memory – of Pope Gregory the Great in particular – here becomes institutional glue.

Who lost out here? Paul Fouracre and Marios Costambeys, from different perspectives, consider the capacity of the established order not only to withstand challenge, but to prevent its being articulated. In his study of 'rebellion' in the narrative sources for the Latin West, Fouracre is struck above all by its absence. Sustained political protest was not part of the lexicon of early medieval polities: the particular equation of 'Thin State: Big Society' did not permit it.

What Marios Costambeys charts is the emergence of a professional cadre – legal notaries – who could ensure that 'justice' always spoke in terms that were controllable. Like priests, they realized they could function without a political master. An institutional culture took over. The voice of the dispossessed was faint at best: listening closely, what Costambeys traces is how they were counted out altogether.

The final two papers cross the millennial threshold, but in very different styles. Both consider what we have called above the 'privatization fable' – the view that after the millennium public power fell into the hands of a

[46] See, for example, M. de Jong, *The Penitential State: Authority and Atonement in the Age of Louis the Pious, 814–840* (Cambridge, 2009); S. Patzold, *Episcopus. Wissen über Bischöfe im Frankenreich des späten 8. bis frühen 10. Jahrhunderts* (Ostfildern, 2008).

rapacious and unaccountable warrior elite. Taking full cognizance of the critique of this view, R. I. Moore insists that there is a wider story here, which we miss at our peril. In the eleventh and twelfth centuries, control over the sacred, which translated into power over justice, was monopolized by a newly defined clerical elite. The *clerici* left the people out of the account – and historians should not collude in their disenfranchisement.

By contrast, Stephen D. White's suspicion is that medieval historians are addicted to narratives of drama and violence. He views the whole account of the 'Transformation of the Year 1000' as a resurgence of the lust for blood that characterized much medieval writing about the feud, before the engagement with Anthropology. Gluckman's 'peace in the feud' holds this bloodlust in check. Whatever its problems as a model, it has a role to play in keeping us sane. For this reason alone, the anthropological turn is not over.

Where does this leave us? There is plenty here that we do not talk about. Our geographical range is restricted: this collection is firmly western Mediterranean in focus. This is also primarily a series of studies in social and cultural history, to the exclusion of classic topics in political and economic history, such as taxation, rent, or pottery. There has been plenty of discussion of these which cheerfully excludes the areas of concern to us. Our immediate concern is to redress a balance – but in the longer term, it is not to institute what child developmentalists call 'parallel play'; the hope must be eventually to play together.

Three other hopes are as follows. The first is to have initiated a conversation that spans the late Roman period and the high Middle Ages. It is not just a fear of Grand Narrative that makes this difficult. There are deep fault lines constraining discussion. Late Antiquity as a field attends to a basically eighteenth-century problem: when did the ancient world end? The study of the early Middle Ages is founded on the nineteenth-century question, 'When did a new order begin?' These spirits from the apparently remote past exert real institutional pressures in the present, as anyone coming onto the job market knows. 'Ancient' or 'medieval' describe not just heirloom questions, but a training and a scheduling: the large-scale conferences, which in the United States are the venue for job interviews, respect traditional periodization. It will take smaller groups and sustained dialogue to get past this.[47]

It follows, second, that we hope to have rendered plausible our title: making early medieval societies. The millennium under discussion here was an intensely creative period for the flourishing of conflict and the formation of new social relationships. These new bonds – we can call

[47] Cf. West, *Reframing the Feudal Revolution*, p. 5.

them 'late ancient' or 'early medieval' as we wish – were not a patch-and-mend strategy for the hole where the State used to be. As these bonds took shape in the later Roman Empire, they were a way of coping with the State's dysfunctional and intermittent presence. In the Latin West, the State, was, or became, the problem; 'making societies' was the solution.

Third, we have sought to write in ways that are accessible to those outside the immediate field or discipline. This is partly a matter of politeness. It is also an attempt to redress a balance of trade. History seems forever to be 'drawing' on Anthropology. Why not the other way round?

1 Property, power, and conflict: re-thinking the Constantinian revolution

Kate Cooper

It has long been recognized that the rise of Christianity and the fall of the Roman state were somehow intertwined. Enlightenment writers including David Hume and, most influentially, Edward Gibbon saw the arrival of Christianity as both cause and product of a lamentable triumph of credulity at the end of antiquity, which decisively weakened both the Roman character and the Roman system of government. More recently, historians have seen the end of the Roman Empire as a question of the changing role of elites. Most influential has been the work of John Matthews, who sees a shift of power away from the state and towards large-scale private land-owners as the decisive development marking the end of antiquity and the beginning of the middle ages.[1] The present essay will attempt to draw these two strands together, considering how the emergence of an imperial Church influenced the changing balance between public and private power.

Gibbon's distorting lens of credulity has distracted scholarly attention, we will suggest, from a more disturbing – and more interesting – historical process. Understood not through the lens of belief and credulity, but rather that of allegiance and accountability, the evidence for the evolution of Christian authority structures tells a surprising story. Two discrete but related developments took place simultaneously in the fourth century: the Christian churches served as a vehicle for contesting the private power of lay landowners, even as the great landowners themselves were successfully encroaching on the power of the Roman state.

[1] See K. Cooper, *The Fall of the Roman Household* (Cambridge, 2007), pp. 9–13 for further thoughts, with J. Matthews, *Western Aristocracies and Imperial Court AD 364–425* (Oxford, 1975), and J.-M. Carrié, 'Developments in Provincial and Local Administration', in A. Bowman, A. Cameron, and P. Garnsey (eds.), *The Cambridge Ancient History, Volume 12: The Crisis of Empire, AD 193–337*, 2nd edn. (Cambridge, 2005), pp. 269–312.

The *Ecclesiastical History* of Eusebius of Caesarea – a 'myth of origins' for an essentially new organization?

In order to gain an accurate understanding of these developments, some far-reaching misconceptions about the nature of the evidence need to be addressed. The most important of these concern the fourth-century historian Eusebius of Caesarea. Traditionally, scholars relied on Eusebius as a guide to the nature of the earliest Christian communities, and it is only with great difficulty that he has been dislodged from his customary position as historiographical gate-keeper for the study of the first three Christian centuries.

Part of the problem is a vicious circle with respect to the survival of evidence from the early centuries. As author of the earliest surviving narrative of the rise of Christianity, Eusebius exerted an incalculable influence on the acquisition policy of medieval librarians, who used his work as a guide to assess the value of material that came into their hands, and naturally wanted to acquire material that he had identified as important. Over time, this led to a corruption of the evidentiary base – evidence for views other than his own was systematically given lower priority, and in some cases actively suppressed. Combined with Eusebius' own practice of pasting in earlier sources which he found valuable, the overall effect is a phenomenally strong distortion of the evidence in favour of his vision of history.[2]

Across the twentieth century, however, it became increasingly clear to scholars that Eusebius wrote at a turning-point in history, and that this influenced his vision of the early churches.[3] Eusebius' vision of history was strongly coloured by the unprecedented circumstances of his own day – first, the crisis situation of the Great Persecution (303–311), and subsequently the Church's reversal of fortune under Constantine, Rome's first Christian emperor. But no firm consensus exists on Eusebius' aims in shaping the story of the rise of Christianity.

What is certain is that his *Ecclesiastical History* stands as both a frame and an obstacle to our view of the first three centuries. This means that the medieval suppression of 'non-Eusebian' evidence is doubly problematic. Put simply, it is extremely difficult to assess whether the concerns and conditions of the historian's own day led him to misunderstand or misrepresent earlier communities.

[2] E. Pagels, *The Gnostic Gospels* (New York, 1979), offers a valuable attempt to re-consider the problem in light of the 'gnostic' library discovered at Nag Hammadi in 1945; see especially chapter 2, '"One God, One Bishop": The Politics of Monotheism', 33–56.

[3] A valuable recent overview of trends in Eusebian scholarship can be found in A. P. Johnson, *Eusebius* (London, 2013); see also A. P. Johnson and J. Schott (eds.), *Eusebius of Caesarea: Traditions and Innovations* (Cambridge, MA, 2013).

Nonetheless, twentieth-century scholarship made valuable progress in identifying Eusebius' tendencies as an interpreter of Christianity's first three centuries. Consider the following Eusebian axioms: positions which the historian does not argue, but rather assumes to be self-evident, each of which has been challenged in recent decades.

First, that the earliest churches were characterized by intellectual and spiritual unity. Eusebius argued forcefully that heretical doctrines were a departure from the pristine spirit of Christian unity that had characterized the earliest churches. Rival authorities had reared up successively, with rival doctrines to justify the self-interested rejection of established authority. (Eusebius saw the fraternity of orthodox bishops as having its roots in the time of Jesus). This first axiom, the Eusebian 'myth of unity', was challenged by Walter Bauer almost a century ago. Bauer suggested that the earliest churches were characterised by diversity, reflecting the independent histories of individual communities. During a secondary stage of Weberian 'rationalization' and institution-building, the charismatic authority of the early missionaries gave way to a network of leaders who reinforced one another's authority by mutual recognition. Bauer's work has served as a fundamental point of reference over the last half-century.[4]

The *second* axiom is that the churches attained a firm institutional structure by the end of the first century, with ascetics providing moral leadership and bishops providing institutional leadership.[5] This view, too, has been challenged in the wake of Bauer's work, and the challenge has been given new support from modern fieldwork on new religious movements. Influentially, in *The Rise of Christianity: A Sociologist Re-considers History*,[6] Rodney Stark argued that the early Christian communities were household-based influence networks which drew on friendship and family ties to achieve a broad 'reach' in the provincial environment of the Roman provinces.

The *third* axiom is that the church had attained a recognized corporate status within the Roman legal system by the mid third century, with the Emperor Gallienus recognizing the churches as holding institutional title to corporate property. This is a view which I have challenged in a previous publication, and the present study will offer further support for the position.[7]

[4] See D. J. Harrington, 'The Reception of Walter Bauer's "Orthodoxy and Heresy in Earliest Christianity" during the Last Decade', *Harvard Theological Review*, 73 (1980), 289–98. T.A. Robinson 'The Bauer Thesis Examined: the Geography of Heresy in the Early Christian Church (Lewiston, NY, 1988). Also valuable is A. Cameron, 'Enforcing Orthodoxy in Byzantium', in K. Cooper and J. Gregory (eds.), *Discipline and Diversity* (Woodbridge, 2007), pp. 1–24.

[5] J. Corke-Webster, 'Violence and Authority in Eusebius of Caesarea's *Ecclesiastical History*', unpublished PhD thesis, University of Manchester (2013).

[6] (Princeton, NJ, 1996).

[7] K. Cooper, 'Christianity, Private Power, and the Law from Decius to Constantine: the Minimalist View', *Journal of Early Christian Studies*, 19 (2011), 327–43. For a recent re-statement of the traditional view on Gallienus and the Christians, see T. D. Barnes, *Early Christian Hagiography and Roman History* (Tübingen, 2010), pp. 98–105.

The *fourth* and final Eusebian axiom, closely related to the third, is that by the mid third century, Christian institutional leaders understood the Church to be a single, universal institution governed by divine authority. Eusebius took the polemical tracts of Cyprian of Carthage as evidence that the overseers (*episkopoi*) of Christian assemblies (*ekklesiai*) in each city were in fact local representatives of an empire-wide and hierarchically governed organization (the Universal Church).

In the light of these challenges, the present chapter aims to re-consider the position of Christianity before, during, and after the Constantinian revolution. Axiomatic to the approach offered here is the centrality of private power in the Roman social and political landscape. The bishop, it will be argued, can usefully be understood not as a strictly institutional figure, but as a distinctive type of Roman *paterfamilias*. Many of his characteristic activities – for example, in dispute resolution within Christian communities – required no distinctive legal status, and indeed were characteristic of the wider class of men from whom he was drawn. Yet his acquisition of new privileges and immunities in the fourth century would have far-reaching results. By the end of the fifth century, it was possible to imagine the Church as a public institution, one carrying more conviction, in fact, than the Roman State. Much like the work of his eighth-century emulator the Venerable Bede, Eusebius of Caesarea's *Ecclesiastical History* offers a stylized vision of history: the blueprint for an ideal future, rather than a warts-and-all view of the past.[8]

Christianity in the first three centuries: when and how did a household-based network become a coherent trans-regional movement?

The task of constructing an alternative to the idealized institutional history offered by Eusebius is a daunting one, but starting-points can be identified. We must begin with what we know about power and communication in the Roman provinces.

In the last quarter of the twentieth century, ancient historians reached a consensus that Roman government was rather more 'reactive' than previous generations of scholarship had acknowledged.[9] Information was difficult to come by, and information about subversive groups especially so. This can be seen in a well-known letter of ca. AD 111 in which the

[8] See P. Wormald, 'Bede, Beowulf, and the Conversion of the Anglo-Saxon Aristocracy', in R. T. Farrell (ed.), *Bede and Anglo-Saxon England: Papers in Honour of the 1300th Anniversary of the Birth of Bede, Given at Cornell University in 1973 and 1974*, BAR 46 (Oxford, 1978), pp. 32–95.

[9] The seminal study is F. Millar, *The Emperor in the Roman World (31 BC-AD 337)* (London, 1977).

Roman provincial governor Pliny the Younger described to the Emperor Trajan a difficult case he had encountered. He had been called on to judge a case involving individuals identified as Christians without actually knowing who the Christians were or what about their behaviour might be cause for suspicion, though he was aware that they were understood to be subversives.[10] And if the inaccessibility of reliable information created difficulties for government officials as well as to outsiders who encountered group members in the course of events, it also created challenges for a group's own members.

The emerging second-century leadership attempted to create an accountability network among local leaders, using the idea of 'heresy' to nominate rival leaders – or simply individuals who challenged their authority – for exclusion from the circle of trust.[11] In the early second century, Ignatius of Antioch (d. ca. 98–117) coined the phrase 'universal assembly' or 'catholic Church' (*katholikē ekklēsia*) to define the eschatological community gathered around the person of Jesus Christ;[12] by the third century, Cyprian of Carthage began to use the idea to suggest that 'The authority of the bishops forms a unity, of which each holds his part in totality.'[13]

The emergence of sacred literature played an important role in establishing a point of reference for inclusion and exclusion.[14] Early in the century, the letters of Ignatius of Antioch indicate that he has been reading the letters of Paul of Tarsus, which had been circulated by the early communities.[15] Book ownership was a rarity. Most Christians had access only to the spoken word, whether read aloud or spoken in preaching and prophecy.[16] In the second century, we begin to have evidence that

[10] On the Pliny–Trajan correspondence, see now J. Corke-Webster, 'Trouble in Pontus: the Pliny–Trajan Correspondence on the Christians Reconsidered' (unpublished manuscript).

[11] Pagels, '"One God, One Bishop"'. See also R. A. Markus, 'The Problem of Self-Definition: From Sect to Church', in E. P. Sanders (ed.), *Jewish and Christian Self-Definition. Vol. 1: The Shaping of Christianity in the Second and Third Centuries* (Philadelphia, PA, 1980), pp. 1–15.

[12] Ignatius of Antioch, *Letter to the Smyrneans* 7.

[13] Cyprian, *Unit. eccl.* 5 (Cyprian, *De lapsis and ecclesiae catholicae unitate*, ed. and trans. Maurice Bévenot, S. J. [Oxford, 1971], pp. 64–7), with discussion in Cooper, 'Christianity, Private Power, and the Law', pp. 333–4.

[14] F. Wisse, 'The Use of Early Christian Literature as Evidence for Inner Diversity and Conflict', in C. Hedrick and R Hodgson, Jr., *Nag Hammadi, Gnosticism, and Early Christianity* (Peabody, MA, 1988), pp. 177–90.

[15] On Ignatius, see R. F. Stoops, Jr., 'If I Suffer . . . Epistolary Authority in Ignatius of Antioch', *Harvard Theological Review*, 80 (1987), 161–78, and now K. Cooper, 'Martyrdom, Memory, and the "Media Event": Visionary Writing and Christian Apology in Second-century Christianity', in D. Janes and A. Houen (eds.), *Terrorism and Martyrdom: British Perspectives in Global Context* (Oxford, 2014), pp. 23–39, at 31–3.

[16] K. Haines-Eitzen, *Guardians of Letters: Literacy, Power and the Transmitters of Early Christian Literature* (Oxford, 2000), with, more recently, Haines-Eitzen, 'The Social

Christians were expected to have access to books, though there was of course no New Testament yet. It was Marcion of Sinope (himself remembered as a heretic) who first put forward the idea of a 'canon' of scripture around the middle of the century.[17] Around 180, Speratus of Scillium was interrogated by Saturninus, Proconsul of Africa, and admitted to having 'books and letters of Paul, a just man'[18] on his person. He carried them in a *capsa* – a small case designed to hold a single scroll; this could easily have been the only text to which his community had access.

Caution must be observed in considering the sources. If modern meanings are 'read back' into early Christian language, a highly distorted picture can emerge. So, for example, if a Greek-speaking listener were to eavesdrop on second-century Christians speaking informally, he might notice that they seemed to acknowledge a mutual *kyrios* – a lord or patron – and that they placed trust in an Anointed One – *christos* – who might perhaps be a king or some kind of demi-god. The listener might also pick up a sense that they claimed to be part of an *ekklesia*, an 'assembly' or 'gathering' – the word could mean anything from the lower assembly (alongside the *boule*) of a provincial city to a small party of friends – and that 'elders' (*presbyteroi*) and 'supervisors' (*episkopoi*) played a part in the group, as did 'sponsors' (*diakonoi*).[19] These terms meant something very different to second-century Christians than they do to the modern churches – they are normally translated as 'Lord', 'Christ', 'Church', 'Priest', 'Bishop', and 'Deacon' respectively, evoking modern cognates that are almost certainly misleading.

News travelled, for the most part, via social networks. A second-century person could easily become involved with a circle of followers of the Anointed One without having too clear an idea of what it was all about. In fact, involvement did not necessarily involve intention – it might simply be a matter of staying put. If one's friends or family became involved followers of the Anointed One, it might seem harsh to insult them by refusing to spend time with their new friends. Modern network theory suggests that listeners are sensitive to emotional and relational cues about shared news – does the story elicit sympathy or indignation? Is the speaker

History of Early Christian Scribes', in B. D. Ehrman and M. Holmes (eds.), *The Text of the New Testament in Contemporary Research: Essays on the Status Quaestionis* (Leiden, 2013), pp. 479–95.

[17] B. M. Metzger, *The Canon of the New Testament: Its Origin, Development, and Significance* (Oxford, 1997), pp. 29–32.

[18] *Acts of the Scillitan Martyrs* 12, in H. Musurillo (ed.), *The Acts of the Christian Martyrs* (Oxford, 1972), pp. 86–9, at 88–9.

[19] For discussion of these terms emphasizing their fluidity in the early period, see G. Macy, *The Hidden History of Women's Ordination* (Oxford, 2008), pp. 23–48.

likeable or worthy of trust? – and comparatively less acute in their assessment of the content aspect of the news being shared.

Judged by modern standards, even the elders and supervisors of ancient communities may have known surprisingly little about their group and its history. One who grew up as a Christian might have heard stories about travelling prophets and miracle-workers, though these individuals did not exist in great enough numbers to keep the flow of information thick on the ground. Their stories would often be re-told by audience members, who in turn might tell them again.

Up to the middle of the third century, there is very little evidence of criteria for Christian overseers other than good character. Our earliest 'job description' for the role, the *First Letter to Timothy* (which most scholars believe to be by an anonymous late first or second-century writer, though it claims to be a letter of Paul) emphasizes that the individual should be a *pater*, faithful to one wife, and sober in managing a household.[20] Significantly, *1 Timothy* specifies both hospitality and ability to teach as desirable characteristics.[21]

Similarly, it is important to remember that the movement had its basis in private relationships. Sociologists have established a correlation between social networking and high growth for modern religious and social movements, and there is every reason to believe that the same principle was at work in the swift expansion of Christianity.[22]

In the absence of archaeological evidence for the period before 250, it seems fair to imagine that gatherings were normally held in the courtyard of the elders' or overseer's homes. A space-poor but well-liked individual who was good at gently commandeering the resources of others would probably not have been disqualified from a leadership role, but access to meeting space would need to be negotiated if a community grew beyond what he or she could accommodate domestically.[23] In any case, it is worth

[20] K. Cooper, 'Closely Watched Households: Visibility, Exposure, and Private Power in the Roman *domus*', *Past & Present*, 197 (2007), 3–33, at 7–8. On the social context of the Pastoral Epistles, see M. Y. MacDonald, *Early Christian Women and Pagan Opinion: the Power of the Hysterical Woman* (Cambridge, 1996).

[21] 1 Timothy 3:2–3 (NIV): 'Now the overseer is to be above reproach, faithful to his wife, temperate, self-controlled, respectable, hospitable, able to teach, not given to drunkenness, not violent but gentle, not quarrelsome, not a lover of money.'

[22] R. Stark, *The Rise of Christianity: a Sociologist Reconsiders History* (Princeton, NJ, 1996), with additional evidence in K. Cooper, 'Ventriloquism and the Miraculous: Conversion, Preaching, and the Martyr Exemplum in Late Antiquity', in K. Cooper and J. Gregory (eds.), *Signs, Wonders, and Miracles, Studies in Church History*, 41 (Woodbridge, 2005), pp. 22–45.

[23] G. F. Snyder, *Ante Pacem: Archaeological Evidence of Church Life Before Constantine* (Macon, GA, 2003), pp. 127–53, and K. Cooper, 'The Household as a Venue for Religious Conversion', in B. Rawson (ed.), *A Companion to Families in the Greek and Roman Worlds* (Oxford, 2010), pp. 183–97. K. Bowes, 'Early Christian Archaeology: a

remembering that the Church was not a formally constituted institution in the early centuries. The evidence suggests that arrangements were improvised according to local need and availability.[24]

The Constantinian revolution

It would be wrong to imagine an overnight transformation of the Church into a public institution under Constantine. The fourth century opened with a decade of civil war, with accompanying purges of dissidents in the provinces which would be remembered by Christians as the Great Persecution of 303–11. But with Galerius' Edict of Toleration in 311, and the so-called Edict of Milan in February of 313, Christian churches began a period of access to targeted privileges and immunities.

In the aftermath of his victory at the Milvian Bridge in October of 312, the Emperor Constantine seems to have sought to establish a definitive network of Christian leaders who were accountable to him and to whom he could extend the benefits of imperial favour. Scholars have yet fully to understand the nature of Constantine's engagement with the Christians – his 'conversion' has been the subject of debate for centuries – but early witnesses suggest that he felt that the God of the Christians had delivered the Milvian Bridge victory, and that as a result he should give honour to the priests of the God's cult.[25] It is also possible that he admired the networks of loyalty and mutual service which the Christian elders were able to foster in the localities – it is clear from the reforms of his grandson Julian the Apostate a half-century later that these aspects of the Christian polity were perceived as enviable.

To begin with, Constantine announced in the winter of 312–13 that he wished to restore property of Christians which had been confiscated during the Great Persecution. As a result, he found himself involved quite quickly in trying to adjudicate disputes between Christian factions in the major cities over which should gain recognition for its chosen leader as the bishop responsible for representing the city to the Emperor and the Emperor to the Christians in that locality. Most significantly, the Christians of Carthage could not agree whether Caecilian or Majorinus

State of the Field', *Religion Compass*, 2 (2008), 575–615. Given the evidence in K. Madigan and C. Osiek (eds.), *Ordained Women in the Early Church: a Documentary History* (Baltimore, MD, 2005), I have allowed for the possibility of female presbyters.

[24] This is true for liturgy as well as for more practical arrangements. On the difficulty of accepting traditional pre-Constantinian dates for the major liturgical collections, see P. F. Bradshaw, *The Search for the Origins of Christian Worship: Sources and Methods for the Study of Early Liturgy*, 2nd edn. (London, 2002).

[25] On Constantine's conversion, see R. Van Dam, *Remembering Constantine at the Milvian Bridge* (Cambridge, 2011).

should be put forward, a dispute which formed the kernel of what would become the Donatist schism.

Constantine seems to have stood firm in his view that each city should have only one recognized bishop. It was a view which flew in the face of the historical reality – Christians had never successfully been organized into a single, multi-city organization, even if some writers had put this forward as an ideal. Part of the vitality of Christianity had been in the fact that rival bishops could foster their own networks in a locality, with only the ability to attract followers as the criterion of viability.

Nonetheless, Constantine tried to build on a third-century tradition of bishops meeting in council in order to resolve the question of precedence definitively. It was an initiative whose results can only be described as disastrous. At Rome in 313 and again at Arles in 314, he called councils to resolve disputes over control of the newly recognized Christian polity, involving bishops of other regions in what was swiftly hardening into a major schism among the Africans. Then he turned his ill-conceived energies to Alexandria, where a personal dispute surrounding the gifted and unruly presbyter Arius would result first in an unsuccessful council at Nicaea in 325, and then in a theological dispute – known to history as the Arian controversy – which would endure for a half-century.

Modern historians continue themselves to dispute over the political effects of imperial Christianity. Was monotheism good for the Empire?[26] The relentless appetite of the Christians for quarrelling with each other was a clear source of frustration to the Emperor, yet theological debates offered a ready mechanism for emerging leaders to test their ability to command a following.

Towards the end of his life, Constantine lost patience with the Nicene bishops: his successors would favour the Arians. But if the failure to achieve uniformity was a disappointment, the existence of rival followings may have been a necessary escape-valve in the new dispensation. Dispute between rival 'orthodoxies' allowed the Empire an element of pluralism and plasticity – easy to achieve under the old gods, harder under the aegis of a single deity.

In any case, disputes were clearly good for institution building. Across the first three centuries, heresy accusations had, largely speaking, been exchanged without institutional consequence. But in the fourth century, access to the imperial transport system meant that bishops could enjoy themselves hurrying from council to council, as Ammianus Marcellinus

[26] See the classic discussion of A. Momigliano, 'Christianity and the Decline of Empire', in Momigliano (ed.), *The Conflict between Paganism and Christianity in the Fourth Century* (Oxford, 1963), pp. 1–16.

observed through pursed lips. At the Council of Constantinople in 381, 150 Eastern bishops gathered in an attempt to bring an end to the Arian dispute. The Council produced a ringing declaration to the effect that the nature of God was unknowable; yet the dispute gained momentum nonetheless.

In fact, Christian bishops may not have intended that it abate. By the later fourth century, theological disputes had become firmly entrenched as a way of negotiating status and competing for resources, with the result that for every dispute resolved, another grew up to replace it. Like Wallace-Hadrill's feuding Merovingian war-lords, fourth-century bishops found a 'peace in the feud' which justified their existence.[27]

What was involved in the restoration of property to the churches?

One of the most difficult questions about the Constantinian revolution is that of Church property. It is well known that Constantine restored confiscated property to the churches – but it is not clear what property is meant, or to whom, precisely, the property was restored. Eusebius and Lactantius both include versions of a letter from Licinius addressed to a Roman governor in June 313 – Eusebius' version was addressed to the Governor of Syria Palaestina, while the nearly identical text known to Lactantius was addressed to the Governor of Bithynia. (This is the letter long known, inaccurately, as the Edict of Milan.) The Licinian directive of 313 gives orders for the restoration of property used by Christian communities – property which had been confiscated and subsequently sold to private individuals. The letter specifies that if property was used by Christian congregations as opposed to private individuals, the emperor will reimburse the costs borne by a purchaser of such property who is required to return it for redistribution.

The letter is often taken as evidence that the Christian communities were constituted in a way that allowed them to hold corporate title to property before 313. However, this is an inference not strictly borne out by the surviving witnesses to the letter.[28] If we look closely at Lactantius' Latin version of the text, we see that Licinius gives directions for restoring confiscated property. He states that if anyone has bought a confiscated

[27] M. Wallace-Hadrill, 'The Bloodfeud of the Franks', *Bulletin of the John Rylands Library*, 41 (1959), 459–87.

[28] Cooper, 'Christianity, Private Power, and the Law', 327–43. See also K. Sessa, '*Domus Ecclesiae*: Rethinking a Category Of *Ante-Pacem* Christian Space', *Journal of Theological Studies*, N.S. 60 (2009), 90–108, and A. Luijendijk, *Greetings in the Lord: Early Christians and the Oxyrhynchus Papyri* (Cambridge, MA, 2008).

Christian meeting-space, whether from the fisc or through an intermediary, the cost will be reimbursed to them. He then goes on to say that the Christians 'are known to have had (*habuisse noscuntur*) not only places where they have had the habit of meeting, but also others relevant to the justice (*ius*) of their body, that is, of the assemblies, not of individual people (*alia ... ad ius corporis eorum, id est ecclesiarum, non hominum singulorum, pertinentia*).'[29] The thrust of the passage seems to be to clarify that in this particular directive reimbursement is offered only if the space was confiscated because it was used by a Christian community for its collective needs, rather than a space in private use. In other words, property used exclusively by individuals is not covered by the directive, even if they were Christian and the property had been confiscated.

The sole manuscript witness to Lactantius' text is an eleventh-century exemplar, Paris BN Lat 2627, and following nineteenth-century tradition, Barnes translates the passage in a way that would have seemed entirely natural to the eleventh-century copyist. But this reading may well distort the meaning of the fourth-century source. Barnes translates *alia ... ad ius corporis eorum, id est ecclesiarum, non hominum singulorum, pertinentia* as 'other property too which belongs by right to their corporation – that is to churches, not individual persons'.[30] There are two problems here. First, the institutionally slanted translation of *corpus* ('body') as 'corporation' reflects a circular reasoning – it is one of many meanings for the word, and absent independent confirmation, it is not the most obvious.

Second and more importantly, 'belongs by right to' is only one of many possible translations for the phrase *ad ius ... pertinentia.* It is certainly very slim evidence on which to hang a full-blown theory of recognized corporate legal personality and institutional title-holding in the pre-Constantinian era. Yet this is precisely what historians have tried to do.

It should be remembered that the eleventh-century canon lawyers who commissioned the Lactantius manuscript were churchmen whose job it was to justify the privileges and immunities of their own churches in the face of emperors and lay lords. Since they had no need to understand late Roman social history, any anachronism in their reading may have done no real harm, even as it worked in favour of their cause. But to those of us who are interested in the fourth and not the eleventh century, further

[29] Lactantius, *De Mortibus Persecutorum*, 48.9; text in J. L. Creed, *Lactantius: De Mortibus Persecutorum* (Oxford, 1984), pp. 72–3.

[30] T. Barnes, *Constantine: Dynasty, Religion and Power in the Later Roman Empire* (Oxford, 2011), p. 97.

work on this text, and on Eusebius' translation into Greek of a variant of the same letter at *Ecclesiastical History* 10.5.2–14, is a desideratum.

Our understanding of the property arrangements underlying Christian congregations even in the fourth century is surprisingly weak. Already in the 1930s Richard Krautheimer and Floyd Filson were arguing that scholarship should move away from imagining that Christian gatherings (*ekklesiae*) met in designated church buildings, to a sociology in which communities co-opted space flexibly, according to need.[31] Krautheimer suggested that even after the great Constantinian building programmes, Christians in Rome and elsewhere probably continued to meet in rented space for the most part.[32] More recently, a valuable study by Kim Bowes has surveyed the landscape of private domestic space, concluding that in both rural and urban contexts landowners continued to host Christian communities on their property, even as Christian bishops began to make efforts to bring this ad hoc liturgical sponsorship under episcopal oversight.[33]

What the evidence does show quite clearly is the vital role played by informal relationships between bishops and prominent landowners. So, for example, the relationship between John Chrysostom, bishop of Constantinople from 398 to 404, and the heiress Olympias, whose ownership of a complex adjoining the city's cathedral made it possible for her to serve as an indispensable support to the bishop and his congregation. Bishops seem to have had mixed feelings about the vitality of lay patronage in the fourth- and fifth-century churches, however. As the bishop's institutional power developed, limits were increasingly imposed on the scope of lay agency.[34]

[31] C. Leyser, '"A church in the house of the saints": Property and Power in the Passion of John and Paul', in K. Cooper and J. Hillner (eds.), *Religion, Dynasty, and Patronage in Early Christian Rome, 300–900* (Cambridge, 2007), pp. 140–62, has updated the classic discussions of Krautheimer and Filson. See F. Filson, 'The Significance of the Early House Churches', *Journal of Biblical Literature*, 58 (1939), 105–12, and R. Krautheimer, 'The Beginnings of Early Christian Architecture', *Review of Religion*, 3 (1939), 127–48, reprinted in R. Krautheimer, *Studies in Early Christian, Medieval, and Renaissance Art*, ed. James S. Ackerman et al. (New York, 1969).

[32] R. Krautheimer, *Three Christian Capitals: Topography and Politics* (Berkeley, CA, 1983), with discussion in Cooper, 'The Household as Venue for Religious Conversion'.

[33] K. Bowes, *Private Worship, Public Values, and Religious Change in Late Antiquity* (Cambridge, 2008), with K. Bowes, 'Personal Devotions and Private Chapels', in Virginia Burrus (ed.), *A People's History of Christianity. Volume 2: Late Ancient Christianity* (Minneapolis, MN, 2005), pp. 188–210. See also J. Hillner, 'Clerics, Property, and Patronage: the Case of the Roman Titular Churches', in *Antiquité tardive*, 14 (2006), 59–68.

[34] K. Cooper, 'Poverty, Obligation, and Inheritance: Roman Heiresses and the Varieties of Senatorial Christianity in Fifth-Century Rome', in Cooper and Hillner (eds.), *Religion, Dynasty, and Patronage*, pp. 165–89.

The fathers of the Church and the hounds of God: bishops, abbots, and their volatile followings

We will turn now from assessing bishops' competition with one another over resources to considering how they engaged with their own followings. Across our period, one of the central roles filled by bishops was as settlers of disputes. This, too, was a role whose shape changed with the Constantinian revolution, but the change was one of degree rather than type. The evidence suggests that the powers accorded to episcopal courts in the fourth century were a formalization of existing practice rather than a new departure.

Historians of later periods tend to imagine the Roman judicial system as far more robust than that of successor states, and to over-emphasize the role played by the state-sponsored apparatus where justice was concerned. As historians of Roman government have learned to see the Roman business of government as improvisational and responsive, with the need to reply to ad-hoc petitions, rather than long-term planning, as the trigger for the lion's share of imperial legislation.[35] There was, to be sure, a central mechanism for the punishment of offences and the arbitration of disputes. There were legal codes, jurists to interpret them, and teachers to train the next generation of specialist practitioners. To bring a case to court, however, was stunningly expensive and cumbersome. As a means of resolving disputes, it was far less effective than less elaborate mechanisms of justice – even the very rich found this to be the case. Far more common was informal arbitration by *patres* – as heads of household – chosen by custom or simple mutual agreement between the disputants.[36]

It is in this light that we must consider the increasingly important role played by Christian bishops within the wider framework of dispute settlement. By the fourth century, the *audientia episcopalis*, or bishop's hearing, was already the central mechanism of dispute resolution within Christian communities. With the involvement of ever greater numbers of citizens in the Christian churches, the bishops' hearings became ever more significant. But recent research has tended to suggest that the episcopal audience did not change dramatically across the reign of Constantine.[37] Just as the legal basis of the third-century bishop seems

[35] Millar, *Emperor in the Roman World.*

[36] For further discussion, see C. Humfress, 'Bishops and Law Courts in Late Antiquity: How (Not) to Make Sense of the Legal Evidence', *Journal of Early Christian Studies*, 19 (2011), 375–400.

[37] The work of J. D. Harries offers a number of valuable starting-points. See, for example, 'Courts and the Judicial System', in C. Heszer (ed.), *The Oxford Handbook of Jewish Daily Life in Roman Palestine* (Oxford, 2010), pp. 85–101; 'Creating Legal Space: Settling

to have been that of an individual *paterfamilias* able to provide arbitration in the way that any respected property-owner could do, so too in the fourth century. The legal basis of the bishop's ruling seems to have continued as a form of arbitration rather than being converted to an exercise of imperially appointed jurisdiction. Like his third-century predecessor, the fourth-century bishop resolved disputes not as a magistrate but as a man of standing within his community, a *pater*.

Yet among the *patres*, the bishop was known to command a distinctively faithful following. As a result, across the fourth and fifth centuries his authority would grow progressively stronger. In the meantime, the moral authority of lay landowners began to erode, even as their economic power began to encroach on that of the Roman state.

Among the bishop's followers, the most committed – and the most volatile – seem to have been the ascetics. It is during the fourth century that the ascetic movement gained momentum. While Eusebius suggests that the movement had its roots already in the Greek-speaking Jewish culture of the first century, with the communities of the Therepeutae described by Philo of Alexandria, this view does not find strong support in first-century sources.[38] At the same time, Eusebius had his own reasons for seeing the ascetic movement as a central element of the earliest Christian communities.[39]

In the fourth century, the monastery was a new kind of household with distinctive properties. The central element was that its continuity was managed through social rather than biological reproduction, but this should not blind us to its similarity to more traditional households.[40] Philip Rousseau has suggested that the roots of the fourth-century ascetic explosion are in the communalism of rural society in the aftermath of the economic crisis of the third century.[41] Rousseau pointed out that the early Pachomian monasteries could be understood as an organic development

Disputes in the Roman Empire', in C. Heszer (ed.), *Rabbinic Law in its Roman and Near Eastern Context* (Tübingen, 2003), pp. 63–81; Resolving Disputes: the Frontiers of Law in Late Antiquity', in R. E. Mathisen (ed.), *Law, Society and Authority in Late Antiquity* (Oxford, 2001), pp. 68–82; 'Constructing the Judge: Judicial Accountability and the Culture of Criticism in Late Antiquity', in R. Miles (ed.), *Constructing Identities in Late Antiquity* (London, 1999), pp. 214–33.

38 Eusebius, *Ecclesiastical History*, 2.17.

39 J. Corke-Webster, 'Author and Authority: Literary Representations of Moral Authority in Eusebius of Caesarea's *The Martyrs of Palestine*', in P. Gemeinhardt and J. Leemans (eds.), *Christian Martyrdom in Late Antiquity: History and Discourse, Tradition and Religious Identity*, Arbeiten zur Kirchengeschichte 116 (Berlin/New York, 2012), pp. 51–78.

40 K. Cooper, 'Approaching the Holy Household', *Journal of Early Christian Studies* 15 (2007), 131–42.

41 P. Rousseau, *Pachomius: the Making of a Community in Fourth-Century Egypt* (Berkeley and Los Angeles, CA, 1985), pp. 3–6.

in response to an ever-tighter administrative structure for collecting taxes, which increasingly held communities collectively accountable for the economic performance of each member. Rousseau's view has much to recommend it. Households certainly faced new pressures in the third century, resulting both from the economic crisis itself and from the administrative reforms of the Tetrarchs in its aftermath, and it makes sense to see the new prominence of the ascetic movement as in part a response to these new pressures.

But again, the property arrangements underlying the ascetic communities may not have differed very much, in the first phase, from those of non-ascetic households. The monasteries of the fourth century seem to have been under private ownership, and indeed in many cases there was fluidity between the monastery and the informally constituted ascetic household of a landowner who offered hospitality to like-minded guests and dependents. Pachomius' successor as abbot, for example, was a rich landowner who seems to have been a patron of the community – though history does not record whether the monastery itself was in fact established on his land.[42] It is not until the fifth and sixth centuries that we begin to have evidence that monasteries could have legal personality as institutions.[43]

Ascetic communities offered a respectable destination for youths of either sex who remained unmarried. This was an important function in a society where access to the marriage market required access to material resources. The female communities on the whole kept a low profile, and indeed female ascetics frequently lived with their own families.

But male communities made themselves visible as a volatile element in the political mix. In the cities, monks acted as sound-boxes for episcopal agendas.[44] Men who had no dependents could take risks that others could not, and a restless and volatile entourage could be an asset to a bishop. But not always: the monks were often unruly and even violent, destroying pagan shrines and terrorizing urban populations for the sake of various righteous causes. Bishops may have encouraged or at least turned a blind eye on the excesses of the monks, but in the end they would find that the independence of the monasteries was a source of persistent difficulty.[45]

[42] Cooper, 'Approaching the Holy Household'.
[43] Cooper, 'Poverty, Obligation, and Inheritance', 173–4.
[44] D. Brakke, *Athanasius and the Politics of Asceticism* (Oxford, 1995).
[45] G. Dagron, 'Les moines et la ville: Le monachisme à Constantinople', *Travaux et mémoires*, 4 (1970), 229–76, with, more recently, E. J. Watts, *Riot in Alexandria: Tradition and Group Dynamics in Late Antique Pagan and Christian Communities* (Berkeley and Los Angeles, CA, 2010), and M. Gaddis, *There is No Crime for Those Who Have Christ: Religious Violence in the Christian Roman Empire* (Berkeley and Los Angeles, CA, 2005).

As a result, in 451, the Council of Chalcedon ruled that abbots and their monasteries must be accountable to the bishop in whose diocese the monastery was established.

Once episcopal oversight was in place, the unyoking of ascetic households from the biological production of legal heirs for a *paterfamilias* – and the orderly transmission of property to those heirs – made monasteries more susceptible to social engineering then more traditional households. Julia Hillner has documented Justinian's use of monasteries as ideal sites for domestic custody of prisoners. This was a role already undertaken by lay householders, but ascetic organizations were perhaps especially well suited to the task.[46]

Lay householders, by contrast, were committed to their own agendas. Seen from the point of view of the bishops, they were certainly valuable as patrons for churches and monasteries. But irritatingly they tended to try to retain control of the use of their funds, preferring one-off gifts to endowments or established incomes, and maintaining their own private churches, monasteries, and chapels well into the sixth century. Augustine had made it known to Melania the Younger early in the fifth century that splashy one-off gifts had far less value than more strategic giving which allowed for plans to be projected into the future: 'The money that you now furnish to monasteries will be used up in a short time. If you wish to have a memorial forever in heaven and on earth, give both a house and an income to each monastery.'[47]

It is by no means a coincidence that the ascetic movement rose to prominence, re-imagining property ownership as a collective enterprise, at the same time as the bishops began to be administrators of legally recognized property-holding corporations. At the same time, bishops and abbots emerged as new rivals for the share of social and political authority that had traditionally been exercised by lay landowners. It is beyond the scope of this essay to assess whether this development was a cause or an effect of the erosion of public power. Constantine's laws creating privileges and immunities for bishops in the first decade after the Battle of the Milvian Bridge reflect his interest in off-loading public services to their care. This could well have been the ancient equivalent of off-loading them from government to the charity sector, but it is also

[46] J. Hillner, 'Monastic Imprisonment in Justinian's Novels', *Journal of Early Christian Studies*, 15 (2007), 205–37.

[47] *Vita Melaniae* 20 (Gorce, *Vie de Mélanie*, 170; trans. Clark, *Life of Melania*, 43), with discussion in Cooper, 'Poverty, Obligation, and Inheritance', at 167–70. [D. Gorce (ed.), *Vie de Sainte Mélanie* (Sources Chrétiennes 90; Paris, 1962); E. A. Clark, *Gerontius, The Life of Melania the Younger: Introduction, Translation, and Commentary* (Lewiston, Lampeter, and Queenston, 1984).]

possible that he perceived the bishops as a new category of public official. It is precisely this blurring of boundaries that makes the role of fourth-century bishops so fascinating.

Conclusion: the two *patres*

It was not till the end of the fifth century that the Latin bishops would begin systematically to challenge the power of lay landowners to dispose of their own property. In Rome at least, the tide turned with the reign of Pope Gelasius (492–96), framer of the doctrine of the two powers, spiritual and worldly, on which the medieval relation of Church and State would be founded. I have suggested elsewhere that Gelasius drew on a tradition improvised during the Vandal period by African bishops, who took the opportunity of political uncertainty to by-pass imperial legal jurisdiction in their dealings with the married laity.[48] During his short reign Gelasius argued for the precedence of divine over human law; at the same time he learned to challenge the spiritual authority of the laity in more intimate ways, issuing a decretal prohibiting lay founders of churches from appointing clergy to serve their foundations without episcopal approval.[49] The lay landowner might well have a long future as a law-giver on his own estate. But in spiritual terms he was no longer its master. This, then, was the future – almost as Eusebius had remembered it.

[48] K. Cooper, 'Marriage, Law, and Christian Rhetoric in Vandal Africa', in J. P. Conant and Susan T. Stevens (eds.), *North Africa under Byzantium and Early Islam, ca. 500–ca. 800* (Washington, DC, 2015), pp. 237–49.

[49] L. Pietri, 'Évergétisme chrétien et fondations privées dans l'italie de l'antiquité tardive', in J.-M. Carrié and R. Lizzi Testa (eds.), *"Humana sapit": Études d'antiquité tardive offertes à Lellia Cracco Ruggini* (Turnhout, 2002), pp. 253–63.

2 Playing with fire: conflicting bishops in late Roman Spain and Gaul

David Natal and Jamie Wood

Introduction

In the reign of Constantine, Eusebius of Caesarea suggested that as early as the third century Roman emperors had recognized the institutional powers of bishops. On this view, Cyprian of Carthage had articulated a vision of the church universal as a network of bishops, law-givers within their own communities, with episcopal powers of arbitration which Constantine ratified in giving them their own courts. His successors found that these powers could be turned against them: before the century was out, Ambrose had rebuked Theodosius for his massacre of civilians at Thessalonica. Next, still in the traditional narrative, we move to the articulation of papal powers under Pope Leo I in the fifth century and from there onto medieval Christendom, with the episcopal ordering of a Christian society.

Plenty of revisionist energy has been directed against such a view. Some years ago Neil McLynn's study of Ambrose, for example, gave us Ambrose as improviser rather than heir to a well-established institutional position.[1] More recently, Kate Cooper, building on the work of Jill Harries, has suggested that up to the time of Constantine, the power of bishops to resolve disputes derived not from institutional office but from their status as local 'big men'. Although some of the disputants tried to claim otherwise, the justice of these bishops was 'private': they exercised power of mediation in the same way that any head of household would expect to. Through rhetorical élan, bishops from the time of Cyprian forward laid claim to something more than this, and after Constantine, by degrees, the dream of an institutional church was made real.[2]

In this chapter we seek to explain this process of institutionalization through two case studies of late Roman episcopal conflicts in the West. First, we will examine the Priscillianist controversy of the late 370s and

[1] N. B. McLynn, *Ambrose of Milan: Church and Court in a Christian Capital* (Berkeley and Los Angeles, CA, 1994).

[2] K. Cooper, 'Christianity, Private Power, and the Law from Decius to Constantine: the Minimalist View', *Journal of Early Christian Studies*, 19/3 (2011), 327–43.

early 380s. Traditionally, this has been seen as a conflict that escalated from the local to the imperial level, culminating in Priscillian's execution by the government of the usurper Magnus Maximus. We will suggest, however, that there were significant extra-local elements in play from the beginnings of the controversy. This has important implications for understanding the course and resolution of a controversy that proved both divisive and integrative for the emergence of a trans-regional church organization.

If Priscillianism has been understood as a 'bottom-up' process, our second case study, the intervention of Pope Zosimus in Gaul in 417, has often been understood as the imposition of a pope's authority 'downwards' onto the regions and cities of Gaul. In our view, such an interpretation fails to take account of the fact that Zosimus could not simply project his authority into Gaul. Rather, any intervention depended on appeals from competing parties within Gaul. Papal intervention in early fifth-century Gaul was thus largely a response to the initiatives of bishops in the province.

The contextual differences between these two conflicts are particularly important for understanding how they developed and were resolved. The Priscillianist controversy was interrupted by a sudden fragmentation of the empire due to the usurpation of Magnus Maximus in the 380s, a development which played a significant role in determining Priscillian's fate. Zosimus initiated his outreach policy to Gaul in the aftermath of two usurpations in Gaul in the early fifth century. It can thus be seen as part of an imperial attempt to reincorporate Gaul into the Roman system. In both cases, the tendency for inter-regional allegiances among bishops to have a decisive influence on local conflicts was enhanced by uncertainty about the reach of the emperor's power.

This chapter argues that rather than threatening the integrity and status of Christian organizational structures, competition and conflict at regional and supra-regional levels contributed to the construction of an increasingly hierarchical and integrated institutional church in the late Roman West. Yet, as we hope to demonstrate, the construction of the institutional church was not a top-down process. Rather, it was the by-product of conflicts which led to the development of systems of appeal and arbitration that helped to establish precedents of collaboration and mutual inter-dependence. Just as people operating at lower levels tried to garner support for their cause from both recognized and emerging authorities – institutional and charismatic – those at higher levels seized every opportunity to exhibit their ability to intervene and assert their authority within individual localities.

This double-edged sword of appeal and interference helped to institutionalize the church hierarchy. The routine of internal competition and conflict put in motion a wide network of relationships and led to frequent dialogue within the church's developing hierarchy and between geographically dispersed bishoprics. The episcopal networks of Spain and Gaul were not imposed by the core on the periphery nor were they dictated from the upper to the lower levels. Instead, such provincial networks resulted from strategic interactions at all levels of a developing ecclesiastical system, and often took place in dialogue with the imperial administration.

Conflict and scale

The productive and generative function of conflict has been a strong strand within functionalist writing in anthropology since the 1950s. In what follows, we will attempt to gain critical purchase on how bishops sought to influence the emergent structures of the late Roman church in the West. In doing so, we will draw on 'scale theory', an approach to analysing systems taken from the natural and social sciences. We argue that conflict could often reinforce such structures and give them clearer institutional definition.

The great advantage of scale theory is that it takes us away from unhelpful models of 'core' and 'periphery' in thinking about how the church was constructed and facilitates a more nuanced understanding of institutional and hierarchical formation. Scale theory allows us to see two processes more clearly: first, how individual and small groups of bishops repeatedly shifted their positions in response to political circumstance; second, how there was a qualitative change in the church as an institution across the late fourth and early fifth centuries. By the middle of the fifth century we are able to discern much more clearly defined procedures and hierarchies within the church. The 'upper' levels have managed to transfer their nominal prestige into institutionalized authority. Or, to put it another way, we suggest that 'the rise of the papacy' owes much to the politics of provincial feud in the later Roman Empire.

Before turning to scale theory, we should pause to consider one of the most influential conceptions of conflict and competition as a medium of social integration: that of Max Gluckman, the anthropologist whose work ultimately led to the conference from which this volume derives. One of Gluckman's most celebrated insights was that in communities governed by weak forms of authority the routine of structured conflicts helps to maintain social order and cohesion.[3] In a series of publications in the

[3] J. M. Wallace-Hadrill, 'The Bloodfeud of the Franks', *Bulletin of the John Rylands Library of Manchester*, 41 (1959), 459–87; see also I. Wood, '"The Bloodfeud of the Franks": a

post-war period culminating in 'The Peace in the Feud' and *Custom and Conflict in Africa* in 1955, Gluckman sought to understand the pressures facing tribal communities at a time when colonial rule was coming to an end, paying particular attention to oppositional relationships, especially those between village and state and between city and country.[4]

Perhaps most relevant to the present discussion is Gluckman's interest in the *interhierarchical role* that chiefs and district commissioners played between the colonial state and individual tribal communities. According to Gluckman, actors in *interhierarchical* roles were able to channel and modify the influence of macro processes taking place outside their communities. Theirs was an enviable position, since it gave them frequent occasion to do so in ways that advanced their own interests.[5] Gluckman was especially interested in how decisions that are taken at the centre of imperial power can often be implemented in unexpected ways by individuals in intermediate social positions. Another of Gluckman's key insights was to identify how conflict often had a legitimating effect on the issue that was being disputed. Those who disagreed had, at the very least, to agree that the subject over which they were disputing was a legitimate venue for conflict. These approaches to conflict and its resolution are peculiarly appropriate to a period of history – whether post-war Africa or the late Roman Empire – in which the 'reach' of a central colonial power is being challenged and re-negotiated.

The scale model takes aim at these interactions from another angle, considering them through the lens of complexity rather than hierarchy.[6] Emerging from the disciplines of geography and ecology, scale theory replaces the emphasis on hierarchy and the concentration of power with

Historiographical Legend', *Early Medieval Europe*, 14 (2006), 489–504, questioning Gluckman's influence on Wallace-Hadrill.

4 M. Gluckman, 'The Peace in the Feud', *Past & Present*, 8 (1955), 1–14. See also: M. Gluckman, J. C. Mitchell, and J. A. Barnes, 'The Village Headman in British Central Africa', *Africa: Journal of the International African Institute*, 19/2 (1949), 89–106; M. Gluckman, 'Tribalism, Ruralism and Urbanism in South and Central Africa', in V. W.Turner (ed.), *Colonialism in Africa 1870–1960. Part III: Profiles of Change* (Cambridge, 1971), pp. 127–66.

5 R. P. Werbner, 'The Manchester School in South-Central Africa', *Annual Review of Anthropology*, 13 (1984), 157–85; see L. Schumaker, *Africanizing Anthropology: Fieldwork, Networks, and the Making of Cultural Knowledge in Central Africa* (Durham, NC, 2001), p. 65, on Gluckman's dependence on intermediaries to do his own work.

6 We are much indebted to Julio Escalona and Santiago Castellanos for allowing us to read their chapters before publication. Much of this introduction on the scale is based on Escalona's paper: J. Escalona, 'The Early Middle Ages: a Scale-based Approach', and S. Castellanos, '*Tributa* and *Historiae*: Scale and Power at a Turning Point in Post-Roman Spain', both in J. Escalona and A. Reynolds (eds.), *Scale and Scale Change in the Early Middle Ages: Exploring Landscape, Local Society, and the World Beyond* (Turnhout, 2011), pp. 9–30, and pp. 187–214.

an emphasis on scale, understood as the level of complexity within a given social system. 'Complexity' does not simply refer to a society with a complex hierarchy. A society with a relatively ill-defined social hierarchy can be characterized by remarkable levels of relational complexity.[7] Since a scale-based approach facilitates analysis of how the collapse of higher complexity levels affects underlying components, it may offer a useful framework for analysing the increasing regionalization of the late antique West, because both social fragmentation (reduction in scale) and supra-regional integration (increase in scale) occurred at various points in the period. An important advantage of such an approach is that it bypasses debates about system-wide continuity and rupture that have long dominated scholarly discussion of the end of the Roman Empire.[8]

The concept of *scale-jumping* may also be useful to the study of late antique and early medieval societies. *Scale-jumping* refers to 'how actors operating at a given scale are able to connect to processes operating at another – higher or lower – scale in order to reinforce claims within their own context'.[9] For example, as we will see later in this chapter, Gallic bishops raised the spectre of Gallic secessionism when appealing to Rome in order to encourage papal intervention. They drew the authority of the higher scale level into their disputes in order to maintain their autonomy in the face of the efforts of the Bishop of Arles to assert his superiority on a regional level.

Although it is perhaps a more dynamic and flexible model, the notion of *scale-jumping* can be related to Gluckman's *interhierarchical roles.* Gluckman emphasized the discontinuities between the tribe and the colonial state, understanding them as two separate economic, social, and ideological systems linked by asymmetric hierarchical relationships.[10] Because these spheres are only partially integrated, people in interhierarchical roles are

[7] B. A. Nelson, 'Complexity, Hierarchy, and Scale: a Controlled Comparison between Chaco Canyon, New Mexico, and la Quemada, Zacatecas', *American Antiquity*, 60/4 (1995), 597–618; J. Wu and Y. Qi, 'Dealing with Scale in Landscape Analysis: an Overview', *Geographic Information Sciences*, 6/1 (2000), 1–5; Escalona, 'The Early Middle Ages: A Scale-Based Approach', pp. 5–10.

[8] Two paradigmatic examples of rupture and continuity are respectively Bryan Ward-Perkins and Walter Goffart, see: B. Ward-Perkins, *The Fall of Rome and the End of Civilization* (Oxford, 2005), and W. Goffart, *Rome's Fall and After* (London, 1989). For a critical revision of this debate see C. Wickham, *Framing the Early Middle Ages: Europe and the Mediterranean 400–800* (Oxford, 2005), p. 3.

[9] Escalona, 'The Early Middle Ages: a Scale-Based approach', p. 19; G. D. Berreman, 'Scale and Social Relations', *Current Anthropology*, 19/2 (1978), 225–45.

[10] M. Gluckman, 'Interhierarchical Roles: Professional and Party Ethics in Tribal Areas in South and Central Africa', in M. J. Swartz (ed.), *Local-level Politics: Social and Cultural Perspectives* (London, 1969), pp. 69–94, at p. 70: 'these persons occupy positions where there are major discontinuities in the total hierarchy and the sets of social relations become radically different'.

often required to engage in a process termed *situational selection*, in which the same actor plays different social roles depending on the sphere of engagement.[11] Although Gluckman emphasized the pressures and constraints to which such interhierarchical actors were subjected by the community and the colonial state, he did not fully explore the challenges and opportunities that engagement with higher scale levels provided for social actors in the tribe and the metropolis.[12]

Such limitations may derive from the strong influence that the *core-periphery* model exerted on Gluckman's thinking. In various ways this model – largely dependent on the European colonial experience – has long been at the centre of the western historical analyses. The core-periphery model has had a major impact on modern historical approaches to many periods of study and has influenced a number of explanations for the end of the Roman Empire in the West.[13] However, aside from some colonial capitalist systems, the empirical basis for this model is open to question. Its applicability to pre-modern, non-colonial, and non-capitalist contexts is therefore in serious doubt.[14]

A scale-based approach has the potential to overcome the limitations of a rigidly applied core-periphery model. As we have demonstrated, scale conceives of the social construct as a complex network of relationships among the different units and levels of a system. Scale can therefore be considered not as a pre-determined social structure, but a result of human activity. As a consequence, it is subject to modifications that arise from the individual perceptions and behaviours of the various agents within the different parts of the system.

Scale theory thus allows for a more nuanced analysis of territorial and social structures because it acknowledges that individuals and groups manipulate and transform systems and their constituent parts through

[11] M. Gluckman, 'Social Anthropology in Central Africa', *Rhodes-Livingstone Journal*, 20 (1956), 1–27, at 17 and 'Tribalism in Modern British Central Africa', *Cahiers d'Études Africaines*, 1/1 (1960), 55–70.

[12] A. Kuper, 'Gluckman's Village Headman', *American Anthropologist*, 72/2 (1970), 355–8; M. Gluckman, 'The Bonds in the Colour-bar', in *Custom and Conflict in Africa* (Oxford, 1955), pp. 137–65; W. M. J. Van Binsbergen, 'The Unit of Study and the Interpretation of Ethnicity', *Journal of Southern African Studies*, 8/1 (1981), 51–81, at 54.

[13] Perceptible for instance in Jones' depiction of the imperial machinery, A. H. M. Jones, *Later Roman Empire 284–602: a Social, Economic and Administrative Survey* (Oxford, 1973). This was rightly criticized by Bickerman: see E. J. Bickerman, 'Review of *Later Roman Empire 284–602*', *The American Historical Review*, 70/3 (1965), 750–1.

[14] M. J. Rowlands, 'Centre and Periphery: a Review of a Concept', in M. Rowlands, M. Larsen, and K. Kristiansen (eds.), *Centre and Periphery in the Ancient World* (Cambridge, 1987), pp. 219–42; see also P. Fouracre, 'Space, Culture and Kingdoms', in P. Linehan and J. L. Nelson (eds.), *The Medieval World* (London, 2001), pp. 366–80.

social action and competition. Scale enables us to envisage 'integration' as occurring without having to assume that uniformity was established or that centralization was happening at the same time. As we seek to demonstrate in the case studies that follow, another benefit of scale theory is its potential for analysing power structures. We suggest that the church of the late fourth and early fifth century was not a 'top-down' hierarchical 'structure' but a social organism constructed by the social and rhetorical actions and reactions of individuals and groups at different levels and in different places. Finally and most importantly, a scale-analysis model makes it possible to chart two simultaneous developments – one, the fragmentation of the Roman political order and the other, the gradual integration of discrete regional ecclesiastical communities into a single trans-regional system (an emerging 'church') – and to assess how the two developments fed into one another.

The growing pains of the Spanish episcopacy: the Priscillianist controversy in its late fourth-century context

We begin with the affair of Priscillian of Ávila, a lay Spanish landowner whose conflict with a group of bishops led first to his consecration as a bishop himself and then to his execution on a sorcery charge. While it is difficult to understand the root cause of the conflict, it is instructive to see Priscillian as a figure who tried and failed to establish an inter-regional network of ecclesiastical support at a time when the political landscape was treacherously unpredictable.

At some point in the mid-380s, after two trials, Priscillian was condemned to death by the government of the usurper Maximus on a charge of sorcery. He was executed at some point between 385 and 387.[15] This is not the place to offer a full-blown narrative of the Priscillianist controversy and the events that followed it, but it will be instructive to pick out a number of key features that illustrate the ways in which disputants sought to create and exploit episcopal and imperial networks across a range of scale levels in order to bolster their position in relation to their enemies.[16] In this case study and the one that follows we will suggest that such competition had the effect, gradually but perceptibly, of more clearly

[15] V. Burrus, *The Making of a Heretic: Gender, Authority, and the Priscillianist Controversy* (Berkeley, CA, 1995), pp. 187–8, surveys scholarship on the likely date of the trial and execution of Priscillian.

[16] For a treatment of Priscillianism that relates the 'movement' to Arianism in the Iberian Peninsula earlier in the fourth century, see: M. V. Escribano Paño, 'Heresy and Orthodoxy in Fourth-Century Hispania: Arianism and Priscillianism', in K. Bowes and M. Kulikowski (eds.), *Hispania in Late Antiquity: Current Perspectives* (Leiden, 2005), pp. 121–50.

defining such scale levels and the networks that had sought to exploit them and thus the concept and structures of the 'church' as an emergent institution.

Priscillian was a well-born landowning intellectual who came either from the north-western Spanish province of Gallaecia or the south-western province of Lusitania. Originally he did not hold ecclesiastical office, yet due to his erudition and ascetic rigour he attracted a mixed following of women and men, including at least two bishops, in the 370s and early 380s.[17] The group's ascetic practices and Priscillian's teachings led Bishop Hyginus of Córdoba to report Priscillian and his followers to the metropolitan bishop of the province of Lusitania, Hydatius of Mérida, in the late 370s.[18]

Hydatius' initial efforts to bring Priscillian and his party to order failed. A council was called at Zaragoza in October 380. Pope Damasus seems to have been consulted in advance of the meeting and had stated that no-one could be condemned in their absence. Priscillian must not have been present at the council because he is not named in its records. However, the topics that were treated leave little doubt that the main intention was to condemn practices labelled as Gnostic, Manichean, and, ultimately, 'Priscillianist'.[19]

The council forbade unauthorized persons from taking the title 'doctor', a not very veiled reference to the fact that at this point Priscillian did not hold office within the church. As we shall see, efforts were soon made to remedy this deficiency and raise Priscillian to the episcopacy, a move that opened up new avenues for competition between the Priscillianists and their opponents.

Of the twelve bishops that attended the council at Zaragoza, two came from Gaul. Bishops from north of the Pyrenees were clearly taking an interest in the matters of ecclesiastical discipline in Spain and Priscillian may have had some support in southern Gaul.[20] This and the effort that was made to consult Damasus prior to the council emphasize that there was a strong trans-regional dimension to the conflict from its inception.

[17] For Priscillian's background, see A. M. C. M. Jorge, 'The Lusitanian Episcopate in the 4th Century: Priscilian of Ávila and the Tensions Between Bishops', *e-journal of Portuguese History* 4/2 (2006), available online at: brown.edu/Departments/Portuguese_Brazilian_Studies.

[18] A. R. Birley, 'Magnus Maximus and the Persecution of Heresy', *Bulletin of the John Rylands Library of Manchester*, 66/1 (1983), 13–43, at 18–19.

[19] Priscillian, *Tractate* 2.35.22–4, ed. G. Schepss, CSEL, 18 (Vienna, 1889); Birley, 'Magnus Maximus', 20. The council was concerned with the practical enforcement of ecclesiastical discipline, placing restrictions on fasting, female attendance at readings with men who were not their relatives, and retreats in country houses or the mountains. Burrus, *Making of a Heretic*, pp. 15–18, and 47–159.

[20] Birley, 'Magnus Maximus', 18–20.

As the conflict intensified, further interventions were made from Gaul and Italy, and both Priscillian and his enemies solicited outside aid repeatedly.

After the council at Zaragoza, we see a reduction in the scale level at which conflict occurred as the Priscillianists attempted to intervene directly in Hydatius' backyard.[21] After he returned from Zaragoza to Mérida, Hydatius was accused – on what charge is not recorded – by one of his own priests and members of the clergy withdrew from communion with him. The charges that had been made against Hydatius were circulated among the Priscillianist churches and two of Priscillian's supporters – the bishops Instantius and Salvianus – decided to go to Mérida to investigate, but they were beaten back by a crowd. It is clear that at this point in the conflict neither side was able to impose its will from the top down and instead looked to local bases of support to gain the upper hand.

Having failed to undermine each other's local power bases, the next stage of the conflict saw both sides attempt to consolidate their position. Significantly, the Priscillianists decided to fight the bishops on their own, ecclesiastical, turf. The Priscillianists produced and circulated a profession of faith to demonstrate their orthodoxy. They also seem to have attempted to raise more members of the movement to the episcopate. As part of this effort, at some time after the council of Zaragoza, Priscillian was consecrated as Bishop of Ávila by his episcopal supporters, Instantius and Salvianus.[22]

Priscillian entered the controversy as a lay aristocrat, and his consecration as a bishop caused as many problems as it solved. His opponents later claimed that his consecration was invalid on the grounds that his consecrators had been condemned at Zaragoza, a charge which was denied repeatedly by the Priscillianists.[23] Hydatius also obtained a directive from Emperor Gratian (r. 375–83) that the 'Manichees and pseudo-bishops' should be deposed.[24] Of interest here is the 'clericalization' of the conflict as both sides fought over the same turf. This process of alignment should, according to the logic of the 'Peace in the Feud', have confirmed the importance of the ecclesiastical turf which was being fought over. In the case of Priscillian, however, the conflict was not to remain a church

[21] The main disputants also engaged in direct controversy with one another. Hydatius wrote a tract condemning the use of apocrypha and Priscillian responded with a spirited defence; Burrus, *Making of a Heretic*, pp. 25–46, 55, 60–1, 64–5, 68; A. S. Jacobs, 'The Disorder of Books: Priscillian's Canonical Defense of Apocrypha', *The Harvard Theological Review*, 93/2 (2000), 135–59.

[22] Sulpicius Severus, *Chronicle*, 2.47.4, ed. Ghislaine de Senneville-Grave, *Sulpice Severe, Chroniques, Sources chrétiennes*, 441 (Paris, 1999).

[23] Ibid., 2.47.2.

[24] Priscillian, *Tractate* 2.40.30, 2.41.1; Sulpicius Severus, *Chronicle*, 2.47.5–7.

matter. No sooner had the dispute veered into ecclesiastical territory, than it jumped tracks again. The calling in of the imperial government was the next stage in the escalation of the conflict. Ultimately, what this suggests is that the borders of 'church' and 'state' were highly permeable at this point. In fact, it may be too early to talk about separate spheres at all.

It is clear, therefore, that from the beginning the controversy was not restricted by geographical or organizational boundaries. The letter from Pope Damasus and the attendance of the Gallic bishops at Zaragoza is good evidence for this. The aristocratic nature of the Priscillianist group may also help to explain why the conflict soon began to shift between the ecclesiastical and the imperial spheres as Priscillian's supporters utilized what were for them entirely normal legal processes, although studies have demonstrated that late Roman bishops were as adept at using imperial law to their advantage as were other members of the elite.[25] Scale theory may therefore offer the most appropriate model for understanding the development of the conflict. The Priscillianist conflict began by operating at a 'pre-hierarchical' stage, where all of the participants attempted to maximize their advantage, on whichever scale level seemed most appropriate. Just as conflict helps to legitimize the territory that is being fought according to 'The Peace in the Feud', so it may help to establish the legitimacy of different levels of a 'pre-hierarchical' scale system.

The conflict escalated formally and geographically, incorporating different levels of the imperial and ecclesiastical hierarchies, as well as aristocratic factions. At first, Priscillian and some of his supporters – including a number of Gallic aristocrats from around Bordeaux – travelled through Gaul and Italy attempting to gain support from important bishops including Pope Damasus and Bishop Ambrose of Milan, both of whom proved reluctant to intervene.

Priscillian and his supporters sought assistance not only from figures within the church in Italy but also from the imperial government there. Priscillian had some success in securing a rescript from the government in Milan allowing him to depose Ithacius from his see. Ithacius fled to Trier and managed to gain the ear of the praetorian prefect there. Priscillian's

[25] Among the extensive literature on late Roman bishops making use of imperial law, notable recent studies include: C. Humfress, 'Bishops and Lawcourts in Late Antiquity: How (Not) to Make Sense of the Legal Evidence', *Journal of Early Christian Studies*, 19/3 (2011), 375–400; C. Humfress, *Orthodoxy and the Courts in Late Antiquity* (Oxford, 2007); K. Uhalde, *Expectations of Justice in the Age of Augustine* (Philadelphia, PA, 2007); E. T. Hermanowicz, 'Catholic Bishops and Appeals to the Imperial Court: a Legal Study of the Calama Riots in 408', *Journal of Early Christian Studies*, 12/4 (2004), 483–523.

Italian connections influenced the matter in his favour and Ithacius had to go into hiding to avoid trial back in Spain.[26]

In the meantime, however, Magnus Maximus (r. 383–8) had taken control of the government of Britain, Gaul, and Spain. In response to an approach from Ithacius, Maximus ordered that a council be convened at Bordeaux to bring the Priscillian affair to a close. At the Bordeaux council, which was probably held in 384, Instantius, one of Priscillian's episcopal supporters, was deposed.

Although we do not know for certain whether he did so before or after his own case had been heard by the Bordeaux council, Priscillian appealed directly to the government of Magnus Maximus in Trier.[27] The decision to place the matter before the imperial government turned out to have been ill-judged. There was a series of hearings in which Priscillian stood accused of the capital charge of sorcery by Ithacius. Bishop Martin of Tours worked behind the scenes to persuade Ithacius to withdraw his charges and Magnus Maximus to act with clemency, yet despite his best efforts Priscillian was eventually found guilty and executed at some point between 385 and 387 on the sorcery charge. A number of Priscillian's supporters were executed and others were exiled to the Isles of Scilly, some after a follow-up trial.[28]

Priscillian must have had some hope that the tribunal at Trier would find in his favour and it has been suggested that he was somewhat unlucky to be caught between the usurper Magnus Maximus and the eastern Roman Emperor Theodosius as they jockeyed to establish their credentials as defenders of Nicene orthodoxy.[29] On this interpretation, Priscillian was simply in the wrong place at the wrong time and his case provided Magnus Maximus with an opportunity to prove that he was a hardliner on religious issues.

However, Priscillianism also illustrates the wide gap that existed between the ideal and reality of conflict resolution processes in the later Roman Empire. This was because the affair was influenced significantly by the murky workings of the imperial bureaucracy in at least three ways. First, Priscillian and his enemies are alleged to have bribed imperial officials to try to gain the upper hand in their dispute.[30] Corruption was far from unknown in the late Roman administration, so this was not

[26] H. Chadwick, *Priscillian of Avila: the Occult and the Charismatic in the Early Church* (Oxford, 1976), pp. 41–2.

[27] Birley, 'Magnus Maximus', 28–9 for uncertainty over whether Priscillian was dealt with at Bordeaux or he appealed before his case could be heard.

[28] Ibid., 34–5 for full details.

[29] Ibid., 32, 37; Chadwick, *Priscillian of Avila*, pp. 114–26.

[30] Chadwick, *Priscillian of Avila*, pp. 40–4; Birley, 'Magnus Maximus', 23.

surprising.[31] Second, rivalry between high officials within the administration was common and seems to have dogged efforts to resolve the dispute.[32] Third, the charge for which Priscillian was finally executed, sorcery, carried the additional punishment of confiscation of property.[33] Such property went to the imperial fisc rather than to the deceased person's family. Although it may not have been the primary motivation for governmental interest in the case, the accusations against Priscillian and his wealthy followers provided the administration of Magnus Maximus with a welcome opportunity to boost its coffers.

The outcome of the Priscillianist controversy hung on the interaction between two overlapping systems: episcopal networks and imperial law. Both sides called for support from ecclesiastics from outside Spain. They also sought to draw members of the imperial administration into their disagreements, with some success. Such support provided them with the means to escalate their disagreement through the different levels of the legal apparatus and attendant appeals processes. Even the judicial process that resulted from this shift was by no means fixed and Priscillian and his supporters were able to appeal for support to external authorities, including illustrious bishops, aristocratic backers, and members of the imperial government.

The Priscillian affair extended across all scale levels within the church at the same time as shifting sideways into the imperial sphere, although, as we have already suggested, the boundaries between the two systems were extremely porous at this period and we should be wary of describing the church as a fully formed institution in this period. We have already seen that the controversy involved disagreements at the provincial level of the ecclesiastical hierarchy. Yet those disputes grew from, and in turn created new, tensions at the micro-level, within individual cities. Certain priests at Mérida withdrew from communion with Hydatius after the council at Zaragoza, suggesting that Priscillian had some sympathizers in the bishopric of one of his main critics. This was met with a strong reaction from Hydatius' supporters, who prevented the Priscillianists from intervening more directly in the affairs of the bishopric.

Contemporary observers, even those who were opposed to Priscillian and his party, were disturbed by the fact that an ecclesiastical dispute was

[31] For a survey of evidence for bribery and corruption in the later Roman Empire, see R. MacMullen, *Corruption and the Decline of Rome* (New Haven, CT, 1988).

[32] Chadwick, *Priscillian of Avila*, pp. 40–4.

[33] Chadwick, *Priscillian of Avila*, pp. 143–5. For a general survey of Roman legal rulings on magic, see J. B. Rives, 'Magic in Roman Law: the Reconstruction of a Crime', *Classical Antiquity*, 22/2 (2003), 313–39, esp. 329, and 332.

judged in an imperial tribunal and horrified that the dispute had ended with Priscillian's execution. In the aftermath of the execution, there was a determined effort to prevent ecclesiastical conflicts from shifting into the imperial sphere.[34] We propose that such efforts may have played an important role in differentiating two systems that had not been clearly distinguishable in the past.

We shall see in a moment how this discussion played out in Gaul. In Spain, the backlash against Priscillian's accusers may have provided his supporters with the breathing space to entrench their position on the moral high-ground in the cities of Spain.[35] They seem to have had some success because our sources indicate that tension may have continued into the fifth century.[36] Not long after Priscillian's execution a council of the Spanish church was held in Toledo (397–400). Most of the council's canons are devoted to attacking Priscillian's doctrine and several forbid actions which are strikingly similar to the accusations which had been levelled at Priscillian in the 380s. The council should therefore be seen as a determined effort to stamp out Priscillian's supporters and their practices once and for all.[37]

This was more than a simple mopping-up operation, however. The records of the council reveal that the Priscillianists were still in the ascendancy in certain cities in the province of Gallaecia in north-western Spain. They had managed to exclude the 'orthodox' bishops from their sees and the council attempted to bring the Priscillianist bishops into line. The Priscillianist party had not been waiting passively for the re-imposition of ecclesiastical discipline from the 'centre' since its founder's execution. Symphosius, one of the bishops reconciled to the orthodox party at Toledo, is said to have ordained Dictinius as a bishop at the urging of the 'people', even though such an action had been forbidden in a letter that had been sent to Spain by Ambrose of Milan.[38] Symphosius was also said to have ordained bishops to other vacant sees, especially those in Gallaecia. The acts from Toledo therefore provide powerful evidence both for attempts to suppress the Priscillianist movement and for its continued vibrancy in parts of Spain in the decade after Priscillian's execution. Priscillian's supporters had tried to bolster their authority and perhaps to secure themselves from prosecution by appointing bishops

[34] Chadwick, *Priscillian of Avila*, pp. 126–65.
[35] Chadwick, *Priscillian of Avila*, pp. 148–65.
[36] Chadwick, *Priscillian of Avila*, pp. 208–17; Burrus, *Making of a Heretic*, pp. 102–25.
[37] *First Council of Toledo*, pp. 20–21 and *Sententiae*, ed. José Vives, *Concilios Visigóticos e Hispano-Romanos* (Barcelona and Madrid, 1963), pp. 25–32.
[38] *First Council of Toledo*, *Sententiae*, pp. 30–1.

and clerics to vacant positions, the same strategy that had been attempted in Priscillian's lifetime.

Disputants in this ecclesiastical conflict were not afraid to play 'wild cards'. They appealed to charismatic superstars of the Christian church who had little or no institutional relationship to their case. For example, Priscillian sought to draw support from Pope Damasus and Ambrose of Milan, while Martin of Tours tried to intervene too.[39] Another option might be to use family connections or powerful patrons to balance a conflict situation in their favour.[40]

The episcopal bias of our sources may not give us a rounded picture of the conflict as a whole. Yet, despite the active intervention of the imperial government and the direct involvement of Priscillian's aristocratic backers throughout the affair, the primary brokers of this conflict were bishops. Bishops, both individually and collectively, played a key role in the inception of the dispute at Zaragoza, in its escalation within Spain, and in its movement between imperial and ecclesiastical systems. Bishops from outside Spain were not reluctant to interfere in matters there and continued to try to intervene in the legal proceedings almost until the last moment of Priscillian's condemnation.

The position of bishop was of paramount importance in this dispute at lower scale levels too. Individual cities became sites of conflict, while efforts were made to bolster the authority of the episcopacy through legal pronouncements in councils. The Priscillianists were willing to play the episcopal establishment at its own game, intervening actively to destabilize the bishoprics of their opponents and trying to build up their own numbers through the ordinations of new bishops. Bishops in council took measures to entrench their power by legislating against the 'flatter' networks of the Priscillianists and reaffirming episcopal primacy within the church.

In this sense, the winner in the Priscillianist controversy was episcopal office; and the lesson learned was that bishops should not play with imperial fire. In turning to Gaul, we see how a somewhat chastened episcopacy moved towards a hierarchical model of conflict. Escalation of a dispute remained, of course, a possibility – but the elements of volatility and complexity characteristic of the late fourth century were contained.

[39] As a result of his attempts to prevent Priscillian's execution, Martin of Tours was accused of the same crimes as Priscillian by Ithacius of Ossonuba.

[40] For an example of the tendency for disputants in Spanish ecclesiastical conflicts to draw on their family connections, see M. Kulikowski, 'Fronto, the Bishops, and the Crowd: Episcopal Justice and Communal Violence in Fifth-Century Tarraconensis', *Early Medieval Europe*, 11 (2002), 295–320.

Papal primacy and Gallic 'particularism': ecclesiastical and imperial politics in the early fifth century

Across the Pyrenees in Gaul, bishops argued with each other during the first two decades of the fifth century in ways that are strikingly similar to the Priscillianist controversy. They invoked the support of emperors and usurpers, and operated across scale levels to draw down the authority of higher powers both within and outside the church.

One bishop, in particular, Proculus of Marseilles, had all the makings of a new Priscillian: ascetic charisma, a network of followers, and a disdain for higher powers who tried to stop him. In 416, the bishop of Rome, Pope Zosimus, intervened, claiming the primacy of Rome over the Gallic sees, and in fact over the whole imperial church. Zosimus' intervention has often been seen in terms of failure: he was unable to realize the kind of papal authority that Pope Leo I would later wield to subdue the unruly Gauls in the middle of the century. From our perspective, however, the Gallic disputes of the early fifth century and papal involvement speak to new a level of orderliness in the conduct of ecclesiastical rivalry – a peace in the feud. Where the Priscillianist case had spiralled out of control, tensions around Proculus remained within relatively circumscribed channels. The 'Proculan controversy' (and it is not an accident that we do not refer to it in those terms) was a dog that did not bark.

Priscillian's execution divided the episcopate in Gaul, and debate continued long after the event. One bishop, Felix of Trier, was outspoken in his defence of Priscillian's punishment, much to the disgust of some of his colleagues. A group of bishops gathered around Martin of Tours, Victricius of Rouen, and Proculus of Marseille, following the precedent set by Ambrose of Milan, and decided to excommunicate Felix and those who were in communion with him.[41] Felix's supporters seem to have maintained strong links with the Gallic regional aristocrats who had supported the usurpation of Magnus Maximus, whereas the anti-felicians initially exploited their connections with Italian bishops, such as Ambrose of Milan and Pope Damasus.

As the debate unfolded Proculus emerged as an ambitious and independent provincial leader in his own right. By the end of the century (although the chronology is disputed), he seems to have made a bid for juridical pre-eminence in Provence – risking the disapproval of more

[41] Ambrose, *Ep.* 30 [24].12, ed. O. Faller and M. Zelzer, CSEL 82.1–3 (Vienna 1968, 1990, 1982).

distant authorities. Whether by accident or design, Proculus' disquiet at Priscillian's execution helped to strengthen links with the Italian bishops, enabling him to assume a position as a local ecclesiastical potentate that was not unlike that of Priscillian.

Proof of Proculus' political abilities and Italian connections was the Council of Turin, an event that is difficult to interpret as the last part of its proceedings is not preserved and there are doubts about its chronology.[42] We follow here Palanque's date of 398, but whichever date is accepted, the records reveal that Proculus was a canny political operator. At Turin he was able to have himself recognized as metropolitan authority over a number of bishoprics around Marseille, even though, strictly speaking, they belonged to the new province of Narbonensis II and Marseille itself was in Viennensis.[43]

So, Proculus, his allies, and his enemies played with fire – but managed to avoid the fate of Priscillian. The conflict over episcopal jurisdiction became even stronger in the first decades of the fifth century due to the deep changes in the social and political fabric of the Western Roman Empire. The invasions of Sueves, Vandals, and Alans in 406/7 and, especially, the usurpations of Constantine III (407–411) and Jovinus (411–413) in Gaul had a major impact on the Gallic episcopacy. As in the case of Magnus Maximus, it is clear that the usurpers paid attention to ecclesiastical affairs and cultivated connections to former anti-felician leaders such as Heros of Arles and Proculus of Marseille. In a period in which Gaul and Italy were separated politically, therefore, Proculus shifted his attention from his Italian connections and started to cultivate a network of contacts within Gaul.[44]

This strategy led to problems after the usurpers had been defeated. The government of Honorius made considerable efforts to stabilize the situation in Gaul, including expelling bishops who had collaborated with the usurpers from their sees. In Arles, Heros was accused of adultery and replaced by Patroclus who, according to Prosper, was a relative of

[42] J. R. Palanque, 'Les dissensions des Églises des Gaules à la fin du IVe siècle et la date du concile du Turin', *Revue d'Histoire de l'Église*, 21 (1934), 481–501. For different proposals, see C. É. Babut, *Le concile de Turin: essai sur l'histoire des églises provençales au Ve siècle et sur les origines de la monarchie ecclésiastique romaine (417–450)* (París, 1904); D. Frye, 'Bishops as Pawns in Early Fifth-Century Gaul', *Journal of Ecclesiastical History*, 42/3 (1991), 349–61; M. Kulikowski, 'Two Councils of Turin', *Journal of Theological Studies*, 47/1 (1996), 159–68. For an account which gives Proculus his due, see S. Loseby, 'Marseille: A late antique success story', *Journal of Roman Studies* 82 (1992), 165–85.

[43] *Acta Concilii Taurinensium* 1, CCSL 148 (Turnhout, 1963).

[44] Prosper Tironis, *Chronicon* (a. 412), ed. T. Mommsen, MGH SS AA IX (Berlin, 1892), pp. 385–485.

Constantius, the main general in the Western court and co-emperor during the last seven months of his life in 421.[45]

Over the next few years the imperial government reorganized Gaul and put in motion a number of measures designed to prevent future usurpations. There was a purge of those members of the Gallic aristocracy that had collaborated with the usurpations in 413.[46] Five years later, the Council of the Seven Provinces was reinstated in Arles.[47] The Council was established as an institution at which the Gallic nobility from the provinces in the imperial diocese of Viennensis gathered annually. Although intended as a forum for preventing future usurpations it has also been blamed for further promoting Gallic particularism.[48]

It was in this context that Pope Zosimus started one of the first initiatives to establish papal primacy over the church in the West. In March 417, four days after he was ordained Pope, Zosimus sent a letter to the Gallic bishops, in which he granted to the See of Arles the authority to ordain bishops in the provinces of Viennensis and Narbonensis I and II. Zosimus also ordered that Gallic clerics who wanted to appeal to the Roman bishop should first obtain commendatory letters (*litterae formatae*) from Patroclus of Arles.

Zosimus must have thought that in the context of a general concern in Rome about Gallic threats of secession, this was a good moment to undertake what was an unprecedented initiative. In the letter that he sent to the Gallic bishops, Zosimus justified the action as a response to the general distress in Gaul and the need to reorganize this problematic territory.[49]

Zosimus' ability to present his authority in Gaul as part of a wider imperial effort at preventing future secession is a classic case of 'scale-jumping' and bears striking similarities with the restoration of the Council of the Seven Provinces by the imperial government. Both were emphatic attempts to delegate power to more regionally based authorities. In this

[45] Prosper Tironis, *Chronicon* (a. 412), see J. F. Drinkwater, 'The Usurpers: Constantine III (407–411) and Jovinus (411–13)', *Britannia*, 29 (1998), 269–98, M. Kulikowski, 'Barbarians in Gaul, Usurpers in Britain', *Britannia*, 31 (2000), 325–45.

[46] *Chron.* 452 (a. 413), ed. R. W. Burgess in 'The Gallic Chronicle of 452: a New Critical Edition with a Brief Introduction', in R. Mathisen and D. Shanzer (eds.), *Society and Culture in Late Antique Gaul: Revisiting the Sources* (Aldershot, 2001), pp. 52–84; M. Heinzelmann, *Bischofsherrschaft in Gallien, Zur Kontinuität römischer Führungsschichten vom 4. bis zum 7. Jahrhundert. Soziale, prosopographische und bildungsgeschichtliche Aspekte*, Beihefte der Francia, 5 (Munich, 1976), p. 220.

[47] *Constitutio Saluberrima* (17 April 418), ed. MGH Epp. III, 13 (Berlin, 1894).

[48] Drinkwater, 'The Usurpers', 269–98; Mathisen, *Ecclesiastical Factionalism*, 42.

[49] Zosimus, *Ep.* 1.3, ed. W. Grundlach, MGH Epp. III (Berlin, 1892), 3.5–6. For Zosimus' letters we will follow the numbering proposed in PL 20, although not always the text of this edition.

way, 'central' authorities tried to normalize and even harness *de facto* regional autonomy and, in the process, to dilute the authority of what they may have considered more dangerous local centres of power. It is likely that Zosimus would have found ready support among imperial authorities, especially given the fact that Patroclus of Arles was related to Constantius.

However, there was one big difference between the Council of the Seven Provinces and Zosimus' effort to grant primacy to Patroclus in Gaul. While the government had formal power over Gaul and could legitimately delegate part of it, the Bishop of Rome did not have such power over the Gallic dioceses. Consequently, Zosimus was delegating to Patroclus a power that the Pope had never before possessed. Zosimus' letter reflected the fact that this was a novelty that lacked precedent. First, although Zosimus described the extraordinary powers of Arles, he did not use a term (such as primacy, for instance) to refer to its new authority. This indicates the overall lack of definition within the institutional framework and Zosimus' lack of authority in this matter because, at least in theory, all bishops were of equal status. Second, Zosimus had to justify the primacy of Arles by resorting to the unconvincing tradition of Trophimus, a supposed bishop of Arles who had allegedly Christianized this area in the middle of the third century.[50]

It should be emphasized here that the main beneficiary of this posturing was not the bishop of Arles, but Zosimus. His old relationship with Patroclus ensured that the bishop of Arles would be a loyal lieutenant of Rome. On another level, however, Zosimus was able to assert the supremacy of Rome because the bishop of Arles was forced to invoke the authority of Rome in order to exert his own authority over his fellow bishops in Gaul.[51] Furthermore, Zosimus' letter also included details of the procedures that were to be followed in the case of appeal to Rome if the decisions of Patroclus were not accepted in Gaul. The potential effect of the letter was therefore to establish the reliance of Arles on Roman authority. It is important to emphasize, however, that Rome's success depended largely on the acquiescence of ecclesiastical authorities at lower scale levels. As we shall see, such agreement was not necessarily forthcoming.

In fact, the protests began shortly after the content of the letter became known. When some Gallic bishops tried to appeal to Rome, they found that Patroclus refused to concede the *litterae formatae* required.

50 Zos. *Ep.* 1.2.

51 Patroclus was in Rome during Zosimus' election in 417; See Zos. *Epp.* 7 and 10; L. Duchesne, *Fastes Episcopaux de l'Ancienne Gaul* (Paris, 1894), I, 98.

Presumably, he was unwilling to allow an appeal that would have threatened his new-found status within Gaul and, in fact, Zosimus' letter did not require Patroclus to grant all requests for such letters.

It is difficult to explain Zosimus' reasons for conceding to Arles what was, in effect, a right to veto any appeal to Rome. Zosimus may have been trying to limit the custom among disgruntled Gallic bishops of appealing to Rome in order to overturn decisions that had been made locally.[52] This practice had, in the past, frequently led to the intervention of a variety of imperial and aristocratic agents in local ecclesiastical matters, with potentially dangerous outcomes, as the experience of Priscillian showed. In fact, Zosimus complained about outside interference when he defended this measure to the metropolitans of Vienne, Aix, and Narbonne.[53] This clause could also have been a way of regularizing and explicitly advertising the fact that Gallic bishops could appeal to Rome, something which may have seemed necessary after a decade of regional fragmentation. In the end, however, nothing prevented the Gallic bishops from appealing directly to Rome without the letters.

Zosimus' other interventions at the imperial level seem to confirm the Pope's determination to establish his overarching authority. For instance, sometime before 418 Zosimus had received an appeal from Apiarius of Sicca, a man who had been deposed by his fellow African bishops. Zosimus decided to reinstate him and finally managed to impose his decision, although a synod of African bishops had refused Zosimus' decisions and had forbidden external appeals.[54]

If intervening in Gallic conflicts had been Zosimus' first intention, things could not have gone better. The bishop of Rome had to answer the complaints of the metropolitan bishops of Vienne, Narbonne, and Marseille. On one interpretation, their appeals to Rome were a clear triumph for Zosimus. Despite their complaints, the metropolitans actually followed the procedure laid down by Zosimus' letter. In effect, their appeals against Zosimus' actions were an implicit recognition of the new dispensation. In order to consider the question of the primacy of Arles (and the papacy) over Gaul, Zosimus convened a council of Gallic and Italian bishops in September 417. Zosimus explained the results of the council in five letters outlining specific problems that his measure caused in Gaul.[55]

[52] R. W. Mathisen, *Ecclesiastical Factionalism and Religious Controversy in Fifth-Century Gaul* (Washington, DC, 1989), p. 48.

[53] Zos. *Ep.* 5, MGH Epp. 3.11.

[54] Bonifacius, *Ep.* 2, PL 20, cols. 749–84. See J. E. Merdinger, *Rome and the African Church in the Time of Augustine* (London, 1997), pp. 111–34.

[55] Zos. *Epp.* 3–7; É. Griffe, *La Gaule chrétienne à l'époque romaine*, vol. II (Paris, 1957), p. 148.

One of those letters was addressed to Simplicius, the bishop of Vienne (theoretically the metropolitan See of Viennensis). In it, Zosimus confirmed his previous decision that the metropolitan rights of Viennensis must be transferred to Patroclus of Arles. However, Simplicius was granted the right to ordain bishops in the small dioceses around Vienne. This represented no change from the situation established at the Council of Turin; Simplicius had ensured that his authority would not be curtailed any further. In the same letter, Zosimus dealt with the problematic bishopric of Aix, the metropolitan of Narbonensis II. Zosimus insisted on the deposition of its bishop Lazarus, who had been ordained during the usurpation of Constantine III sometime after 407. Following Zosimus' orders, Lazarus was substituted by his predecessor, Remigius, a former felician and one of Proculus of Marseilles' adversaries.[56]

The reinstatement of Remigius suggests that Zosimus' main target was Proculus of Marseille. Unlike Heros of Arles or Lazarus of Aix, Proculus had rather surprisingly managed to remain in office in spite of the loyalist reactions that followed the suppression of the Gallic usurpations of the early fifth century. This seems to have been because Proculus was a powerful figure in his city and province, and it is likely that the imperial authorities preferred to make an exception in order to maintain the peace in the important city of Marseille.[57]

Further evidence of the pressure that Zosimus brought to bear on Proculus can be gleaned from the same letter that sanctioned the primacy of Arles. In the letter, Zosimus ordered that the parishes (*paroeciae*) of Cytharista and Gargaria – in Narbonensis II but still within the orbit of Marseille – must be transferred to Arles.[58] Rather than appealing to Rome and thereby recognizing the nascent authority of Zosimus to intervene in Gaul, Proculus based his strategy on establishing his authority at lower scale levels, relying on his power within the local community and the environs of Marseille. Proculus also ordained two bishops, Ursus and Tuentius, in the parishes of Cytharista and Gargaria.[59] By ordaining bishops Proculus positioned himself as a metropolitan authority and symbolically contradicted Zosimus' vision of a hierarchical progression from the still poorly defined parish level to that of the imperial (and papal) centre of authority at Rome. In practical terms, the immediate result of Proculus' action, as in the case of the Priscillianist episcopal

[56] Zos. *Ep.* 3.3–5, CSEL 35, 103–8; about the old confrontation between Proculus and Remigius see *Chron. 452* (a. 409).

[57] Acta Conc. Taur. 1.

[58] Zos. *Ep.* 1.3. The relationships between the *pagus* of Gargaria and the *civitas* of Arles were old, as an inscription from the second century confirms, *Cf. CIL* XII, 594.

[59] Zos. *Ep.* 4.4, MGH Epp. 3.7–9.

appointments several decades beforehand, was that he would have two more supporters at the provincial councils of Narbonensis II.

Proculus' decision to retrench his position locally seems to have led him to shift alliances in pursuit of local cohesion. It is very probable, for example, that the new bishop, Ursus, was the same person with whom Proculus had been disputing at the Council of Turin in 398.[60] This was not the first time that Proculus demonstrated his willingness to form alliances with former enemies: in 398 he had been in conflict with Lazarus, who later became an ally after being elected as bishop of Aix.

Zosimus' response to Proculus' strategy of withdrawal was to try to present the defiance of the bishop of Marseille as a matter of universal concern. In September 417, Zosimus ordered the deposition of the two bishops of Cytharista and Gargaria in a letter that, significantly, was addressed to the bishops of Hispania, Gaul, and Africa.[61] Here Zosimus strained consciously to advertise the overarching authority of the Roman Church.[62] The effectiveness of Zosimus' measures in Gaul was limited and did not last beyond his death in December 418.[63] The new Pope, Boniface, was not the enthusiastic supporter of Patroclus that Zosimus had been. In addition, in 423 a new usurper, Joannes, seized power in Gaul. In this new context the balance of power in Gaul shifted again and forced Gallic bishops to realign themselves once more.

The fate of Proculus is not known, although it is likely that he remained in office until his death, which came at some point after 428. However, it is possible that he, or his successors, lost responsibility for the parishes of Cytharista and Gargaria.[64] Patroclus of Arles, on the other hand, began to focus now on cultivating relationships within Gaul, relying on Joannes' support and exploiting the usurper's political weakness to exert his own authority there. In fact, Patroclus' commitment to the usurpation caused his execution in 426, a year after Joannes' usurpation had been defeated.[65]

Zosimus' measures in Gaul have traditionally been considered as part of a failed attempt at imposing Roman authority over the church.[66] For Mathisen, Zosimus' intervention in Gaul unified opposition to the papacy and Patroclus and pushed Gallic anti-felicians, such as Proculus, into an isolationist position.[67] We argue, however, that the isolationist position of

[60] Conc. Taur. 6. [61] Zos. *Ep.* 4, MGH Epp. 3.7–9 [62] Zos. *Ep.* 4.
[63] Zos. *Epp.* 10–11, ed. J.-P. Migne, PL 673–5; Bonifacius *Ep.* 12.
[64] In the sixth century Caesarius of Arles is recorded as visiting the 'parish' of Cytharista, *Vita Caesarii* 2.21, ed. B. Krusch, MGH SRM III (Hannover, 1896), pp. 457–501.
[65] Prosper Tironis, *Chronicon* a. 426.
[66] See, for instance, L. Duchesne, *Histoire ancienne de l'Église* III (Paris, 1910), 227.
[67] Mathisen, *Ecclesiastical Factionalism*, 48–60.

some Gallic bishops was not ideological, but the result of the constraints imposed above all by competition between Gallic bishops within an unstable overall socio-political context of which periodic regional usurpations and the reimposition of central imperial control were regular features. It would not be wise, however, to assume that Zosimus' measures left things unaltered. On the provincial level, they contributed to the definition of an emerging institutional hierarchy in the Gallic church that ranged from the metropolitan sees to the small parishes that would be the main topic of debate at sixth-century Gallic councils.[68] On an imperial level, Zosimus contributed in large part to the integration of the Gallic church into a network that gradually came to converge on Rome. After Zosimus' papacy, the bishopric of Rome was increasingly perceived as an alternative arena for the playing out of local or regional competition. This emerging large-scale system was beneficial to agents operating at various levels. Gallic bishops from minor sees could make use of it to undermine the attempts of more powerful regional ecclesiastical 'hubs' to establish their superiority, while Rome could use local conflicts to slowly establish what its bishops gradually came to regard as its universal (and universalizing) vocation.

Conclusion

Blessed are the peacemakers? This chapter has suggested that breaking the peace was actually an episcopal speciality, quite as much as making it. Bishops, as they emerged in the later Roman Empire, were combative creatures. As they jockeyed for position and promotion, bishops engaged in competition on a continuous basis and this frequently resulted in conflict. Quarrelling, most often with each other, became a modus operandi.

Such competition and conflict was a risky strategy: conflicts were volatile, and could spin out of control. The tendency for competition and conflict to run out of control was not helped by the fact that in the late fourth century and well into the fifth the 'church' did not yet exist as a clearly defined entity. The conflicts that we have analysed in this chapter were important to the complementary processes of institution-building and episcopal identity formation.

Processes of fragmentation and integration into the imperial superstructure had a decisive influence on episcopal conflicts. Priscillian, Ithacius, and Proculus attempted to traverse a rapidly changing and

[68] See Council of Agde 506, Cnn. 21, 30, 38, ed. C. Munier, CCSL 148 (Turnhout, 1963).

unpredictable imperial landscape. Both Priscillian and his opponents tried and sometimes succeeded in cultivating connections with the imperial government – both with that of Gratian before the usurpation of Magnus Maximus and with Magnus Maximus afterwards. Proculus and his opponent Patroclus of Arles also knew how to exploit social and political connections and take advantage of the progressive detachment of Gaul from the empire.

In this chapter we have observed several examples of *scale-jumping* in which actors exploited connections between local conflicts and higher-scale levels in order to reinforce their position at the lower level. We have seen how conflicts about metropolitan and episcopal authority within Gaul and Spain were drawn into and became subsumed within empire-wide processes of usurpation or secession. *Scale-jumping* could also operate 'downwards': large-scale processes such as purges by the imperial government after usurpation were exploited in conflicts at local and provincial levels.

We have also seen how bishops transformed, and in some senses even brought into being, the scale levels of the ecclesiastical system through collective and individual action. Ecclesiastical competition and conflict did not necessarily end in fragmentation. On the contrary, integration also occurred through dialogue between individuals and their networks at different levels and in different geographical locations and through the establishment and refinement of new conflict management procedures. In our second case study, for example, the continued construction and reconstruction of alliances against papal interference helped to bind the Gallic episcopacy together and to further refine the mechanisms of conflict management. Dialogue between the different parts of the emerging ecclesiastical system was frequently triggered by competition and conflict, creating opportunities for the lower levels to appeal 'upwards' and for the upper levels to assume and then display their status as arbiters of disputes. Zosimus, for example, legitimized his intervention in Gaul through reference to the inability of the Gallic bishops to settle their own conflicts.[69]

Episcopal competition and conflict also led to the establishment of new conflict management procedures. In the case of the bishops of late antique Spain and Gaul, the 'Peace in the Feud' may be found in the gradual efforts that the ecclesiastical establishment made to clarify and restrict the *fora* in which conflict could be carried out and the ways in which it could be articulated. Episcopal legislators responded to circumstances in which disputes had gone too far and sought to restrict their future scope, for example by trying to snuff out the possibility of placing

[69] Zos. *Ep.* 1.1–3.

ecclesiastical disputes before imperial tribunals and closing off the involvement of bishops from nearby provinces or even further afield in local and regional conflicts. The aim was not to end conflict but to constrain the terms on which it could be carried out and resolved in future and to reinforce the point that it was bishops, as dual representatives of individual communities and the church as a whole, who were responsible for its identification and resolution. In this respect, we have suggested that the execution of Priscillian actually marked a watershed in terms of episcopal willingness to 'play with fire'. The dispute showed the success of the episcopacy in magnetizing a social world around them. The clearest sign of this is Priscillian's decision to become a bishop himself.

Priscillian's execution, however, seems to have been experienced as a defining moment in the gleefully fractious culture of the Spanish and Gallic higher clergy. For some, such as Felix of Trier, such a drawing down of the fearsome mechanics of imperial justice was wholly appropriate. For others, from Martin of Tours to Proculus of Marseille, theocracy stopped here.

Evidently, Proculus and his followers did not foreswear conflict. In the following generation, the bishop of Marseille did everything he could to 'push the envelope' in terms of extending his reach. His greatest achievement, perhaps, was in avoiding the fate of Priscillian. He survived at least three usurpers. When his enemies came after him, they did so through ecclesiastical channels. We should not let the vengefulness of Patroclus of Arles and Pope Zosimus distract us from this point: like Priscillian's ordination as bishop, what we see here is 'churching' of dispute settlement.

The intervention of Zosimus against Proculus seems in turn to have established another important script for future conflicts: appeal to Rome. In the case of Priscillian, Gallic and Italian bishops were called into what was originally a Spanish conflict. In early fifth-century Gaul, the routine of appeals and the need to find alliances outside Gaul facilitated the integration of the Gallic episcopacy into wider networks. This process increased the complexity and interconnectedness of the church. Variations in Roman episcopal policy wrought changes in the organization of the Gallic church and conflicts in Gaul fostered changes in the Roman attitude towards provincial churches.

Episcopal competition and conflict in Spain and Gaul led to a gradual but perceptible increase in hierarchy and moves to define the different institutional levels of the church. Conflicts created a vital opportunity for bishops to showcase their nominal authority. Yet, as we have stressed repeatedly, the process of increasing hierarchy was far from mechanical. Rather than the manifestation of a regularized structure, the various levels of the church were linked organically. Across at all of the geographical units and scale levels both individual actors and networks of actors contributed to developing the system as a whole.

The authority of the upper levels of the institutional church – or to be more precise a church that was in the process of institutionalizing – relied to a large extent on what they could offer to lower levels. The means by which this authority could be enforced were few and high-risk, as the execution of Priscillian showed. The construction of the institutional church was therefore not only a top-down, centre-to-periphery process. Lower and what would normally be considered 'peripheral' levels played a decisive part in it too. Actors at the lowest scale levels had room for manoeuvre even in the face of concerted imperial and ecclesiastical opposition. The combative activities of the Priscillianists in Spain after the execution of their 'leader' and Proculus' ability to use his power base in Marseilles to resist whatever charges were thrown at him are ample demonstrations of this phenomenon.

Social scientists have long recognized that disputants have a tendency to invoke higher levels in their conflicts and in the process to bring such higher levels into being.[70] In order to resolve disputes through appealing 'outside' or 'upwards' within legal systems, it is necessary for disputants and other interested parties to accept that such higher authority figures exist. It is therefore unsurprising that bishops promoted an image of the church as a universal entity at the same time as they were invoking the idea of a universal church as a resource within their local conflicts. Ecclesiastical competition and conflict in late Roman Spain and Gaul both called for and constituted ideas of episcopal authority, Christian community, and the church as an institution. The upshot of such conflicts was to provide the medieval papacy and the churches of the successor kingdoms to the Roman Empire with the ideological and practical resources to assert their independence and, at times, their supremacy.

[70] B. C. Cartwright and R. D. Schwartz, 'The Invocation of Legal Norms: an Empirical Investigation of Durkheim and Weber', *American Sociological Review*, 38/3 (1973), 340–54. E. Eriksen and J. M. Parent, 'Central Authority and Order', *Sociological Theory*, 25/3 (2007), 245–67.

3 After Rome, before Francia: religion, ethnicity, and identity politics in Gregory of Tours' *Ten Books of Histories*[1]

Helmut Reimitz

Despite the best efforts of a generation of revisionist scholarship, Gregory of Tours is still presented in most of the general handbooks of the early Middle Ages as the historian of the Franks. There are at least three reasons for this. The first has nothing to do with Gregory. No matter that he called his principal work *Ten Books of Histories*: to an English-speaking audience, this text remains most accessible in the translation of Lewis Thorpe, *The History of the Franks*.[2] The second, again, is extraneous. Gregory is our principal source for the Franks and their kings in the sixth century: no matter what he says, he is their historian by default. The third reason does have to do with Gregory. In the second half of his *Histories*, from Book V onwards, Gregory shows his readers that he kept company with Frankish kings. He is at once their courtier, their victim,

[1] I should like to thank the editors of this volume Kate Cooper and Conrad Leyser for their, as ever, generous support in correcting and improving the English of this chapter and their insightful suggestions and comments. I should also like to thank the participants of the History Seminar at Johns Hopkins University for discussing this essay with me, in particular Gabrielle Spiegel who organized the seminar. Research on this article has been generously supported by the Austrian Science Fund (FWF).

[2] See W. Goffart, *Narrators of Barbarian History (AD 550–800): Jordanes, Gregory of Tours, Bede and Paul the Deacon*, 2nd edn. (Notre Dame, IN, 2005), p. 119, with a discussion of the modern translations, which apart from the German translation of Rudolf Bucher all entitle the *Histories* as a *History of the Franks*; see already his discussion in 'From *Historiae* to Historia Francorum and Back Again: Aspects of the Textual History of Gregory of Tours', in Th. F. X. Noble and J. J. Contreni (eds.), *Religion, Culture and Society in the Early Middle Ages: Studies in Honour of Richard Sullivan* (Kalamazoo, MI, 1987), pp. 55–76. M. Heinzelmann, 'Grégoire de Tours "père de l'histoire de France"?' in Y.-M. Bercé and Ph. Contamine (eds.), *Histoire de France, historiens de France* (Paris, 1994), pp. 19–45; the translation of Lewis Thorpe (London, 1974) interestingly does not use the latest edition of Krusch and Levision published in 1951 where the *Histories* were entitled *Decem libri historiarum*. For some reason Thorpe decided to translate the edition of Henri Omont and Gaston Collon (published in two fascicles 1886 and 1893) of two manuscripts of the *Histories* (tr. Thorpe, p. 53). A very good new translation of parts of the *Histories* has been published by A. C. Murray, *Gregory of Tours, The Merovingians, Readings in Medieval Civilizations and Cultures* X (Peterborough, ON, 2006).

and their would-be adviser – in whatever role, at his own insistence, he is in the frame with them.[3] For all that, this chapter suggests, Gregory sought to hold the Franks and their kings at arm's length. He resisted Frankishness, just as he resisted Romanness. Both as an actor in and as an author of *Histories*, Gregory avoided too strong identification with all the kingdoms of this world.

Gregory lived and wrote, it is argued here, at a liminal moment: after the collapse of the Roman imperial dispensation, but before the crystallization of a new order.[4] He could see what shape that order might take: plenty of his contemporaries, whether bishops or kings, Frankish warriors or Gallo-Roman grandees, increasingly promoted or acquiesced in Frankish identity as a rallying point and a centre of signification at precisely the time when Gregory was working on his *Histories* from the 570s onwards. Gregory, however, stood against the closing down of a broader, more inchoate politics of identity.[5] As is clear from his preface, he saw himself as a narrator of confusion: 'a great many things keep happening, some of them good, some of them bad'.[6]

Many of the contradictions and incoherencies in Gregory's *Histories* have been taken as evidence that Gregory was unable to erase or reconcile all of these by the final revision he made to the text at the end of his life. This may well have been the case in some instances. But we should also remember Gregory's stern injunction that no one was to change one word of his text after his death.[7] If his text is disorientating, then that is the effect he sought to create. Later readers could, indeed did, extract a *History of the Franks* from his works, but that was not at all his intention.[8]

[3] See I. N. Wood, *Gregory of Tours* (Bangor, 1994); M. Heinzelmann, *Gregory of Tours: History and Society in the Sixth Century*, tr. C. Caroll (Cambridge, 2001); Goffart, *Narrators*, ch. 3 with the updated bibliography in the second edn. pp. XX–XXVII, Murray, ed. and tr., *Gregory of Tours*, pp. xxix–xli, see also the forthcoming *Companion to Gregory of Tours* ed. by A. C. Murray (Leiden, 2015).

[4] See now P. Brown, *Through the Eye of a Needle: Wealth the Fall of Rome and the Formation of the Christian West* (Princeton, 2012), esp. pp. 481–526.

[5] See H. Reimitz, *History, Frankish Identity and the Framing of Western Ethnicity*, AD 550–850 (Cambridge, 2015), with further literature.

[6] Gregory of Tours, *Decem Libri Historiarum* (hereafter *Historiae*), preface, ed. B. Krusch and W. Levison, MGH SRM I,1 (Hannover, 1951), pp. 1, tr. L. Thorpe, 63.

[7] Gregory of Tours, *Historiae* X, 31, ed. Krusch and Levison, p. 536, see M. Heinzelmann, *Gregory of Tours: History and Society in the Sixth Century*, tr. C. Caroll (Cambridge, 2001), pp. 94–101.

[8] This is however only true for the Fredegar-Chronicle and the *Liber historiae Francorum* whose authors turned Gregory's text upside down in their excerpts, but not for the Merovingian abbreviation of Gregory's *Histories*, generally known as the six-book version; for a comprehensive discussion see my *History*, ch. 6.

There was, of course, one clear point of reference in Gregory's universe. Having announced his intention to chronicle the vicissitudes of his era, Gregory took his stand as 'a Catholic', and set out his understanding of such a commitment. The opening chapter of his *Histories* is a credal statement.[9] This is not to say that Gregory's approach to the contemporary political order was based in 'personal piety'. One of the achievements of the past generation of Gregory research has been to take him seriously as a Christian bishop – a brilliant impresario of the cult of St Martin and of other saint cults in Gaul – and a Christian narrator, highly attuned to the way his stories aligned with sacred history of the Old and New Testament,[10] theology, and the Christian narrative since, in particular Eusebius, Jerome, and Orosius.[11]

What remains to be done, however, is to offer a systematic discussion of religion and ethnic identity as figured in Gregory's texts and in his world. Historians tend to assume that in the post-Roman dispensation, barbarian warlords and Roman provincial bishops worked for a common cause. But Christianity and Frankishness did not necessarily go together. Gregory knew this. Sometimes he was prepared to create the impression that all was well: as Ian Wood showed several years ago, Gregory's account of the conversion of the Frankish King Clovis to Catholic Christianity glides over the uncomfortable fact that the Franks had been Arian before they were Catholic.[12] Elsewhere, however, tension between Frankish kings and Christian bishops is at the very centre of his story. And he is not afraid to go further analytically. Ultimately, Catholicism offered Gregory what anthropologists call 'a rival cognition' – an alternative

[9] Gregory of Tours, *Historiae* I, 1, ed. Krusch and Levison, p. 3.

[10] P. Brown, 'Gregory of Tours. Introduction', in K. Mitchell and I. N. Wood (eds.), *The World of Gregory of Tours* (Leiden, 2002), pp. 1–28; and *The Rise of Western Christendom: Triumph and Diversity, 200–1000*, 3rd edn. (London, 2013), pp. 154–65, Heinzelmann, *Gregory*, esp. ch. 3.

[11] See C. Leyser, 'Divine power flowed from this book: Ascetic Language and Episcopal Authority in Gregory of Tours' *Life of the Fathers*', in K. Mitchell and I. N. Wood (eds.), The World of Gregory of Tours (Leiden, 2002), pp. 281–94; for Gregory's models for his *Histories* see Heinzelmann, *Gregory*, pp. 101–15, and 'La réécriture hagiographique dans l'œuvre de Grégoire de Tours', in Heinzelmann and M. Goullet (eds.), *La réécriture hagiographique dans l' occident médieval: transformations formelles et idéologiques*, Beihefte der Francia, 58 (Sigmaringen, 2003), pp. 15–70; on Eusebius' *Church History* in this context, see G. Halsall, 'The Preface to Book V of Gregory of Tours' Histories: Its Form, Context and Significance', *The English Historical Review*, 122 (2007), 297–317, and H. Reimitz, 'Cultural Brokers of a Common Past: History, Identity and Ethnicity in the Merovingian Kingdoms', in W. Pohl and G. Heydemann (eds.), *Strategies of Identification: Early Medieval Perspectives* (Turnhout, 2013), pp. 257–302.

[12] I. N. Wood, *The Merovingian Kingdoms*, 450–751 (London 1994), pp. 41–50; I. N. Wood, 'Gregory of Tours and Clovis', *Revue belge de philologie et d'histoire*, 63 (1985), 249–72.

interpretative paradigm that justifies those who would refuse to fulfil the expectations of networks of identity and obligation.[13]

We need to follow Gregory in his analysis of the competing claims of religious and ethnic identities. In what follows, we look at Gregory's representation both of conflict and of order as a way of assessing his 'identity politics'. The problem, as ever with Gregory, is to determine the value of his witness – given both his idiosyncrasy as a narrator and investment as a political actor. In what sense does he speak for anyone other than himself? Our approach here is that he gave as good as he could. His stories of dispute and hierarchy speak to the shifting matrices of identity and solidarity within which he was operating.

Law and spheres of obligation: the case of Praetextatus of Rouen

In 577, King Chilperic I (d. 584) summoned a council of all the bishops of the kingdom in Paris, Gregory among them, to hold trial against Praetextatus, bishop of Rouen, who was accused of high treason. The king was obliged to assemble the *audientia sacerdotalis* because he could only condemn the bishop of Rouen with the other bishops' agreement.[14]

The value of following this episode in some detail is that it shows us the stakes in the politics of the epoch. The dispute reveals not only conflicts of interest between the parties – dynasts and churchmen – but more fundamentally, a disagreement about how to resolve such conflicts. As Stefan Esders has shown in his insightful discussion of the case, Gregory's altercation with King Chilperic himself is not only about how to deal with Praetextatus but also about different parameters of rule and justice.[15] What were the limits of obligation and accountability, and who was to define them? Thus a clash between 'royal' and episcopal jurisdictions is in fact a debate about the nature of law and the social order of the time.

The pretext of the council leads us again into the ongoing power struggles among the Merovingian kings of Gregory's time – and

[13] For an application of the concept in late antiquity and further references see K. Cooper, 'Gender and the Fall of Rome', in P. Rousseau and J. Raithel (eds.), *A Companion to Late Antiquity* (Oxford, 2009), pp. 187–200.

[14] Gregory of Tours, *Historiae* V, 18, ed. Krusch and Levison, p. 216.

[15] S. Esders, *Römische Rechtstradition und merowingisches Königtum. Zum Rechtscharakter politischer Herrschaft in Burgund im 6. und 7. Jahrhundert*, Veröffentlichungen des Max-Planck-Instituts für Geschichte, 134 (Göttingen, 1997), pp. 443–9 and his discussion of another example in 'Der Reinigungseid mit Helfern. Individuelle und kollektive Rechtsvorstellungen in der Wahrnehmung und Darstellung frühmittelalterlicher Konflikte', in Esders (ed.), *Rechtsverständnis und Konfliktbewältigung. Gerichtliche und außergerichtliche Strategien im Mittelalter* (Cologne, Weimar, and Vienna, 2007), pp. 55–77.

Gregory seems to have been deeply involved in them. The story begins with the death of King Sigibert of Austrasia in 575. To his half-brother Chilperic, and to his widow Brunhild, Sigibert's death was both an opportunity to exploit and a danger to contain. Other parties at court, in particular Chilperic's son Merovech, and various bishops, Gregory among them, were drawn into the machinations. In the *Histories*, as Guy Halsall has recently emphasized, Gregory staged this as a point of particular crisis[16] – and this was also the point at which he, Gregory, enters the stage of his own narrative.

Sigibert's widow Brunhild tried to secure her position as queen of the eastern kingdom by building an alliance with Merovech. Chilperic had Brunhild sent to Rouen, where Praetextatus was bishop. At the same time, he sent his son Merovech with an army to Poitiers. Merovech, however, spent Easter with Gregory in Tours, a city that Chilperic had once wanted to incorporate into his kingdom even though it belonged to the kingdom of Sigibert and Brunhild. In Tours, Merovech's plans began to diverge considerably from those of his father. He went to Rouen, where he formed an alliance with his aunt Brunhild, and she took him as her husband. The marriage was performed by the local bishop, Praetexatus, who was Merovech's godfather.[17] Chilperic did succeed shortly thereafter in taking Merovech captive and exiling him to a monastery. But Merovech had planted enough seeds of opposition against Chilperic, especially within the former territory of the recently deceased Sigibert, to activate serious resistance to the king. And Merovech also soon escaped back to Austrasia.[18] Only slowly, beginning in 577, did Chilperic manage to get Merovech's rebellion under control. Eventually in the Champagne, where Merovech had looked for support in vain, he was killed at Chilperic's behest by one of his men.[19]

In the same chapter that Gregory ends with the death of Merovech, he also gives a detailed report of Chilperic's trial against Bishop Praetextatus, who had married Merovech to the widow of his uncle Sigibert in 575. Chilperic appears to have been well prepared for the trial. As Karl Ubl has shown, this political context is likely also reflected in the additions of one

[16] Halsall, 'The Preface to Book V'.

[17] See the discussion of this aspect in B. Jussen, *Patenschaft und Adoption im frühen Mittelalter*, Veröffentlichungen des Max Planck Instituts für Geschichte, 98 (Göttingen, 1991), pp. 177–98.

[18] B. Kasten, *Königssöhne und Königsherrschaft: Untersuchungen zur Teilhabe am Reich in der Merowinger- und Karolingerzeit*, MGH Schriften 44 (Hannover, 1997), pp. 45–9; Julia Hofmann, 'The Men Who Would be Kings: Challenges to Royal Authority in the Frankish Regna, c. 500–700', unpublished PhD thesis, Queen's College, University of Oxford (2008), pp. 112–50.

[19] Gregory of Tours, *Historiae* V, 18, ed. Krusch and Levison, pp. 223–5.

of the *Lex Salica* redactions. The text was expanded from its exemplar through (among other things) regulations on incest, which included the addition of a prohibition regarding a man and the wife of a dead uncle.[20] At the same time, Chilperic was also able to build on the church's regulations of incest. These were straightforwardly articulated in councils in the decade before the trial – 567 in Tours and 573 in Paris – as particularly pressing demands.[21] The policy on incest in the council of Tours is transmitted as the longest canon in Merovingian conciliar history. In the midst of misunderstandings and lazy excuses, the incest regulations of older councils were repeated and summarized. As the bishops announced in their preamble to the canon: the compendium should be distributed and shown to the people as a whole.[22]

Chilperic also refers to these ecclesiastical regulations in Gregory's account of the trial. The king opened the proceedings by accusing the bishop not only of high treason, but also of violating the laws of the church:

> What was in your mind, bishop, when you married my enemy Merovech, who should have been my son, to his own aunt, the uncle's widow? Surely you know what the canons of the church have prescribed for such a case? What is more, it is proved that you not only did wrong in this, but that you have conspired with Merovech to bribe certain people to encompass my death.[23]

But Gregory portrays the proceedings against Praetextatus as a show-trial. False witnesses appeared and presented fake evidence. Most of the bishops were either bribed or intimidated by the king, or both. This perspective becomes particularly obvious in Gregory's account after the king leaves the room and the bishops begin to discuss the case among themselves. Here Gregory the actor enters the stage of his text again, and he admonishes the bishops in a dramatic sermon: *Audite me, o sacerdotes domini, qui in unum collecti estis . . .*[24] The bishops should be aware of their responsibility. It was not the king's task to tell them what was right or wrong; that was precisely their duty. In his address Gregory attempts to convince his episcopal colleagues with examples from history. Rulers such

[20] K. Ubl, *Inzestverbot und Gesetzgebung. Die Konstruktion eines Verbrechens (300–1100)* (Berlin, 2008), pp. 176–9; for the *Pactus legis Salicae* see now his, 'L'origine contestée de la loi salique: une mise au point', *Revue de l'Institut français d'histoire en Allemagne*, 1 (2009), 208–34; and É. Renard, 'Le *Pactus legis Salicae*, reglement militaire romain ou code de lois compilé sous Clovis?', *Bibliothèque de l'École des chartes*, 167 (2009), 321–52.

[21] Ubl, *Inzestverbot und Gesetzgebung*, pp. 157–67.

[22] *Propterea placuit etiam de voluminibus librorum pauca perstringere et in canonibus inserere, ut scarpsa lectio de aliis libris in unum recitetur ad populum, Concilium Turonense (567)*, ed. F. Maassen, MGH Concilia, 1 (Hanover, 1893, repr. 1989), p. 131.

[23] Gregory of Tours, *Historiae* V, 18, ed. Levison and Krusch, p. 217, tr. Thorpe, p. 275.

[24] Gregory of Tours, *Historiae* V, 18, ed. Levison and Krusch, p. 217, tr. Thorpe, p. 275.

as Maximus, who had acted against the advice of St Martin, or more recently, Clovis' son and successor Clodomer (d. 523/524), who had refused to take the advice of the abbot Avitus, both lost their empires and their lives through the *iudicium* of the *rex aeternus*.[25]

When Chilperic hears of this, he has Gregory summoned before him. Their debate, the centrepiece of the whole episode, concerns the nature and the politics of justice. Chilperic begins the discussion by accusing Gregory of denying him, the king, *iustitia* by protecting Praetextatus. Gregory replies that the king has the power to correct anyone who strays from the path of *iustitia*. But who, asks Gregory, is supposed to correct the king when he himself acts against justice? Chilperic reacts angrily to this fundamental question, and he subverts it by challenging Gregory's own sense of *iustitia: Cum omnibus enim inveni iustitiam et tecum invenire non possum*. 'With all I have found justice and with you only I cannot find it'.[26] If not even the king can agree with his bishop on what is just, what chance do the common people have of finding justice? Chilperic threatens to turn Gregory's own bishopric against him by advertising his unjust behaviour to the *populus* of Tours.

At the threat of political agitation, Gregory tries to bring the argument to a close. *Quid plura?* There was nothing more to say. He points out only that the king has access to the *leges* and *canones*, which he ought to know well, for they warn that he will be judged by the *iudicium Dei* if he does not heed their commandments. This was a proposal that seems to have satisfied Chilperic. He invites the bishop to dine with him, but Gregory refused to accept, unless the king swears to behave according to the *leges* and *canones*. Chilperic does swear, and Gregory presents this resolution to his readers as his own victory.

But this did not help the bishop of Rouen, who, according to Gregory, was innocent. Gregory – who might well have been involved himself in plotting Merovech and Brunhild's alliance – explains that it was a trick alone that made it possible to sentence the falsely accused Praetextatus. A few bishops on Chilperic's side manage to convince the bishop of Rouen that the best solution for him would be publicly to admit his guilt; this would guarantee him the king's pardon. Praetextatus takes their advice and confesses. But instead of forgiving him, Chilperic has a

[25] Gregory of Tours, *Historiae* V, 18, ed. Levison and Krusch, p. 218, tr. Thorpe, p. 277. Gregory included the history of both rulers in previous books of his *Histories*, Maximus only briefly (*Historiae* I, 43, p. 28) but Martin's encounters with Maximus were well known through the works of Sulpicius Severus, in particular his Chronicle (*Chronicon* II, 46–51, ed. C. Halm, CSEL [Vienna 1866], pp. 103–5) – and for Chlodomer and Avitus, see *Historiae* III, 6, p. 102.

[26] Gregory of Tours, *Historiae*, V, 18, ed. Krusch and Levison, p. 219.

liber canonum brought out, which Gregory says had a 'new quire' attached to it – a *novus quaternio, habens canones quasi apostolicus*. Among these canons was the assertion that 'a bishop convicted of murder, adultery or perjury shall be expelled from his bishopric'.[27] On the basis of these 'pseudo-canons'(or so Gregory figured), Praetextatus is eventually deposed and exiled. Gregory protested the conviction, at least in his text, which he insists was not based on valid ecclesiastical law.

The episode by Gregory is still used today to illustrate the fundamental antagonism of a Roman bishop and a barbarian king – an episode about the clash of cultures in sixth-century Gaul with a barbarian mentality on the winning side.[28] But as I have argued elsewhere at greater length this is a serious misinterpretation of the episode.[29] In fact Chilperic is not criticized for his barbarian behaviour but for his adoption of Roman models, thus resorting to models of rule and representation that in Gregory's view belonged to the past. Chilperic's success in restoring law and order lulled the king into a false sense of security regarding the prospects of the kingdom's and the king's own future. As Peter Brown has recently underlined Gregory's collections of history and hagiography were written to warn the powerful (Romans and Franks alike) that Christ was still present in their world and that He would return in the last days to judge them:

> Gregory was convinced that the great of the land needed such reminders. He opened his *Histories* with a chronological survey that reminded them, abruptly, that time was running out. He left speculation on the exact date of the coming of Antichrist and the Last Days to others. But 5574 years, patiently calculated from the making of Adam to the death of king Sigibert in 575, was already a long enough respite to make one feel anxious. How much longer could God's patience last?[30]

In this respect Gregory's account of the Praetextatus case demonstrates how open the negotiations about the social and political structures of the Merovingian *regnum* remained at the end of the sixth century. Gregory actually discusses with Chilperic two different understandings of *iustitia*. Chilperic wanted to find justice *with* somebody. In his view, justice was consensual and malleable. It was based on mutual loyalties, agreements,

[27] Gregory of Tours, *Historiae* V, 18, ed. Krusch and Levison, p. 222.

[28] G. Scheibelreiter, *Die barbarische Gesellschaft. Mentalitätsgeschichte der europäischen Achsenzeit, 5. – 8. Jahrhundert* (Darmstadt, 1999), pp. 189–90.

[29] H. Reimitz, 'Contradictory Stereotypes: "Barbarian" and "Roman" Rulers and the Shaping of Merovingian Kingship', in N. Panou and H. Schadee (eds.), *Evil Lords: Theory and Representations from Antiquity to the Renaissance* (Turnhout, forthcoming).

[30] P. Brown, *The Ransom of the Soul: Wealth and the Afterlife from Late Antiquity to the Early Middle Ages* (Cambridge, MA, 2015), p. 155; I should like to thank Peter Brown for letting me read his lectures in advance.

and consent. Chilperic had found this kind of justice with everybody – *cum omnibus* – but not with Gregory, who promoted a different idea of justice. The *iustitia* that the bishop of Tours stood for was not a malleable parameter but an absolute truth. Consent could only come from the shared efforts of society's members to establish just practices in the Merovingian kingdom which aligned with eternal justice.

Certainly, one could never be sure about this truth, this eternal justice, and Gregory was not claiming to be. But one could at least build on the holy traditions and wisdom of the Christian Church, seeking to explore the truth through history. In his sermon at the beginning of Praetextatus' trial, Gregory also exhorted his fellow bishops to take into account the *exempla* of history. The 'history' he referred to was not only the past of the emperor Maximus and St Martin but also the more recent past of Chilperic's uncle Clodomer and the abbot Avitus. Gregory had portrayed Clodomer's history at length in one of the previous books. And by referring to it in his sermon, Gregory became part of the same story: Martin of Tours, the emperor Maximus, King Clodomer, Avitus, Chilperic, and Gregory became part of a history in which Gregory the shaping author constantly negotiated the *Spielräume* (room[s] for manoeuvre) in which Gregory the bishop promoted a radical Christian vision of the world.

This vision should link the different realities to a 'larger social whole' to be shared by all of the (real or imagined) social groups in the Merovingian regnum.[31] But this larger social whole was greater than the Merovingian *regnum*. Neither Gregory nor Chilperic was able to comprehend its full reality. Gregory tried to emphasize that one had to accept its existence and should strive to understand its meaning for the communities of the kingdom. In his *Histories* Gregory offered in his different personas, as actor, *auctor*, and *auctoritas*, his expertise in the business of truth to explore the reality of the *regnum Dei*. In order to fulfil his pastoral duty, however, he needed the cooperation of his audience. In his conflict with Chilperic Gregory tried in vain to convince the king of the reality of the *iudicium Dei*. Gregory lost the case of Praetextatus. But Chilperic lost his soul. If one continues to read the *Histories* one hears that after Chilperic had died, his grisly posthumous fate was vouchsafed in a vision seen by Gregory and by Chilperic's brother King Guntram.[32] But Chilperic, in Gregory's view, was not the problem: he was a symptom. His manipulative treatment of the bishops, and his self-seeking attitude towards the law

[31] On changing *Spielräume* for social, political, and cultural brokerage in post-Roman Gaul, see my forthcoming *History*, ch. 9.
[32] Gregory, *Historiae* VIII, 5, ed. Krusch and Levison, p. 374.

were typical, in Gregory's view, of the exercise of power in the kingdoms of this world. Any form of political solidarity in the here and now was provisional, and should not be mistaken for the peace and order in the world which was to come.

One such form of this-worldly solidarity was 'Frankishness'. Gregory proposes no theory of ethnic identity: as far as he was concerned, it was a problem to be solved. Ethnic identity threatened to instantiate a political culture – networks of obligation and allegiance – which stood in the way of the enactment of God's justice. Gregory set himself the task of working against the establishment of collective identities in history which his contemporaries might have understood in terms of social and political integration. But integration without divine *iustitia* was an illusion.

In response to this problem Gregory employed history as a medium not only to develop a genealogy of pastoral power in Gaul. He also used history to contrast the potency of pastoral power with the instability and vulnerability and transience of social frameworks that were not held together by the will of its members to belong to the Christian community.

These strategies of deconstruction can well be observed in Gregory's employment of the terms *regnum* and *gens*. The post-Roman world of Gregory inherited wide *Spielräume* for the interpretation of the term and the reinterpretation of its legacy by Christian writers, who increasingly called the Roman Empire a *regnum* too. The successor kingdoms in the West were all called *regna* in the political terminology of the world but they all represented still quite different and still relatively open political and social experiments when Gregory was writing his *Histories.*[33] Kings sought to use 'kingdoms' to define and focus their power: for Gregory, a kingdom was a transitional space, a temporary venue for the Christian community on its way to eternal salvation.

Gregory seeks to school his readers in his understanding of politics. He is especially explicit in the preface to Book V, which frames his account of the fallout at the death of Sigibert we have just discussed. As Guy Halsall has persuasively argued, this preface may have been based on a sermon given by Gregory at Easter of 576.[34] Gregory used it to announce to readers his own entry as an actor into the course of events – not least to underscore to them that they should pay particular attention.

[33] H. Wolfram, 'Das römische Königtum der Germanen', in W. Pohl and V. Wieser (eds.), *Der Frühmittelalterliche Staat – Europäische Perspektiven*, Forschungen zur Geschichte des Mittelalters, 16 (Vienna, 2009), pp. 3–10; H.-W. Goetz, J. Jarnut, and W. Pohl (eds.), *Regna and Gentes: the Relationship between Late Antique and Early Medieval Peoples and Kingdoms in the Transformation of the Roman World* (Leiden, 2003), pp. 21–54, in particular the contribution by H.-W. Goetz, '*Gens*, Kings and Kingdoms: the Franks', pp. 307–44.

[34] Halsall, 'The Preface to Book V'.

In the preface, Gregory addresses the *regnum Francorum* in the very first sentence: 'I am weary of calling to mind the details of the civil wars that mightily plague the *gens* and *regnum Francorum*'. As he continues, he intertwines well-known biblical citations and equally familiar experiences of the present with eschatological imagery in a drastic effort to bring the woeful situation of the kingdom before the public eye:

We now seem to see the moment draw near which our Lord foretold as the real beginning of our sorrows: "The father shall rise up against the son, and the son against the father; brother shall rise up against brother, and kinsman against kinsman". *(Matthew 24: 8)*

Gregory then addresses the kings personally: 'If only you—*o reges*—had occupied yourselves with wars like those in which your ancestors larded the ground with their sweat!' From this follows a detailed and forceful admonition to keep the peace, without which the kings could not receive God's favour.

"What is your object? What do you seek?" What have you not got in plenty? In your homes there are luxuries in abundance. In your storehouses wine, grain and oil abound; gold and silver are piled up in your treasuries. But one thing you lack: without peace, you have not the grace of God.[35]

In this address to the kings, through 'stylistic devices' and through the careful arrangement of biblical citations and eschatological associations – he tries to convince his audience that as bishop of Tours, he was an arbiter of peace and not a broker for a particular political faction.[36] Evoking the name of the Franks in the opening section might well have been part of Gregory's strategy to underline his position as a mediator between the different groups.

As a pastor the bishop of Tours also linked the *regnum* in the 'sermon' with his Christian vision of community. Though he first invokes the military model of Clovis, the *magnus et egregius pugnator* of Book II,[37] he develops his speech into an exhortation to the *reges* of his time, urging them to fight the real battle of the body and soul.

Beware then of discord, beware then of civil wars which are destroying you and your people ... If internal war pleases you – *o rex* – turn your attention to the

[35] Gregory, *Historiae* V, praefatio, p. 193, tr. Thorpe 254.

[36] Halsall, 'The Preface to Book V', pp. 297–9, on stylistic devices; cf. the still monumental study M. Bonnet, *Le latin de Grégoire de Tours* (Paris, 1890), for a recent reconstruction of Gregory's *Latinitas* see K. Hilchenbach, *Das vierte Buch der Historien von Gregor von Tours: Edition mit sprachwissenschaftlich-textkritischem und historischem Kommentar*, 2 vols. (Bern et al., 2009).

[37] Gregory, *Historiae* II, 12, ed. Krusch and Levison, p. 62.

struggle which according to the apostle is waged deep inside the every man: so that your spirit may lust against the flesh and your vices be overcome by your virtues.[38]

In the preface to the fifth book, Gregory not only presents himself in a mediating role between different factions and competing kingdoms; he also links the future of the Merovingian *regnum* to the continual efforts of its individual members, first of all the kings, to long for the eternal kingdom. The tension between the earthly and eternal *regnum* creates the interpretative framework for the history of the *regnum Francorum* and indeed any *regnum* in Gregory's *Histories*.

This tension is developed and sustained throughout the ten books of the *Histories*. From the first book onward, Gregory carefully builds up the tension between the earthly *regna* and the *regnum caeleste*. It begins with tight and carefully selected examples from Old Testament history.[39] From the history of the *regnum* of the Israelites[40] he mentions the *regnum Salomonis*, or *Roboae*.[41] Of course, the *regnum* of King Ninus should not be left out, since (as Gregory explains) that was when Abraham lived, *id est Abraham initium fidei nostrae*.[42] But so as not to give the impression that he was only interested in reporting on the *gentes Hebreae*, he also briefly enumerates *reliqua regna* which existed in the time of the Israelites – *tempore Israhelitarum*.[43] The chapter on Jesus Christ, who preached penance, bestowed the grace of baptism, and promised the *caeleste regnum* to all peoples – *cuncti gentes* – forms a sharp caesura in this respect.[44] From then on, *regnum* in the rest of the first book almost always signifies the heavenly *regnum* alone.[45] The sole exception is the *regnum* of Constantine I, which can hardly be seen as a realization of the heavenly *regnum*: Gregory reports that Constantine had his son and his wife killed out of fear that they could rob him of his rule (*regnum eius*).[46]

The connection between the earthly with the heavenly *regnum* does not stand out clearly in the *Histories* – this was an ongoing process. Gregory's *regnum* remained in the space in between human endeavours and the divine plan, semantically open-ended. So Gregory frequently employs the names of reigning kings to define a *regnum* more precisely – just as

[38] Gregory, *Historiae* V, *praefatio*, ed. Krusch and Levison, p. 193, tr. Thorpe, p. 254.
[39] For the version Gregory used see the comments of Bonnet, *Le latin de Gregoire de Tours*, pp. 54–62.
[40] Gregory, *Historiae* I, *capitulatio*, ed. Krusch and Levison, p. 2.
[41] Gregory, *Historiae* I, 13 and 14, ed. Krusch and Levison, p. 14.
[42] Gregory, *Historiae* I, 7, ed. Krusch and Levison, p. 9.
[43] Gregory, *Historiae* I, 17, ed. Krusch and Levison, p. 16.
[44] Gregory, *Historiae* I, 20, ed. Krusch and Levison, p. 17.
[45] Gregory, *Historiae* I, 25, ed. Krusch and Levison, p. 19, 3 (*regnum Dei*); ibid. I, 31, p. 24, 8 (*regnum Dei*); ibid. I, 33, p. 25, 12 (*regna caelorum*).
[46] Gregory, *Historiae* I, 36, ed. Krusch and Levison, p. 27.

Constantine sought to conserve *regnum eius*, Clovis extended *regnum suum per totas Gallias* – or Gregory orders *regna* politically and geographically by recourse to Roman geographical terminology.[47]

After the end of the second book, except for a few instances where Gregory connects the concept of *regnum* to the name of the Franks, there are only two additional moments in which Gregory defines *regna* through a collective identity. In the first, he localizes the city of Agde as (still) being in the *regnum Gothorum*; in the second, he tells of the three kings of the Thuringians, who divided the *regnum gentis illius* between them.[48]

In Gregory's own world, however, *gentes* structure the political geography only for a short period in history of Gaul. But as the main agents of history, they appear only in the second book and their role changes dramatically from the end of this book onwards.[49] Gregory subjects the term *gens* itself to this transformative process. In particular starting with the end of Book II, Gregory explores the 'playing field' of the meaning of *gens*. *Gentes* appear as subject to a *regnum*, as in *gentes ultra Rhenum*, who were an important military power base of the eastern Merovingian kings ruling in Rheims and Metz.[50] *Gentes* can be other peoples, too; the Lombards are called a *gens* several times.[51] But Gregory also uses the term to denote a family or familial network, not least that of the Merovingian kings.[52] And *gentes* could also be contingents of the *exercitus (Francorum)*, which alongside Burgundians and Saxons consisted of *Byturgi, Sanctonici or Petrocorici* – the people from cities such as Bourges, Saintes, or Périgieux.[53] In Gregory's Christendom, these

[47] For example, Gregory, *Historiae* III, 5, ed. Krusch and Levison, p. 101 and III, 31, p. 126 (Italy under the rule of Theoderic); III, 1, p. 97 (*Hispania*), II, 3, p. 40; (*Africa*) for the political-geographical terminology Goetz, '*Gens*, Kings and Kingdoms'; cf. also W. Pohl, 'Gregory of Tours and Contemporary Perceptions of Lombard Italy' in I. N. Wood and K. Mitchell (eds.), *The World of Gregory of Tours* (Leiden, Boston and Köln, 2002), pp. 131–44.

[48] Gregory, Historiae III, 4, ed. Krusch and Levison, p. 99: *Porro tunc apud Thoringus tres fratres regnum gentis illius retinebant* ... VI, 2, p. 266: ... *Agathae urbem, quae in Gothorum regno sita est* ...

[49] Cf. H. Reimitz, 'The Providential Past: Visions of Frankish Identity in the Transmission of Gregory of Tours' *Historiae*', in W. Pohl, C. Gantner, and Richard Payne (eds.), *Visions of Community: Ethnicity, Religion and Power in the Early Medieval West, Byzantium and the Islamic World* (Farnham, 2012), pp. 109–36.

[50] See E. Ewig, 'Die fränkischen Teilungen und Teilreiche (511–613)', in Ewig *Spätantikes und Fränkisches Gallien*, 1 (Munich, 1976), pp. 114–71, at 166–71.

[51] For example, Gregory, *Historiae* VI, 6, ed. Krusch and Levison, p. 272–3; ibid. IX, 25, p. 444; ibid. IX, 29, p. 447; ibid. IX, 3, p 483; see Pohl, 'Gregory of Tours'.

[52] Cf. Guntram's reproach of Berthram of Bordeaux, whom Guntram regarded as a relative for his support of Gundovald: 'Gratias', inquid [Guntram] 'agimus, quod sic custodisti fidem generationi tuae. Scire enim te oportuerat, dilectimisse pater, quod parens eras nobis es matre nostra, et super gentem tuam non debueras inducere pestem extraneam', Gregory of Tours, *Historiae* VIII, 2, ed. Krusch and Levison, p. 372.

[53] Gregory, *Historiae* VIII, 30, ed. Krusch and Levison, p. 393.

various forms of *gentes* do not structure the history of the *regnum*. Instead they merge into its perspective for a common future.

Gregory had already primed this process in the first book of the *Histories*. He begins with the Old Testament's representation of history, and yet he orientates this in selections from the chronicle of Eusebius-Jerome. These selections synoptically juxtapose biblical history with the histories of other *regna*.[54] At the same time that Gregory borrows liberally from his sources, he cites them verbatim only sometimes.[55] He treats the history of the world from Adam to Moses in only a few chapters. When he reaches the exodus of the Iraelites out of Egypt, however, he grants the crossing of the Red Sea a longer chapter in his retelling.

Many historians had already commented on this episode, and Gregory too chose to include a few remarks on the location of the place and on the crossing – *transitus* – itself. He extensively described the details of an account that was very important to him, for he saw it as the archetype of Christian baptism – *tipum nostri baptismatis*.[56] He enters into a small exegetical treatment in response to the widely shared understanding that the tribes – *tribus* – of Israel had gone through the Red Sea in separate groups, and that the sea had opened up more pathways to accommodate them. Gregory rejected this interpretation. When the Israelites undertook their *transitus* through the Red Sea, the division of the *tribus* did not play any part. In the end, Gregory cites the Apostle Paul who forcefully emphasized that all were baptized beneath the cloud: *Omnes patres nostri sub nube fuerunt et omnes in Moysen baptizati sunt in nube et in mare*.

Such differences played no role in baptism. They dissolved – as they did at the end of the second book, when, after the baptism of Clovis and the three thousand *de exercitu suo*, the different individuals and groups that were previously identified as *Franci* merge into the spiritual and social texture of Gaul.

[54] On the Christian world chronicles see the concise and excellent discussion of Brian Croke, *Count Marcellinus and His Chronicle* (Oxford, 2001), pp. 145–69; on the ancient and late Antique chronicle tradition see now R. Burgess and Michael Kulikowski, *Mosaics of Time: The Latin Chronicle Tradition from the First Century BC to the Sixth Century AD* (Turnhout, 2013); on chronicles in sixth century Gaul, see Ian Wood's discussion of Marius of Avenches, 'The "chain of chronicles" in London BL 16974' in Richard Corradini and Maximilian Diesenberger (eds.), *Zwischen Niederschrift und Wiederschrift: Historiographie und Hagiographie im Spannungsfeld von Edition und Kompendienüberlieferung*, Forschungen zur Geschichte des Mittelalters, 15 (Vienna, 2010), pp. 67–78; for Eusebius and Jerome see A. Grafton and M. Williams, *Christianity and the Transformation of the Book: Origen, Eusebius and the library of Caesarea* (Cambridge, MA, 2006), in part. ch. 3.

[55] See the remarks of Bruno Krusch, in the preface of his edition of the *Histories*, p. XIX.

[56] Gregory, *Historiae* I, 10, ed. Krusch and Levison, pp. 11–13: *tipum nostri baptismatis* (p. 13).

This was not only true for the Franks, however, but also for other collectives in the *regnum*. Parallel to the Franks, other *gentes* such as the Alemans, Thuringians, Burgundians, and even the Saxons appear in the *Histories*, and the *regnum* similarly absorbs them.[57] But it seems that Gregory did not find it necessary to work as hard as he had in the case of the *Franci* to argue against a privileged role for the identities of these other groups.

After Rome

It is significant that we can observe parallels to Gregory's efforts in regard to Frankish identity in only one other case: that of Roman identity. At the beginning of his history, Gregory explicitly refers to the Chronicle of Eusebius and Jerome as a chronological model.[58] In certain places Gregory actually takes passages from Jerome and his ordered list of Roman rulers, albeit very selectively. The only Roman king he mentions in the first book is Servius, to show that he knows to account for groups other than the *gens Hebrae*. But his remark on *Romanorum sextus Servius* is all he includes of early Roman history.[59] Right after this he mentions Julius Caesar, the first Roman ruler *qui tutius imperii obtenuit monarchiam*, and his successor Augustus. Gregory reports that not only was Jesus Christ born during the reign of Augustus; it was also the time when Lyon was founded – the city whose name was later made famous through the blood of martyrs – *quae postea, inlustrata martyrum sanguine, nobilissima nuncupatur.*[60]

Gregory's featured list of Roman emperors is extremely incomplete and it hardly serves as a chronological framework for apostolic and martyrial history in Gaul.[61] In many places, his adapted dating system highlights his alternative historical focus. Gregory does not count the succession of emperors since Caesar and Augustus, but instead he counts the succession of persecutors of the Church: Trajan, for example, was the third emperor since Nero to order the persecution of Christians.[62] After

[57] Cf. G. Krutzler, 'Die Wahrnehmung der nichtfränkischen Völker in der fränkischen Historiographie', in W. Pohl and G. Heydemann (eds.), *Post-Roman Transitions: Christians and Barbarian Identities in the Early Medieval West* (Turnhout, 2013), pp. 487–547.

[58] *De subpotatione vero huius mundi evidenter chronicae Eusebii Caesariensis episcopi ac Hieronimi presbiteri prolucuntur et rationem de onmi annorum serie pandunt.* Gregory, *Historiae* I, preface, p. 5.

[59] Gregory, *Historiae* I, 17, ed. Krusch and Levison, p. 16.

[60] Gregory, *Historiae* I 18, ed. Krusch and Levison, p. 17.

[61] Gregory, *Historiae* I, 25, ed. Krusch and Levison, p. 20; ibid. I, 30, pp. 22–3.

[62] Gregory, *Historiae* I, 27, ed. Krusch and Levison, p. 21.

Trajan, only Gallienus, Diocletian, and Constantine are mentioned as rulers of the *Imperium Romanum*. Along with the context of these dates, Gregory also uses the names of the Roman emperors to put the bishops of the city of Rome in chronological order.[63]

Only one instance of the *Romani* in the first book deals with them directly. In the Battle of Adrianople, after the Romans had suffered a catastrophic defeat against the Goths, the emperor Valens forced monks to fight in the war. The Jerome Chronicle extensively recounts the circumstances which culminated in this event. But here Gregory conspicuously stresses the agency of the *Romani*. In Jerome, it was the *legiones Romanae* who had been wiped out by the Goths.[64] Gregory, however, adds the name of the Romans to Jerome's text twice: *Post haec bellum saevissimum in Thracias Romani gessire, in quo tanta stragis fuit, ut Romani, amisso equorum praesidio, pedebus fugirent.*[65]

In the second book, the *Romani* are localized above all in Gaul. With the appearance of the *Franci* in the ninth chapter of this book, Gregory gives a short overview of the political and ethnic geography of the Gaul they had entered. After the Franks had settled along the Lower Rhine, the *Romani* became their southern neighbours in the territories up to the Loire.[66] From that point in time, they appear as allies or opponents of the Franks in Gaul: under the *magister militum* Aegidius *ex Romanus*,[67] *Romani* and *Franci* fought together against the *Saxones*. When Clovis' father Childeric – *cum esset nimia in luxuria* – was driven out by the Franks for having raped his daughter, Aegidius even ruled over the Franks for a short time.[68]

In Gregory's text, Aegidius' appointment as *magister militum* follows the brief account of the Emperor Avitus, whose short reign from 455 to 456 was founded on his power base in Gaul.[69] A little over a hundred years

[63] See Krutzler, 'Die Wahrnehmung nichtfränkischer Völker'.

[64] *Lacrimabile bellum in Thracia, in quo deserente equitum praesidio Romanae legiones a Gothis cinctae usque ad internecionem caesae sunt*, Jerome, *Chronicon*, ed. R. Helm, Eusebius Werke, 7: *Die Chronik des Hieronymus, Die griechischen christlichen Schriftsteller der ersten Jahrhunderte*, 47 (Berlin, 1956), p. 249.

[65] Gregory, *Historiae* I, 41, ed. Krusch and Levison, p. 28.

[66] In his *autem partibus, id est ad meridianam plagam habitabant Romani usque ad Ligerem fluvium*, Gregory, *Historiae* II, 9, ed. Krusch and Levison, p. 58.

[67] Gregory of Tours, *Historiae* II, 11, ed. Krusch and Levison, p. 61

[68] Gregory of Tours II, 12, p. 61f; see J. Jarnut, 'Gregor von Tours, Frankengeschichte II, 12: Franci Egidium sibi regem adiscunt: Faktum oder Sage', in K. Brunner and B. Merta (eds.), *Ethnogenese und Überlieferung. Angewandte Methoden der Frühmittelalterforschung*, Veröffentlichungen des Instituts für Österreichische Geschichtsforschung, 31 (Vienna, 1994), pp. 129–34; and G. Halsall, 'Childeric's Grave, Clovis' Succession and the Origins of the Merovingian Kingdoms' in R. Mathison and D. Schanzer (eds.), *Society and Culture in Late Roman Gaul* (Aldershot, 2001), pp. 116–33.

[69] Gregory of Tours II, 11, ed. Krusch and Levsion, p. 60; cf. G. Halsall, *Barbarian Migrations and the Roman West, 376–568* (Cambridge, 2007), pp. 257–62.

before Gregory, the chronicler Hydatius had outlined a largely positive picture of the Gallic *Augustus* as a capable and accomplished ruler.[70] It is entirely possible that Hydatius, who was a bishop in northern Spain, fixed on Avitus a hope for greater political stability in the region where he lived. However, Gregory represents the Gallic emperor less favourably. Avitus, a senator from Gregory's hometown of Clermont, had by excessive ambition claimed to control the *imperium Romanum*. In any case, the senators soon overthrew him, when he started to act *luxuriosae*. Gregory does not tell us what kind of *luxuria* Avitus liked. But the seventh-century chronicler Fredegar would add to Gregory's epitome a story with some graphic jokes about Avitus abusing the senators' wives.[71] Even in Gregory's text, the parallels between Clovis' father, Childeric, who was likewise deposed by the Franks because of his *luxuria*, are striking.

One important difference, however, was that Childeric managed to return, whereas Gregory states that Avitus was succeeded by the emperor Martianus, and in Gaul Aegidius *ex Romanus* took over as *magister militum*. Gregory, furthermore, calls Aegidius' son *rex Romanorum*, who rules over one of the *regna* in Gaul before Clovis extended his rule *per totas Gallias*. From that point on, the *Romani* are completely absorbed into Gregory's *regnum*. After the end of the second book, the name completely disappears in Gregory's *Histories*.

Linked to the Roman past of Gaul, and appearing beyond the end of the second book, is the identity of the *senatores*. Gregory often uses the term for members of the upper class in southern Gaul.[72] Their culture and education make them particularly well suited for episcopal office.[73] Not surprisingly, Gregory portrays his own family as members of this class.[74] But even here in the history of the *senatores*, we can observe how Gregory confronts the dangers of a common past to serve his Christian vision. Gregory does not let his readers forget that like the Franks, the *senatores* had a pagan past. Just as with Childeric's and Avitus' *luxuria*, the *Histories* depict the pagan past of the Franks and of the *senatores* with striking terminological similarities. Gregory's chapter on the paganism of the

[70] Hydatius, Chronicon, ed. and tr. R. W. Burgess, *The Chronicle of Hydatius and the Consularia Constantinopolitana* (Oxford, 1993), pp. 105–9.

[71] Fredegar, *Chronicon* III, 7 and 10, ed. B. Krusch, MGH SRM II (Hanover, 1888, repr. 1984), pp. 94 and 95.

[72] Heinzelmann, *Gregory*, pp. 8–11.

[73] Gregory, *Historiae* VI, 9, ed. Krusch and Levison, p. 279.

[74] See for instance on his own predecessor as bishop of Tours: *Eufronius presbiter ordinatus, ex genere illo, quod superius senatores nuncupavimus*, Gregory, *Historiae* X, 31, p. 534; see Heinzelmann, *Gregory*, p. 7–11, but cf. the statistics in S. Patzold, 'Zur Sozialstruktur des Episkopats und zur Ausbildung bischöflicher Herrschaft in Gallien zwischen Spätantike und Frühmittelalter', in M. Becher and S. Dick (eds.), *Völker, Reiche und Namen im frühen Mittelalter, Festschrift für Jörg Jarnut* (Munich, 2010), pp. 121–40.

Franks, which immediately follows his inconclusive search for the early Frankish kings, starts with the sentence: *Sed haec generatio fanaticis semper cultibus visa est obsequium prabuisse.*[75] This was something that the *Franci* shared with the *senatores* of earlier times. For when the *septem viri* came to preach Christianity in Gaul, Gregory tells us that the *senatores* were likewise committed to paganism: *Senatores vero reliqui meliores loci* [Bourges] *fanaticis erant tunc cultibus obligati.*[76]

In Gregory's representation, members of the senatorial class had much better credentials for taking on important social and political roles. But their background did not legitimate this position. As one could see from the example of Gregory's compatriot, the emperor Avitus – *cives Avernus* and *unus ex senatoribus* – not all senators were equally equipped to act responsibly for their communities. The legitimacy of their position was based, as it was for all others, on taking responsibility for the Christian community and on the vision of a common future.

Post-Roman perspectives

But Gregory was well aware that his present was different. He knew that his vision of a Christian community stood in competition with other efforts promoting different social identities and frameworks, some of them even building on the providential aspect of Christian identity. Evidence for this competition is included in one of the oldest extant collections of Gallic canons, which was probably compiled in the last years of Gregory's life or shortly after his death. The collection contains the resolutions of the first general council of Gaul in the Merovingian kingdoms – the council of Orleans under Clovis' reign in 511. The copyist ended the text with the sentence: *Expliciunt canones Francisci* – here end the Frankish canons.[77] It was against everything Gregory had worked for in his *Histories.* If he was already dead by that point he would have rolled in his grave to see the very thing he had been challenging come to life even within his *ecclesia.*

But we should not see this just as the anti-frankish resentment of a bishop who presented himself as a descendant of one of the most important and noble Roman families of Gaul. Gregory was actually engaged in

[75] Gregory, *Historiae* II, 10, ed. Krusch and Levsion, p. 58.

[76] Gregory, *Historiae* I, 31, ed. Krusch and Levison, p. 24.

[77] Cologne, Erzbischöfliche Diözesan– und Dombibliothek cod. 212, fol. 40r; for the dating of the manuscript see CLA VIII, 1162 and the catalogue entry published with digital publication of manuscripts of the Kölner Dombilbliothek, Codices Ecclesiastici Electronici Colonienses at www.ceec.uni-koeln.de/; see also the edition *Concilium Aurelianense,* A. 511, ed. F. Maassen, MGH Conc. I (Hannover, 1893), p. 10.

a wider conversation about the social and political organization of a world after the end of the Western Roman Empire. As Peter Brown has observed, Gregory was a man of a new age and was determined to use the *Spielräume* of this new age to promote his vision of a Christian community and future.[78] But he also knew that his contemporaries were using those *Spielräume* too to forge their own visions of community for the social and political integration of the kingdom. In this respect Gregory seemed to have seen efforts to build on the prestige and flexibility of Roman identities as well as the cultivation of Frankish identity as powerful alternatives to his vision of society.

To be sure Gregory's *Histories* can only be used as a negative blueprint for efforts using Frankish or Roman *identities* as a focus for social and political integration. The focus for the integration of the kingdom was Gregory's view of Christianity, or Gregory's vision of a Gaulish Christendom. Consequently, the conception of the larger social whole in and around this Christendom was organized along the powerful dichotomies of Christianity and paganism, orthodoxy and heresy. But his *Histories* might still help us to pay more attention to the social and political developments to which the bishop of Tours reacted. Gregory had most likely started to work on the first four books of his *Histories* before he became bishop of Tours.[79] But as recent research has emphasized Gregory took up his historiographical project with renewed energy from 584 onwards, after the death of Chilperic I.[80] It was in the time following the death of Chilperic that Gregory became an influential adviser of the last remaining son of Clothar I, Guntram. The 'senior king of the royal family' (as Eugen Ewig has described the powerful position of Guntram after the death of Chilperic), issued an edict in 585 which is our oldest extant royal document that uses the title *rex Francorum.*[81] And it was roughly at the same time when Guntram's designated successor, the young Childebert II, started to use the Intitulatio *rex Francorum* in his official correspondence with the Byzantine empire.[82] In earlier letters

[78] Brown, *Through the Eye of a Needle*, pp. 506–22. [79] See Wood, *Gregory*, pp. 1–4.

[80] See the discussion in A. C. Murray, 'Chronology and Composition of the *Histories* of Gregory of Tours', *Journal of Late Antiquity*, 1 (2008), 157–74.

[81] *Gunthramni regis Edictum*, ed. A. Boretius, MGH Capit. I (Hanover, 1883, repr. 1984), pp. 10–12; For the date, see M. Weidemann, 'Zur Chronologie der Merowinger im 6. Jahrhundert', *Francia*, 10 (1982), 471–513; and I. Woll, *Untersuchungen zur Überlieferung und Eigenart der merowingischen Kapitularien*, Freiburger Beiträge zur mittelalterlichen Geschichte, 6 (Frankfurt am Main, 1995), pp. 33–6.

[82] *Episulae Austrasicae*, 25, 28, 31, 33 ed. W. Gundlach, MGH Epp. III (Hanover 1892), p. 138, 140, 141, 142; the dating of the letters is controversial, the MGH editor Gundlach assumed 584; whereas Goubert dated it to 588; the recent Italian study and translation of the Epistulae by E. Malaspina, *Il Liber epistolarum della cancelleria austrasica (saec. V-VI)* (Rome, 2001), p. 181 suggests 'end of 587'. Thomas Lienhard, who is preparing a

Childebert had – just like his predecessors as Merovingian kings—used the title *rex* without the ethnic definer *Francorum*.[83] It seems that the intensified use of the name of the Franks to address the *regnum* as a common political and social framework was a relatively recent phenomenon when Gregory was writing his *Histories*. As I have argued elsewhere at greater length, it was most likely the result of the intensified competition between the sons of Clothar I, particularly after the death of Charibert I in 567.[84] The *bella civilia*, as Gregory called the numerous conflicts between Clothar's sons, have not only made it possible for a new governing class to emerge.[85] This new governing class, which confidently relied on their wealth, land, and military power, had also helped to establish a vocabulary of consensus in which the name of the Frank was increasingly used to address the common good.[86]

This process was also supported by the intensified diplomatic interaction of the Merovingian kings with Byzantium during the last decades of the sixth century in the context of Byzantine efforts to win support against the Lombards, who had just invaded Italy. As Averil Cameron has shown, it was precisely this context in which the Byzantine historian Agathias presented the Frankish kingdoms as perfectly compatible with Byzantine culture. The new *Germani* had not only changed their name but were also transformed into good Christians and peer successors to Roman rule and culture in Gaul.[87] As Averil Cameron suggested, Agathias seemed to have built on information of Merovingian envoys in his portrait of the Franks, and one can indeed easily imagine that the intensification of diplomatic exchange opened to Merovingian envoys a new stage for representing

French translation and commentary, however, does not think that one could be more exact than between 584 and 590. I would like to thank Thomas Lienhard for sharing the results of his unpublished study with me.

83 For the titles of the Merovingian kings, see H. Wolfram, *Intitulatio I. Lateinische Königs – und Fürstentitel bis zum Ende des 8. Jahrhunderts*, Mitteilungen des Instituts für Österreichische Geschichtsforschung, suppl. vol. 21 (Graz, Vienna, and Cologne, 1967), pp. 108–27.

84 Reimitz, *History*, pp. 98–123. for the *bella civilia* see Wood, *Merovingian kingdoms*, pp. 88–93; and now S. Esders, 'Avenger of all perjury in Constantinople, Ravenna, and Merovingian Metz. St Polyeuctus, Sigibert I, and the division of Charibert's Kingdom in 568', in A. Fischer (ed.), *Cultural Transfers in the Mediterranean, 5th – 9th Centuries* (Bangor, 2014), pp. 17–40.

85 Brown, *Ransom*, pp. 152–3

86 This is well documented in the accounts of the Fredegar-chronicle, where the name of the Franks is particularly emphasized in contexts where the 'Frankish' elite resolved conflicts between different kings and their factions; for a more comprehensive discussion of this process see my *History*, ch. 7.

87 See A. Cameron, 'Agathias on the Early Merovingians', *Annali della Scuola Normale Superiore di Pisa. Classe di lettere e filosofia* ser. 2, 37 (1968), pp. 95–140, who compares the portrayal of the Franks in Agathias with the one of Procopius, who presents the Franks largely as 'true' barbarians.

themselves as Romano-Christian Franks. But the diplomatic plays in Constantinople affected the arenas for self-identification in the Merovingian kingdoms themselves too. In their constant conflicts over territories and power, each ruler worked hard to present himself as superior to the others in order to maintain the loyalty of his followers and subjects. Byzantium's endorsement certainly played an important role in these efforts. With Merovingian elites going to Byzantium and Byzantine envoys coming to the Merovingian court, the intensive diplomatic exchange became a race, a competition for becoming the accepted king of the Franks.

To be sure, the extant evidence shows identifications with the name of the Franks still as situational constructs.[88] However, Gregory seems to have observed that the situations in which people resorted to Frankish or Roman identity as a focus for social and political integration had considerably increased in the last decades of the sixth century and he might also have observed that the name of the Franks appeared more and more in relation to institutions such as the *regnum* or even the Christian church. Gregory's historiographical response tried to undermine this process in emphasizing the incoherent and contradictory nature of these identities. In his eyes, the social and political structures of the Roman Empire belonged to the past while Frankish identity should have no future.

This was, however, not only about the reinvention of Romanness or the increasing salience of the Frankish name as foci for political and social integration. It was also about the increasing salience of an 'ethnic' ordering of the world as a world divided among distinctive and analogous groups – *gentes*.[89] This is above all well documented by the reactions to Gregory's views on the history and identity of the Franks by later chroniclers and historians, such as the Fredegar-Chronicle or the *Liber historiae Francorum*, which wrote directly against Gregory's conception of history and identity in their efforts to promote Roman-Frankish identity.[90] But these texts not only presented different views on the relative importance of Frankish, Roman, or Christian identities. They also developed different conceptions of the larger social whole, which in turn gave meaning to a

[88] See the classic study of P. Geary, 'Ethnic Identity as a Situational Construct in the Early Middle Ages', *Mitteilungen der anthropologischen Gesellschaft in Wien*, 113 (1983), 15–26.

[89] For a comprehensive discussion about recent approaches on ethnic identities and ethnicity and their application to early medieval studies see W. Pohl, 'Introduction. Strategies of identification. A methodological profile', in Pohl and G. Heydemann (eds.), *Strategies of Identification: Ethnicity and Religion in Early Medieval Europe* (Turnhout, 2013), pp. 1–64.

[90] See Reimitz, *History*, for a more comprehensive discussion of debates about the meaning and social function of Frankish identity and their impact on the formation of a Western conception of ethnicity in the early Middle Ages.

social identity. Thus the debates about Christian, Roman-Frankish, and ethnic identity in Gregory's *Histories* can also be explored as debates about the organization of a larger social whole and competing efforts to establish a specific world view. In order to study the precise formation of these world views as historically open processes we also need to take into consideration the competition, overlaps, interactions, and interferences of different efforts to organize the social world.

4 'To mistake gold for wealth': the Venerable Bede and the fate of Northumbria[1]

Martin J. Ryan

Introduction

In the final decades of his life, Bede (d. 735) appears as a man disquieted. His biblical commentaries speak increasingly of a Church in decline, beset by avaricious leaders, false brethren, even nests of heretics.[2] In current events, Bede saw ominous harbingers of the approaching End of Days: strife, iniquity, natural disasters, and heavenly portents[3]. The hopes and strength of his native Northumbria had likewise ebbed and fallen away.[4] No longer, as it had been in the seventh century, the pre-eminent English kingdom, Northumbria now faced the growing might of Mercia to the south and the resurgence of hostile British communities to the north[5].

[1] The title is taken from 'An Anachronism; or, Missing One's Coach' a story about a time-traveller encountering the Venerable Bede, published anonymously in *The Dublin University Magazine* in June 1838. As well as the other contributors to this volume, whose observations and insights have proved invaluable, I would like to thank the participants of the Medieval Discussion Group at the University of Sheffield, the members of the University of Manchester Centre for Late Antiquity, the Old English reading group of the Manchester Centre for Anglo-Saxon Studies, and those attending the M6 Medieval Seminar series for their comments on various versions of this paper. Rosa Vidal Doval's input has been equally significant. Over the years I have benefitted immeasurably from my many discussions with Nick Higham about Bede and Anglo-Saxon England; this paper is offered as a small, and now much belated, token of my gratitude to him, on the occasion of his retirement.

[2] A. Thacker, 'Bede's Ideal of Reform', in P. Wormald with D. Bullough and R. Collins (eds.), *Ideal and Reality in Frankish and Anglo-Saxon Society: Studies Presented to J. M. Wallace-Hadrill* (Oxford, 1983), pp. 130–53; A. Thacker, 'Bede, the Britons and the Book of Samuel', in S. Baxter et al. (eds.), *Early Medieval Studies in Memory of Patrick Wormald* (Farnham, 2009), pp. 129–47; S. DeGregorio, 'Bede's *In Ezram et Neemiam* and the Reform of the Northumbrian Church', *Speculum*, 79 (2004), 1–25.

[3] For detailed and expert analysis of Bede's eschatological thought across the whole of his corpus, see P. Darby, *Bede and the End of Time* (Farnham, 2012).

[4] *Historia ecclesiastica gentis Anglorum*, ed. and tr. B. Colgrave and R. A. B. Mynors (Oxford, 1969) [henceforth *H.E.*] IV 26 (24).). For background see N. J. Higham, *Ecgfrith: High-king of Britain* (Donington, forthcoming) – I am grateful to Nick for sight of this prior to publication.

[5] For the rise of Mercia see N. J. Higham and M. J. Ryan, *The Anglo-Saxon World* (London, 2013), pp. 181–6 and for the Strathclyde Britons, C. Stancliffe, *Bede and the Britons* (Whithorn, 2007), pp. 12–32.

Not just Northumbria but the Anglo-Saxons as a whole seemed to Bede to stand at the edge of a precipice. The first book of the *Historia ecclesiastica* lays out the fall from God's grace of the once-favoured Britons. By the close of the final book, the unmistakable signs of sin and corruption imply that without reform the Anglo-Saxons risk a similar fate.[6]

How many of his contemporaries shared this gloomy outlook is unclear: Anglo-Saxon England at the opening of the eighth century is now seen almost exclusively through Bede's eyes. Once, Bede's unease might have been understood as a product of his isolation – he was long seen as a man fundamentally at odds with the outlook of his society, viewing the world beyond his cloister with incomprehension or condemnation and frequently with both.[7] Yet it is now clear that Bede was actively engaged with his world. His writings were works of contemporary advocacy, designed to remedy or ameliorate the ills that he, and perhaps others, perceived in his own times. Scripture served as the ultimate guide here – the Bible gave Bede a means of scrutinizing his own society and of discovering solutions for its problems. In his biblical commentaries, Bede repeatedly emphasized the contemporary relevance of the messages of Scripture.[8] The words of the Bible spoke to the present; they had been written for our instruction and correction.[9] Thus exegesis – which made up the bulk of Bede's written output – was not an abstruse or abstract occupation, of relevance only to the few, but a vital tool of reform.

Attention to Bede's exegesis also confirms a remarkable unity of purpose across much of his output. Certain themes and concepts clearly had particular resonance and relevance to Bede and he explored these through the differing perspectives offered by the various genres in which he worked. Exegesis, history, and hagiography provided different means of approaching the same end. Much work has already been done in this regard, not least concerning Bede's sustained intervention in debates about the provision of pastoral care and ecclesiastical leadership; that much more still can be said is simply a reflection of the riches of Bede's

6 O. Szerwiniack, 'L'*Histoire ecclésiastique* ou le rêve d'un retour au temps de l'innocence', in S. Lebecq, M. Perrin, and O. Szerwiniack (eds.), *Bède le Vénérable entre Tradition et Postérité*, Histoire de l'Europe de Nord-Ouest 34 (Villeneuve d'Ascq, 2005), pp. 159–76.

7 See the discussion by W. Goffart, *The Narrators of Barbarian History (A.D. 550–800): Jordanes, Gregory of Tours, Bede, and Paul the Deacon* (Princeton, NJ, 1988), pp. 236–8 and N. J. Higham *(Re-) Reading Bede: the Ecclesiastical History in Context* (London, 2006), pp. 50–1.

8 S. DeGregorio, 'The Venerable Bede and Gregory the Great: Exegetical Connections, Spiritual Departures', *Early Medieval Europe* 18 (2010), 43–60, at 60.

9 G. H. Brown, 'Bede's Neglected Commentary on Samuel', in S. DeGregorio (ed.), *Innovation and Tradition in the Writings of the Venerable Bede* (Morgantown, WV, 2006), pp. 121–42, at 127.

output.[10] This paper explores four inter-related issues within Bede's writings – kingship, violence, wealth, and imperfection. At its heart is the premise that Bede's lifetime had witnessed significant and thoroughgoing changes in the nature of the Anglo-Saxon Church and Anglo-Saxon society as a whole and that Bede's writings acknowledged and responded to these changes. Ultimately, what Bede presented across his works was a vision of reform that encompassed the entirety of his own society; his writings were an attempt to remake Northumbria.

Authority, power, and violence

Michael Wallace-Hadrill observed 'Bede's mind was full of kings; so, too, his writings'.[11] Such a focus was not surprising: kingship had become a problem in eighth-century Northumbria. The death of Aldfrith in 705 ushered in a period of dynastic upheaval, with short-lived kings, dissolute rulers, regicide, and coups. Something approaching stability would return only with the accession of King Eadberht in 737.[12] Negotiating this shifting political terrain was not easy and such upheavals threw into sharp focus questions about the proper extent of loyalty and obedience. The rapid rise and fall of monarchs likewise demanded explanation – what should a king do if he sought to prosper, what behaviour was pleasing to God and what would bring down his wrath? What, ultimately, was kingship for?

If Bede's mind was full of kings his writings were full not so much of kings as of the allegorical and tropological potential of the word 'rex'. Though the *Historia ecclesiastica* is in many ways a mirror for princes, Bede's attention to kingship and secular power in his biblical commentaries is far more muted. Bede tended to interpret descriptions of kings or secular rulers as references to the holders of religious offices, to the saints, or to Christ.[13] Even his commentary on 1 Samuel – a book of the Bible with much to say about earthly kingship – follows this pattern.

[10] In addition to the items in note 2 see also S. DeGregorio, '*Nostrorum socordiam temporum*: the Reforming Impulse of Bede's Later Exegesis', *Early Medieval Europe*, 11 (2002), 107–22 and his, 'Footsteps of His Own: Bede's Commentary on Ezra and Nehemiah', in Gregorio (ed.), *Innovation and Tradition*, pp. 143–68.

[11] J. M. Wallace-Hadrill, *Early Germanic Kingship in England and on the Continent* (Oxford, 1971), p. 72.

[12] N. J. Higham, *The Kingdom of Northumbria: AD 350–1100* (Stroud, 1993), pp. 144–6 and D. Rollason, *Northumbria, 500–1100: Creation and Destruction of a Kingdom* (Cambridge, 2003), pp. 190–3.

[13] H. Vollrath-Reichelt, *Königsgedanke und Königtum bei den Angelsachsen* (Köln, 1971), pp. 22–3. There are notable exceptions, such as the discussion of the letter of Artaxerxes to Ezra in Bede's commentary on Ezra and Nehemiah, see R. A. Markus, *Bede and the Traditions of Ecclesiastical History* (Jarrow, 1975), p. 398 and below pp. 86–7.

Thus Bede's exploration of the first meeting between Samuel and Saul, including Saul's anointing, is an extended discussion of Christ's encounter with John the Baptist rather than a meditation on kingship and rule.[14] In general, Bede seemed unwilling to draw explicit comparisons between biblical rulers and contemporary Anglo-Saxon kings in his exegesis,[15] although he did on occasion draw such parallels in his historical writings.[16] Where secular rule was discussed by Bede, it was most often to draw distinctions, expressed in general terms, between the type of kingship exemplified by Christ and that by earthly rulers.[17] Bede's reading of the Bible, particularly the historical books of the Old Testament, must have informed his understanding of contemporary Anglo-Saxon kingship, but in practice it is hard to draw anything more than the most general connections between his commentaries and his historical works in this regard.[18]

Though Bede had little to say about earthly kingship *per se* in his commentaries, his exegesis does evince a particular attitude to secular authority and worldly power. As so often, Bede's writings show here the clear imprint of the thought of Gregory the Great. Rulers had been set over the people by God and to rebel against them, however sinful they were, was an offence to the Lord.[19] Commenting on 1 Peter, Bede rehearsed St Paul's assertion that authority derived ultimately from God and stressed that all should be subject to the worldly powers.[20] Unjust treatment in no way permitted rebellion against worldly authority: tyranny and persecution were to be borne patiently and the blameless servant punished by his master was an imitator of Christ's passion.[21] Such ideas may have had an immediate contemporary relevance. Bede's commentary on the Catholic Epistles was probably completed sometime

[14] *In primam partem Samuhelis libri III*, ed. D. Hurst, CCSL, 119 (Turnhout, 1962), pp. 81–6.

[15] See, for example, G. H. Brown, 'Le Commentaire problématique de Bède sur le premier Livre de Samuel', in Lebecq et al (eds.), *Bède le Vénérable*, pp. 87–96.

[16] The classic comparison is between Æthelfrith of Northumbria and Saul, *H.E.* I 34. See also Wallace-Hadrill, *Early Germanic Kingship*, p. 78.

[17] For example, *In Lucae evangelium expositio*, ed. D. Hurst, CCSL, 120 (Turnhout, 1960) pp. 32 and 345 (quoting Augustine).

[18] Wallace-Hadrill, *Early Germanic Kingship*, pp. 76–9 and J. McClure, 'Bede's Old Testament Kings', in Wormald et al. (eds.), *Ideal and Reality*, pp. 76–98.

[19] See, for example, Gregory, *Regula Pastoralis*, PL, 77, 55d-62a.

[20] *In epistolas VII catholicas*, ed. D. Hurst, CCSL, 121 (Turnhout, 1983), p. 239; *Commentary on the Seven Catholic Epistles*, tr. D. Hurst, Cistercian Studies 82 (Kalamazoo, 1985), p. 90.

[21] *In epistolas VII catholicas* pp. 239–42; *Seven Catholic Epistles* pp. 91–3; See also *Homiliarum euangelii libri ii*, ed. D. Hurst, CCSL, 122 (Turnhout, 1955), p. 341; *Homilies on the Gospels: Book Two, Lent to the Dedication of the Church*, tr. L. T. Martin and D. Hurst, Cistercian Publications 111 (Kalamazoo, MI, 1991), p. 219.

after 710.[22] As such, the composition of at least parts of it is likely to have coincided with the final years of the reign of King Osred. Though Bede had initially entertained great hopes for Osred – describing him as a new and illustrious Josiah – the later years of his reign were marked by debauchery and tyranny and he was killed, perhaps murdered, in 716.[23]

To the pious Christian, accepting with humility the governance of unjust and persecuting rulers, Bede would contrast implicitly the proud and impious Pharisees. Despite the peace and security brought by Roman rule, the Pharisees did not believe that the people of God should be subject to human laws. This sedition would lead ultimately to the destruction of Jerusalem by the Romans.[24] As he did elsewhere, here Bede employed Jews as negative exemplars, their behaviour representing the inversion of behaviour that was – or should be – characteristic of Christians.[25] The pride of the Pharisees led them to rebel against worldly authority, even when this authority brought them peace, and so their destruction followed; the Christian who endured tyranny and misrule would, by contrast, achieve a greater glory.

If unjust leaders were to be endured patiently, Bede was clear, nevertheless, of the fate that awaited such sinful rulers. Those rulers who gave themselves up to idle pleasures and, worse still, incited those subject to them to sin would be damned.[26] As Samuel's speech to the Israelites confirmed, rulers and their subjects who did not fear God would face the Lord's wrath; such kings would eventually lose their kingdoms and face captivity and death. Though Samuel had been prophesying about Saul and the Israelites, Bede asserted that all earthly kingdoms were encompassed by the prophet's words.[27] Contemporary readers could scarcely have missed the significance of this: Bede's commentary on 1 Samuel was composed in the years around 716, the date of King Osred's death.[28]

Secular authority was, then, bestowed and, indeed, revoked ultimately by God. Nevertheless, particular manifestations of such authority, kingship included, were human constructions that had origins and histories that could be traced. In his commentary on Genesis, Bede explored the

[22] For discussion see Darby, *Bede and the End of Time*, pp. 67–8.
[23] Thacker, 'Bede, the Britons', pp. 144–6. [24] *In Lucam*, p. 356.
[25] The most detailed study to date of Bede's attitude towards the Jews is A. Scheil, *The Footsteps of Israel: Understanding Jews in Anglo-Saxon England* (Ann Arbor, MI, 2004), although the corpus of works Scheil investigates is relatively restricted. For more recent comment see W. T. Foley and N. J. Higham, 'Bede and the Britons', *Early Medieval Europe*, 17 (2009), 154–85 and Thacker, 'Bede, the Britons', pp. 136–44.
[26] *In Lucam*, p. 259.
[27] *In primam partem Samuhelis* pp. 98–9 and Wallace-Hadrill, *Early Germanic Kingship*, p. 76.
[28] Thacker, 'Bede, the Britons', p. 140 and Darby, pp. 167–70.

common Patristic theme of the gradual falling away of man from a primitive and pastoral state and his embrace of cities, technology, and government.[29] As Bede saw it, even after the Fall, if man observed the natural law then all human artifices and technology would be unnecessary. Their manufacture and use, even by the virtuous, was an indication of how far the human race had fallen away from its original, primitive purity.[30] Nimrod, grandson of Noah, occupied a pivotal place in this schema. He corrupted mankind with a new mode of life; having raised up an army and exerted hitherto unknown tyranny over the people, Nimrod finally claimed a kingdom for himself and constructed mighty cities.[31]

Bede does not quite state that Nimrod was the first king, simply that Scripture records he was the first to do such things. Nevertheless, there is the sense in Bede's commentary that kingship was, in origin, a result of the imposition of tyranny and yet one more facet of man's continuing fall away from a primitive and more innocent mode of living. The Israelites' request for a king, as set out in 1 Samuel 8, offered another example of the embrace of kingship as a falling away. As Bede would have read, this request was a rejection of God's rule, a rejection of Him who had 'brought them up out of Egypt'. Even when Samuel had rehearsed the oppressions and appropriations that such a king would enact, still the Israelites wished to be like other peoples and have a king who would judge them and lead them into battle. Bede's allegorical interpretation of this passage only served to underline the anti-theocratic nature of the Israelites' request. Just as the elders of Israel rejected God in favour of an earthly king at the time of Samuel, so the elders of Israel rejected Christ at the time of His incarnation, preferring instead to be like the Gentiles, who had never known God, and like the kingdoms that had never called upon the name of the Lord.[32]

Bede was, though, no anti-monarchist. If he thought kingship to be in origin an inessential adjunct of human society, he gave no indication, nevertheless, that any other political system was desirable or even possible amongst the Anglo-Saxons.[33] The issue for Bede was not whether the

[29] J. M. Dean, 'The World Grown Old and Genesis in Middle English Historical Writings', *Speculum*, 57 (1982), 548–68.

[30] *In principium Genesim*, ed. C. W. Jones, CCSL, 118a (Turnhout, 1967), p. 88; *On Genesis*, tr. C. B. Kendall, Translated Texts for Historians 48 (Liverpool, 2008), p. 156.

[31] *In principium Genesim* p. 144; *On Genesis* p. 218.

[32] *In primam partem Samuhelis*, p. 71. For discussion and translation of the key passages see G. H. Brown, 'Bede's Style in his Commentary *On 1 Samuel*', in J. Roberts and A. Minnis (eds.), *Text, Image, Interpretation: Studies in Anglo-Saxon Literature in Honour of Eamonn Ó'Carragáin* (Turnhout, 2007), pp. 233–51.

[33] Though Bede was aware that the Continental Saxons had satraps instead of kings he offers no indication that such a situation ever prevailed amongst the English, *H.E.* V 10.

existence of kingship in the present was a good or a bad thing but how kings should act and how royal power should be used. Kingship, like all worldly institutions, civil structures, and technologies was of benefit only to the extent that it was employed to further true religion. Bede noted that the wicked delighted in things made by human skill for their own sake, whereas the virtuous shunned them or used them only for some fitting purpose.[34]

Again, Bede found confirmation in the First Book of Samuel. In the first year of his reign, Saul had, according to Bede, remained humble and private, neither clothing himself in royal garments nor desiring to take up the other trappings of kingship; only in the second and third years of his reign did Saul begin to deviate from this course.[35] Yet renouncing the adornments of worldly status did not necessarily mean giving them up. Though Saul had done so, rejection of the trappings of rule was not a necessary requirement of the pious exercise of authority. Proper attitude and proper purpose were key. Commenting on Luke 20:46, Bede noted that Christ did not forbid those whose rank permitted it to receive greetings in the marketplace, or to sit in the highest seats in the synagogues, or in the chief rooms at feasts. For Bede, such marks of distinction were not the problem; rather it was love of them for their own sake that was the issue.[36]

Though Bede's theory of kingship and rule must, for the most part, be pieced together from a variety of sources, his commentary on the books of Ezra and Nehemiah does contain sustained comparisons of Old Testament rulers and contemporary Christian kings. Such comparisons occur in two places in particular: commentary on the decree of King Darius in Ezra 6 and the discussion of the letter of Artaxerxes in Ezra 7.[37] For Bede, Darius represented those kings who aided the Christian faith through their decrees and enriched the Church through their gifts.[38] Artaxerxes likewise brought to Bede's mind contemporary royal benefaction as well as those kings who ensured their subjects gave all that was asked of them by the Lord and the archbishop.[39]

Bede also devoted considerable time to discussion of the exemption from taxation enjoyed by the Levites. He praised the foresight of

[34] *In principium Genesim*, p. 88; *On Genesis*, p. 156.

[35] *In primam partem Samuhelis*, p. 102 and Wallace-Hadrill, *Early Germanic Kingship*, p. 77.

[36] *In Lucam*, pp. 360–63.

[37] Markus has referred to the latter commentary being 'a short … treatise on Christian kingship', see *Traditions of Ecclesiastical History*, p. 38.

[38] *In Ezram et Neemiam libri iii*, ed. D. Hurst, CCSL, 199a (Brepols, 1969), pp. 294–6; *On Ezra and Nehemiah*, tr. S. DeGregorio, Translated Texts for Historians 47 (Liverpool, 2006), pp. 88–91.

[39] *In Ezram et Neemiam* pp. 312–19;*Ezra and Nehemiah* pp. 118–26. For the translation of 'pontifex' as 'archbishop', see *Ezra and Nehemiah*, p. xxxiv.

Artaxerxes in ensuring that those constantly occupied with religious worship would be free from tribute and servitude to him, noting that the exemption showed the Persian king to have understood well the needs of those who performed the divine services.[40] The issue of exemption from royal tribute would have had a direct contemporary relevance to Bede's audience. The Church in Kent had been freed from royal taxation in the final decade of the seventh century and that in Wessex by the beginning of the eighth. The evidence from Northumbria is more ambiguous but the case has be made that Church lands were free from some royal dues and obligations.[41] Yet, curiously, this is one of the few occasions where Bede did not draw a direct comparison between the actions of Artaxerxes and those of Christian rulers. Such an omission may point to an otherwise unattested debate about the validity or desirability of such exemptions in eighth-century Northumbria. Equally, it may suggest the Northumbrian Church had not been so exempted and that Bede was wary of explicitly criticizing current royal policy. Whatever the reasons for such an omission, Bede was, through Artaxerxes, making the case that ecclesiastical exemptions from royal taxation were vitally necessary and the mark of a pious and foresighted king.

The overall message from Bede's discussion of kingship in his commentary on Ezra and Nehemiah is the need for close co-operation, for king and Church to work in harmony towards the shared goal of the maintenance and extension of Christianity. It is a message reinforced by a number of Bede's other works closely contemporary to the commentary on Ezra and Nehemiah, particularly his *Historia ecclesiastica* and his letter to Bishop Ecgberht of York in 734.[42] Bede's excursus on kingship in his commentary thus provided both biblical exemplars and historical precedents for his vision of what contemporary kingship should be and the rulers invoked therein can be seen as both evidentiary and hortatory.

One aspect of Bede's treatment of Darius and Artaxerxes is worth further exploration: the connection between royal power and violence. Royal violence was of issue for Bede for a number of reasons. First, much of the wealth and prosperity of the Northumbrian Church must have been, directly or indirectly, the result of conquest and plunder.[43] Second, there is evidence that the later seventh and eighth centuries

[40] *In Ezram et Neemiam*, pp. 317–18; *Ezra and Nehemiah*, p. 125.

[41] See, for example, S. Foot, *Monastic Life in Anglo-Saxon England, c. 600–900* (Cambridge, 2006), p. 188. For Northumbria, see E. John, *Land Tenure in Early England: A Discussion of Some Problems* (Leicester, 1960), pp. 44–45.

[42] For the former see *Ezra and Nehemiah*, p. 88–9, n. 4; for the latter Higham *(Re-) Reading Bede*, p. 151.

[43] J. Campbell, 'Elements in the Background to the Life of St Cuthberht and his Early Cult', in J. Campbell, *The Anglo-Saxon State* (London, 2000), pp. 85–106, at 86–8.

witnessed an increase in the exercise of royally sanctioned judicial violence. The law-codes of Wihtred of Kent and Ine of Wessex contain the first references to corporal and capital punishment in English legal texts, with the latter code also including the earliest mention of the judicial ordeal in Anglo-Saxon England (in this case the ordeal by hot water).[44] Though neither code presents such punishments as innovative, the sense that by the later seventh century Anglo-Saxon kings were increasingly asserting – or arrogating – their right to inflict judicial violence is strengthened by evidence from mortuary archaeology. Specialized execution cemeteries were in use by the late seventh or early eighth century, with their location and layout and the nature of insults and injuries inflicted on those buried therein suggesting rulers were employing public execution as a means of displaying and affirming their power and authority.[45]

If the right to inflict this judicial violence was increasingly claimed as a royal prerogative, the Church was, nevertheless, implicated in its practice and operation. Later Anglo-Saxon legal texts show the ordeal to have been conducted in churches with clerics officiating,[46] while the so-called *Laws of Edward and Guthrum*, written in the eleventh century, suggest that it was in the gift of the bishop whether those who had been judicially mutilated and left for dead could be aided.[47] Nearer to Bede's own day, the *Dialogus* of Archbishop Ecgberht of York states that those who could not render the necessary compensation for offences against the Church should be handed over to the secular arm for punishment.[48] Likewise, though the rights of sanctuary and asylum claimed by churches throughout the Anglo-Saxon period offered at least a temporary bulwark against some forms of judicial violence, the demarcation of certain spaces as especially privileged nevertheless implicitly acknowledged the legitimacy of such violence elsewhere.[49]

[44] A. Reynolds, *Anglo-Saxon Deviant Burial Customs* (Oxford, 2009), pp. 21–4. For discussion of the ordeal in Ine's code, see S. L. Keefer, '*Đonne se cirlisca man ordales weddigeð*: the Anglo-Saxon Lay Ordeal', in Baxter et al (eds.), *Early Medieval Studies*, pp. 353–68, at 354–5.

[45] Reynolds, *Anglo-Saxon Deviant Burial Customs*, p. 237.

[46] F. Liebermann (ed.), *Die Gesetze der Angelsachsen* 3 vols (Halle a.S., 1903–1916), I (1903), pp. 386–7.

[47] Ibid. pp. 132–4.

[48] *Succinctus dialogus ecclesiasticae institutionis*, ed. A. W. Haddan and W. Stubbs, *Councils and Ecclesiastical Documents Relating to Great Britain and Ireland*, 3 vols (Oxford, 1869–71), III (1871), pp. 408–9. See also M. J. Ryan, 'Archbishop Ecgberht and his *Dialogus*', in A. Rumble (ed.), *Leaders of the Anglo-Saxon Church from Bede to Stigand*, Pubns. of the Manchester Centre for Anglo-Saxon Studies (Woodbridge, 2012), pp. 41–60.

[49] For a useful survey of sanctuary and asylum in the Anglo-Saxon period see T. B. Lambert, 'The Evolution of Sanctuary in Medieval England', in P. Dresch and H. Skoda (eds.), *Legalism: Anthropology and History* (Oxford, 2012), pp. 115–44, at 123–30.

Turning to Bede's writings to determine his understanding of the legitimacy and purpose of violence is initially disappointing. In his exegesis, Bede tended not to interpret references to violence and destruction in strictly physical or literal terms. Thus Hannah's exultation, 'the Lord killeth and maketh alive', was interpreted by Bede as referring to the passing of Divine favour from the Jews to the Christians – 'he kills the Synagogue and gives life to the Church'. Equally, her 'the bows of the mighty are broken' was taken to refer to God's humbling of those who study logical and secular philosophy.[50] Likewise, though Bede described numerous battles in his *Historia ecclesiastica* he offered little indication of what justified these.[51]

Yet it is clear from Bede's writings that violence, or the threat of it, were legitimate tools for kings. His discussion of Darius underlined that a key role of secular power was the creation and maintenance of the kind of peace that would ensure the survival and growth of the Church. In his commentaries on the Gospels of Luke and Mark, as well as in a number of his homilies, Bede repeated the common idea that Christ chose to be incarnated during the reign of Augustus so that his birth would coincide with a period of universal peace.[52] Such peace not only fulfilled the prophecies of Isaiah, but also facilitated the spreading of the Gospel, as it allowed the Apostles to travel more easily than would have been possible had the Roman Empire not brought the world under a single ruler.[53] However, peace was not simply passive: it needed to be actively cultivated and enforced. This could be achieved in part through royal edicts – such as those Bede wrote of in his discussion of Darius. Yet just as Darius had threatened death to ensure the observance of his decrees, so too Christian kings had to be able to intimidate, to provoke fear, and to threaten violence.[54] Indeed, all with authority over others had to be able to provoke fear in their subjects. Bede observed that rulers ('rectores') had to be

[50] *In primam partem Samuhelis*, p. 23.

[51] For the one possible exception – battle of *Deniseburn* see J. M Wallace-Hadrill, *Bede's Ecclesiastical History of the English People: a Historical Commentary* (Oxford, 1988), p. 89 and C. Stancliffe, 'Oswald "most holy and most victorious king of the Northumbrians"', in C. Stancliffe and E. Cambridge (eds.), *Oswald: Northern King to European Saint* (Stamford, 1995), pp. 33–83, at 44–5.

[52] For example, *In Lucam*, p. 44.

[53] *Homiliae euangelii*, p. 38; *Homilies on the Gospels: Book One, Advent to Lent*, tr. L. T. Martin and D. Hurst, Cistercian Studies 110 (Kalamazoo, MI, 1991), pp. 53–4.

[54] Higham, *(Re-) Reading Bede*, p. 156: 'in the last resort, Bede believed that kings should be scary'. Such applied also to non-Christian kings if they were the instruments of Divine wrath, see the discussion of Æthelfrith's slaughter of the monks of Bangor-on-Dee in J. Campbell, 'Questioning Bede', in M. Henig and N. Ramsay (eds.), *Intersections: the Archaeology and History of Christianity in England, 400–1200. Papers in Honour of Martin Biddle and Birthe Kjølbye-Biddle*, BAR British Series 505 (Oxford, 2010), pp. 119–27, at 124.

feared by those under their authority if these subjects evinced no fear of God.[55] Moreover, those new to the faith or inexpert in it would sometimes need to be brought to good works through terror.[56] For Bede, the fear-inducing power of kings had to encompass foreign peoples and nations as well as their own subjects. In his invocation of a seventh-century Golden Age in the *Historia ecclesiastica*, Bede noted that the English had 'such brave Christian kings, they were a terror to all the barbarian nations'.[57] David provided confirmation. In his commentary on 1 Samuel, Bede stated his belief that David had taken the head of Goliath to Jerusalem in order to strike terror into the heart of the Jebusites, who believed their citadel to be impregnable.[58]

Yet peace was not always desirable and sometimes warfare was necessary. Bede wrote how the prophet Habakkuk had seen the peace of sinners, accompanied by the affliction and persecution of the righteous.[59] Similarly, Bede noted the need for a good war to break asunder an evil peace – that is, when the world was divided against itself in matters of the faith, with each and every household containing both infidels and believers.[60] Kings might also deliberately provoke warfare and strife. By surrounding himself with powerful men and with those ready for war, Saul had stirred up the Philistines and neighbouring peoples against Israel.[61] Such a situation brought to Bede's mind the battle against sin; the enemy would attack most fiercely when the sinner was stirred out of his lethargy and sought to win the battle against temptation and vices.[62] Warfare also offered a means of channelling the violent or worldly ambitions of some. Bede noted that wages were paid to soldiers so that those striving after gain would not roam in search of victims like thieves.[63] Likewise, it was legitimate to claim the spoils of warfare. It was because he was a despiser of wealth that Abram was to be praised for rejecting the plunder offered him by the king of Sodom, not because accepting such spoils would necessarily have been wrong. Indeed, because he was one who loved justice, Abram ensured that the other warriors under his command would get their share of the plunder.[64]

If terror, violence, and warfare were weapons appropriate to kings and others in authority, what justified their deployment was not simply the behaviour of those targeted but the motivations and interior dispositions

[55] *In principium Genesim*, p. 13; *On Genesis* p. 204. [56] *In Lucam*, p. 142.
[57] *H.E.* IV 2. [58] *In primam partem Samuhelis*, p. 162.
[59] *In Habacuc*, ed. J. E. Hudson, CCSL, 119B (Turnhout, 1972), p. 381; *On Tobit and the Canticle of Habakkuk*, tr. S. Connolly (Dublin, 1997), p. 65.
[60] *In Lucam*, p. 262. [61] 1 Sam 14:52 – the causal connection is Bede's, see note below.
[62] *In primam partem Samuhelis*, p. 125. [63] *In Lucam*, p. 79.
[64] *In principium Genesim*, pp. 192–3; *On Genesis*, pp. 270–1.

of those who wielded them. Violence had to be inspired by love and carried out with a calm mind, free from thoughts of anger or hatred. This was what had made it justifiable for Phinehas, Samuel, Elijah, and Peter to kill sinners with the sword or with the word, not simply that these victims were sinners.[65] Likewise, when a Samaritan village refused to receive Christ, James and John asked Jesus whether they could call down fire from heaven to destroy just as Elias had done; Jesus' response was to rebuke his disciples. For Bede, Christ reproached his disciples not because they wished to follow the example of Elias but because they were motivated by hatred rather than love. After Christ had taught them to love their neighbours, examples of such vengeance were not lacking, although they were rarer than in the Old Testament.[66] Such was the importance of interior disposition that if good works were carried out with good intentions and with no evil thoughts, even if such actions resulted in injury or in harm the doer would nevertheless receive divine reward.[67]

Bede cannot have imagined that his strictures concerning violence would have had much impact upon the mores and behaviours of the lay elite of Northumbria. As Bede knew, even St Cuthbert had been unable to prevent King Ecgfrith's needless assault on Ireland.[68] Rather, Bede looks to have sought to offer his clerical and monastic audience a means of interpreting the violence that was a fixture of their society. The Church could not avoid being implicated in royal violence, either as a recipient of its proceeds or as an active participant in it. What Bede supplied were the tools to assess the legitimacy or otherwise of this violence and the methods through which the Church could refine its response to it.

Church and wealth, poverty and mediocrity

Examples of the dangers of wealth abound in Bede's writings. Love of riches disturbed the equilibrium of the mind and allowed it no peace.[69] Always the avaricious sought more wealth, and yet however much they possessed it could never be enough – twice Bede cited the Horatian maxim 'semper avarus eget'.[70] Even in their tombs, the avaricious could not be without their riches,[71] and after their deaths they would be tormented by the memory of the wealth that could so easily have gained them

[65] *In epistolas VII catholicas*, pp. 190–91; *Seven Catholic Epistles*, pp. 18–19.
[66] *In Lucam*, p. 212. [67] Ibid. p. 240. [68] *H.E.* IV 26 (24).
[69] *In Marci euangelium expositio*, ed. D. Hurst CCSL, 120 (Turnhout, 1960), pp. 482–83.
[70] *In prouerbia Salomonis*, ed. D. Hurst CCSL, 119B (Turnhout, 1983), p. 72, and *Homiliae euangelii*, p. 213; *Homilies on the Gospels*, p. 39.
[71] *In Lucam*, p. 408. If Bede was here thinking of the Anglo-Saxon furnished burial rite, nevertheless the words he employed were taken from Jerome.

absolution from their sins.[72] Riches themselves were like thorns, piercing the soul with its own evil desires and choking off the other virtues.[73] The dangers were not only personal. The lust for riches and for material possessions was at the root of much discord and warfare.[74] Earthly things could not always be defended and for the sake of wealth many were captured or killed.[75]

Wealth and its possession were perilous things and so it had proved to be for the Anglo-Saxon Church. Bede's own lifetime coincided with a remarkable increase in ecclesiastical wealth. From the 670s onwards, there was a massive upsurge in monastic foundation and patronage. First kings and then their nobles founded and endowed countless monasteries, supplying some with vast landed patrimonies. The extent of this patronage was such that over the course of little more than a generation the Anglo-Saxon Church was enriched.[76] If Bede showed little enthusiasm for detailing this newly acquired prosperity of the Church, near-contemporaries, such as Aldhelm of Malmesbury, Stephen of Ripon, and Alcuin of York, showed no such reluctance, describing a world of churches ablaze with precious metals and gemstones and monasteries controlling vast estates.[77]

This enrichment of the Anglo-Saxon Church took place, not coincidentally, at the same time as wider societal changes, now best discerned in the archaeological record. The evidence from both rural settlement sites and from the wider landscape points to a marked intensification in the exploitation of landed resources.[78] This intensified production was made more profitable by the growth in long-distance trade – the later seventh and eighth centuries was the age of the emporia, with the establishment and expansion of the great entrepôts at London, Southampton, York, and Ipswich and the constellation of smaller sites and centres that formed

[72] *In epistolas VII catholicas*, pp. 216–17; *Seven Catholic Epistles*, p. 55.
[73] *In Marcum*, p. 483.
[74] *In epistolas VII catholicas*, p. 213; *Seven Catholic Epistles*, p. 47.
[75] *In prouerbia Salomonis*, p. 97.
[76] J. Blair, *The Church in Anglo-Saxon Society* (Oxford, 2005), pp. 79–91. This is not to suggest that all monasteries were themselves wealthy institutions, this was clearly not the case, rather that taken as a whole the Anglo-Saxon Church became enriched from the 670s onwards.
[77] Campbell, 'Elements in the Background', p. 88 and, more generally, C. R. Dodwell, *Anglo-Saxon Art: a New Perspective* (Manchester, 1982).
[78] For recent comment and more detailed bibliography see S. Rippon, 'Landscape Change during the "Long Eighth Century" in Southern England' and S. Oosthuizen, 'Medieval Field Systems and Settlement Nucleation: Common or Separate Origins?' both in N. J. Higham and M. J. Ryan (eds.), *The Landscape Archaeology of Anglo-Saxon England* (Woodbridge, 2010), pp. 39–64 and 107–31 respectively. For an overview of the settlement evidence see H. Hamerow, *Early Medieval Settlements: the Archaeology of Rural Communities in North-West Europe, 400–900* (Oxford, 2002).

their hinterlands.[79] This growing international trade – in which churches and monasteries played key roles – as well as the levels of coinage in circulation point to a rapidly expanding economy.[80] Yet such expansion brought with it increasing social stratification and inequalities. Along with the growing demands and burdens placed on the rural peasantry and the concomitant decline in their status, the existence of the truly destitute and the utterly impoverished can be discerned, imperfectly but increasingly, in written sources from the eighth century onwards.[81] The contrasts in this new world could be stark. In Æthelwulf's *De abbatibus*, the poor gathered at the gates of the monastery to warm themselves in the ashes from the monastic fires while inside upon the altar rested a golden chalice, encrusted with gems and picked out in silver.[82]

The response to the swelling coffers of the Church in the later seventh and eighth centuries took numerous forms. For many Anglo-Saxon writers, the Church had become excessively tangled in secular affairs and there was an extended discussion amongst churchmen on the right relationship between the secular and religious worlds. At the same time, there was growing lay suspicion about the levels of ecclesiastical wealth. For Stephen of Ripon, at the root of St Wilfrid's troubles with King Ecgfrith of Northumbria was jealousy. Ecgfrith's queen, like a latter-day Jezebel, poured poison into the heart of the king, eloquently describing to him Wilfrid's vast wealth and his numerous royally arrayed followers.[83] More general concerns were voiced at the south-Humbrian Church council that met at *Clovesho* in 747. Kings and their nobles were said to believe that churchmen envied them their worldly goods and their most favourable prosperity and were insincere in their affections towards them.[84]

[79] The literature is vast, but for recent general survey see R. Fleming, *Britain after Rome: the Fall and Rise, 400–1070* (London, 2010), pp. 183–212 and Higham and Ryan, *The Anglo-Saxon World*, pp. 193–203. For introductions to the specific sites see the essays in B. Hardh and L. Larsson (eds.), *Central Places in the Migration and Merovingian Periods* (Lund, 2002). For 'productive sites' and the hinterlands of the emporia see, for example, T. Pestell and K. Ulmschneider (eds.), *Markets in Medieval Europe: Trading and Productive Sites, 650–850* (Macclesfield, 2003). The phrase 'the age of emporia' is taken from R. Hodges, *The Anglo-Saxon Achievement* (London, 1989).

[80] The levels of coinage are discussed in M. Blackburn, '"Productive Sites" and the Pattern of Coin Loss in England, 600–1180', in Pestell and Ulmschneider (eds.), *Markets in Medieval Europe*, pp. 20–36.

[81] There has been relatively little work on the destitute in Anglo-Saxon England, for brief comment and some typically insightful examples see J. Campbell, 'The Church in Anglo-Saxon Towns', in J. Campbell, *Essays in Anglo-Saxon History* (London, 1986), pp. 139–54, at 142.

[82] *De abbatibus*, ed. A. Campbell (Oxford, 1967) for the chalice p. 37, for the poor at the gates p. 39.

[83] *The Life of Bishop Wilfrid by Eddius Stephanus*, ed. and tr. B. Colgrave (Cambridge, 1927), p. 48.

[84] Haddan and Stubbs, *Councils and Ecclesiastical Documents* III, p. 375.

If Bede's writings give little detail about the nature and extent of ecclesiastical wealth, he grappled, nevertheless, with the problems such riches presented. His response to concerns that the Church was excessively wealthy was to recast the terms of the debate. What mattered was not whether the Church was or was not wealthy but whether the Church fulfilled its pastoral obligations. It was the duty of the rich materially to support the Church – the wealthy who could not preach the word of God ought to sustain those who could.[85] Similarly, it was the duty of the rulers of the Church to protect and maintain it and to ensure that its members did not fall into despair for lack of material possessions.[86]

The problem was not worldly goods, for a flow of wealth into the Church was necessary and to be expected, but what was done, or not done, to earn such. Drawing on Matthew 6:1–8, Bede condemned those who practised outward shows of excessive religiosity – praying on street corners that they might be seen by others – in order to gain not only praise from their fellow man but also money. Such men did not hesitate to accept money from the sick or from those troubled by their consciences, pretending that they would be their advocates at the Last Judgement. These men would spend whole nights in prayer if it meant they could rob the poor of their money.[87] Yet Bede was clear that the receiving of money or possessions for performing religious services was not in itself wrong; carrying out of such duties solely to gain wealth was.[88] Worse still, however, were those churchmen who demanded money and rewards from those in their care yet failed to carry out any of their religious obligations. A repeated theme of much of Bede's later writings is that enrichment of the Church was acceptable only if the Church fulfilled its pastoral and educative duties. Bede complained of those Churchmen who accepted or, indeed, exacted, offerings and gifts from the people but in no way laboured to rectify or to drive out their sins. Yet the only justification there could be for churchmen to receive these offerings was that they led those assigned to their care back to the path of truth, correcting their behaviour and preaching to them of heavenly things.[89]

[85] *In Ezram et Neemiam*, p. 248;*On Ezra and Nehemiah*, p. 17

[86] *De Tabernaculo*, ed. D. Hurst, CCSL, 119a (Turnhout, 1969), p. 51; *On the Tabernacle*, tr. A. Holder, Translated Texts for Historians 18 (Liverpool, 1994), p. 55. The word rendered above as 'despair' is 'tristitia', one of the members of Gregory the Great's heptad of vices in his *Moralia in Iob*. If Bede was using the word in this technical sense he may have been suggesting that a lack of resources could actually lead to avariciousness amongst churchmen, see *Moralia in Iob* X, PL, 76, 621d-22a.

[87] *In Lucam*, p. 361.

[88] *Retractatio in Actus Apostolorum*, ed. M. L. W. Laistner CCSL, 121 (Turnhout, 1960), pp. 143–44.

[89] *De Tabernaculo*, p. 115; *On the Tabernacle*, p. 133. see also *In Marcum*, pp. 592–3.

The wealth of the Church was, Bede strove to assert, different from other forms of wealth; it was not to be reckoned by the same calculus. Rather than personal or private property, it was the means by which the pastoral needs of the whole of the faithful could be met. The Church did not, or should not, accrue lands and possessions for their own sake but only to further the faith. Indeed, Bede stressed that the more assiduously individuals preached the word of God the less they were concerned about the acquisition or possession of worldly goods.[90] To borrow Peter Brown's phrasing, ecclesiastical wealth did not cause 'the coarse adrenalin of lordship to surge within those who owned it'; ecclesiasts were the stewards not the possessors of the riches that flowed into the Church.[91]

If the Church was to be enriched by the pious gifts of the faithful, Bede was, nevertheless, aware that the sources of these offerings and the intentions behind them could be problematic. The growing wealth of Anglo-Saxon England was troublesome not only for the institutional Church but also for the rich themselves. Bede noted that many people gave much to the poor but what they gave had been seized from others, either by force or by fraud.[92] Here Bede was voicing concerns that would be raised also at the council of *Clovesho* in 747. Canon twenty-six of this council, an extended discussion of almsgiving, decreed that alms should not be given from goods unjustly plundered or otherwise extracted through force or cruelty.[93]

As well as outright violence, both Bede and the council seem to be acknowledging the potentially exploitative nature of Anglo-Saxon lordship. Given the intensification of agricultural production in this period, the boundary between the collection of legitimate rent, tribute, or labour dues and the exploitation and oppression of the rural workforce must have been an uncertain and unsettled one.[94] Certainly, Bede would write of those who not only refused charity to the poor but also denied to their hirelings and servants the wages owed for their labour.[95] Likewise, when commenting on the famine and the poverty of the Jews detailed in Nehemiah 5:1–4, Bede spent considerable time expounding the literal meaning of the passage. He noted that the famine had been

[90] *In Ezram et Neemiam*, p. 248; *Ezra and Nehemiah*, p. 17.
[91] P. Brown, *Through the Eye of a Needle: Wealth, the Fall of Rome and the Making of Christianity in the West, 350–550 AD* (Princeton, NJ, 2012), p. 485.
[92] *In Prouerbia Salomonis*, p. 40
[93] Haddan and Stubbs, *Councils and Ecclesiastical Documents* III, p. 371.
[94] For a possible example of this in action, see the discussion of Ine 67 in T. Charles-Edwards, 'The Distinction between Land and Moveable Wealth in Anglo-Saxon England' in P. H. Sawyer (ed.), *English Medieval Settlement* (London, 1979), pp. 97–104 at pp. 101–103.
[95] *In epistolas VII catholicas*, p. 217; *Seven Catholic Epistles*, p. 56.

caused not only by the failure of crops but also by the oppressive taxation demanded by avaricious rulers. The desperation of those affected was such that they sold their children or their lands for food or borrowed from moneylenders to pay the taxes that they owed. The sense that these passages had contemporary relevance for Bede is furthered by his analysis of Nehemiah 5:7–8. Rather than seek for the allegorical meaning of these verses, Bede stated that instead we should observe their literal sense. During times of famine not only should we give aid to those in need but also we should excuse those subject to us from their customary dues.[96]

Bede also made reference to those who, weighed down with riches and sins, believed that the frequent giving of alms would be sufficient to absolve them, despite not giving up their dissolute way of life. Bede explicitly compared such people to the Jews, who, he claimed, neglected justice, mercy, and faith but believed that through their sacrifices and offerings they were able to placate God.[97] Again, such concerns were shared by those present at the council at *Clovesho*. The twenty-sixth canon condemned those who gave alms so that they could more freely indulge in feasting, drunkenness, and other bodily pleasures.[98] Canon thirty similarly introduced the example of a certain rich man who thought that he could purchase with bribes the fasting and psalmody of others to atone for his own sins. Indeed, he believed – and had been assured by others – that so fully had his sins been expiated by such methods that if he were to live for another three hundred years any penance imposed on him was already paid for.[99] Both Bede and the members of the council sought to underline that greater wealth did not allow the rich to sin more freely nor, likewise, could they gain absolution simply through the payment of money. To accept otherwise not only implied that God's mercy and forgiveness could be bought and sold but also undermined the coercive power of the institutional Church itself. If ecclesiastical censure and the imposition of penance could be circumvented by the wealthy then the Church's ability to direct the morality and behaviour of the lay elites was compromised.

If wealth presented problems, so too, Bede acknowledged, did poverty. The expansion of Christianity away from a relatively restricted elite over the course of the seventh century brought with it questions about the role of the growing lay community within the Church and the demands and expectations placed upon it: what did it mean to be Christian in the eighth

[96] *Ezra and Nehemiah*, pp. 183–5; *In Ezram et Neemiam*, pp. 359–60.
[97] *In primam partem Samuhelis*, p. 133
[98] Haddan and Stubbs, *Councils and Ecclesiastical Documents* III, p. 371.
[99] Ibid. pp. 373–4.

century?[100] The avenues open to the Anglo-Saxon elite to express their religious devotion and dedication – patronage of churches and monasteries and the distribution of alms – would have been closed off to large numbers of the laity. Certainly, Bede was aware that the fulfilment of the command to give alms was a problem for the poor and impoverished. He noted that there were many who wished to fulfil God's commandments and carry out their Christian duties but were hindered by poverty or lack of means – some, indeed, were hindered by the oppression and unjust exactions of others.[101] Bede's solution to these problems was to make clear that the giving of alms was not just about material possessions. Alms were not to be understood solely as the giving of food to the hungry, drink to the thirsty, clothes to the naked, or hospitality to pilgrims; those who forgave the offences of others also gave alms.[102] Nor was the value of any good given important. God was pleased by what was given with a good heart; he did not weigh the value.[103]

Just as there were pious Christians who were less wealthy, who lacked material means, so too for Bede were there pious Christians who were less perfect – the ordinary faithful. Within Bede's exegesis there is frequent, albeit scattered, exploration of the ways in which these ordinary faithful, these less perfect, can ensure their salvation. Bede was at pains to stress that many of the most stringent demands made of Christians by Jesus – chastity and poverty, for example – applied only to the more perfect of the faithful, to those who had been endowed by God with greater gifts. For the ordinary faithful, it was enough that they obeyed the Ten Commandments, gave alms, and carried out other charitable works.[104] The more perfect, those able to follow a stricter way of life, would ultimately enjoy greater rewards but nevertheless all of the faithful who fulfilled what was expected of them could hope for a place in heaven.[105] Mediocrity was not a cause for despair: not everyone could ascend to the highest heights nor were they expected to. Such divisions of the faithful were not the result of a falling away or a decline over time; they had been present from the earliest days of Christianity. Even in the early Jerusalem

[100] B. Dumézil, *Les racines chrétiennes de l'Europe: Conversion et liberté dans les royaumes barbares V^e^ – VIIIe siècle* (Paris, 2005), pp. 317–8 and M. Dunn, *The Christianization of the Anglo-Saxons c. 597-c.700: Discourses of Life, Death, and Afterlife* (London, 2009), partic. pp. 187–94.

[101] *In Ezram et Neemiam*, p. 360; *Ezra and Nehemiah*, p. 18.

[102] *In Lucam*, p. 241.

[103] Ibid. p. 362.

[104] See, for example, *De Templo* (ed.) D. Hurst C.C.S.L. 119A (Turnhout, 1969) pp. 162–63; *On the Temple* tr. S. Connolly, Translated Texts for Historians 21 (Liverpool: Liverpool University Press, 1995), p. 25. *In principium Genesim*, p. 225; *On Genesis*, pp. 303–04.

[105] See, for example, *In Lucam*, p. 259.

community, as detailed in Acts of the Apostles, not all of the faithful had given up their property or embraced celibacy.[106]

Bede's vision of the Christian community was, then, a hierarchical one with a clear distinction between the majority of the faithful and the spiritual elite. But it was one in which all had a part to play. Spiritual renewal in Northumbria could come about only through the reform of both the elite and the ordinary Christian. Bede's ideas about spiritual renewal – his ideal of reform as Alan Thacker termed it – have been explored in some detail by scholars.[107] As suggested above, Bede saw a Northumbrian Church in spiritual decline. Effective leadership was scarce and too many in positions of authority were venal and avaricious. Numerous members of the clergy were unable or unwilling to provide adequate pastoral care to the laity and such provisions as existed were perilously overstretched. Bede's solution, inspired by the writings of Gregory the Great, was renewal and reform spearheaded by a spiritual elite whom he most frequently termed *doctores* or *praedicatores*. These elites were essentially non-institutional – *doctores* and *praedicatores* could be found amongst the laity as well as amongst the clergy and monastics – but they would possess deeper spiritual knowledge than the rest of the faithful and would be able to balance the demands of the active, pastoral life with the necessity for asceticism and solitary withdrawal. Bede's reforming vision, though found throughout his writings, comes to the fore in his later writings, particularly his commentary on the books of Ezra and Nehemiah which features repeated and extended discussion of the pastoral obligations of the clergy and the failings of the contemporary Church.[108]

If Bede's focus in his writings was on the spiritual elite, his reforming agenda, nevertheless, also had a place for the rest of the faithful.[109] Indeed, for reform to be truly successful *doctores* and *praedicatores* required, and could further inspire, an active and engaged audience – *auditores*. For Bede, progress in the Church depended not only on preachers and teachers spreading the Word of God but also on *auditores* listening to and obeying what was said and, crucially, entreating these *doctores* and *praedicatores* to provide further guidance and instruction.[110] The decline of the Northumbrian Church was not simply or not exclusively a failure of leadership. Bede likened the Israelites lack of weaponry when facing the Philistines to the spiritual indolence of his contemporary Northumbrians;

[106] G. Olsen, 'Bede as Historian: The Evidence from his Observations on the Life of the First Christian Community at Jerusalem', *Journal of Ecclesiastical History*, 33 (1982), 519–30.

[107] Thacker, 'Bede's Ideal of Reform'.

[108] For example, DeGregorio, 'Bede's *In Ezram et Neemiam*', or DeGregorio, '*Nostrorum socordiam temporum*'.

[109] See, for example, DeGregorio, 'The Reforming Impulse', pp. 113 and 117–8.

[110] *In Ezram et Neemiam*, p. 277; *Ezra and Nehemiah*, p. 62.

through their sluggishness in reading and in questioning spiritual teachers they allowed the devil to bring to bear the weapons of impiety against all their other virtues.[111] This enemy could not be defeated through the cultivation of human wisdom but through divine grace and the importuning of the exhortations of *doctores*. Just as Bede longed for a new Nehemiah to lead the spiritual renewal of Northumbria,[112] so too he wished that a great crowd of faithful listeners would once more throng around the teachers of the word as they had done during the ministry of Christ.[113]

For Bede, the spiritual elite, however important, could be only one part of the story. First, it was clear to Bede that teachers could not always offer the guidance needed by the individual Christian; at times personal responsibility and examination were required. As Bede put it, *doctores* were the fishermen of the Church, gathering up believers in the net of the faith. Yet just as nets were sometimes open to catch fish and at other times folded away, so not all times were suitable for teaching. Sometimes *doctores* should speak, at other times the faithful should look to their own welfare.[114] Given the limits of human perception and judgement, that such personal responsibility was necessary was unsurprising. Bede wrote of those who seemed perfect in the eyes of the world and yet would be judged imperfect by God.[115] Human judgement erred frequently because it could only weigh up the deeds of another; it could not look into their hearts.[116] Second, the spiritual elite themselves were not and could not be perfect. Not even the greatest *doctores* could free themselves from earthly concerns when they attended to the salvation of those under their care.[117] Moreover, those who found a respectful and attentive audience and secured many souls for God risked falling into arrogance, while those whose audience was neither humble nor conscientious risked being stung into anger.[118] Bede would also stress the frailty and fears of those entrusted with teaching, who worried that they were unfit for such a task or longed to return to the peace and tranquillity of private contemplation.[119]

[111] *In primam partem Samuhelis*, pp. 112–13.
[112] *In Ezram et Neemiam*, p. 360; *Ezra and Nehemiah*, p. 184. [113] *In Marcum*, p. 510.
[114] *In Lucam*, pp. 113–4. [115] *Homiliae euangelii*, pp. 320–21; *Homilies* II, p. 191;.
[116] *Homiliae euangelii*, p. 371; *Homilies* II p. 259. Though Bede assumed that the Apostles and others of the spiritual elite had greater perception than ordinary men as they would aid Christ in the Last Judgement, see *In Ezram et Neemiam* p. 322 and also *Homiliae euangelii*, p. 89.
[117] *In Lucam*, pp. 216. See also *In Regum librum xxx quaestiones*, quaest. 30, ed. D. Hurst, CCSL, 119 (Turnhout, 1962), p. 321.
[118] *In Cantica Canticorum*, ed. D. Hurst CCSL, 119B (Turnhout, 1983), p. 277; *On the Song of Songs and Other Selected Writings*, tr. A. Holder (New York, 2011), p. 147.
[119] Ibid., p. 278; p. 148.

Just as Bede used his hagiography and history to draw unfavourable comparisons, largely implicit, between the spiritual leaders of the Northumbrian past and those of the present, so too he contrasted implicitly the sluggishness of the faithful in the present with the behaviour of those in the past. When describing St Cuthbert travelling from village to village, Bede noted that it had then been customary that whenever a cleric or priest arrived at a settlement that all the inhabitants gladly gathered together to listen to them preach and then eagerly put into practice what they had been taught.[120] The implication of Bede's words was that in the eighth century, such was no longer the custom. Bede likewise implied that a virtuous pastorate and a respected clergy could inspire just this kind of piety amongst the laity. Discussing the Northumbrian Church in the time before the Synod of Whitby of 664, Bede observed that 'the religious habit was held in great respect at that time, so that whenever a cleric or monk went anywhere he was gladly received by all [. . .] great attention was also paid to his exhortations, and on Sundays the people eagerly flocked to the church or the monastery, not to get food for the body but to hear the word of God'.[121] Bede's reference to food, as well as pointing to a little-studied aspect of early Anglo-Saxon church attendance, must be read in the light of his exegesis. Discussing Mark 3:20, 'And the multitude cometh together again, so that they could not so much as eat bread', Bede described the crowd as so eager for salvation that they did not allow Christ even time to eat. Bede then offered up a prayer, asking Christ to bestow his grace so that now, too, the faithful would sometimes be prepared to go without their daily bread in their assiduousness to learn from *doctores*.[122]

Bede's writings also contained models for emulation, *auditores* whose behaviour could be imitated. Bede's treatment of the conversation between Nicodemus and Christ in John 3 filled out the Gospel account extensively, presenting the Pharisee as an eager pupil, diligently seeking out knowledge from Jesus and deservedly receiving enlightenment.[123] In Bede's hands, Nicodemus became an idealized *auditor* and his exchange with Christ a model for the interaction between teacher and pupil.[124] Elsewhere in his writings, Bede would repeatedly stress the need for the active seeking out of spiritual insight and wisdom that he saw in Nicodemus. Thus the followers of John the Baptist inquired of Christ

[120] *Vita Cuthberti*, ed. and tr. B. Colgrave, *Two Lives of Saint Cuthbert* (Cambridge, 1940), p. 187.
[121] *H.E.* III 26.
[122] *In Marcum*, pp. 473–4. See also M. T. A. Carroll, *The Venerable Bede: His Spiritual Teachings* (Washington, DC, 1946), pp. 139–40.
[123] *Homiliae euangelii*, pp. 311–17
[124] Scheil, *The Footsteps of Israel*, pp. 37–9.

where he was dwelling that they might meet with Him more frequently and be instructed more fully in the divine secrets. Seeing 'that they were asking, seeking, and knocking well', Christ willingly shared with them the knowledge and instruction that they sought.[125] Bede used the same ask, seek, knock formula from Matthew 7:7 when writing of Nathanael-Bartholomew, presenting him as a pious *auditor* whose actions made him worthy of receiving the light of truth.[126]

Bede's discussions of *auditores* are by no means as extensive as his discussions of *doctores* and *praedicatores* – unsurprising given the intended elite clerical and monastic audience for much of his exegesis. Yet his vision of reform necessarily encompassed both groups: for reform to succeed, all the faithful had to play their part. As Bede wrote of the period of Christ's ministry, the great happiness of that time could be discerned both in the efforts of teachers and in the eagerness of learners.[127]

Conclusions

As he grappled with the problems facing his society, Bede cannot have been unaware of his own power and influence. Though debates continue about Bede's own social status,[128] it is clear that he was a privileged and well-connected member of a privileged and highly important institution. The monastery at Jarrow was closely tied to the Northumbrian royal dynasty, particularly in the person of King Ecgfrith and was located in the heartlands of royal power.[129] Bede's own connections were equally impressive. Alongside King Ceolwulf of Northumbria to whom he dedicated the *Historia ecclesiastica*, Bede could include a future archbishop of York and a future archbishop of Canterbury amongst his correspondents and his writings show him in contact with a wide range of churchmen and women across Anglo-Saxon England, sending already completed works to some and receiving commissions and requests for information or explication from others. Such requests and commissions show Bede's intellectual abilities were recognized and well regarded by his contemporaries. That Nothhelm, a priest in London, a visitor to the papal archives in Rome and, from 735, the archbishop of Canterbury, sought the opinion of a Northumbrian monk on various cruces in the Book of Kings demonstrates

[125] *Homiliae euangelii*, pp. 112–13; *Homilies* I, pp. 158–59.
[126] *Homiliae euangelii*, p. 123; *Homilies* I, p. 171. [127] *In Marcum*, p. 510.
[128] For recent comment see Campbell, 'Questioning Bede', pp. 119–20.
[129] For example, I. Wood, 'The Foundation of Bede's Wearmouth-Jarrow', in S. DeGregorio (ed.), *The Cambridge Companion to Bede* (Cambridge, 2010), pp. 84–96, partic. pp. 91–2 or I. Wood, 'The Gifts of Wearmouth and Jarrow', in P. Fouracre and W. Davies (eds.), *The Languages of Gift in the Early Middle Ages* (Cambridge, 2010), pp. 89–115 partic. 99–100.

the strength of Bede's reputation.[130] Bede had, then, good reason to believe that his ideas would be read and taken seriously by leading figures within Northumbria and Anglo-Saxon England as a whole.

Pre-eminent among Bede's patrons was his diocesan bishop, Acca of Hexham, who commissioned or otherwise encouraged a number of Bede's exegetical works – in some cases going to great lengths to persuade Bede of the need to undertake particular tasks.[131] Whether Acca shared or promoted Bede's vision of reform or other of the ideas explored in this piece is harder to determine. Was Acca actively seeking from Bede comment on the Northumbrian Church and society alongside interpretation of biblical passages and précis of Patristic wisdom and, if so, to what end? Or was Bede using these commissions as the opportunity to communicate to Acca his own concerns about the present and to set out the remedies he had devised? Such questions are now largely unanswerable. Though much is known about the subsequent transmission of Bede's writings in medieval Europe, their immediate reception and audience in Northumbria, beyond their dedicatees, are for the most part unknown.[132] Acca presumably circulated copies of the works he had commissioned but to whom and for what purpose is now unknowable. Some have argued that these works were intended to be the standard text-books or guides for clergy and monks within Acca's diocese, and perhaps Northumbria as a whole, but such is no more than supposition.[133]

Bede himself thought highly of Acca, praising him in the *Historia ecclesiastica* as 'of great energy and noble in the sight of God and man ... as well as a very learned theologian, untainted in his confession of the catholic faith and thoroughly familiar with the rules of ecclesiastical custom'.[134] Such may suggest Bede saw in Acca a kindred spirit or at the very least a patron worth cultivating but this is a long way from establishing a shared agenda or common goals. Certain themes in Bede's writings may have had particular appeal or utility for Acca, not least, given the turbulent politics of eighth-century Northumbria and Acca's apparent involvement therein, Bede's insistence on the need for close cooperation between king and Church. On the other hand, Bede's

[130] *In Regum librum* preface.

[131] See the letters prefatory to *In Lucam* and, for comment, M. Stansbury, 'Source-marks in Bede's Biblical Commentaries', in J. Hawkes and S. Mills (eds.), *Northumbria's Golden Age* (Stroud, 1999), pp. 383–9.

[132] J. A. Westguard, 'Bede and the Continent in the Carolingian Age and Beyond', in DeGregorio (ed.), *Companion to Bede*, pp. 201–15.

[133] J. Raine (ed.), *The Priory of Durham* 2 vols (London, 1864), I, p. xxxii.

[134] *H. E.* V 20. Though not so learned a theologian that he could not fundamentally misunderstand a passage from Bede's commentary on the Book of Samuel, see *De eo quod ait Isaias* PL, 94, 702–10.

resolute rejection of rebellion or revolt against secular powers, however unjust or tyrannical, could have been an implicit criticism of the involvement of Acca and other churchmen in factional politics. Certainly, Acca fled from his see in 731, probably in the aftermath of an attempted coup against King Ceolwulf and perhaps as a result of his involvement in it. Likewise, as a diocesan bishop Acca would have played a central role in the provision of pastoral care and so Bede's exploration of the responsibilities of *doctores* and *praedicatores*, as well as their *auditores*, would have had especial relevance for him. Yet the criticism of the current state of affairs that runs through these discussions necessarily implicated Acca – would he have welcomed, or even recognized, Bede's assessment of the situation?

In the last resort, though Bede's engagement with his own times is clearly apparent in his writings how his contemporaries responded to his work, what they made of his ideas, and what use they put them to is far from clear. One final point is, however, worth stressing: Bede believed change to be possible. His letter to Bishop of Ecgberht of York, his final surviving work, envisages a partnership between bishop and king that will transform the Northumbrian Church and it is not difficult to imagine that Bede saw such a partnership as recreating the fruitful relationship between Bishop Aidan and King Oswald in the 630s. It is this belief that change is possible and that the best of the past can be recaptured that arguably explains one of the cruces of the *Historia ecclesiastica*. Bede brings his work to a close with a survey of the English kingdoms in the present noting 'in these favourable times of peace and prosperity, many of the Northumbrian race, both noble and simple, have laid aside their weapons and taken the tonsure, preferring that they and their children should take monastic vows rather than train themselves in the art of war. What the result will be, a later generation will discover.'[135] Scholars have often suggested that here Bede was hiding his true feeling for this monastic boom and that the strident criticisms of sham and secularized monasteries expressed in his letter to Ecgberht better reflect what he actually felt.[136] The passage may even have an eschatological sting in its tail.[137] Yet, could Bede have been genuinely suspending judgement here? Through his extensive corpus of writings Bede had provided his contemporaries with the tools necessary, as he would see it, to construct a better Christian society and to channel this religious enthusiasm into productive forms. Bede must have known as he finished his history that it was likely to be his last major work; he would not see the results of his endeavours but he could at least hope that they would bear fruit.

[135] *H. E.* V 23. [136] Wallace-Hadrill, *Historical Commentary*, p. 200.
[137] Darby, *Bede and the End of Time*, pp. 213–4.

5 The incidence of rebellion in the early medieval West

Paul Fouracre

Early medieval societies may have had weak governing institutions, but they had them nonetheless. Office and authority were always in principle separable from favour and personal power, and if states were weak, the vocabulary of public authority and fiscal resource nevertheless survived from Roman times. So did the idea of legitimate power held over all of the inhabitants of a wide area designated as a single political entity, and some of these areas in early medieval Europe were just as wide as the modern states that would eventually grow out of them. In theory, therefore, people were aware of the wider entity. Elsewhere in this volume we see how a mentality of interregional contact and support survived the breakdown of imperial government and of the widespread exchange networks that underpinned it.[1] For reasons of social strategy, in a given polity wider authority might, as Roberts suggests, be invoked where it was otherwise absent.[2] Where that authority conferred legitimation and provided access to rights and resources, it might be fought over. Governing institutions, the collectivity of which is perhaps as close as we can get to a definition of the 'state', could thus have a bearing on any area of social interaction, including feud, or on other institutions, such as the church. Where such intervention was successful, those institutions could be co-opted by or even absorbed into the state. This is particularly true of the church, which came to articulate notions of statehood based on its own moral hegemony.[3] According to the early ninth-century *Annales Mettenses Priores*, the rise to power of the Carolingians began with a blood feud and ended with a *coup d'état*, passing by way of the

[1] See the chapter by D. Natal and J. Wood, 'Playing with Fire: Conflicting Bishops in Late Roman Spain and Gaul', in this volume.

[2] S. Roberts, 'The Study of Dispute: Anthropological Perspectives', in J. Bossy (ed.), *Disputes and Settlements: Law and Human Relations in the West* (Cambridge, 1983), pp. 1–24.

[3] M. de Jong, 'The State of the Church: *Ecclesia* and Early Medieval State Formation', in W. Pohl and V. Wieser (eds.), *Der frühmittelalterliche Staat – europäische Perspektiven* (Vienna, 2009), pp. 241–54.

Church.[4] Yet of all the possible socio-political options that the weakness of government allowed, overthrowing authority, or seceding from a given authority to form a new one, was very rarely taken. The incidence of rebellion in the early medieval west was strikingly low. This paper examines those incidents the Latin sources termed *rebelliones* to see if we can understand the infrequency. That it was apparently so hard to conceive of the overthrowing of authority or the invention of new political entities has a bearing on how we understand the maintenance of order in the wider frame.

The term 'rebellion' is a problematically broad one. If we allow 'rebellion' to comprehend 'revolts' of all kinds, then the incidence of risings against rulers appears to be much higher. The term 'revolt' is, however, a modern coinage or borrowing. Originally meaning 'a turning back' it first appears with the meaning of 'rising against a ruler' in the early sixteenth century, initially in French and then in English.[5] 'Revolt' is often used in English as a synonym for the term 'rebellion', but equally 'revolt' can signify a more restricted rising. One can revolt against an element of a regime, rule, or restriction, whereas 'rebellion' retains its Latinate sense of a more profound challenge to authority. The term *rebellio* is used sparingly in early medieval sources, from which one may conclude that such profound challenges to authority were themselves rare in our period. There is, nevertheless, a rich vocabulary of conflict which reveals the personal and generally small-scale nature of political revolt. Motivation for revolt is often given an emotional framing: it is occasioned by hatred (*odium*) or envy (*invidia*) or unexplained personal enmity (*inimicitia*). It is the reaction to personal insult, injury, or a sense of unjust treatment. The results are plots: *seditiones, insidiae, conjurationes, contentiones*, and so on. Action is generally taken by small groups, often structured around linked families. The term faction (*factio*) perhaps comes closest to our notion of a grouping of a political nature, and its use typically reveals a grouping within the elite organized to gain or increase a hold over peers. The vocabulary of conflict therefore supports the impression that early medieval sources have relatively little to say about rebellion against a given authority or order, as opposed to revolt against a particular set of rulers. Whereas the former entailed challenging the ruling elite as a whole, the latter sought a redistribution of power within an elite, that is, within the same political order. What follows will try to account for why there are relatively few accounts of rebellions in our sources. It will ask why some

[4] *Annales Mettenses Priores*, ed. B. von Simson, MGH SRG (Hannover and Leipzig, 1905), years 687–725 tr. with commentary P. Fouracre and R. Gerberding, *Late Merovingian France: History and Hagiography 640–720* (Manchester, 1996), pp. 350–70.

[5] W. von Wartburg, *Französisches Etymologisches Wörterbuch*, vol. 10 '*R*'.

areas produced more than others, and seek to understand what conditions produced which kind of violent conflict. My base-line observation is the relatively unchanging configuration of political entities or states in Western Europe in the period roughly 560–760.

Let us begin with late antiquity when rebellions were apparently more common than in the later period. The late Empire witnessed much political and military disturbance. And in the course of that disturbance, numerous new political entities were formed, whether short or long lived. There is an obvious contrast here with the situation from the later sixth century onwards, when very few new entities came into being. Formation was by both rebellion and invasion, the two being interrelated in cause and effect, but having a common consequence in that a new entity was formed when a group ceased to respond to Imperial command and began to signify itself as having an independent authority. An example of rebellion leading to separation would be that of Tibatto. According to the *Chronicle of 452*, in the year 435, one Tibatto rebelled in *Gallia Ulterior*, that is Western Gaul north of the Loire, including Armorica. As a result the region *discessit a Romana societate* and fell under the sway of the *Bacaudae*.[6] Whether or not the *Bacaudae* were rebels against the social order is, of course, an open question, but at the very least they were regarded as a threat to Roman authority.[7] An example of rebellion against Imperial authority within the senatorial elite would be Aegidius' assumption of independent rule, also in Gaul north of the Loire, after the death of the Emperor Majorian in 461. According to Gregory of Tours, though he is perhaps not reliable on this point, Aegidius' son Syagrius, who ruled in the Soissons area, would be styled *rex Romanorum*.[8] In Spain, the uprising of Burdunellus in 496 was rebellion against the growing power of the Visigoths, who were claiming authority in Spain. It may have been the threat posed to the Hispano-Roman elite in the *Tarraconensis* by newly arriving settlers that provoked Burdunellus. Our source, the *Chronicon Caesaraugustana*, says nothing about the causes of the rebellion, although it does provide the exotic detail that Burdunellus was executed in Toulouse by being incinerated in a bronze bull.[9] *Foederati* rebelled against the authorities when conditions were poor, as Gildas tells us that the

[6] *Chronicon Gallica a CCCCLII a DXI*, ed. T. Mommsen, MGH AA IX, *Chronica Minora* 1 (Berlin, 1892), pp. 646–62, XII, p. 660.

[7] For the difficulty in categorizing the *bacaudae* given that there are very few references to them, see J. Drinkwater, 'The Bacaudae of Fifth-Century Gaul', in J. Drinkwater and H. Elton (eds.), *Fifth-Century Gaul: a Crisis of Identity?* (Cambridge, 1992), pp. 208–17.

[8] Gregory of Tours, *Decem libri Historiarum* II, 27, tr. L. Thorpe, *Gregory of Tours: History of the Franks* (Harmondsworth, 1974), p. 139.

[9] *Chronicorum Caesaraugustanorum Reliquiae*, ed. T. Mommsen, MGH AA XI, *Chronica Minora* 2 (Berlin, 1894), pp. 221–3.

Saxons did against the Britons when their supplies were not renewed.[10] In this context, invasion and rebellion overlapped. And in relations between different barbarian groups, warfare, resistance, and rebellion intermingled, as we can see over a century in relations between the Visigoths and Sueves, for example. In addition, there were usurpations, or bids for power, by army leaders such as Constantine III in 407 and these, it has been said, accounted for the bulk of the fighting in the late Empire.

What is striking here is the sheer variety of ways in which disorder came to Western Europe as Roman government unravelled in the fifth century. Hence the frequency of rebellion as provincial elites were challenged, or were themselves forced to create independent authorities, or when newly established elites were in their turn confronted either by the natives or by fresh incomers. Multiple political entities were formed, most of which failed to survive. All of this appears to have calmed down over the sixth century – 'appears' is a necessary caveat because we must also ask whether the appearance of less complex conditions is the effect of that lowering of horizons, or simplification of political language, which came with the Christian curriculum and the monastic chronicler.[11]

In the first instance, what we see is the rise to domination of a few kingdoms based around barbarian peoples, and these rose to domination at the expense of smaller or weaker groups.[12] The rise of the Franks is the best documented and most studied example.[13] I shall begin with them and make observations about authority and lack of resistance in Francia before making brief comparisons with other regions. It was the Franks who in 486 put an end to Syagrius' independent statelet or kingdom of Soissons, thus in effect ending the rebellion begun by Aegidius. By the middle of the sixth century they had control over a territory that included nearly all of Gaul and Provence, and stretched from the Pyrenees to the Scheldt estuary, and from the Rhine to the Atlantic coast, having defeated and then absorbed or expelled all other groups within this massive territory.[14] Thereafter, despite the size and heterogeneous nature of their territory, the Franks faced virtually no rebellion.

[10] Gildas, *De Excidio et Conquestu Britanniae* 23, tr. M. Winterbottom, *Gildas, the Ruin of Britain* (London and Chichester, 1978), pp. 26–7.

[11] On this cultural transition, J. Fontaine, 'Education and Learning', in P. Fouracre (ed.), *The New Cambridge Medieval History*, I (Cambridge, 2005), pp. 735–59.

[12] Of this process there are numerous recent accounts. See, for instance, G. Halsall, *Barbarian Migrations and the Roman West 376–568* (Cambridge, 2007), pp. 414–98.

[13] On the centrality of Francia in the historiography of early medieval Europe, see P. Fouracre, 'Francia and the History of Early Medieval Europe', *Journal of the Haskins Society*, 23 (2011), 1–21.

[14] One reason for the centrality of this account is the detailed narrative provided by Gregory of Tours, *Decem libri* I-IV.

In the earliest Frankish law-code, the *Pactus legis Salicae*, early sixth century, and in the *Lex Ribuaria* of the early seventh century, we see measures aimed at keeping social order by remedying injury and offence in ways that honoured social status.[15] The codes do not touch on questions of authority, except indirectly when they outline procedures to be followed in legal proceedings, that is, these presuppose the working of the count's court, the *mallus*, or something like it; a court in which the president wielded authority in the name of the king. Royal legislation from the sixth and early seventh centuries did talk about order and disorder and on occasion called for *pax et disciplina*, but, as far as I am aware, with the possible exception of what one might term emergency measures in 614, it never did this as a reaction to rebellion or even widespread disobedience.[16] Measures concerned policing and peace keeping in the context of normal government rather than any reaction to extraordinary events. Formularies, the earliest of which contains material relating to the sixth century, deal with both ordinary and extraordinary situations. There is, for instance, a form to be used when violence and disorder have resulted in the loss of a person's documents (*appennis*), but there is no form to deal with the aftermath of rebellion.[17]

Nor do narrative sources mention rebellion. The only people termed 'rebels' in Gregory of Tours' *Ten Books of Histories* are the Saxons who rebelled in 555.[18] Frankish sources up to the late eighth century would continue to refer to the Saxons as 'rebels'. This reflects the fact that the Franks periodically managed to impose overlordship over the Saxons, forcing them to pay a cattle tribute, but were unable to rule directly in Saxony before the late eighth century. The Saxons were therefore able to throw off that overlordship, breaking any oaths of submission they had made at times of weakness. To the Franks this was rebellion against their authority, and the oath-breaking made the Saxons a perfidious people. Elsewhere too rebellion came to be associated with oath-breaking, as the maintenance of political authority rested on the keeping of oaths.

[15] The earliest version of *Lex Salica* is *Pactus Legis Salicae*, ed. K. Eckhard, MGH Legum, sectio I, vol. IV (Hannover, 1926); *Lex Ribuaria*, ed. F. Beyerle and R. Buchner, MGH Legum sectio I, vol. 3 pt. I (Hannover, 1954).

[16] See, for instance, *Clotharii Edictum*, ed. A. Boretius, *Capitularia Regum Francorum* I, MGH Legum, sectio II, i (Hannover, 1883), pp. 20–3: '*Ut pax et disciplina in regno nostro sit, Chritso propitiente, perpetua, et ut revellus vel insullentia malorum hominum severissime reprimatur*'. Issued in 614, this legislation re-established peace after Clothar II had reunified all three Frankish kingdoms. For comment on how this legislation has been (wrongly) interpreted, see P. Fouracre, *The Age of Charles Martel* (Harlow, 2000), pp. 12–14. On the possible element of rebellion, see below p. 110.

[17] For examples of *appennis*, see *Formulary of Angers* 31, 32, 33, trans A. Rio, *The Formularies of Angers and Marculf: Two Merovingian Legal Handbooks* (Liverpool, 2008), pp. 73–6.

[18] Gregory of Tours, *Decem libri* IV, 10.

The notion of perfidy also struck a religious chord, placing those who broke with authority in spiritual jeopardy. This was of course particularly appropriate in the case of the Saxons who were not Christians.

Gregory of Tours' narrative is notoriously full of violent incident, but lacking in tales of revolt as well as of rebellion. Apart from the episodes in which the Franks fought with other peoples in the earlier books, it was either the *bella civilia* between the descendants of Clovis, or a kind of mindless interpersonal conflict that produced violence.[19] There was much plotting by magnates to increase their power and to damage rivals, but this took place by and large through the medium of struggles between kings. The closest we come to a challenge to Merovingian authority is the attempt by the pretender Gundovald to seize power in the years 582–5.[20] This affair Ian Wood (unlike Gregory) refers to as a 'rebellion', but he goes on to say that it was 'in the first instance an act of Merovingian family politics', support for Gundovald being aimed against King Guntram of Burgundy with the connivance of his rival Childebert, king of Austrasia.[21] The various magnates involved may have been trying to strengthen their own power by weakening that of Guntram, but they were not challenging the political order in the wider sense. If they had been successful, what would have emerged was a new ruler, but a ruler that was still a Merovingian. Commentators on Gregory, such as Ian Wood, Guy Halsall, Edward James, or Martin Heinzelman, can offer plausible analyses of the whys and wherefores of Gregory's *bella civilia*, but Gregory himself never said why the kings and others were so often at each other's throats.[22] According to Walter Goffart, Gregory held back from such an analysis because he wished to emphasize the arbitrary stupidity of people who felt their actions needed no guidance from God. This, argues Goffart, was part of a rather subtle project on Gregory's part, that is, to argue for complete submission to the divine power.[23] So, perhaps there was something like rebellion in sixth-century Gaul/Francia, but it is not revealed in Gregory of Tours' narrative because Gregory did not wish to talk about motives other than greed, vanity, and stupidity. Alternatively,

19 On Gregory's agenda in stressing the mindlessness of the conflicts, see the seminal work of W. Goffart, *The Narrators of Barbarian History: Jordanes, Gregory of Tours, Bede and Paul the Deacon* (Princeton, NJ, 1988), pp. 112–234.

20 Gregory of Tours, *Decem libri* VI, 24, VII,10, 26, 34–8, 36.

21 I. Wood, *The Merovingian Kingdoms, 450–751* (Harlow, 1994), p. 94.

22 Wood, *Merovingian Kingdoms*; G. Halsall, 'Nero and Herod? The Death of Chilperic and Gregory's Writing of the Histories', in K. Mitchell and I. Wood (eds.), *The World of Gregory of* Tours (Leiden, 2002), pp. 337–50; E. James, *The Origins of France: From Clovis to the Capetians, 500–1000* (London, 1982); M. Heinzelmann, *Gregor von Tours (538–594) 'Zehn Bücher Geschichte'. Historiographie und Gesellschaftskonzept im 6 Jahrhundert* (Darmstadt, 1994).

23 Goffart, *Narrators*, pp. 227–34. See also H. Reimitz in this volume.

either Gregory was such a poor historian that he was not capable of dealing with more complex issues, or there really was nothing to report. It is arguable that Goffart's approach rather flatters Gregory as a writer. He was by no means a subtle historian, but, nevertheless, he could narrate events in sufficiently coherent detail to allow modern historians to discuss Merovingian politics of the sixth century quite plausibly. His near silence on rebellion would therefore seem to be worth taking seriously. It is, after all, a silence shared with the two law codes, royal legislation, and the formularies. Another reason for thinking that we should accept Gregory's silence as evidence here is that the sources of the seventh century, different in kind and orientation, also have very little to say on the subject of rebellion.

The main narrative source for the Francia in the first half of the seventh century is the *Fourth Book of the Chronicle of Fredegar.*[24] From the second half of the century there is an increasing body of hagiography, charters, and another Chronicle, the *Liber Historiae Francorum*, completed by the year 727.[25] Fredegar referred to rebellion, using the noun *rebellio* or the verb *rebellare*, four times for the period 612–41, and he reserved the term for challenges to authority. Other violence was for Fredegar, as for Gregory, occasioned by greed, hatred, revenge, or ambition.[26] The first rebellion in Fredegar took place in 613/14 as Clothar II, the king of Neustria, took over the kingdoms of Austrasia and Burgundy after a period of fighting between Merovingians: the last of the *bella civilia* as it were. It may be that it was this incident that forms the only reference to rebellion in legislation, for the Edict in question[27] was promulgated in 614, but the reference is vague: 'that the rebellion and insolence of wicked people will be most severely suppressed'. Clothar had sacked Eudila, count of the Jura, and replaced him with a Frank, Herpo. Herpo was vigorous in imposing his will in the area, at which the *pagenses*, in league with the *patricius* Aletheus, the local bishop, and another count, *per rebellionis audatiam* killed Herpo.[28] Clothar had the rebels killed, but not Aletheus, who in the next chapter tried to seduce Clothar's queen. Since

[24] *The Fourth Book of the Chronicle of Fredegar with its Continuations* [hereafter Fredegar], ed. and tr. J. Wallace-Hadrill (London, 1960).

[25] *Liber Historiae Francorum*, ed. B. Krusch, MGH Scriptores Rerum Merovingicarum II (Hannover, 1888), the last nine chapters, tr. with commentary Fouracre and Gerberding, *Late Merovingian France*, pp. 79–96. On the use of hagiographic sources for this history, P. Fouracre, 'Merovingian History and Merovingian Hagiography', *Past & Present*, 127 (1990), 3–38.

[26] On the portrayal of violence in Fredegar, P. Fouracre, 'Attitudes Towards Violence in Seventh- and Eighth-Century Francia', in G. Halsall (ed.), *Violence and Society in the Early Medieval West* (Woodbridge, 1998), pp. 59–75.

[27] This chapter, Note 16. [28] *Fredegar* IV, 43.

he was himself of royal Burgundian blood, he argued, he could become king in Clothar's place. As soon as his plot came to light, Aletheus was also killed. Eudila is an East Germanic name, that is, non-Frankish. The *pagenses* of a remote region were involved, and Aletheus claimed descent from the pre-Frankish (Burgundian) rulers of the area. So was this a rebellion by Burgundian separatists, and an attempt to replace the dynasty and the Franks in the Jura? That there was such a separatist movement was certainly an idea popular in the early twentieth century, but there is simply no clear evidence for it.[29] Aletheus wanted to be king of all Francia, not to separate from it. The trouble may, however, have been the fruit of resentment at the imposition of Clothar's followers at the expense of locals, rather than a 'nationalistic' movement. This would happen again in the later seventh century, when an Austrasian king replaced Neustrians, but then it would be clear that the politics of resentment revolved around the palace. The second rebellion in Fredegar is a much clearer case. This was when the Slavs threw off the rule of the Avars in the 620s.[30] The language here is very clear. The *oppressiones* of the Avars against the whole people of the Wends became unbearable, and so they began to rebel against this *dominatio*, with the help, remarkably, of a Frankish merchant called Samo, who would become the king of a newly created Slav political entity. So here we see a challenge to the domination of a whole group, which led to that group being driven off. The next rebellion was in 635/6. Fredegar simply says that the Basques *forteter revallerent*.[31] No more needed to be said: like the Saxons the Basques were always rebelling, that is to say, the Franks had been unable to impose their authority upon them.[32] The fourth and last reference is revealing. After Samo had become king of the Wends, there was war with the Franks, who expected that Samo would submit to them. The Wends raided deep into Thuringia, until a Frank called Radulf was made duke of Thuringia and began to push them back. Elated by his victories, and because he was in conflict with duke Adalgisel of Austrasia, Radulf began, 'little by little', to rebel against his king, Sigibert.[33] Then having risen in open rebellion in 639, he was attacked by a large Austrasian

[29] M. Chaume, *Les origines du duché de Bourgogne* (Dijon, 1926) was the champion of the notion of Burgundian separatism in a study which exhibited a large degree of regional patriotism. A similar belief in a regional separatist mentality is found in relation to Aquitaine in a much more recent work, M. Rouche, *L'Aquitaine des Wisigoths aux Arabes, 418–781. Naissance d'une region* (Paris, 1979). Both works were convinced of regional differences and mentalities which could only lead to rebellion.

[30] *Fredegar* IV, 48. [31] *Fredegar* IV, 78.

[32] *Fredegar* IV, 21: The Franks supposedly conquered the Basques in 602, but *Fredegar* IV, 54, which relates to 626, mentions in passing that they had already rebelled.

[33] *Fredegar* IV, 77 Radulf; 'paulatem contra Sigybertum iam tunc ciperat revellare.'

army.[34] This looks at first sight like a border duke with his own army and strongholds defying royal authority and separating himself off from the rest of the elite to form a new political entity. On closer inspection we see that Radulf's so-called rebellion was part of a deep rift within the Austrasian elite. Amongst Radulf's supporters was one Fara, a member of the Agilolfing family, whose father Chrodoald had been by killed by King Dagobert at the urging of Pippin of Landen and Arnulf of Metz. After Dagobert and Pippin were dead, Pippin's son Grimoald, an ally if not a blood relative of Adalgisel, was excluded from power. The attack on Radulf should be understood as part of Grimoald's fight for the position of 'mayor of the palace' that his father had held. Fara, the Agilolfings, Otto who was the actual mayor of the palace and Grimoald's principal rival, and Radulf were all part of a faction which opposed him. In the event, the attack on Radulf was a disaster. Radulf was triumphant. He dealt with the Wends as an independent ruler and he strutted around like a king, but, said Fredegar, 'he would not in so many words actually deny that Sigibert was his king'.[35] That is to say, he did not go on to form a new kingdom as Samo had done. Is this because Samo was a merchant adventurer, not part of the Frankish ruling elite, whereas Radulf was very much a part of it and unable to cut his ties? This episode does much to help us understand why the massive Frankish polity did not simply break apart: by the middle of the seventh century, Francia had an elite of regional leaders who were in social, cultural, and religious terms well integrated into a single political community, which revolved around a centre that had its focus in the palaces of the Merovingian kings.[36] Life outside such a community seems to have been inconceivable.

The existence of an integrated elite is, as suggested earlier, reflected in the use of the word *factio* to refer to the different interest groups, that is, factions, within it, a use first seen in Fredegar: it was the *factio* of Pippin and Arnulf bishop of Metz that in 613 had urged King Clothar II to take over the kingdom of Austrasia.[37] In the sources for the second half of the seventh century, there is much about infighting within the elite, but hardly anything about rebellion. It is possible to see that there were periodic outbursts of conflict when one faction was thought to have too much power. Since power, legitimation, and privilege were mediated through office which was derived from royal authority, conflict revolved around control of the royal palace, the source of

[34] *Fredegar* IV, 87. [35] *Fredegar* IV, 87: 'in verbis ... Sigiberto regimini non denegans'.

[36] P. Fouracre, 'The Nature of Frankish Political Institutions in the Seventh Century', in I. Wood (ed.), *Franks and Alemanni in the Merovingian Period: an Ethnographic Perspective* (Woodbridge, 1998), pp. 285–316.

[37] *Fredegar* IV, 40

office.[38] Periodic conflict was in effect a way of redistributing power, and this could be done without rebellion. The factions might have a regional basis, but, as already suggested, the leaders of even the most peripheral regions had strong ties to the centre. Patrick Geary showed this 25 years ago for the supposedly peripheral region of Provence where the leading family was related to Neustrian, that is, North-Western French, 'mayors of the palace'.[39] The 'mayors' were key figures as having control of the palace gave them access to the treasury (*fiscus*) and to military resources. They also controlled access to the king, and so could exclude political enemies from the centre. Given the ties between locality and centre, kings, or mayors and queen-regents when kings were minors, could play people in the localities off against each other by offering support to allies or withdrawing support from opponents.[40] Here they could tap into the energy of local rivalry. We can see that there were actually relatively few people we could call 'magnates' in Francia. Ganshof estimated that there were about three hundred comital families in the time of Charlemagne, and less than this, presumably, in the smaller Merovingian kingdom. Alongside these we should count bishops and a much smaller number of special people such as dukes and *domestici*. Such highly coveted positions made the holder dominant in the county. Whatever resources the holders might otherwise have, they needed office and royal approval to legitimate their power in giving them the right to raise revenue, organize military forces, and oversee the judicial system. Offering that legitimation to a rival worked political wonders. Competition thus led people to support an authority that might reward them, and the fact that both local rivals and the collective power of the magnates could be mobilized against dissenters meant that it would have been very hard to mount a rebellion. The Franks held assemblies each spring. The right to attend was jealously guarded: magnates wished, as we would say, to be kept in the loop. It was at these assemblies that collective power could be mobilized. They might also explode into violence as different factions came face to face, but they were nevertheless moments expressing a consensus about the nature of authority, even if they saw bickering about the distribution of power.[41]

[38] P. Fouracre, 'Conflict, Power and Legitimation in Francia in the Late Seventh and Eighth Centuries', in I. Alfonso, H. Kennedy, and J. Escalona (eds.), *Building Legitimacy: Political Discourses and Forms of Legitimation in Medieval Societies* (Leiden, 2004), pp. 3–26.

[39] P. J. Geary, *Aristocracy in Provence: the Rhône Basin at the Dawn of the Carolingian Age* (Stuttgart, 1985).

[40] For three examples of this interplay between centre and locality, see Fouracre, 'Merovingian History'.

[41] Fredegar ends with the violence between magnates that followed on from such a meeting: *Fredegar* IV, 90.

In our sources, including Fredegar for the earlier part of the seventh century, there is a notable emphasis on the moral quality of power, that is, on how power was exercised. Those who ruled unjustly, or in the words of the *Liber Historiae Francorum*, who 'cruelly oppressed the Franks', would get their comeuppance. To prepare *insidias* (*Liber Historiae Francorum* again) against such people was morally justified.[42] Where a ruler was harmful, they should be replaced and their authority should be transferred to someone else. Authority was understood in concrete terms as the right to issue binding commands. The right itself could not be challenged, hence the emphasis on the personal quality of the rule. We may see here the influence of the reductionist language of hagiography, which was, after all, the most common form of writing in this period. That is to ask whether our impression of an integrated elite which found rebellion inconceivable was actually the product of a simplified moral universe in which the devil stirred up trouble, but the Christian community always remained intact. Even the mayor of the palace, Ebroin, demonized as a ruler, was on his way to mass when struck down for his sins. Proper rebels were those like the Basques or the Saxons, who were perceived to resist the Christian truth. One can argue, however, that it is as much the other way round: hagiography of the later seventh century is marked by the use of legal and political language. Misbehaviour was indeed prompted by the devil but the devil worked through greed, pride, and envy, which correlates with the domination of certain factions and with the use of local rivalry as a political tool. The saints, many of whom were political leaders, were attacked by rivals in whom the devil had stirred up a deadly *invidia*. Legal terminology and even bureaucratic procedure find their way into these narratives. This is so much the case that the Merovingian Church has been regarded as feeble and its saints as distinctly unholy.[43]

The earliest *Passio Leudegarii*, composed probably in the 680s, is the most detailed account of violent political conflict that we have for the seventh century anywhere in Europe.[44] It centres on events between 672 and 676 in which there was a complex factional struggle for control of the royal palace. But given the nature of links between the palace and the provinces, its effects were felt throughout Francia. We can, moreover, see references to them in several other contemporary sources. The two main

[42] The *Liber Historiae Francorum*, 45 is here referring to the assassination of King Childeric II in 675 for having treated the 'Franks' harshly. The only note of regret in the *Liber* is that Childeric's pregnant wife was killed along with him. The source does not mention the fact that an infant son was also murdered.

[43] Fouracre and Gerberding, *Late Merovingian France*, pp. 38–47.

[44] *Passio Leudegarii*, tr. with commentary, Fouracre and Gerberding, *Late Merovingian France*, pp. 193–253.

protagonists were the mayor of the palace, Ebroin, and Leudegar, bishop of Autun. The trouble began when Ebroin tried to exclude opponents from Burgundy from the palace. But he was ousted when the king died and he could not prevent the wider magnate community from assembling. Raising the new king, Theuderic III, had to be done in a way that was open for all to see to give each magnate access to him; otherwise, in the words of the *Passio*, if he [Ebroin] 'kept the king in the background and just used his name, he would be able to do harm to whomsoever he wished'.[45] So the assembly turned on Ebroin. Leudegar replaced him, Theuderic was deposed and replaced by his brother Childeric, who was already king in Austrasia. But, Childeric also became unacceptable when he favoured his Austrasian followers over the Neustrians and Burgundians, or as the *Liber Historiae Francorum*, a partisan Neustrian source, put it, because he 'was too frivolous' and 'oppressed the Neustrians'. They killed him.[46] There followed a mighty struggle for the palace, which Ebroin eventually won, and then he had Leudegar put to death. With Theuderic III restored to the throne, Ebroin took up where he had been forced to leave off. This is cutting a very long story short, but there is enough here to show that getting rid of unwanted rulers, coming from behind to regain power, and changing the personnel and direction of government all could take place without rebellion, and though military force would decide the day, it was control of the palace and the legitimation of power that sealed victory. When Childeric became king, he issued a series of edicts guaranteeing the privileges of the magnates in the different regions of the kingdom, and also stating that the key position of mayor had to be open to all, that is, it could not be monopolized by a single faction.[47] Just as the king's name could do harm, it could also be used to put things right, and it could do this because royal decrees were legally binding. When Ebroin returned to power, according to the *Passio Leudegarii*, he issued an edict restoring order.[48] The wording here may reflect the *Theodosian Code*, where it dealt with the aftermath of barbarian attack and limited recriminations for damage done in the confusion.[49] Our author says that this showed just how wicked Ebroin was because this allowed him to hold on to property wrongly seized in the troubles, but we might say that it shows the persistence of Roman notions of government through legally binding orders, just as royal charters show dispositive power. When Ebroin returned to office he acquired the *ius potestatis*, 'the right of power',

[45] *Passio Leudegarii*, 5. [46] Note 42. [47] *Passio Leudegarii*, 7.
[48] *Passio Leudegarii*, 28.
[49] *The Theodosian Code* XV.14, tr. C. Pharr, *The Theodosian Code and Sirmondian Constitutions* (Princeton, NJ, 1952).

which greatly magnified the harm he could do.[50] It may be this sense that legitimation was the necessary adjunct of power that made the concept of rebellion difficult to express.

The only source that mentions the word rebellion in this sequence is an original charter for 679, which dealt with Chramlinus, the bishop of Embrun, who had been deposed, presumably in the context of the conflict. Chramlinus, said this royal document, had been found *in infidelitate nostra*, and he had become bishop fraudulently 'either though his own audacity, or by using false documents, or *per revellacionis audacia*, but not through our order'.[51] So not much to go on rebellion-wise here, but it merits mention out of interest for the phrase *audatia rebellationis*, which was the phrase used by Fredegar to refer to Aletheus' rebellion in the Jura – a region like that of Embrun, which had been at the heart of the old Burgundian kingdom.[52] One wonders whether this is somehow a regional usage. The only other reference to rebels in this period comes from the Sornegau, adjacent to the Jura. Again it comes from a contemporary Saint's Life, the *Vita Germani Grandivallensis*. Adalric, duke of Alsace, who was one of the belligerents of the troubles of the 670s, was trying to extend his power into Grandvalle. He accused the inhabitants of the valley of having been rebels against his predecessors. He then ordered the *centenarii* out of the valley, before getting in an Aleman war-band to help him take control of it.[53] Is this a unique example of rebellion from below? That would depend on whether the accusation was just a convenient excuse for Adalric to extend his power beyond Alsace, as the hagiographer suggests. The inhabitants are certainly presented as vigorously denying the charge. That the *centenarii* should be exiled is an interesting but rather baffling detail. All in all, I do not think we can use this as an example of rebellion.

We have seen that references to rebellion in Gaul/Francia are rare from the time of Gregory of Tours to the early eighth century, when the author of the *Liber Historiae Francorum* signed off. In the sixth century, the struggles between kings provided an outlet for dissent that made rebellion less likely. Frankish hegemony floated on a cultural accommodation in which no other groups were obviously excluded, oppressed, and forced to revolt. By the seventh century we see an elite that was too integrated, and too aware of their privileges derived from co-operation to rebel. No

[50] *Passio Leudegarii*, 28.
[51] T. Kölzer (ed,), *Die Urkunden der Merovinger*, MGH. Diplomata regum Francorum e stirpe Merovingica, 2 vols. (Hannover, 2001), I, 312.
[52] Above, p. 110.
[53] *Vita Germani Gandivallensis*, ed. B. Krusch, MGH SRM V (Hannover, 1910), pp. 33–40, here chapters 10–12.

alternatives to the relatively light touch of Merovingian rule seem to have been imaginable. Nor was there a standing army that could throw up alternative rulers backed by force – there could never be a Frankish Phocas. What of elsewhere in Europe?

Visigothic Spain is much less well documented than Francia, and apparently suffered much more rebellion. Whereas Frankish hegemony in Gaul was quickly established and became synonymous with Merovingian kingship, it was not until the campaigns of Leovigild in the 570s that the Visigothic rulers controlled the Spanish periphery, and not until the 620s that they ruled over all of Spain. Although Visigothic rule, like Frankish rule, depended on a convergence of interest between locality and centre, the partnership seems to have been much more fragile than in Francia.[54] Pressure from outside, initial religious difference, the failure to establish dynastic rule, and not least geography, made integration around a central power more difficult. In the localities, as far as we can see (and that is not much) there were *castros* and *oppida* in the hands of local nobles, which meant that the magnates of the *civitas* could not necessarily deliver loyalty at regional level as their equivalents could in Francia. Through into the seventh century we hear of groups of people, such as the Astures, the Roccones, and the Sappones, whose rebellion and defeat seems to be part of their integration into the Spanish kingdom, or who, in other words, had up to this time resisted, or been largely untouched by, the authority of the kings.[55] The *Chronicon* of John of Biclaro, though brief, is clear that rebellion and integration were closely linked. Take, for instance, the account of Leovigild's conquest in 572 of Cordoba, a *civitas* 'for a long time in rebellion against the Goths'. To hold it down Leovigild occupied the *urbes* and *castella* of the region. He also killed a 'multitude of *rustici*'.[56] And in 577 he invaded the neighbouring region of Orospeda, occupied its *civitates* and *castella*, and made it 'his province'. Once the Goths had 'oppressed the rebellious *rustici* they held all of Orespeda'.[57] The resistance of the *rustici* in these cases has been described as 'peasant revolt'[58] (though note that Biclaro's term is *rustici rebelantes)*. It would,

[54] See Natal and Wood in this volume. Also S. Castellanos and I. Martin Viso, 'The Local Articulation of Central Power in the North of the Iberian Peninsula (500–1000)', *Early Medieval Europe*, 13 (2005), 1–41 and C. Wickham, *Framing the Early Middle Ages: Europe and the Mediterranean, 400–800* (Oxford, 2005), pp. 93–102 and pp. 219–32.

[55] For the narrative of integration, see A. Barbero and M. I. Loring, 'The Formation of the Sueve and Visigothic Kingdoms in Spain', in P. Fouracre (ed.), *New Cambridge Medieval History*, I, pp. 162–92.

[56] John of Biclaro, *Chronica Minora II*, ed. T. Mommsen, MGH AA XI (Berlin, 1894), pp. 207–20, at p. 213.

[57] John of Biclaro, *Chronica Minora* II, p. 215.

[58] Barbero and Loring, 'Formation', p. 185.

however, seem likely that the *rustici* incorporated at least some elements of the nobility who might wish to resist the imposition of authority from outside – the leaders of *castros* and *oppida*, perhaps.

The third and final rebellion mentioned by John of Biclaro was that of Hermenegild in 579.[59] In the narrative sequence this appears as the last attempt of the region of Baetica to resist Leovigild's drive to impose royal authority in the South. John of Biclaro typically has little to say about it. Heremenigild, Leovigild's son, was incited by the *factio* of his mother Goswintha to make himself a *tyrannus* – a ruler without legitimate power – in the Seville area. This was to *rebellare* against his father, drawing other *civitates* and *castella* into the rebellion, a disaster for all concerned. This episode was famously covered by Gregory of Tours at about ten times the length of John of Biclaro's account.[60] This was because Gregory was interested in the fate of Hermenegild's wife Ingund, who was a Frankish princess, and because Hermenegild converted to Catholicism, which allowed the rebellion to be presented as Catholic resistance to Arianism. From Gregory's narrative we can see that this was indeed a major rebellion. It took Leovigild four years to suppress it and it drew in the Byzantines and the Sueves, with the Franks hovering in the background. In the next generation three of these elements in the rebellion would disappear: religious difference, the presence of the Sueves, and the capacity of the Byzantines to intervene in the South. What would remain to determine – but also to limit – the scope of future disturbances in Spain were the *factiones* of magnates grouped around people who by family history had a claim to the Visigothic throne. At this point, the situation in Spain comes more to resemble that in Francia.

Gregory of Tours had written that the Goths had a nasty habit of killing their kings if they did not like them, and Fredegar called this 'the sickness of the Goths' (*morbum gothorum).*[61] But such killing and usurpation was not rebellion against Visigothic authority, rather, it came from competition to hold it. As Fredegar goes on to explain, King Chindaswinth, diagnosing the illness, attempted to cure it by massacring the opposition. From the evidence of councils and laws, Chindaswith, Reccaswinth, and Wamba, kings between 641 and 680, attempted to strengthen royal authority by building up palatine offices and reinforcing military and judicial powers at comital level, as well as conferring responsibilities on *servi fiscales*, a kind of royal *ministeriales.*[62] It may be that this strengthening of the centre created the conditions for fresh rebellion. Unlike the

[59] John of Biclaro, *Chronica Minora* II, p. 215.

[60] Gregory of Tours, *Decem libri* V, 38, VI, 42. [61] *Fredegar* IV, 82.

[62] A. Barbero and M. I. Loring, 'The Catholic Visigothic Kingdom', in Fouracre (ed.), *New Cambridge Medieval History*, I, pp. 346–70, at pp. 365–60.

Franks, the Visigoths did not hold annual assemblies at which dissent might have been defused. The famous 'councils of Toledo' were held infrequently, and in this mid seventh-century period, hardly at all, for, as Joaquin Martinez Pizzaro has recently pointed out, they were held when the kings felt they were in need of support, and not when they felt their position was strong.[63] A rebellion against Wamba on his accession in 672 would seem to be a reaction to this lengthy period of dominant kingship. We know of this through the contemporary *Historia Wambae* by Julian of Toledo, a whole work dedicated to a rebellion.[64]

Shortly after Wamba's inauguration as king, Ilderic, duke in Narbonnensis/Septimania, rose in rebellion. Wamba sent one Duke Paul to put this down, but Paul joined the rebels and declared himself 'king of the East'. The *Historia* is an account of Wamba's successful campaign to defeat Paul and bring the Narbonnensis back into line. We can call it a rebellion as Julian of Toledo did, because it most definitely involved a rejection of authority and the creation of a new political entity. Julian used the language of the usurpations of late antiquity, particularly the panegyrics of Claudian, to describe these events, but the idea of provincial separatism is there, and the treachery is cast as perfidy – the rebels had broken solemn oaths and stood condemned in a religious as well as secular sense. Since these events took place at the same time as the conflict between Ebroin and Leudegar in Francia one wonders if there is a connection – there was certainly a Frankish element involved in the rebellion. Perhaps all one can say is that conflict in Francia might have made it seem a propitious time to bid for independence in Narbonnensis, for the province had always been a Gothic outpost vulnerable to Frankish attack. The other notable feature of the *Historia* is the leniency with which the rebels were treated, despite a law which said that traitors should at the very least be blinded. In this case they were pardoned, and even eventually got their lands back. Perhaps this shows the essentially weak position of Wamba at the beginning of his reign. Thereafter he tried to strengthen it by introducing more stringent military obligations.

Kings after Wamba seemed to row back from attempts to strengthen the centre at the expense of the regional elites. Paul's may have been the last Visigothic rebellion. We hear rather vague tales of upsets thereafter in the so-called *Chronicle of 754* or *Mozarabic Chronicle*, and there are coins minted by what may have been a breakaway king at the very end of the

[63] J. Martinez Pizarro, *The Story of Wamba: Julian of Toledo's 'Historia Wambae Regis'* (Washington, DC, 2005), pp. 59–61.

[64] *Historia Wambae*, (tr.) J. Martinez Pizarro, *The Story of Wamba*.

seventh century.[65] The end of Visigothic Spain famously came with more infighting around the crown in 711. The North African invaders of that year headed straight for the royal city of Toledo. That with its fall the Visigothic regime should collapse more or less of its own accord suggests that the weak hold that the centre had had over the regions in the earlier period, and which had allowed rebellions to occur, had never really been remedied. A postscript is the Asturian rebellion against the Berbers, which took place after the battle of Covadonga in 718; a typical Visigothic rebellion of a local elite against the centre, in a region remote enough to get away with it.

Italy suffered even more disturbance than Spain in the sixth century and would thereafter be un-unifiable. Each of the several political entities in the peninsula has its own history of rebellion, of which we can see very little, but one might assume that the proximity of rival powers and Frankish and Byzantine sponsorship provided opportunities and encouragement here. Benevento in the late 780s would provide a useful example of the interplay of local, regional, and international powers.[66] In Byzantine Italy the remoteness of the central power and resources available to military leaders provided opportunities – a case in point would be Mezetius' attempt to seize Sicily in 668. In the Lombard kingdom, however, rebellion may have been relatively rare. In the *Historia Langobardorum* Paul the Deacon used the term for only five incidents.[67] Although three of these involved dukes on the borders of the kingdom, the rebels were not trying to separate themselves from the Lombard kingdom, but were aiming for the throne itself. The most detailed account of a rebellion in the *Historia* is that of Alahis against Cuniperct in the 680s. It reads like a protracted civil war that revolved around control of the palace in Pavia. Unlike the Franks, the Lombards had their palace in a fixed location. Physical control of this space was the prerequisite for holding power. One wonders whether there might have been Byzantine influence here. Rebels, if indeed this is the right term, for Paul the Deacon uses the term more loosely than other authors, tended to head for the centre rather than seek to escape authority on the periphery, which helps explain the long term territorial integrity of the Lombard kingdom. We should also note that it is only in later books of the *Historia* that Paul the Deacon used

[65] *Chronicle of* 754, ed. E. López, *Cronica mozarabe de 754. Edición critica y traduccion* (Zaragoza, 1980); Barbero and Loring, 'Catholic Visigothic Kingdom', p. 368.

[66] As seen in the letters of the *Codex Carolinus*, tr. P. D. King, *Charlemagne: Translated Sources* (Lambrigg, 1987), pp. 269–307, nos. 32, 34, 33, 37, 38, 39, and in the *Royal Frankish Annals*, tr. W. Scholz, *Carolingian Chronicles* (Ann Arbor, MI, 1972), pp. 37–125, sa. 787.

[67] *Historia Langobardorum*, ed. G. Waitz, MGH SRL (Hannover, 1878), IV, 3, V, 18–20, V, 36, 38, VI, 55.

the term *rebellio*. At this stage of the work Paul was attempting to show that Lombard kingship had matured into a fully legitimate Catholic monarchy. To describe what might have been factional fighting as *rebellio* was a way of enhancing the image of Lombard kingship.[68] As we shall see shortly, the early Carolingians would also use the term to this effect, and we know that Paul had contributed to the articulation of Carolingian legitimation whilst writing in Francia.

England is the last area this chapter shall briefly consider. There is no rebellion in Bede's *Historia Ecclesiastica*. There are, of course, plenty of struggles for power, both between kingdoms and within them, but where this conflict was occasioned by the need to profit from warfare, we can say that it was itself a means of ruling, or of establishing authority. Only when one group became dominant on a more permanent basis can we describe rebellion in England, and this would seem to come with the rise of Mercian power in the later seventh century. This we see, for instance, with a rebellion in Kent after the death of Offa of Mercia (796). It is clear that Offa and his family had been helping themselves to minsters formerly in the hands of the Kentish ruling families, and charters show Mercian intervention in Kentish land transactions. The archbishop of Canterbury was also a Mercian.[69] The uprising of 796 and the brief re-establishment of a kingdom of Kent under the rule of Eadbehrt Praen involved the driving out of the Archbishop and, presumably, other Mercians. It was indeed a rebellion, and one that had to be put down with force.

So far we have seen that when authors used the term 'rebellion' they were generally distinguishing a major upheaval in which authority was challenged from the kind of plotting and feuding and fighting through which individuals tried to increase or defend their standing. In Francia in the second half of the eighth century we see a more frequent and subtle use of the term. The context for this was the generation-long struggle of the Carolingians, principally under Charles Martel, to bring all of Francia under their control. The first Continuator of the *Chronicle of Fredegar*, writing shortly after 751, used it no less that ten times when dealing with events between 724 and 751.[70] Terming an opponent a rebel was a way of drawing attention to the legitimate nature of one's own power, that is, that it constituted a legitimate authority that was being challenged. In this sequence, those who resisted Charles Martel and his sons are termed rebels. Interestingly, in some later sources it would be the other way round, with Charles Martel the *tyrannus*, one whose power was not

[68] I am grateful to Christopher Heath for discussion on this point.
[69] N. Brooks, *The Early History of the Church of Canterbury* (Leicester, 1984), pp. 114–27.
[70] Fredegar, *Continuations*, 1, 14, 17, 19, 20, 26, 27, 29, 31, 32.

legitimate, but based purely on force. Modern historians tend to agree with this latter view, seeing the so-called rebels in Burgundy, Alemannia, Bavaria, and Provence as legitimist defenders of the Merovingian order.[71] Curiously, neither the first nor the second Continuator of Fredegar ever referred to the Aquitainians as rebels, even though they resisted Carolingian conquest to the bitter end.

Writers in Francia from the later eighth century onwards developed that strand of thought that concentrated on the morality of power, for this could be worked into a thorough justification for the Carolingians' seizure of the Frankish throne – something that could otherwise itself have been seen as ultimate rebellion. The sense of moral urgency went hand in hand with a narrative of papal sanction to present the Carolingians as having had a duty first to take and then to exercise a power that was aimed at bringing Christian order to all. Logically, this hardening of moral certitude would seem to have set the bar lower for rebellion in that any disobedience was now perfidious and a challenge to a God-given order. In fact, rebellions were just as rare under the Carolingians as under the Merovingians. Only two spring to mind for the period before 800: one an Italian rebellion of 776 that sought to re-establish Lombard rule,[72] and the other a rebellion by Hardraad and other leaders in eastern Germany, who seem to have found the regime too intrusive and wished to get rid of the new dynasty.[73] And of course, the Saxons remained perfidious rebels. It is conventional to say that the Carolingians obviated dissent at home by plundering abroad. It may also be that their control of the written word worked to silence the record of dissent – Hardraad's rebellion, for instance, is not mentioned in the original version of *The Royal Frankish Annals*, a work that can be more or less regarded as the mouthpiece of the regime. But by the same token, one might argue that a regime that had the wherewithal to control the media could well also have had the means to suppress dissent in the field. This is an impression one can get from Charlemagne's capitularies, where, for instance, he ordered counts to keep lists of potential dissidents in their region.[74] At the same time we see the regime banning *coniurationes* and *gildonia*, except for small mutual self-help groups. That is to say, no political or social association that depended on binding oaths could be formed except under the aegis of the regime, and certainly not in opposition to it. Here we may have a hint of resistance or opposition at a social level below that of the elite, for we later meet a *coniuratio* or sworn association that was made up of peasants.

[71] Fouracre, *Age of Charles Martel*, pp. 79–120. [72] *Royal Frankish Annals* sa. 775, 776

[73] *Revised Royal Frankish Annals, Lorsch Annals, St Nazarius Annals*, all sa. 786, tr. King, *Charlemagne*.

[74] *Articles sent by 'missi' to counts*, 3, tr. King, *Charlemagne*.

It is interesting to note that on this famous occasion in 859 when the population of the Channel coast did form an association to resist the Vikings, the elite were quick to stop their own infighting and had no difficulty in massacring the confederation.[75]

It could be objected that this study has given too much weight to Frankish evidence and has therefore arrived at an unrepresentative picture of Western Europe as a whole. This might be the case, but in its defence I would argue that Francia is more knowable because there is simply more evidence from this area. The juxtaposition of different narratives, charters, law codes, formularies, and the plentiful hagiography allows us to get a slightly more three-dimensional view of conflict. We can see more of local conditions to set alongside the usual high-political narrative. Where we can do this elsewhere, say in the setting of the *Lives of the Fathers of Merida*[76] alongside John of Biclaro, the interplay of local rivalry and intervention from the centre looks much like what we see in Francia: the situation of local rivalries in Merida in the later sixth century very much resembles that in Clermont and the Auvergne as described by Gregory of Tours. Both also bear significant similarities to the fields of episcopal contestation described by David Natal and Jamie Wood elsewhere in this volume. It is therefore valid to maintain that the picture we get from Francia, of competition for power within a single political system, rather than rebellion against established authority, or attempts to create separate political entities, is one than can be generalized. Of course, different conditions and histories throw up contrasts, particularly between England and the Continent, and between areas more or less vulnerable to outside pressure. But I would like to end by returning to the base-line observation that the large polities that emerged in the sixth century were remarkably stable – for centuries, no new states were created. This leads to a final question, one the late Timothy Reuter asked in a similar discussion several years ago, namely, 'how did they get away with it?', by which he meant, in large states with relatively weak governing institutions but massive and brutal inequalities of wealth and privilege, and one might add, at a time of apparent labour shortage, why was there no social rebellion? All we have are the possible hints of John of Biclaro's rebellious *rustici*, and in an even wilder flight of romantic imagination, the *centenarii* of the Sornegau as the focus of resistance to unwelcome impositions – prototype Clay Cross councillors, perhaps? One can point to three basic points which might inform an answer. First, we can observe that

[75] *Annals of St Bertin*, sa. 859, ed. and tr. J. Nelson, *Ninth-Century Histories: the Annals of St Bertin* (Manchester, 1991).

[76] *Lives of the Fathers of Merida*, tr. A. Fear, *Lives of the Visigothic Fathers* (Liverpool, 1997), pp. 46–105.

every pulse of cultural development strengthened the social hierarchy.[77] As Marios Costambeys demonstrates, even where the records seem to reveal institutions that were objective and rhetorically impartial, detailed analysis shows those institutions being worked by the elite in a way that reinforced the social hierarchy.[78] Second, competition within that hierarchy made each level biddable in relation to the level above, and resistant to pressure from the level below, and third, later when and where we do see resistance at the bottom, this was invariably protest against very local conditions rather than against any wider authority.[79]

The study of rebellion shows us that the large political entities that dominated early medieval Europe were not about to unravel. The stability of the larger political units along with a social hierarchy that was conservative and an elite that was well integrated were key ingredients in the making of medieval Europe. We can trace them back to the inter-regional networks of ecclesiastical association with which this volume began, and likewise back to common social benchmarks in late antiquity: elites across Europe dressed off from those who ran the late Empire. They, like their forebears, were in a strong enough position to keep hold of what little surplus production there was, and to keep the producers in the state of dependence necessary to achieve this. This was not fertile ground for rebellion. As Bob Moore shows in relation to the so-called Feudal Revolution,[80] when change did come after the fading of the Carolingian hegemony this was more a question of widening the elite than of weakening it.

[77] P. Fouracre, 'Cultural Conformity and Social Conservatism in Early Medieval Europe', *History Workshop Journal*, 33 (1992), 152–60.

[78] See the essay by Marios Costambeys, 'Disputes and Documents in Early Medieval Italy', in this volume.

[79] For example, the disputes over olive production in Limonta in Northern Italy: R. Balzaretti, 'The Monastery of Sant'Ambrogio and Dispute Settlement in Early Medieval Milan', *Early Medieval Europe*, 3 (1994), 1–18, esp, 7–8.

[80] See the essay by R. I. Moore, 'The Weight of Opinion: Religion and the People of Europe from the Tenth to the Twelfth Century', in this volume.

6 Disputes and documents in early medieval Italy

Marios Costambeys

Introduction

When, in 832, the scribe Rodoaldus sat down to write up the dispute between the bishop of Piacenza and the descendants of Hermefrit, he seemed to have a template ready to hand. The bishop claimed that Hermefrit's descendants owed labour service for their land, but did not want to perform it. There being a matter in dispute, Rodoaldus therefore followed the standard model of a dispute charter, a *notitia iudicati*, along adversarial lines: he quoted each party laying out their case in turn, in direct speech. Having done so, however, he abruptly switched models. The parties had reached a 'friendly agreement' (*amica pactuicio*), and he wrote the rest of the charter according to the template for a written agreement, a *cartula convenientia*.[1] The impression, then, is that although the bishop of Piacenza initially pursued his claim through the formal judicial process, his 'opponents' – tenants of the bishopric – quickly proved willing to settle 'out of court'.

Documents like this serve to undermine the intuitive image of an early medieval Europe in which often violent conflict was endemic, even normal.[2] It is an easy characterization, encouraged by sources that tend to foreground strife and discord, and that have influenced a historiography that accommodates conflict more easily than peace: 'simply because [medieval] society was so contentious, order, community and consensus

[1] *Chartae Latinae antiquiores: Facsimile-Edition of the Latin Charters. 2nd Series, Ninth Century*, ed. G. Cavallo and G. Nicolaj, vol. LXVIII (Zurich, 2006) [hereafter *ChLA* with volume and document no.], no. 20 = P. Galetti (ed.), *Le carte private della cattedrale di Piacenza* (Parma, 1978), no. 27; cf. R. Volpini, 'Placiti del "Regnum Italiae" (secc. IX–XI). Primi contributi per un nuovo censimento' in P. Zerbi (ed.), *Contributi dell'Istituto di storia medioevale*, III (Milan, 1975), pp. 245–520 [hereafter Volpini with document no.], *compositio* 1, pp. 447–51, issued 1 October 832. For comment, see A. Castagnetti, *Arimanni in 'Langobardia' e in 'Romania' dall'età carolingia all'età communale* (Verona, 1996), pp. 21–2. For the *convenientia*, A. J. Kosto, 'The *Convenientia* in the Early Middle Ages', *Medieval Studies*, 60 (1998), 1–54, esp. 40–9.

[2] For observations on the stereotype of violent conflict, see W. Brown, *Violence in Medieval Europe* (Harlow, 2011), pp. 1–23.

become the problem, not the explanation'.[3] In Rodoaldus' document, however, where the parties were a bishop and his peasant tenants, the potential for class conflict quickly gives way to social peace; where we might expect to hear discord, we in fact get harmony. The case therefore bears witness to an increasing trend in the documentation of intra-social conflicts (or 'conflicts') in early medieval Italy, towards narratives of acquiescence, if not agreement, rather than dispute. It stands in marked contrast to northern Europe, especially west Francia, where the increasing willingness of scribes to set down elaborate, less formulaic, descriptions of conflicts has directly fed a debate among historians over a perceived rise in conflict and concomitant weakening, or 'privatization', of mechanisms of conflict regulation: the 'feudal anarchy' of classic historiography.[4] Over precisely the same period, from the ninth to the twelfth centuries, Italian court-case documents of the *notitia iudicati* type become more formulaic, frequently adopting limited forms of words which attested not argument, but agreement: instant, unchallenged, and decisive. This chapter examines the history of that development, and draws out some of its implications. In particular, in noting the unhelpfulness of court-case charters, it will consider the evidence for early medieval Italian conflicts in other types of document, and what they can tell us about the way in which conflicts were managed in this period.

Discouraged by the absence of real conflict in *notitiae iudicati*, one could, of course, turn instead to narrative sources, which often relate with relish the clashes of aristocrats, churchmen, and rulers, both within the judicial court and outside it. These give plenty of material for studies of attitudes to conflict and the kinds of processes through which they were managed. Empirically, though, there is always the problem of their

[3] G. Koziol, 'Review Article: the Dangers of Polemic: Is Ritual Still an Interesting Topic of Historical Study?', *Early Medieval Europe*, 11 (2002), 367–88, at 383. Being inherently revealing of the dynamics of the societies that generate it, conflict is naturally especially prominent in our sources; which is not to say that its necessary corollaries, peace and peacemaking, are especially obscure. A bit of effort, and intelligent analysis, can bring out their full significance too: see P. J. E. Kershaw, *Peaceful Kings: Peace, Power and the Early Medieval Political Imagination* (Oxford, 2011).

[4] For a cogent statement of the effect of changes in documentation on historians' perceptions of social change, see D. Barthélemy, *The Serf, the Knight and the Historian* (Ithaca, NY, 2009), pp. 12–36, a lightly revised version of Barthélemy's, *La mutation de l'an mil a-t-elle eu lieu?* (Paris, 1997), pp. 29–56. For summaries of the debate, see P. Fouracre, 'Marmoutier and its Serfs in the Eleventh Century', *Transactions of the Royal Historical Society*, 6th ser., no. 15 (2005), 29–49, and W. Brown and P. Górecki, 'What Conflict Means: the Making of Medieval Conflict Studies in the United States', in W. Brown and P. Górecki (eds.), *Conflict in Medieval Europe: Changing Perspectives on Society and Culture* (Aldershot, 2003), pp. 1–35, at pp. 26–33.

authors' very disparate literary agenda.[5] However plausible the story of a conflict's progress and resolution, it was related for reasons other than to give insight into its progress and resolution.[6]

Seeking evidence of conflicts that reveals genuine social norms and disputing strategies, historians have not unnaturally tended to look to legal documents, which have been thought to offer objective reflections of the societies that produced them. Taken as a single genre, the legal document is a complex category of evidence. All literate societies produce texts that can be seen as contracts, including formulae that encapsulate accepted norms, whether for arranging a marriage, undertaking a piece of work, or transferring some land. It is documents in this latter category, dealing with transfers of property, that constitute the vast majority of those that survive, in many thousands, from early medieval Western Europe. Very largely this is because they related to, where they did not actually prove, the ownership of particular pieces of landed property, and so might retain some utility for successive owners of that property. Some of them are extant in their original form, at first written on a variety of media but increasingly on single sheets of parchment (and known as charters); others are preserved as copies made later (often centuries later), either on single sheets or collected into books (cartularies).[7]

[5] On the problem of narrative sources about violent conflicts, see G. Halsall, 'Violence and Society in the Early Medieval West: an Introductory Survey', in Halsall (ed.), *Violence and Society in the Early Medieval West* (Woodbridge, 1998), pp. 1–45, at pp. 6–7.

[6] A good example of conflict related for another purpose (here, to demonstrate the power of a saint), occurs in the *Miracula sancti Columbani*, ed. H. Bresslau, MGH SS XXX/2 (Hannover, 1934), pp. 993–1015. For a summary, perceptive analysis, and partial French translation, see F. Bougard, 'La relique au procès. Autour des miracles de saint Colomban', in *Le règlement des conflits au Moyen Âge*, Actes du XXXIe congrès de la Société des historiens médiévistes de l'enseignement supérieur public (Paris, 2000), pp. 35–66.

[7] A good English-language introduction to charters across the entire period for which they constitute important evidence – from the late Roman to the early modern eras – remains a desideratum, though see L. E. Boyle, 'Diplomatics', in J. M. Powell (ed.), *Medieval Studies: an Introduction*, 2nd edn. (Syracuse, NY, 1992), pp. 82–113, and P. Delogu, *An Introduction to Medieval History* (London, 2002), pp. 159–82. I use the term 'charter' here to encompass all documents of a legal or contractual kind. Some strands of historiography – especially those influenced by classic French diplomatic scholarship – define 'charter' (French *charte*, Latin *carta*) as a subjective, dispositive document (i.e., purporting to be issued by or on behalf of one person, and itself enacting the legal act it describes), and contrast it with 'notice' (Latin *notitia*), which is defined as an objective document (a third-party narration of an act), with merely probative force: see, for example, G. Declercq, 'Originals and Cartularies: the Organization of Archival Memory (Ninth-Eleventh Centuries)', in K. Heidecker (ed.), *Charters and the Use of the Written Word in Medieval Society* (Turnhout, 2000), pp. 147–70. This strikes me, and has struck others, as too rigid a distinction, of strictly limited utility when applied to actual surviving documents: see, for instance, Barthélemy, *The Serf, the Knight and the Historian*, pp. 14–15, and further this chapter, p. 130.

The insights that individual charters offer into their societies are very limited. But when they survive in collections from discrete places and periods, they can reveal general patterns of activity, property, and social condition in that place and time.[8] Even in these cases, however, there are significant filters between the charters and the realities from which they sprang. The most obvious and widely acknowledged of these is that the vast majority of the documents that survive to us from early medieval Western Europe do so because they were preserved by ecclesiastical institutions. What we can see is not just what was preserved, but what churchmen preserved. It is not a safe assumption that those churchmen's archival strategies were always especially careful or systematic or consistent, nor that every preserved document directly concerned the institution that preserved it: many of our documents do not mention churches or monasteries at all, let alone the institution in which they ended up, but embody the ordinary legal business of laymen and women.[9] In general, however, the majority of the surviving documents comprise those of particular use to the institutions that kept them, especially by providing a record of their property transactions, whether as proof against future claims or as the building blocks of institutional memory (or, most often, both).[10] While these are reasons for, rather than strategies of, archiving, they gave ample incentive for shaping the record, both by selecting what to keep and what to lose (or destroy), and, in a number of demonstrable cases, by creating a new record of a past event – in a word, forging.[11] This brings us to a further filter between the charter and the real event: the charter scribe, his assumptions, his training and, in particular, his models. The requirement that charters be formulaic, so that they could be

[8] Noted as a general point by C. Wickham, 'Problems of Comparing Rural Societies in Early Medieval Western Europe', *Transactions of the Royal Historical Society*, 6th ser., no. 2 (1992), 221–46, at 227.

[9] For full exploration of the use of documents by the early medieval laity, see W. Brown, M. Costambeys, M. Innes, and A. Kosto (eds.), *Documentary Culture and the Laity in the Early Middle Ages* (Cambridge, 2012).

[10] For ecclesiastical institutions' archives and institutional memory, see now A. Sennis, The Power of Time. Looking at the Past in Medieval Monasteries', in A. Müller and K. Stöber (eds.), *Self-Representation of Medieval Religious Communities. The British Isles in context* (Berlin, 2009), pp. 307–325.

[11] On the destruction of documents, see A. Sennis, '"Omnia tollit aetas et cuncta tollit oblivio". Ricordi smarriti e memorie costruite nei monasteri altomedievali', *Bullettino dell 'Instituto Storico Italiano per il Medio Evo*, 106 (2004), 93–135, at 101–14. For a positivist introduction to the identification of forged charters, see C. Brühl, 'Die Entwicklung der diplomatischen Methode im Zusammenhang mit dem Erkennen von Fälschungen', in *Fälschungen im Mittelalter. Internationaler Kongreß der Monumenta Germaniae Historica München, 16.-19. September 1986*, vol. III (Hannover, 1988), pp. 11–27; on the problem of defining forgeries, however, see M. Mostert, 'Forgery and Trust', in P. Schulta et al. (eds.), *Strategies of Writing* (Turnhout, 2008), pp. 35–59.

recognized as valid, not only constrained their scribes' ability to describe the actions and transactions before them; it sometimes meant that the description distorted the action to fit a preconceived legal paradigm. Thus, for instance, historians are increasingly noticing that some of the transactions in Italian charters that take the form of a sale were actually describing loans of money, in which the transferred land was collateral.[12] In some circumstances, then, the writers of charters could cast events differently to suit their own polemical purposes – which raises the familiar problem of how we can understand the reality behind the text. Are charters to be included among those texts from which, as one suggestion has it, we can recapture only 'epiphenomena of textuality', that reveal something of the ideological and textual influences of their scribes, and of the authorities that sponsored the documents, but little of the social realities?[13]

The formulaic nature of charters certainly constitutes another filter between such texts and their contexts. In many parts of early medieval Europe, the use of documents in Latin to communicate and to sanction the rights of the socially empowered followed a continuous tradition from late antiquity, so that most of the formulae that made them up originated in the late Roman legal environment. Their critical study began in the second half of the seventeenth century, partly because claims to property by some age-old institutions, especially ecclesiastical ones, continued even then to be based on medieval documents. The need to show anew that these documents were valid – in the face of the more sceptical attitude of the early modern period – gave rise to the discipline of diplomatics: the identification and analysis of a document's formal characteristics, including textual elements – formulae – that help to indicate a document's period and place of production, and so to sift genuine text from later interpolation or outright forgery. Latterly the task of diplomatics has expanded to cover not only the extraction of factual information from documents but also their analysis in order to gain insights into ideologies, cultural traits, and social attitudes. It has nevertheless tended to retain a long-established basic distinction between what are generally called 'public' *acta* – documents drawn up according to established forms by institutional authorities to bestow rights of one kind or another (for instance, to grant land, or office) – and private

12 F. Bougard, *La justice dans le royaume d'Italie de la fin du VIIIe siècle au début du XIe siècle*, Bibliothèque des Écoles Françaises d'Athènes et de Rome, 291 (Rome, 1995), p. 328; M. Costambeys, 'The Laity, the Clergy, the Scribes and their Archives: the Documentary Record of Eighth- and Ninth-Century Italy', in Brown, Costambeys, Innes, and Kosto (eds.), *Documentary Culture and the Laity*, pp. 231–58; L. Feller, A. Gramain, and F. Weber, *La fortune de Karol. Marché de la terre et liens personnels dans les Abruzzes au haut moyen âge*, Collection de l'École française de Rome, 347 (Rome, 2005), pp. 90–1.

13 G. Spiegel, Review of P. Buc, *The Dangers of Ritual* (Princeton, NJ, 2001), *American Historical Review*, 108/1 (2003), 148–9.

documents, whether more formal (private *acta*), or less so (*brevia, notitiae*), which dealt with a wider range of legal business, including notes about different stages of contracts, transactions, and disputes.[14]

Dispute documents and social change

Searching for documents about disputes, historians have understandably turned first to those generated by law courts, which, since courts are generally thought of as public entities, have tended to be classified as 'public acts'. Thus, the most formal and initially widespread records of court proceedings – subjective, because written in the voice of the judges, and kept as proof of the judgement by the winning party – have traditionally been distinguished as a sub-set of the 'public' class of documents, generally known by the Latin terms of art they have been given by diplomaticists of *placitum* or *notitia iudicati*.[15] This kind of document has provided the grist for sustained consideration of early medieval disputes. With an acknowledged debt to the anthropology of dispute, late twentieth-century historians have seen many of them as attesting practical solutions to conflict, aired in public before the peer group who would ultimately be responsible for their enactment, and aimed at managing, rather than entirely eradicating, social tensions.[16] They have observed some important fundamental features of these documents: their limited reference to written law codes, the prevalent use of writing as a means of both proof and record and the preponderance of landed property as the focus of the dispute records that survive.

It is worth underlining, however, that the law court was not the only forum in which disputes were played out. Plaintiffs could choose to use courts or not, but other forms of settlement were always available.

[14] See this chapter, p. 127, for the distinction between 'charters' and 'notices', which, though it reflects some differences in the formal characteristics of particular classes of document, is nonetheless only of very limited use in understanding what those documents meant to, and how they were used by, those who drew them up. The document written by Radoaldus cited at the beginning shows that in practice scribes could and did creatively blend their models.

[15] Basic introduction in Bougard, *La justice*, pp. 119–33. Strictly speaking, *placitum* referred to the actual judicial assembly, *notitia* (*iudicati*) or *iudicatum* to the document issued at the order of the judges as a record of those proceedings. For a detailed description of the basic formula for a judicial document as it is generally found north of the Alps, see W. Brown, *Unjust Seizure: Conflict, Interest and Authority in an Early Medieval Society* (Ithaca, NY, 2001), pp. 108–12.

[16] The landmark, anthropologically informed, study of early medieval disputes is W. Davies and P. Fouracre (eds.), *The Settlement of Disputes in Early Medieval Europe* (Cambridge, 1986). Twentieth-century anthropology on dispute is most easily accessible in S. Roberts, *Order and Dispute: an Introduction to Legal Anthropology* (Harmondsworth, 1979).

To limit ourselves just to property disputes in Italy, we can note remissions of fines,[17] lease-backs of property,[18] the offer of alternative pieces of property,[19] the discontinuance of a suit,[20] or, in general, the kind of 'friendly agreement' (*amica pactuacio*) that may have lain behind the Piacenza case with which we started.[21] Evaluating the relative merits of judicial and extra-judicial dispute mechanisms has been one of the most important aspects of recent work, especially since the effectiveness of courts has been taken as an indication of the effectiveness of the state, itself a concept of debateable value for the early medieval West. Some have therefore emphasized the preferability of courts' adjudication over extra-judicial compromise – 'what was attractive about the [formal process of the law court] was its ability to produce a decision'.[22] Even in the era of robust Carolingian government, though, the two need not be seen as distinct alternatives.[23] Warren Brown has shown how the Bavarian aristocracy of the Carolingian period adopted disputing strategies that gave different weight to formal and informal mechanisms depending on political circumstance.[24] State structures were only one option for directly managing disputes, and the historian's task becomes one of trying to discern under what conditions disputants chose that structure or

[17] For example, Gregory of Catino, *Regestum Farfense*, ed. I. Giorgi and U. Balzani, *Il Regesto di Farfa*, 5 vols. (Rome, 1879–1914) [hereafter *RF*, cited with vol. and document no.], vol. II, no. 56 (=*I placiti del regnum Italiae*, ed. C. Manaresi, 3 vols. (Rome, 1955–60) [hereafter Manaresi with document no.], no. 28, *a.*764).

[18] For example, *RF* II.25, with *RF* II.31 (a.750–1).

[19] For example, Manaresi, no. 64, with *Codex Diplomaticus Langobardiae*, ed. G. Porro Lambertenghi, Historiae Patriae Monumenta, 13 (Turin, 1873), no. 208 (*a.*859); see C. Wickham, 'Land Disputes and their Social Framework in Lombard and Carolingian Italy', in Davies and Fouracre (eds.), *The Settlement of Disputes*, pp. 105–24, reprinted with additions in C. Wickham, *Land and Power: Studies in Italian and European Social History* (London, 1994), pp. 229–56, cited at 250–1.

[20] Wickham, 'Land Disputes', p. 252; S. Roberts, 'The Study of Dispute: Anthropological Perspectives' in J. Bossy (ed.), *Disputes and Settlements: Law and Human Relations in the West* (Cambridge, 1983), pp. 1–24, at p. 23.

[21] The *amica pactuacio* could in fact be judicial, extra-judicial, or both: it illustrates especially well that disputes often drifted into, through and out of the setting of the court. Examples are given by Wickham, 'Land Disputes', p. 252; for a general definition, see Davies and Fouracre (eds.), *The Settlement of Disputes*, p. 269.

[22] P. Fouracre, 'Conclusion: Procedure and Practice in the Settlement of Disputes', in Davies and Fouracre (eds.), *The Settlement of Disputes*, pp. 214–28, at p. 219. See also S. D. White, '"*Pactum ... legem vincit et amor judicium*": the Settlement of Disputes by Compromise in Eleventh-Century Western France', *American Journal of Legal History*, 22 (1978), 281–308, at 308.

[23] Though this view has been moderated more recently: P. Fouracre, 'Carolingian Justice: the Rhetoric of Improvement and Contexts of Abuse', *La giustizia nel altomedioevo (secoli V-VIII)*, Settimane di studio del CISAM 42 (Spoleto, 1995), pp. 771–803, at p. 797, citing P. J. Geary, 'Extra-Judicial Means of Conflict Resolution' in the same volume, pp. 569–602.

[24] Brown, *Unjust Seizure*, esp. pp. 191–200.

mechanism over another. When we come to the societies of the tenth and eleventh centuries that are sometimes labelled 'stateless', the barrier between adjudication and compromise seems entirely to have dissolved. Patrick Geary has argued that in societies in which public courts were weak or wholly lacking, what we would generally label 'judicial' and 'extra-judicial' mechanisms existed symbiotically, and disputing was all the more explicitly a matter not of resolving conflict, but of managing it.[25]

This balancing of attention between texts that were written up at a court and those produced outside the formal judicial process has become central to a debate over actual social change. For fifty years the paradigmatic account of shifts in social relations in the post-Carolingian centuries (the ninth to the twelfth) was Georges Duby's study of the Mâconnais, based on the documents preserved in the archives of the cathedral of Mâcon and the abbey of Cluny.[26] Duby noticed a distinct change, in the period around 1030, in the form of these documents, from tightly structured texts using time-honoured formulae (which he termed 'charters') to freer compositions with greater narrative content ('notices'), and he paid particular attention to documents emanating from and/or recording judicial proceedings, which he categorized according to the involvement of comital authority. The surviving documentation of dispute in the Mâconnais increasingly through the late tenth and early eleventh centuries becomes that of the numerous but relatively ineffectual castellans' courts, of arbitrations, and of extra-judicial agreements, while the count's court itself seems to shrink in remit and the range of personnel it involved.[27] These trends, Duby thought, faithfully reflect an actual change in the administration of justice, when 'public' powers exercised by the count through his court and through lesser aristocrats in his name, passed definitively to the latter, becoming their 'private' rights.

The notion of abrupt social change around the year 1000 rests on a documentary typology that has been significantly undermined in recent years.[28] To distinguish as 'public' those court documents that record the presence of the count, and as 'private' those with no discernible

[25] P. J. Geary, 'Living with Conflicts in Stateless France: a Typology of Conflict Management Mechanisms, 1050–1200', in Geary, *Living with the Dead in the Middle Ages* (Ithaca, NY, 1994), pp. 125–62 (a revised translation of 'Vivre en conflit dans une France sans état. Typologie des méchanismes de règlement des conflits, 1050–1200', *Annales ESC*, 41 (1986), 1107–33. For a similar point in a slightly different context, see J. G. H. Hudson, 'Court Cases and Legal Arguments in England, c.1066–1166', *Transactions of the Royal Historical Society* 6th ser., no. 10 (2000), 91–115, at 113–14.

[26] G. Duby, *La société aux XIe et XIIe siècles dans la region mâconnaise* (Paris, 1953), here esp. pp. XII–XV.

[27] Duby, *La société*, pp. 161–6, pp. 196–204.

[28] The now-classic critique of the notion of documentary transformation is D. Barthélemy, 'Une crise de l'écrit? Observations sur des actes de St-Aubin d'Angers (XIe siècle)',

comital involvement, has proved difficult in the numbers of cases even among the Mâconnais documents where, for instance, the court presidents were men regularly associated with the count or ecclesiastical dignitaries who presided sometimes alongside the count, and sometimes on their own.[29] Equally, the distinction between 'dispositive' and 'probatory' documents – between documents that effected and documents that recorded – does not allow for the possibility that we find realized in many documents of a degree of hybridization between these two functions: these are intrinsically complementary principles; and the notion of 'dispositive' in any case masks differing degrees of legal effectiveness.[30] The balance of document types in our record does change in the late tenth and eleventh centuries, and may even include types that were genuine innovations, but older types did not disappear, even among survivals, and the changes are in part attributable to the increased number of those survivals, itself a product of monasteries' improved archiving.[31] These texts seem therefore to bear witness not to social transformation, but to the effects of 'monastic reform'.[32]

Law court notices and 'undefended cases' in early medieval Italy

In current historiography, these observations are overwhelmingly based on material from, and therefore valid for, west Francia or France. How far they are useful for Italy depends especially on taking account of the very different nature there of the same genre of evidence, the surviving charters. These texts present historians of Italy with a problem that in one sense is the reverse of that at the heart of the 'transformationist' debate in France. For where the latter arose from the increasing emphasis on more verbose, less formulaic notices that become more prevalent in the record around 1000, in Italy an increasing number of the formal *notitiae* issued by courts were couched in legal and bureaucratic formulae that differ remarkably little from one document to another. As with all instances of

Bibliothèque de l'École des Chartes, 155/1 (1997), 95–117, elaborated in his *The Serf, the Knight and the Historian*. For a comparative survey of the evidence from the various documentary cultures of the early medieval West, see now F. Bougard, 'Écrire le procès. Le compte rendu judiciaire entre VIIIe et XIe siècle', *Médiévales*, 56 (2009), 23–40.

[29] F. L. Cheyette, 'Georges Duby's *Mâconnais* after Fifty Years: Reading it then and Now', *Journal of Medieval History*, 28 (2002), 291–317.

[30] Barthélemy, *The Serf, the Knight and the Historian*, p. 15.

[31] Barthélemy, *The Serf, the Knight and the Historian*, pp. 12–34

[32] O. Guyotjeannin, '*Penuria scriptorum*. Le mythe de l'anarchie documentaire dans la France du Nord (Xe-première moitié du XIe siècle)', *Bibliothèque de l'École des Chartes*, 155 (1997), 11–44.

standardization, therefore, the particular details of individual cases become harder to see. Yet historians searching for disputes and their underlying social tensions have tended to concentrate on these documents to the neglect of other types of source that might shed light on the whole process of a dispute. This is perhaps explicable simply by the exceptional number of such documents that Italy preserves: far more for the earlier centuries (from the eighth century to *c.*1000) than does Francia.[33] Another contrast with Francia is that a majority of those who physically wrote the Italian documents were laymen, whose understanding of the Christian notion of justice was filtered through a bureaucratic training in civic institutions, in contrast to the monastic backgrounds of Frankish (and, later, French) charter scribes, which may have encouraged in them a more literary style, and certainly exposed them to a highly moralized view of justice.[34]

The moral aspect of justice found its way into Italian court case *notitiae* through the development in the ninth century of formulae that effectively emphasized social peace. Although she almost certainly did not have them in mind when she formulated the idea, ninth-century Italian *notitiae* increasingly bear witness to what Laura Nader called an 'ideology of harmony'; an ideology that in this case developed in the West under Christian influence, and reinforced social control by the powerful.[35] The necessary conservatism of diplomatic formulae means that identifiable signs of change are inevitably small and gradual. Nonetheless, the first *notitia* to move away from a strictly adversarial format dates from 814, a document issued by a judicial tribunal headed by the king's envoy (*missus*) meeting in Spoleto, which is preserved in Farfa's eleventh-century cartulary.[36] Specifically, it is the first case in which the defending party denies, in its reported speech, that it wishes to dispute the material fact asserted by the opposing party. While taken on its own it seems

[33] For an imbalance in the evidence for disputes and their resolution, see M. Marrocchi, 'Scritture documentarie e librarie per la storia di S. Salvatore al Monte Amiata (secc. XI–XIII)', *Quellen und Forschungen aus Italienischen Archiven und Bibliotheken*, 88 (2008), 34–60. For the numbers of documents surviving from Italy in comparative terms, see Costambeys, 'The Laity, the Clergy, the Scribes and their Archives'.

[34] On the education of Italian charter scribes and the formation of documentary culture, see G. Nicolaj, 'Formulari e nuovo formalismo nei processi del *Regnum Italiae*', in *La giustizia nell'alto medioevo (secoli IX-XI)*, Settimane di studio del CISAM XLIV (Spoleto, 1997), pp. 347–79; on French monastic scribes, Barthélemy, *The Serf, the Knight and the Historian*, p. 17; on a moral rhetoric of justice, P. Fouracre, 'Carolingian Justice'.

[35] L. Nader, *Harmony Ideology: Justice and Control in a Zapotec Mountain Village* (Stanford, CA, 1990), p. 291; see also E. Colson, 'The Contentiousness of Disputes', in P. Caplan (ed.), *Understanding Disputes: the Politics of Argument* (Oxford, 1995), pp. 65–82.

[36] Manaresi, no. 28 (= *RF* II.207). For further comment on this case, see M. Costambeys, 'Disputes and Courts in Lombard and Carolingian Central Italy', *Early Medieval Europe*, 15 (2007), 265–89, at 286–7.

simply to attest one party's rather inept and self-contradictory attempt to plead their case, the recurrence of a similar form of words in subsequent *notitiae* suggests that in fact it marks the beginning of a change in the scribal template, perhaps unconnected with what was really being said in court. Developing a new form of words that strikingly distinguishes them from their north European and Catalan counterparts, scribes in central and northern Italy started to employ a rhetoric of harmony, stressing that the submitting party should 'be at peace' (*quiescere*),[37] or, in another formula, 'quiet and content' (*tacitus et contentus*),[38] and to include willing admissions of the apparent opponents' case: 'truly, we do not dispute with that party'.[39] By the last quarter of the ninth century, whole templates had emerged that categorically obscured any real arguments that may have taken place in court, and replaced them with anodyne agreements and concessions.

The earliest such form to appear among the surviving documents is known as *finis intentionis* (*finis intentionis terrae* or *finis intentionis status*), which first appeared in the 870s.[40] Here, the plaintiff made a statement of his rights in a thing (that is, rights – such as ownership – associated with a legally recognized entity – such as a piece of property), declared himself ready to confront an opponent, and requested a formal recognition of his rights from a 'defendant'. Generally, this latter party would then simply state that he had, or could make no claim to, rights in the thing. A related form was the *ostensio cartae*, first appearing in 880/1, in which a plaintiff presented a charter expressing his rights in a thing, other parties were asked if they wished to contradict it, and they declined to do so.[41] The main difference from the *finis intentionis* was that the text of the charter was copied out in extenso in the *notitia*.[42] The third procedure, appearing first in 874 (but not again then until 896), was the *investitura salva querela*,

[37] Manaresi, no. 74; further examples are 75, 79, 80, and so on.

[38] *Codex diplomaticus Amiatinus. Urkundenbuch der Abtei S. Salvatore am Montamiata. Von den Anfängen bis zum Regierungsantritt Papst Innozenz III. (736–1198)*, 4 vols. (Tübingen, 1974–2004) [hereafter *CDA*], no. 164 (= Manaresi, no. 95).

[39] *CDA* 180 (= Manaresi, no. 115).

[40] Manaresi, nos. 74, 75, 79, 80, 82, 83, 84, 85, 86 (all from Casauria).

[41] Manaresi, no. 91 (from Piacenza = *ChLA* LXX.6, where its authenticity is convincingly established); further examples until 900 are nos. 99, 105, 106, 107.

[42] Bougard, *La justice*, pp. 312–14, argues that this procedure was developed as a necessary response to the practice in which properties were initially occupied illegally and then successively alienated, or their usufruct granted and re-granted, until the original owner's rights were lost sight of. The *finis intentionis* offered the opportunity to 'wipe the proprietorial slate clean', as it were: either the original owner could revindicate his rights, or he would lose them, and a new owner would be invested. This need not mean that a dispute, as such, lay behind this kind of document; its more certain purpose was to give authoritative approval to already-existing possession – in other words either to turn possession into, or to reaffirm it as, ownership.

in which the plaintiff stated his rights in a property, no defendant appeared, and the court formally invested the plaintiff with possession, while leaving open the possibility that a defendant could press a claim to the property in the future, within a certain period.[43] All three forms can be termed 'undefended cases'. Their spread among our surviving documents is strikingly rapid: by 900 – within just over twenty years – they account for two out of every three surviving *notitiae*, and for four out of five by the later tenth century. By the later eleventh century, the 'traditional' form of the *notitia*, relating a true dispute (*altercatio*) between two parties, has virtually disappeared from the record.[44]

The speed with which these new forms were taken up by law courts' scribes in the kingdom of Italy prompts questions about their origins. It suggests a controlling hand, and that hand has generally been located at the royal court in Pavia, where was based the cadre of professional judges that had evolved by the 870s from the royal *notarii* of the early ninth century.[45] It is straightforward to see these men as the principal agents of change; but the reasons for change are less clear and have provoked a good deal of debate, not least because they concern how we interpret the formulae themselves.[46] The issue is in fact a reflection of the debate about the social reality behind shifts in documentation in late tenth-century France, though paradoxically, because where the French notices become less standardized, ninth-century Italian ones become more so. In both cases the dilemma is to know how far scribes' initiatives were driven by procedural considerations, and how far they were responding to shifts in political and social realities. Did they develop new forms because disputes were occurring differently, or because they wanted to write documents differently? The degree of standardization of these forms and their rapid spread seem to indicate central control from Pavia, which by the last quarter of the ninth century was the base of operations for the royal notary-judges who had become the key officials in the judicial system. Since the 'undefended case' formats follow those of earlier *notitiae* up to the end of the plaintiff's statement, at which point their narratives jump immediately to the concession (*professio*) by the other party, some historians have seen them as arising from a simple desire on the part of these

[43] First in Manaresi, no. 77, then 101, 102. Bougard, *La justice*, pp. 314–19, argues that this was simply the logical progression from a series of previous norms and procedures aimed at combatting contumacy.

[44] Bougard, *La justice*, p. 308. [45] Bougard, *La justice*, pp. 193–4.

[46] For the roots of the controversy, compare J. Ficker, *Forschungen zur Reichs– und Rechtsgeschichte Italiens*, I (Innsbruck, 1868; repr. Aalen, 1961), vol. I, pp. 40–1, and G. Mengozzi, *Ricerche sull'attività della scuola di Pavia nell'alto Medio Evo* (Pavia, 1924), pp. 43–158, with C. Manaresi, 'Della non esistenza di processi apparenti nel territorio del Regno', *Rivista di storia del diritto italiano*, 23 (1950), 179–217; 24 (1951), 7–45.

notaries to omit details of the hearing that were ultimately irrelevant, and to record only the court's decision. They may have been prompted, it is suggested, by the growing dominance of charters as modes of proof: even in the more traditional *notitia* format, the display of a valid charter before the court was increasingly likely to end the case.[47] Certainly, the 'undefended' formats show signs of having developed from the forms of words used to deal with particular types of procedural problem, such as contumacy.[48] What we cannot tell is whether this was a development only in formulae, or whether the actual procedures followed in court developed along with them. The language of the 'undefended case' charters constitute a logical conclusion to the development in earlier *notitiae* of a rhetorical attitude that the court could and did achieve finality. Already in the Lombard era, the concluding statement of the body of the text (*conclusio*) tended to follow the simple formula 'Et finita est causa' – the case is closed, the dispute concluded.[49] In the Carolingian

[47] Declercq, 'Originals and Cartularies', pp. 168–9, sees original charters as continuing to be the dominant mode of proof in Italian courts throughout the period, and links this with the relatively late appearance in Italy of the cartulary: courts, that is, required original documents as proofs of title. There is a danger of circularity in this argument, however. Since the *ostensio cartae* and *investitura salva querela* forms required that a charter be presented, it is their dominance among the surviving *notitiae* that creates the impression of the charter's dominance among modes of proof. Archives of charters, moreover, were as susceptible as cartularies to deliberate shaping through selection and omission. In other words, we have to take account of the factors that created our.

[48] This is essentially the argument of Bougard, as observed in Notes 42 and 43.

[49] Variations are minimal. The whole formula can be summed up thus: 'Et finita/um est (inter eos) (causa/causatio/intentio).' The first instance is in *Codice Diplomatico Longobardo* [hereafter *CDL*], vol. IV/1, ed. C. Brühl (Rome, 1981), no. 12, issued in Rieti in 750. It does not appear before the Carolingian conquest in either Tuscan or north Italian charters, but is in use fairly consistently thereafter: see Bougard, *La justice*, p. 126 with n. 57 and p. 129 with n. 81. By the later ninth century in the duchy of Spoleto the formula had changed, though the meaning remained much the same: for example, 'quod ita et factum est' (*RF* II.286, = Manaresi, no. 50, of 845); see also, for example, 'ita factum est, et est causa finita' (Manaresi, no. 75, a Casauria charter of 873: also Manaresi, nos. 76 and 85). Occasionally, after this would be added an admonition (*admonitio*) stressing the settlement's permanence, which at its simplest took the form 'Unde qualiter acta vel deliberata est causa, hanc notitiam (iudicati) N. scribere admonuimus'. Its use begins early in our run of evidence, as do additions to it: for example, *CDL*, vol. I, ed. L. Schiaparelli (Rome, 1929), no. 17: 'ne in posteris exinde … aliqua revolvatur causatio'; see further Bougard, *La justice*, p. 129 with n. 82. Tuscan scribes used different additional expressions, for example, 'ut nulla … de hac causa oriatur intentio', though this is last attested in 807 (Manaresi, no. 20: see Bougard, *La justice*, p. 126 with n. 58 and p. 127 with nn. 66 and 67). Spoletan examples begin with *CDL* IV/1.15 of 761: 'ut a modo non repromoveatur, sed a modo et semper in eadem deliberatione ambae partes debeant permanere'. Compare *CDL* IV/1.35 (= *RF* II.135, Manaresi, no. 5) of 781: 'et pars … de hac causa sibi esset contenta'; and *Die Urkunden Pippins, Karlmanns und Karls des Großen*, ed. E. Mühlbacher, MGH Diplomata Karolinorum,

period, many *notitiae* directly express the royal aspiration 'to make and deliver justice to each man'.[50] The intensification of this language from the 820s onwards suggests that notaries were starting to recognize a shift in the ideology underpinning their task. As the stated aim of courts became increasingly to 'iustitia facere' – to bring about the decisive stability, and therefore harmony, that Carolingian capitularies regularly extolled – their *notitiae* moved away from the task of describing how to manage disputes in a practical way.[51] It encouraged them rather to prefer a form for their *notitiae* which formalized the adversarial process, and focused on a case's 'winner'.[52]

This interpretation can be taken further by looking a little more closely at examples of the *ostensio cartae*, in which the provisions of pre-existing documents received confirmation before the court. Where we can date these pre-existing documents, they are mostly very recent: they were being brought before a court very soon after their redaction. Since there was in these cases no time for a real dispute to arise, the court, or at least the *notitia* of *ostensio cartae* that it produced, seems to be functioning not as a forum for resolving a dispute, but rather as a final corroborative stage in the validation of a transaction.[53] This in turn indicates that the language of 'dispute' in these documents is fictive. While there have been plausible arguments that some of these 'undefended case' *notitiae* were based on real disputes, historians have tended latterly to prefer to see

I (Hanover, 1906), no. 146 of 782, a diploma of Charlemagne evidently written by the beneficiary, the abbey of Farfa: 'sit inter ipsos causatores omni tempore subita vel finita causatio' (see Bougard, *La justice*, p. 120, n. 10).

[50] The first, relatively isolated, incidence of this clause ('ad singulorum hominum iustitiam faciendum ac deliberandum') is in a Pistoiese *notitia* of 806: Manaresi, no. 19. But the life of this formula really begins with a Spoletan document of 845: *RF* II.286 (= Manaresi, no. 50: 'pro singulorum hominum iustitia facienda'). For Tuscan examples, see Manaresi, nos. 61, 62, 69, 70, 102, 127; for northern Italy, Bougard, *La justice*, p. 129, n. 77 (Manaresi, nos. 59, 66, 67, 77, 88, 99, 100, 101, 107, 110). This development indicates that the Italian formula gradually became more similar to, although never identical with, its counterpart north of the Alps: one example among many is T. Bitterauf, *Die Traditionen des Hochstiftes Freising* (Munich, 1905), no. 186, p. 179: ' … ad examinandas causas et cum lege atque iustitia terminandas.' For general comment, see Fouracre, 'Carolingian Justice', esp. pp. 784–6 (for the Freising charters) and 800–2; also E. Magnou-Nortier, 'Note sur l'expression "iustitiam facere" dans les capitulaires carolingiens', in C. Lepelley et al. (eds.), *Haut moyen age: culture, éducation et société. Études offerts à Pierre Riché* (Paris, 1990), pp. 249–64, and R. McKitterick, 'Perceptions of Justice in Western Europe in the Ninth and Tenth Centuries', in *La giustizia nell'alto medioevo (secoli IX-XI)*, Settimane di studio del CISAM 44 (Spoleto, 1997), pp. 1075–102.

[51] Bougard, *La justice*, pp. 122–3. [52] Wickham, 'Land Disputes', p. 246.

[53] Corroboration of the relatively recent date of most of the charters reaffirmed in *ostensio cartae* documents is provided by S. H. Brunsch, 'The Authority of Documents in Early Medieval Italian Pleas', in B. Bolton and C. Meek (eds.), *Aspects of Power and Authority in the Middle Ages* (Turnhout, 2007), pp. 277–88.

these documents as the products of notaries exploring new possibilities for their traditional documentary forms.[54] There is a recognition that looking for 'real' disputes here runs the risk of missing the true point of this evidence. Attesting the fact of a dispute's existence is not really enough – there are always disputes. To gain any significance from that fact we need to know how the dispute progressed and what was its substance. But in the absence of any other evidence the dispute's process is entirely lost to history if its only product is a document that does not spell that process out.[55]

The question, then, is how to treat texts that are too rigidly formulaic to be read as literal narratives of real events. We might begin with the notion that the court was a 'public' institution. Although some previous historiography has seen recourse to a court as an index of the strength of the state, it would be wrong prima facie to think of early medieval law courts as 'public' in the sense of being invariably intertwined with a state apparatus, any more than they were necessarily detached from particularist interests, or automatically objective towards matters in dispute. Nor is it helpful to think of the documents emanating from law courts as possessing a peculiarly 'public' character. Pleas that give the names of the presiding tribunal at a court, and notices that give the names of witnesses to matters in dispute, could each be used creatively in the actual process of disputing, in ways that eroded boundaries between private interest and any distinct 'public sphere'. In a sense, it is the latter that dispute *notitiae* help us to define, though there is a danger of circularity: the *notitiae* are public because drawn up in the presence of those there named; but 'the public' are those named in *notitiae*. Nonetheless, it is certainly crucial to the intended meaning of *notitiae* – including, perhaps especially, those of 'undefended case' formats – that they were written before an audience.

There is an obvious sense in which dispute *notitiae* resemble scripts. They generally include forms of words that are supposed to have been spoken by the parties at court, the actors in the drama: formulae that training and tradition had conveyed to scribes, judges, disputants, and bystanders.[56] To view *notitiae* as scripts also implies that the actions that

[54] C. Wickham, 'Justice in the Kingdom of Italy in the Eleventh Century', in *La giustizia nell'alto medioevo (secoli IX-XI)*, Settimane di studio del CISAM XLIV (Spoleto, 1997), pp. 179–255; Bougard, *La justice*, pp. 307–39. For an earlier view, with references to the arguments for these documents' validity as evidence for real disputes, see Wickham, 'Land Disputes', p. 246 with n. 33.

[55] I here mostly follow Bougard, *La justice*, pp. 323–9, and in part Nicolaj, 'Formulari e nuovo formalismo', pp. 357–8, though without sharing all of the assumptions there about the relationship between surviving notices and legal reality.

[56] My approach here parallels to some extent that taken to law court records in the next phase of Italian history by F.-J. Arlinghaus, 'From "Improvised Theater" to Scripted

they describe can be seen as rituals.[57] Many of them conform to the definition of ritualized behaviour as repeated, standardized, and performative.[58] This goes not only for deliberately ceremonial gestures, such as oath-swearing or the use of symbolic objects like the *festuca* or, in ninth-century Italy, the *fustis*.[59] It is also true of more material actions like the seizure of land, the offering of pledges and the brandishing – and reading – of charters. Even the procedural activities of the parties in trooping off to court and offering claims and counter-claims were, on this definition, essentially ritualistic in that they were standardized performances. The law court was a theatre in which parties could air issues and grievances before their peers, and before those who were perhaps greater than them in social status and/or coercive power. It allowed legal norms to be rehearsed and, where they conflicted, reconciled. And although there were other, extra-judicial, stages on which to play out disputes, what distinguished the law court was the opportunity it offered to publicize issues before a particular audience, and in a context of ideological authority. Although texts as stylized as the Italian *notitiae* had become by the late ninth century are untrustworthy guides to real events, bearing out fully Philippe Buc's complaint that literary narrativization of medieval rituals makes real actions inaccessible,[60] they nonetheless constitute the best evidence for the court's key function of publicizing business that would otherwise remain private: best, because they were themselves its written witness – literal 'publications'. Transactions that would otherwise have been known only to the parties themselves, confined to documents that only they would see, became known to the tribunal and the often numerous

Roles: Literacy and Changes in Communication in North Italian Law Courts (Twelfth-Thirteenth Centuries)', in K. Heidecker (ed.), *Charters and the Use of the Written Word in Medieval Society* (Turnhout, 2000), pp. 215–37.

57 P. Fouracre, '*Placita* and the Settlement of Disputes in Later Merovingian Francia', in Davies and Fouracre (eds.), *The Settlement of Disputes*, pp. 23–43, at p. 34; J. L. Nelson, 'Dispute Settlement in Carolingian West Francia', in the same volume, pp. 45–64, at pp. 58–9. Despite this, Geary has called for more research into 'the rituals by which conflicts were directed and transformed': 'Living with Conflicts', p. 129.

58 See C. Bell, *Ritual Theory, Ritual Practice* (Oxford, 1992), p. 74; and compare E. Muir, *Ritual in Early Modern Europe*, 2nd edn. (Cambridge, 2005), pp. 9–10.

59 Examples of ceremonial transfer of disputed property 'per fustem': Manaresi, nos. 45, 47, 64, 66, 68, 71, 77, 101, 102, 110, 111, 132, 135, 140, ranging in date from 823x840 to 941. For transalpine comparators, see M. Innes, *State and Society in the Early Middle Ages: the Middle Rhine Valley, 400–1000* (Cambridge, 2000), pp. 137–8.

60 P. Buc, *The Dangers of Ritual: Between Early Medieval Texts and Social Scientific Theory* (Princeton, NJ, 2001), esp. pp. 67–79 on different texts' views of the deposition of Archbishops Gunthar of Cologne and Theutgaud of Trier at the Roman synod of 863. For trenchant criticism, Koziol, 'The Dangers of Polemic'.

crowd that attended the law court.[61] The script may have been fiction, but the audience was real.

In 'undefended case' *notitiae*, those named among the tribunal and bystanders performed a crucial role in confirming the rights embodied in the documents presented to them. It was a role for which, by the ninth century, there was a pressing need. As I have suggested elsewhere, the traditional form of seeking public validation for property transactions through registering them in civic archives had probably ceased to exist; at the very least, it had become far less reliable than formerly.[62] The later Roman Empire had developed a widely used mechanism by which written acts that had not been issued by a public authority could still attain a fair degree of legal security by being registered in municipal offices established to keep track of property ownership for the purpose of taxation, the *gesta municipalia*. Although these offices disappeared – gradually, erratically, but eventually – all over Western Europe after the end of Roman government, the essential quality that registration in the *gesta* had bestowed on a document – its publicization, lending it greater formality – continued to be valued, and scribes even in the Carolingian period included in documents formulae for registration in the *gesta municipalia* long after there is any evidence for such an office in the relevant area.[63] This creative way of overcoming an absence of legal security therefore seems to indicate a durable desire to lend weight to documents. Given this continued need, coupled with the profound institutional changes of the Carolingian period, it is plausible to think that the procedures of law courts, and especially the documents they produced, could have come to perform this function.[64] While the 'state' and the 'public' were by no means synonymous, they did overlap in the law court, and there could lend force to legal acts.

Non-judicial documents about disputes: the Sarnaglia donation, 762

If the 'undefended case' form that came to predominate among those documents that were ostensibly about disputes was essentially a creation of the notaries' bureaucratic mindset, it offers only very limited access to

[61] For a similar conclusion, see Bougard, *La justice*, pp. 319–29.

[62] Costambeys, 'The Laity, the Clergy, the Scribes and their Archives'.

[63] W. Brown, '*Gesta municipalia* and the Public Validation of Documents in Frankish Europe', in Brown, Costambeys, Innes, and Kosto (eds.), *Documentary Culture and the Laity, pp. 95–124.*

[64] An argument along similar lines is put forward by F. Bougard, '"Falsum falsorum judicum consilium". L'écrit et la justice en Italie centro-septentrionale au XIe siècle', *Bibliothèque de l'école des chartes*, 155/1 (1997), 299–314.

real disputing processes. For these, we need to turn to documents that relate to a dispute, but were not the end-product of a formal court hearing. A donation charter issued in Lombard northern Italy in 762 records within it the dispute that gave rise to the donation.[65] It relates that a man named Audiris gave property to the church of S. Maria in Sarnaglia, the priest of which was Odo; that Audiris' brother Gildiris 'entered' that property 'contra racionem'; that as a consequence many hearings followed, culminating in one before the duke of Ceneda (modern Vittorio Veneto), Ursus. Ursus' court ruled that Gildiris should pay composition for his action 'qualiter in aedicti pagina nuscitur esse' ('as is known to be in the pages of the Edict': i.e. written Lombard law). But Gildiris did not have the wherewithal to pay the composition, so had to hand over all his property to Odo, and confirmed this with a charter. It is not clear whether this included the land that Gildiris' brother had given to the church. With the current charter, Odo transferred all the confiscated property back to Gildiris' son, Troctovus. The charter included a stipulation that if Gildiris owed a payment from the property to a certain Ado or any other man, the charter about this was to be invalid. Finally, there is a fairly standard sanction clause, requiring a payment of double the property's value if Gildiris or Troctovus (or any other) tried to revive the dispute, and a statement of the return gift or *launegild* that Troctovus had given to Odo: a shirt.[66]

This charter is particularly valuable because it relates the whole process of the dispute, rather than just the odd snapshots that most *notitiae* provide. There are a number of different actions, events, and outcomes. Seeing the process as a whole enables us to read it along the lines established by current historiography. It is very clear, for instance, that written documents were essential to the processing of the dispute, with new documents being produced at each stage. In addition to the surviving, final, donation charter, there was certainly a donation charter enacting Audiris' initial gift to the church and one embodying Gildiris' transfer of his property to Odo. There are likely also to have been *notitiae* setting

[65] *CDL* vol. II, ed. L. Schiaparelli (Rome, 1933), no. 168. The charter scribe, Rimfrid *clericus et scriptor*, spells Audiris once as 'Audrisis'. For a similar case, see Costambeys, 'Disputes and Courts', discussing *CDL* IV/1 12 and *CDL* vol. V, ed. H. Zielinski (Rome, 1986), no. 16.

[66] On *launegild*, see C. Wickham, 'Compulsory Gift Exchange in Lombard Italy 650–1150', in W. Davies and P. Fouracre (eds.), *The Languages of Gift in the Early Middle Ages* (Cambridge, 2010), pp. 193–216. Setting the Sarnaglia case alongside Wickham's observation, at p. 197, that 'almost none of the many thousands of documents recording gifts of land to the church in the next several centuries [after 726] contain *launegild*' shows the fuzzy boundary between what was and was not *pro anima* in transactions with the church: clearly, the transfer of Gildiris' property to Odo as composition, and the latter's re-grant of it back to Gildiris' family, did not fall into that category.

down the proceedings at each of the hearings following Gildiris' violation of the gift; brief records of the pledges that were made around each hearing for the attendance of disputants and witnesses and the enactment of the court's judgement – examples survive from other parts of Italy;[67] and a document setting out Gildiris' debt to Ado. The narrative also allows us to follow the recommendation to evaluate the role of the court in relation to other procedures. In this case, that role was fairly limited: the earlier hearings (presumably at the court of the local *sculdahis*) had been entirely ineffectual, and the judgement of the ducal court was overridden by Odo's 'act of mercy' in handing back all the confiscated property to the defeated defendant's son. We would have been ignorant of this if all we had were the court-produced *notitia*, as in so many other cases. The extensive use of writing in both judicial and extra-judicial, formal and informal, procedures suggests in fact that no real distinction between the two existed in contemporary mentality, and that this document therefore bears out Patrick Geary's point that disputes were managed through a symbiotic process, as well as depicting parties adopting the kinds of strategies that Warren Brown has revealed in Bavaria.[68] While *notitiae iudicati* privilege the role of the court in managing disputes, documents of other types reveal that early medieval disputants had a pragmatic sense of the possibilities available to them, according no preference or superiority to institutions that we would associate with the state.

It is possible to see this mid-eighth century case as a stepping-stone towards the 'undefended' cases that emerge in *notitiae* a century later. Since neither party ultimately lost anything in relation to their original position, and Gildiris and Troctovus may have gained the land of Audiris, and certainly gained by having a troublesome debt annulled, there is a suspicion of fictitiousness about the roles of Gildiris as malefactor and Odo as wronged plaintiff. This document could therefore have been concocted in order to affirm property rights while relieving Gildiris and Troctovus of their obligation to Ado. An alternative reading, just mentioned, is that Odo's return of the confiscated property conforms to an 'act of mercy' script, one that we find written into a number of charters of the period from both north and south of the Alps: Odo declares himself to have been 'incited by the inspiration of almighty God'.[69] If, at the risk of defying my own warning not to read too much into one document, we

[67] For example, *ChLA* LXIX.33, of 875, in which one Lucebert pledged to testify to Gontardus' possession of property, in the latter's court case with the bishop of Piacenza.

[68] See this chapter, Notes 24 and 25.

[69] *CDL* vol. II, no. 168: 'Dei omnipotentis inspiracionem conpulsi'. On the 'act of mercy' script, see Brown, *Unjust seizure*, pp. 130–5.

engage in some plausible speculation, we might suggest that Odo's mercy was appropriate: that is, that Gildiris tried to take his brother's land because he was indeed dirt poor, lacking enough property of his own even to pay the court's compensation.

There is of course a danger of circularity in suggesting this interpretation, because this is only one document, which does not specify the nature of the social relationship between the parties. To see Odo as the powerful/higher class actor, and Gildiris and Troctovus as the poorer/lower class ones, is, after all, to impose on the situation the assumptions of a modern 'bourgeois subject' (me). But we can avoid it in practice because our assumptions depend ultimately on the many thousands of pieces of evidence from this society that allow us to calibrate the social level or role of, say, the priest. In that context, we are fortunate that what we have in this case is the charter at the end of the process, which reveals that a *pro anima* gift had provoked a number of different property transactions: an appropriation, a confiscation, a restitution, a return gift, and the cancellation of a debt (and that is not counting whatever heavenly return gift Audiris might have enjoyed). It is significant, moreover, that the ultimate solution to the dispute was a gift, because despite their limitations the surviving dispute *notitiae* and other charters reveal that a range of alternative transactions was available: a lease-back, for instance, or a time-limited restitution of usufruct. Taking the charters of Lombard and Carolingian Italy as a whole, documents enshrining the latter – essentially lease arrangements of some kind – increase as donations decrease through the ninth century.[70] The land at the apparent heart of the dispute in this eighth-century case was not especially central to this document – it is nowhere specified, and no place names are given – and since anthropology teaches us that gifts are not just about objects (even if the object is a piece of land), but that property connotes status too, we can see Odo's act of mercy here as intended to enhance his own status as well as to preserve (albeit at a low level) that of Gildiris and Troctovus.[71] On one reading, the latter's meagre patrimony constituted what Annette Weiner categorized as an 'inalienable possession': a property imbued with the identity of one owner even while another might be enjoying its fruits.[72] We might,

[70] W. Kurze, 'Lo storico e i fondi diplomatici medievali. Problemi di metodo – Analisi storiche', in W. Kurze, *Monasteri e nobiltà nel senese e nella Toscana medievale. Studi diplomatici, archeologici, genealogici, giuridici e sociali* (Siena, 1989), pp. 1–22.

[71] M. Godelier, *The Enigma of the Gift*, trans. N. Scott (Chicago, 1999), pp. 10–107.

[72] A. Weiner, *Inalienable Possessions: the Paradox of Keeping-While-Giving* (Berkeley, CA, 1992); see also the remarks of R. Le Jan, 'Introduction', in *Les transferts patrimoniaux en Europe occidentale, VIIIe-Xe siècle*, I, *Mélanges de l'École Française de Rome. Moyen Âge*, 111/2 (1999), 489–97, and compare C. Wickham, 'Conclusion', in Davies and Fouracre (eds.), *Languages of Gift*, pp. 238–61, at pp. 257–8.

indeed, characterize the initial gift, that Audiris made to S. Maria in Sarnaglia, in the same way. These are of course speculations, as the subjunctive indicates.[73] They reveal the possibilities, but also the limits, of anthropological insights into early medieval evidence. But simply being able to raise these suggestions also shows what was at stake in these processes, and underlines that parties had a good deal of power to shape their own social roles through their performances during them, and their production and use of written documents within them.

If the balance of power lay with the disputants, we should see the court as nonetheless important to the process. We can accept the idea of Gildiris' and Troctovus' poverty without having to suppose that in insisting on compensation that could not be paid the court tribunal was making itself irrelevant. Rather, it surely reveals both awareness of the Lombard law of the time, which was invoked in the charter in a relatively common formula, and its limits.[74] In ensuring that the dispute took the course that it did, the court and the parties were skirting around Liutprand's law on defaulting debtors, which stipulated that they be punished by enslavement.[75] Though a debtor to Ado, Gildiris was spared this fate. As for his other transgression – the illegitimate seizure of property – the Lombard law code gives no clear idea of the circumstances in which composition should be required, let alone on its level, so in ruling for an unattainable level here, and leaving it at that, the court was effectively shifting responsibility back to the victorious plaintiff, Odo. It may even have been inviting the act of mercy that followed.

The Sarnaglia case therefore indicates important features of the disputing process in the late Lombard period. First, written law was not absolutely authoritative. It was a point of reference for procedural strategies.[76] There was therefore, second, a hazy and constantly permeable boundary between formal and informal disputing processes – and

[73] Ultimately, we are in no position satisfactorily to explain the contradiction between Troctovus' apparently elevated social status – the charter introduces him as 'vir magnificus exercitalis' – and his father's inability to pay his fine: 'menime habuet unde talem conposicionem facere potuisset' (the poor orthography and syntax here are familiar features of Italian charters of this period: traditional rules of written Latin overlap with a spoken language slowly becoming Romance).

[74] For references to the *aedicti pagina* – the Lombard law code – in dispute documents, see N. Everett, 'Literacy and the Law in Lombard Government', *Early Medieval Europe*, 9 (2000), 93–127, Wickham, *Early Medieval Italy*, pp. 120–6, and F. Sinatti d'Amico, 'L'applicazione dell'Edictum in Tuscia', *Atti del V°Congresso internazionale di studi sull'alto medioevo* (Spoleto, 1973), pp. 745–81.

[75] *Liutprandi leges*, in *Leges Langobardorum (643–866)*, ed. F. Beyerle, *Die Gesetze der Langobarden*, Germanenrechte Neue Folge, Westgermanisches Recht, 2nd edn. (Witzenhausen, 1962), c. 152 states that a debtor who had no means of repayment had to become a debt slave.

[76] Further on this, see Costambeys, 'Disputes and Courts'.

between the written and the oral within them. Chris Wickham has noted how the balance between written and oral shifts slightly in the surviving *notitiae* from the late eighth and early ninth centuries: in particular, written proofs – always documents – ceased to have to be supported by oaths.[77] As for written documents themselves, the Sarnaglia case shows how little guidance the law codes provided about how to draw them up and how to treat them. It also shows that their scribes nonetheless followed interlocking sets of non-legislative norms: the legal formulae handed down through the bureaucratic traditions in which they were schooled, and customary norms that established acceptable ways in which to script the performance of the dispute. Neither formulae nor norms were absolutely fixed: both were subject to development as the requirements of courts and disputants changed. The Sarnaglia donation charter includes a number of such formulae, though none that would put it in the category of 'undefended' cases. The hint of 'fictitiousness' in the Sarnaglia case comes rather from the circularity of an apparent confiscation subsequently entirely restored. While it does not therefore sit on a direct line of evolution towards the fully fledged 'undefended case' *notitia* that emerges a hundred years or so later, it nevertheless points to an important contributing factor in that development: the strategic deployment of written documents to shape a dispute, in this case not just the surviving donation charter but the others that it mentions in the process.

Managing disputes with documents: Piacenza

Taking our search for documents about disputes forward into the ninth century, we can sensibly focus on the collections preserved at and from Piacenza. For one thing, it is there that we can trace the most straightforward development from earlier ninth-century charters to the 'undefended case' format proper: as we have seen, the first fully developed *ostensio cartae* formula is generally held to be a Piacenza charter of 880/1. That said, it should immediately be added that Piacenza cannot be taken as in any sense peculiar in its development of 'undefended case' *notitiae*. Earlier examples of undefended cases – but whose documents do not adopt the *ostensio cartae* formula – do survive from elsewhere: Piacenza documents may be important among survivals, but they can also be taken as broadly representative of developments occurring far more widely, across the Lombard kingdom and its Carolingian successor.[78] Nonetheless, the

[77] Wickham, 'Land Disputes', pp. 243–5.
[78] One of the earliest undefended cases is Manaresi, no. 28, on which see Costambeys, 'Disputes and Courts'; also Wickham, 'Land Disputes', p. 245 with n. 32.

profile of Piacenza's dispute *notitiae* is significant in itself. There is a complete lacuna in such documents between 911 and 976: a hiatus in archiving that did not affect the type of documents being kept.[79] Those that survive either side of that gap (i.e. 880/1–911 and 976–1077) nearly all follow one or other of the 'undefended case' models. Of the thirty-four Piacenza charters classed as dispute *notitiae* (or *placita*) by Manaresi and Volpini (ranging in date from 830 to 1077), twenty adopt a fully fledged 'undefended' model (ten take the *ostensio cartae* form, and five each the *finis intentionis* and *investitura salva querela*), two conclude with an *amica pactuacio*, and a further six can be regarded as early versions of these forms.[80] Of the remaining six, two are instalments of the very long-running squabble over their boundaries between the dioceses of Piacenza and Parma: a different class of dispute altogether, which can also be said to include a record of an inquisition into property contested between two monasteries.[81] Another two involve the exercise of the power of royal *bannum*,[82] leaving only one that might record a dispute resolved through a court.[83] Furthermore, when we examine just the dispute *notitiae* surviving after the long lacuna (that is, from 976 through to the final pre-1100 example, from 1077) we find a far greater concentration on the activities of the very highest in society. Of sixteen such *notitiae*, seven involve the bishop of Piacenza and other parties including another bishop and members of current or recent comital families.[84] Three involve marquises who were prominent landowners in the region, and one a count of the palace.[85] Four embody legal actions by prominent local clerics (a deacon, an archdeacon, an abbess, and an abbot) and the

[79] Manaresi, no. 123, *a.*911, is an original charter from the cathedral archive of the *investitura salva querela* type, featuring the nunnery dedicated to the Resurrection, and S. Sisto and Fabiano, in Piacenza and Herardus the son of a vassal of the *vicecomes* Elmericus. Manaresi, no. 192, *a.*981, is a twelfth-century copy from Cremona of a *notitia* using the *finis intentionis* format to affirm the possession of a large pasture by the same nunnery, and to limit the grazing rights of Gislebert, count of the palace.

[80] *Ostensio cartae*: Manaresi, nos. 91, 99, 105, 107, 114, 181, 213, 273, 337, 418; *finis intentionis*: Manaresi, nos. 192, 212, 233, 375, 385; *investitura salva querela*: Manaresi, nos. 123, 247, 248, 298, Volpini, no. 27 (in abbreviated form as Manaresi, no. 325); *amica pactuicio*: Manaresi, no. 97, Volpini, *compositio* 1 (see above); early forms: Manaresi, nos. 40, 63, 77, 93, Volpini, nos. 4 and 5.

[81] Manaresi, nos. 59 and 87; Volpini, no. 3.

[82] Manaresi, no. 438; Volpini, no. 6, on which see F. Bougard, 'Pierre de Niviano, dit le Spolétin, sculdassius, et le gouvernement du comté de Plaisance à l'époque carolingienne', *Journal des savants*, juillet-décembre (1996), 291–337.

[83] Volpini, no. 22, a lacunose document probably dating to 1014, in which both parties eschew combat in favour of oath-taking as a means of resolution.

[84] Manaresi, nos. 181, 212, 233, 298, 375 and Volpini, nos. 22 and 27 (a better copy of Manaresi, no. 325).

[85] Manaresi, no. 192 involved the count of the palace Gislebert. Manaresi, no. 247 involved Marquis Boso and a daughter of Count Bernard, Manaresi, no. 248 Marquis Boso and

final one is the grant of royal *bannum* to the canons of S. Antonino.[86] We no longer find preserved documents relating to figures a rung or two down the social ladder, such as the *sculdahis* from Niviano, Petrus, whose dossier of documents, extending for forty years from the 870s, found its way into the archives of S. Antonino.[87] To judge from the *notitiae*, therefore, archivists at Piacenza became increasingly selective about what they preserved. Moreover, the nature of their selection, preserving only those *notitiae* in which their own institutions' property rights were negotiated with the most influential in their society, points to the true purpose of the undefended case format: to strengthen property title, rather than to record the management of real disputes in court.

We are fortunate, therefore, that there survive from Piacenza non-judicial charters that tell us something about real disputing there. Some of them show that the developments in archival competence just noted had an effect not only on what documents were preserved by posterity but also on the way documents were used in disputes at the time. Perhaps the most striking of them indicates how mutable 'real' dispute documents – as opposed to traditional *notitiae* – could be, and how they operated both within and outside the court, and combined legal formulae creatively. It was drawn up at Areglia in June 898 by the *notarius* Gumpertus, who describes it as a 'breve donacionis adque confirmacionis' (a brief of donation and confirmation); and though it does indeed involve a transfer, it was not primarily of landed property, but of what is here termed a *calumnia*.[88] In Roman law, *calumnia* was a false accusation (parties had to swear in court that their suits were not false).[89] By the late empire it had

Count Lanfranc, and Manaresi, no. 337 saw Marquis Hugh of the dominant Obertenghi family have confirmed the testament of Gerard, son of Genesius, who had acquired most of the properties of the Gandolfingi: see further F. Bougard, 'Entre Gandolfingi et Obertenghi. Les comtes de Plaisance aux Xe et XIe siècles', *Mélanges de l'École Française de Rome. Moyen Âge*, 101/1 (1989), 11–66, esp. 23–7 and 32–6.

86 Manaresi, nos. 213, 273, 385 and 418 involved respectively Piacenza's archdeacon Aginus, the deacon Domninus, Adelaida, abbess of S. Sisto, and Richezo, abbot of S. Savino. Manaresi, no. 438 is a grant by Henry IV of royal *bannum* over the possessions of the canons of the church of Piacenza.

87 Petrus' dossier provides the raw material for, and is conveniently re-edited in, Bougard, 'Pierre de Niviano'.

88 *ChLA* LXXI.25; also edited in G. Petracco Sicardi, 'Indicazioni etniche germaniche nelle carte altomedievali piacentine', *Archivio storico per le provincie parmensi* 4a ser., 27 (1975), 139–74, no. III, 171–3.

89 *Digesta* 25.2.11–14, ed. T. Mommsen, *Corpus Iuris Civilis*, vol. 1, 16th edn. (Berlin, 1954). Many of the protagonists in the Piacentine charters claimed to live by Roman law, a lingering attachment that may have been a legacy of Emilia's relatively late incorporation into the Lombard kingdom in the seventh century. Nevertheless, it would seem wrong in the context of the late ninth century to give ethnic significance either to the type of document adopted here or to the procedure it details (as does C. Mantegna, *ChLA* LXXI, p. 6).

come also to refer to actions that were merely ill-considered, rather than malicious.[90] Which of these was the case here is not clear from the rather obscure wording of the *breve*. It seems to record that John of 'Marrade', son of Stadevertus, had acquired property as a result of his accusation that Andreas of Avuario, son of Adelbert, had abducted, beaten, and raped his wife Adeltruda, and that he now 'transferred and entrusted' ('tradavit vel perdonavit') that property to Rapert, abbot of S. Paolo di Mezzano Scotti, and his advocate Dagifredus. He did so presumably because his accusation had been judged, or at least had been claimed, to be false or unfounded (hence, a *calumnia*).[91] In fact, then, this document was part of the settlement of a criminal case: the transaction of property arose from a situation of conflicting accusations in which the monastery took a quasi-public role in what appears to have been a compromise settlement. This case therefore involved the original charges, the admission of *calumnia*, or malicious prosecution, and a quitclaim to landed property. In conveying these in a single document, this *breve* resembles the one written by Rodoaldus with which we started. Both demonstrate a certain competence in the use of documents: the combination of what we would term 'criminal' and 'civil' formulae was a creative act by the issuer and his scribe.

A document of this sort – and there are not many among survivals, whether from Piacenza or anywhere else – reveals the skill with which some, at least, of the commissioners and writers of charters could use them in these contexts. The willingness to be creative with the use of documents is evident too in other charters produced by real disputes, which, however, also speak of anxiety on the part of others when faced with their opponents' competence in this respect. Thus, for example, a *breve* written by the *notarius* Giselpertus in April 883 relates how a priest, Agustinus of S. Antonino in Piacenza, had forced a certain Grasevertus to draw up a charter relinquishing any claim on lands that the latter's father had transferred by charter to his sisters, because Agustinus doubted Grasevertus' claim that his father's charter had been lost.[92] Possession of charters was also at issue in a *notitia* of August 892 written by the *notarius* Gausus, which records that Daniel of Godi came to the church of S. Giovanni in Piacenza to swear an oath on the altar along with six *sacramentales*, as was required by the *Lex Salica* under which he lived.

[90] G. Mousourakis, *The Historical and Institutional Context of Roman Law* (Aldershot, 2003), p. 317.

[91] *ChLA* LXXI.25: 'qualiter presiset muliere sua nomine Adeltruda, eam detrassiset et flagellasset eciam cum ea fornicaset'. I have translated the earlier-appearing phrase 'tradavit vel perdonavit' as 'transferred and entrusted'; other meanings are possible.

[92] *ChLA* LXV.40; for Agustinus see also *ChLA* LXV 10, 13, 34 (a.882).

He swore that he did not possess the charters that had been claimed by Andelberga, widow of Rotcari of Godi, and her daughter Rotrada.[93] The importance of pledges here is underlined by another document, written by the priest Raginaldus, recording the testimony of nine pledged men (presumably peasant tenants) concerning pig-grazing rights in a wood. This gives some sense of the amount of oath-making that went on, and suggests how much of it was documented: that is, nearly all of it.[94] Formulae about criminal procedures, property rights, pledges, oaths, and the loss and renewal of documents were among the devices that those with skill and experience in the handling of legal writing could call upon in late ninth-century Piacenza to further their interests; and, it is worth repeating, Piacenza was not at all unusual in this respect.

In a situation where the writing of documents was so central to legal business, litigants must clearly have found it important to have access to those who performed such writing best, and the Piacenza documents offer hints at how that access was constrained. By themselves, the examples just cited raise the familiar problem that our picture of contemporary practices is dictated by the circumstances of later preservation. In other words, these charters all ultimately worked to the benefit of the institutions that kept them. The transfer of property following John's *calumnia* was written by the *notarius* Gumpertus and passed to S. Paolo in Mezzano Scotti; Grasevertus' quitclaim, written by the *notarius* Giselpertus, allowed property that was initially possessed by women to pass to the church of S. Antonino in Piacenza; similarly, Daniel's oath, recorded by the *notarius* Gausus, relinquished a claim to the possessions of a widow and her daughter, which then passed to S. Giovanni in Piacenza; and the priest Raginaldus wrote a document specifying grazing rights in a wood controlled by the cathedral church of Piacenza (probably his own). It is straightforward to think that these charters were preserved, just like traditional court case *notitiae*, because they supported the property rights of the institutions that kept them. Fortunately, however, we also possess evidence that our record is not simply a product of what we might call 'beneficiary archiving'. One Piacenza document, undated but probably to be put in the decade or so before 890/891, lists transactions and pledges associated with the figure of Petrus de Niviano, who was a *sculdassius* in

[93] *ChLA* LXVI.36. The two women were represented by Ratcausus of Muradello, who had pledged to hear the oath on their behalf; further on Ratcausus, see *ChLA* LXVI 25, 35, 39 and E. Falconi ed., *Le carte più antiche di S. Antonino di Piacenza* (Parma, 1959), no. 86.

[94] *ChLA* LXVIII 15, dated 15 Jan. 823; for comment, see Bougard, 'Entre Gandolfingi et Obertenghi', p. 14.

the Piacentino from 880/1 to 891.[95] Since different pledges are entered in different hands, it seems to be a running record of judicial actions made as and when they took place, usefully demonstrating that lay officials kept track of the cases and documentation that passed before them. Since, furthermore, at least one of the hands is identifiable as that of a Piacentine notary known from other documents, this rough-and-ready text shows that laity as well as clergy could possess the institutional clout to command the expertise of those well-practised in document writing. In Piacenza as elsewhere, the men who possessed these skills were clearly professionals. The list of Piacentine charter scribes of the ninth century reveals two significant features.[96] First, most gave themselves no clerical designation (such as *presbiter* or *clericus*), but preferred *notarius* (occasionally with *scriptor*) – a statement, in other words, of their occupation, which implied nothing about their lay or clerical status either way. Second, those who appear on more than a handful of occasions wrote charters preserved in the archives of more than one institution: that is, they were not 'house' scribes, but performed their task for a number of different 'employers' (it is impossible to say whether they did so for money, though this seems likely, prima facie). Taken as a whole, then, the Piacenza evidence indicates that it was created by a professional cadre of charter scribes. It also shows that increasingly through the ninth century this group worked most readily and most often in the interests of the best-organized and most powerful in their region: churches, monasteries, lay officials, and the most prominent families.[97]

Conclusion

The 'undefended case' format is therefore an especially stark example of a wider phenomenon: creativity in the use of documents in disputes. As anxiety over their loss shows, legal documents were valued as objects to wield in the course of disputes. But it was not only the fact of their existence that was valuable: it was what they said and how they said it. The primary function of many was to assert, if not to strengthen, rights to property, and some were simply textual devices to that end. The 'undefended case' types can certainly be seen as such: epiphenomena of a

[95] *ChLA* LXVI.42. On Petrus' career, see Bougard, 'Pierre de Niviano', pp. 292–4. At least three hands wrote the entries, one of which seems to be that of the scribe identified by the editors of the Piacenza charters as Petrus (VI).

[96] A register of ninth-century Piacentine charter scribes appears very handily (as 'Anagrafe dei notai piacentini del IX secolo'), in *ChLA* LXXI, pp. 12–15.

[97] The importance of notaries' dexterity with documentary forms has been recognized for the eleventh century by Bougard, '"Falsum falsorum judicum consilium"'. I am here suggesting that the development began rather earlier, in the ninth century.

documentary culture that had developed its own rationale. But documents of that kind themselves also demonstrate that forms of words – formulae – could be manipulated; and for some that meant that their meanings shifted with context. Though nearly all charters were preserved ultimately because they had something to do with the ownership of property, this was not always their only function at the time they were written. At S. Maria in Sarnaglia, a donation charter was a vehicle for strengthening the social ties of patronage of its priest; similarly, in the case of *calumnia* from Piacenza John can be seen as putting himself under the patronage of the abbot of S. Paolo di Mezzano Scotti. It is no coincidence, moreover, that these two parties were ecclesiastical institutions. The Piacenza charters demonstrate that by the late ninth century expertise in the use of documents was not accessible to all equally. Churches, monasteries, and influential laymen were more likely than the ordinary laity to command the skills of those who could write documents most effectively, and ecclesiastical institutions in particular were better able to store documents for the long term. The latter ability in particular may lie behind the increasing social exclusivity of the 'undefended case' types that we saw at Piacenza. It may be, that is, that ecclesiastical archivists were choosing to preserve not just particular types of documents – court-case *notitiae*, or even just those of 'undefended case' type – but only those with particular protagonists – the politically powerful, especially an emerging and relatively narrow group of signorial families. Very useful as they may have been in validating rights, 'undefended case' *notitiae* may have been increasingly open only to those with the notarial and archival resources to generate and keep them.[98]

It might seem surprising, then, that over the long term, the 'undefended case' type proved a dead end. Ultimately, the history of Italian judicial documents saw the triumph of informal and mediatory procedures and the unformulaic notices that recorded them: a development linked definitively to the growth of communal jurisdiction in north Italian and Tuscan cities.[99] The 'undefended case' format would not have a future

[98] Wickham, 'Land Disputes', pp. 252–3 notes that compromise and arbitration, rather than definitive judgement, are more frequent in documentation emanating from 'lower courts'. In the Sabina, for example, the formal *placitum* headed by a count or royal *missus* became rare. This simply underlines the point that the proceedings of these 'higher courts' were coming to be about something other than disputes: they were for validating documents and the rights expressed in them.

[99] C. Wickham, *Courts and Conflict in Twelfth-Century Tuscany* (Oxford, 2003), pp. 6–9; J.-P. Delumeau, 'Sociétés, cadres de pouvor et règlement des conflits en Italie du Xe siècle à l'émergence des juridictions communales', *Actes des congrès de la Société des historiens médiévistes de l'enseignement supérieur public. 31e congrès* (Angers, 2000), pp. 169–88.

much beyond 1100. Yet we can perhaps see reasons for this in the alternative tradition of documenting disputes that has been touched on here: the non-judicial documents, *brevia* and *notitiae*, which provide our best evidence for real social conflicts. They show that law courts were not central to such conflicts: the disputing process did not begin and end in court. And they also show that success in that process increasingly came to depend on a certain expertise with documents that some were better able to wield than others. As charter scribes became more adept at using formulae that were originally restricted to property transactions for all sorts of other business – for taking on power of attorney in a rape case, or guarding against fraud – so the documents they produced became both expressions and instruments of power within their local societies. The powerful therefore had an increasing incentive to monopolize this expertise.

The archival expertise that developed alongside this notarial competence might be another reason for the atrophy of forms such as the *ostensio cartae*. The *notitiae* generated by law courts remained valuable for as long as the court bestowed on their documents, and the transactions and rights that they embodied, a quality that litigants could not find elsewhere: that of public validation. This should not be seen as a stamp bearing the authority of a 'state'; it derived rather from acknowledgement by a peer group in a formal setting, recognized as such. But an institution with a well-managed archive that reliably preserved documentary proofs had less need of the imprimatur of public validity that law courts had given to transactions through the 'undefended case' forms. Moreover, once other formal settings became available, and acquired some of the authority that had surrounded the royal courts – once, in the early twelfth century, imperial power had started to decline and communal government to assume greater competence – those seeking to affirm their rights could and did turn to these new sources of validity instead. In other words, the 'undefended case' formats shared their fate with that of the royal law court, and the disappearance of the latter was the effect of declining royal power, not its cause.

The link between documentary change and social transformation operated in Italy at a different level from that proposed for a 'transforming' tenth- and eleventh-century west Francia. Certainly, there is no strong parallel to draw between the decline of royal power in west Francia, and the change in documentary format with which it coincided, and that of imperial power in Italy a century or more later. Although in twelfth-century Italy the 'undefended case' format shared the fate of royal-imperial law courts, it is also disproportionately prominent in the record because of archivists' priorities and preferences: there are plenty of other types of document that get less attention and do not 'fit' the rise and fall of imperial power in the same way. In Italy – and this may also be the case in west Francia – it is not that the production of legal documents responded to social change; it is, rather, that the documents were themselves instruments of that change. We can see this as early as the eighth century, and not so much in 'undefended case' types as in those many other types of documents that disputes generated, but that got preserved more haphazardly. The successful deployment of these documents in the course of disputes depended to a large extent on the skill of the scribes who drew them up. This fact in itself encouraged the greater institutionalization of scribes, whether they were the notary-judges who emerged at Pavia, those who came to work for bishops as the latter increasingly assumed civil administrative roles, or those who could draw on their knowledge of burgeoning institutional archives – of monasteries and of signorial families. By helping their institutions to secure their property rights, extend their landed wealth, and impose their power over others, the documents that those scribes produced were themselves instruments of social transformation. By giving written permanence to dues that had hitherto been only temporary, Rodoaldus' documentary manoeuvre, with which we began, meant that the bishop of Piacenza could thereafter count on regular labour services from Hermefrit's descendants, and their heirs. In the ninth century, the professional skill of notaries and the power of institutions were mutually reinforcing, to the benefit of both, and to the detriment of those who had once looked to law courts to uphold their meagre rights.

7 Divorce and remarriage between late antiquity and the early middle ages: canon law and conflict resolution

Riccardo Bof and Conrad Leyser

> And the apostolic Innocent, Leo, and Gregory, and the African Council, Ambrose, John of Constantinople, Origen in his books amended by Saint Jerome, the venerable priest Bede and all other catholic doctors all agree with this gospel truth and apostolic doctrine.[1]

The 'gospel truth' here proclaimed is that the bond of marriage cannot be broken – except in particular circumstances. The speaker is Hincmar of Rheims, writing in the spring of 860 on the case of the Carolingian king Lothar II (r. 855–69) and his wife Teutberga.[2] Lothar sought to be rid of his wife and to remarry. He claimed that she had committed sodomitical incest with her brother, and that these were grounds for annulling the marriage. Two councils held in the royal palace had ratified this, but some of those present had their reservations. As Hincmar tells us, a group of bishops and laymen had sent him a record of the councils, along with a number of questions. These ranged from the theoretical – was repudiating a spouse really permissible? – to the awkwardly personal – had Hincmar in fact backed Lothar? Hincmar did not stint on the challenge

[1] Hincmar of Rheims, *De divortio Lotharii regis et Theutbergae reginae*, ed. L. Böhringer, MGH Conc. IV suppl. I (Hanover, 1992), p. 143, ll. 8–11. All subsequent citations are from this edition; translation by Rachel Stone and Charles West, available online at www.hincmar.blogspot.com, and forthcoming, with introduction and commentary, from Manchester University Press. Our thanks to both for their generosity in sharing their work, and for their comments on this chapter. Thanks also to Helmut Reimitz, Jan Van Doren, and in particular to Abigail Firey for help and advice; and to fellow contributors, as to friends and colleagues in Manchester, for support and suggestions.

[2] See in the first instance K. Heidecker, *The Divorce of Lothar II: Christian Marriage and Political Power in the Carolingian World*, tr. T. M. Guest, Conjunctions of Religion and Power in the Medieval Past (Ithaca, NY and London, 2010); and the galvanizing contribution of S. Airlie, 'Private Bodies and the Body Politic in the Divorce Case of Lothar II', *Past & Present*, 161 (1998), 3–38. D. d'Avray, *Dissolving Royal Marriages: A Documentary History, 860–1600* (Cambridge, 2014), and his *Papacy, Monarchy, and Marriage, 860–1600* (Cambridge, 2015) appeared too recently to be taken into account here.

of replying. The result, the treatise known to its modern readers as *On the Divorce of Lothar and Teutberga*, was a masterpiece of equivocation, despite, or because of, its appeal to authoritative truths.[3]

In the event, Lothar did not prevail. Clerical opinion and family politics conspired against him. In many accounts, his defeat appears as a milestone in the history of Christian marriage in Latin Europe. As told, for example, by Georges Duby what we see is here the first stage in the clerical takeover of marriage.[4] According to Duby, from the Carolingian period onwards, Christian bishops began to insist that marriage was a once-and-for-all commitment before God, not a short-term easily dissolved contract for the material advantage of two families. The power of celibate priests to dictate the lives of married lay people is seen as a process that will gather pace through the Middle Ages. We know what happens next: nearly seven hundred years after the humbling of Lothar, England's Henry VIII has to establish his own Church before he can get his own matrimonial way.

This familiar account of the 'rise of Christian marriage' assumes, without warrant, a fixity in the position both of 'the Church' and of the laity. Thus, scholars often follow Hincmar in asserting that the Church's position on marriage has been set more or less in stone from the earliest times.[5] As Hincmar did, they draw a line from New Testament texts, through Church Councils, in particular in Africa, and Church Fathers, in particular Augustine, down to the ninth century and then beyond. One scholar has dubbed Augustine's views as 'the normative Western position'.[6] *Pace* this view, we argue here that, at least until the ninth century, there was no 'normative' position in the Latin West. Christian

[3] Hincmar's original title is lost. We use the modern title for convenience, but under protest. Hincmar does not discuss 'divorce': what Lothar sought was an annulment. See further below, pp. 173–4.

[4] G. Duby, *Le chevalier, la femme et le prêtre. Le mariage dans la France féodale*, La force des Idées (Paris, 1981), in a tradition established by P. Daudet, *Études sur l'histoire de la jurisdiction matrimoniale. Les origines carolingiennes de la compétence exclusive de l'Église (France et Germanie)* (Paris, 1933). More recent work, in whose tracks we follow, sees ecclesiastical legislation in the context of dispute settlement. See L. Böhringer, 'Gewaltverzicht, Gesichtswahrung und Befriedung durch Öffentlichkeit. Beobachtungen zur Entstehung des kirchlichen Eherechts im 9. Jahrhundert am Beispiel Hinkmars von Reims', in S. Esders (ed.), *Rechtsverständnis und Konfliktbewältigung. Gerichtliche und außergerichtliche Strategien im Mittelalter* (Cologne, Weimar, and Vienna, 2007), pp. 255–90, at 256.

[5] See, for example, H. Crouzel, *L'Église primitive face au divorce*, Theologie historique, 13 (Paris, 1971).

[6] P. L. Reynolds, *Marriage in the Western Church: the Christianization of Marriage during the Patristic and Early Medieval Periods*, Supplements to Vigiliae Christianae. Texts and Studies of Early Christian Life and Language, 24 (Leiden, New York, and Cologne, 1994), pp. 176–7 and 417–18. See also J. Brundage, *Law, Sex, and Christian Society in Medieval Europe* (Chicago, 1987), p. 80.

tradition spoke with many voices, and we need to distinguish between them. If Hincmar appeals to a consensus, it is our task to establish how, or indeed whether, he was able to produce one.

The position of the laity is in no less need of differentiation. Early medievalists have already set to work on the assumption made by Duby that there was a 'Germanic' model of pair-bonding in play in the Lothar–Teutberga case. Before he married Teutberga, Lothar had fathered a child with another woman, Waldrada. Thanks especially to the intervention of Ruth Karras, we need no longer entertain the notion that this relationship constituted a Frankish 'love-match' which Lothar sought to justify in the face of clerical disapproval. Lothar took his stand on Christian law: he had clerical experts on his side, making a learned case for repudiating Teutberga.[7]

This is not to say that the laity had no independent agency or culture of marriage. If we reach behind the 'Germanic', and indeed also 'the Christian', we can in fact start a history of marriage in the late Roman period. As Kate Cooper has shown, in the fourth century, a new valorization of the conjugal bond arose not from clerical dogma, but from within lay political society.[8] The newly constituted imperial courts of the Dominate, from the Emperor Diocletian (r. 284–305) onwards, needed to recruit talent: their magnetism destabilized the structure of provincial society. Sons straining to escape the leash of paternal authority started to marry 'down' in order to make themselves freer to answer the metropolitan call of imperial patronage. A socially inferior wife was 'portable' in a way that a prominent local heiress was not. The Roman *pater* lost control, to a degree, of his children; conversely, the Roman husband gained power over his wife. In response, imperial legislation sought to foster a sense of responsibility among husbands, setting limits to non-consensual divorce. Christian pronouncements about the marriage bond trailed in the wake of these social storms.

The 'Christianization of marriage' is altogether too narrow a description for what we see happening in the late and post-Roman West.[9] A full-scale reorganization of the family is underway, given extra impetus in the law codes issued in the post-Roman kingdoms. To pick out the most salient developments: women's legal right to hold property collapsed; the practice of adoption, at the centre of Roman family planning, fell away;

[7] R. Karras, 'The History of Marriage and the Myth of Friedelehe' *Early Medieval Europe* 14 (2006), 119–51.

[8] K. Cooper, *The Fall of the Roman Household* (Cambridge, 2007) esp. pp. 23–30.

[9] See A. Guerreau-Jalabert, 'La parenté dans l'Europe médiévale et moderne: à propos d'une synthèse récente', *L'homme* 29 (1989), pp. 69–93, reviewing J. Goody, *The Development of Family and Marriage in Europe* (Oxford, 1983).

we witness the rise of godparenthood, incest prohibitions, and vows to sexual continence.[10] With regard to the marriage bond and its dissolution, we need to track and explain a shift from a late Roman culture of ready divorce to an early medieval one of reluctant annulment. None of this can be attempted here: suffice it to say that pointing the finger at 'the Church', as though this can explain what are new developments within Christian tradition, is a weak alibi for the real task of analysis.

Underneath these lurching transformations, one element of continuity does stand out: the need to keep the peace. The more important the bonds of marriage, in fact, the greater the need to minimize the fallout from their collapse. Hincmar's *De divortio*, for all its dogma and bluster, is a test case of this. His treatise was at once a masterly synthesis of tradition, and, in context, a pastoral, not a doctrinal intervention. As we examine the twists and turns of his reasoning, what we see is a concern to amass the resources of Christian lore, with the goal of expanding, not contracting, the room for manoeuvre. The situation required the balm of expertise, not an intransigent assertion of principle. Equivocation – as the Jesuit who coined the term was well aware – has its moral problems, but also its real uses.[11]

Divorce and conflict management in the later Roman Empire

1 *Christian ethics and Roman law*

Christian teaching on marriage and divorce was, at least in theory, at odds with its cultural setting. In the ancient world, marriage was conceived primarily as a contract between two families, whose main purpose was the transfer of a woman's procreative power to the service of her husband's family, in order to produce legitimate heirs.[12] Once the contract had served its purpose, it could be dissolved.[13] Broadly speaking, Roman legislation and Hellenistic practices allowed divorce[14], even when

[10] On incest, see now K. Ubl, *Inzestverbot und Gesetzgebung: Die Konstruktion eines Verbrechens (300–1100)* (Berlin, 2008).

[11] See F. L. Huntley, 'Macbeth and the Background of Jesuitical Equivocation', *Proceedings of the Modern Languages Association of America*, 79 (1964), 390–400.

[12] Cooper, *Fall of the Roman Household*, p. x.

[13] The case of Cato and his wife is a striking example of the 'contractual' Roman approach to marriage: Y. Thomas, 'Fathers as Citizens of Rome, Rome as a City of Fathers (second century BC – second century AD)', in A. Burguière et al. (eds.), English trans., *A History of the Family, Pt 1: Distant Worlds, Ancient Worlds* (Cambridge, MA, 1996), pp. 228–69, at 256–7.

[14] S. C. Saar, *Ehe – Scheidung – Wiederheirat*, Ius vivens: Abt. B, rechtsgeschichtliche Abhandlungen, 6 (Münster u.a., 2002), p. 7, with extensive bibliography. According to

initiated by the wife, while the Jewish tradition, from which Christianity itself sprang, permitted it to the husband only (at least until the Middle Ages).[15] By contrast, in Christian texts, such as the Gospels of Mark or Luke, there are several passages prohibiting or limiting the dissolution of the conjugal bond.[16]

Christian teaching was not, however, without ambivalence. Take, in particular, the Gospel of Matthew:

They were told, 'A man who divorces his wife must give her a certificate of dismissal.' But what I tell you is this: If a man divorces his wife *for any other cause than unchastity* he involves her in adultery; and whoever marries her commits adultery. (5: 31–32)

I tell you, if a man divorces his wife *for any other cause than unchastity*, and marries another, he commits adultery. (19:8–9)[17]

Matthew raised but only partially answered some pressing questions: were there terms on which divorce was acceptable? Was remarriage ever permissible, either to those who had dismissed their spouses, or to those dismissed (hereafter 'repudiators' and 'repudiatees', with apologies for the inelegance of the terms). Matthew took the line that 'unchastity' (*fornicatio*, usually understood to mean adultery) was grounds for divorce. A female repudiatee could not remarry; but a male repudiator could only remarry if his wife was an adulteress. While further consideration of Matthew's immediate context is beyond the scope of this chapter, it should be borne in mind that polygamy was the norm in first-century Palestine. Interpreting what the Gospel meant in the context of Roman monogamy proved problematic.[18]

In the early Church, divorce was not easily policed. The bishop, the highest figure in the local Christian community, could not rely on any formal power to force the members of his congregation to respect the norms of Christian behaviour, where these did not coincide with Roman law. Only spiritual sanctions, such as excommunication or penance, could be wielded against sinners. While the value of such sanctions in

Treggiari, 'the most important feature of Roman divorce throughout the classical period is that it was free': S. Treggiari, *Roman Marriage: Iusti Coniuges from the Time of Cicero to the Time of Ulpian* (Oxford, 1991), p. 459.

[15] J. D. Rayner, *Jewish Religious Law: a Progressive Perspective*, Progressive Judaism Today, 3 (New York and Oxford, 1998), pp. 162–70.

[16] Mark 10: 11f., Luke 16: 18, and 1 Cor. 7: 39.

[17] Translations from J. M. Suggs, K. Doob Sakenfeld, and J. R. Mueller (eds.), *The Oxford Study Bible: Revised English Bible with Apocrypha* (New York, 1992), p. 1272 and p. 1289 our italics.

[18] See Reynolds, *Marriage in the Western Church*, pp. 173–213. See also E. A. Clark, 'Constraining the Body, Expanding the Text: the Exegesis of Divorce in the Later Latin Fathers', in W. E. Klingshirn and M. Vessey (eds.), *The Limits of Ancient Christianity* (Ann Arbor, MI, 1999), pp. 153–71, at p. 160.

the management of face-to-face communities must not be underestimated, the bishops' capacity legally to enforce their judgement was limited, since their judicial power depended on the authority conferred on them by their own congregations.[19]

We turn now to review the legal landmarks with respect to divorce in the later Empire. Constantine was the first Roman emperor to limit the traditional Roman freedom which allowed both men and women to repudiate one's spouse unilaterally. In 331, he ruled that the repudiator had to be punished if s/he could not justify this action by specified faults committed by the repudiatee.[20] These faults, itemized in the law, were serious crimes carrying grave punishment (exile, forced labour, or the death penalty).[21] In fact, a woman could only be repudiated if she was an adulteress, a poisoner, or a procuress; a man, only if convicted of murder, poisoning, or profanation of tombs. Crucial to note, however, is that this law leaves consensual divorce untouched. Constantine restricted unilateral divorce, repudiation initiated by one partner against the other, and without the latter's consent.

Post-Constantinian imperial legislation on divorce was to fluctuate. Each limit to the right of repudiation was followed by a correction, when it became clear that the limits were too severe. Constantine's law seems to have been repealed by Julian (ca. 362), but another similar ruling was issued in the western Empire by Honorius, in 421.[22] The pattern was repeated in the following three decades.[23]

Much later, in the sixth century, imperial legislation went further. The Emperor Justinian (527–66) issued several laws on unilateral divorce; then, in a radical departure from previous tradition, he prohibited divorce by mutual consent, which had remained unrestricted since the classical

[19] J. D. Harries, *Law and Empire in Late Antiquity* (Cambridge, 2004), pp. 210–11.

[20] *Codex Theodosianus* 3,16,1; English translation: J. Evans Grubbs, *Women and Law in the Roman Empire: a Sourcebook on Marriage, Divorce and Widowhood* (London and New York, 2002), p. 203.

[21] Evans Grubbs, *Law and Family*, p. 229. See also G. S. Nathan, *The Family in Late Antiquity: the Rise of Christianity and the Endurance of Tradition* (London and New York, 2000), p. 64.

[22] Reynolds, *Marriage in the Western Church*, pp. 130–1. See also C. Fayer, *La familia romana. iii. Concubinato, divorzio, adulterio*, Problemi e ricerche di storia antica, 22 (Rome, 2005), pp. 145–6. Fayer leans towards the possibility that Constantine's law was not repealed, but simply disregarded after Julian's reign. It has been suggested that Julian's successor, Jovian, reintroduced restrictions to repudiation, but there is little evidence to support this: see M. Kuefler, 'The Marriage Revolution in Late Antiquity: the Theodosian Code and Later Roman Marriage Law', *Journal of Family History*, 32 (2007), 343–70, at 356.

[23] Laws by Honorius (421, *Codex Theodosianus* 3.16.2), Theodiosius II (439, novel 12; 449, *Codex Iustinianus* 5.17.8), Valentinian III (452, Novel 35,11); English translation: Evans Grubbs, *Women and Law in the Roman Empire*, pp. 204–8.

age of Roman jurisprudence (from the first century BCE).[24] But again, the measure was short-lived; it was repealed by Justinian's immediate successor, Justin, in 566, the very first year of his reign. Justin explained that he reintroduced the right to consensual divorce in response to the many petitions he had received from spouses pleading to be released from married lives which had become unbearable.[25] In general, the Roman lawgivers' goal was not to limit the dissolution of marriage, but rather to limit conflict between the parties involved.

There is evidence to suggest that Christian leaders took much the same position. In late Roman Egypt, as revealed in papyri studied by Roger Bagnall, divorce remained a common practice, and priests and bishops were involved in arbitrating these cases; conversely, there is no indication that these clerics sought to prevent or to forbid the dissolution of these unions.[26] They were rather trying to find an amicable settlement between the contending spouses. It would be facile to say that these churchmen were just making their own lives easier, by going along with local practice or secular law: pragmatism may have been the soundest pastoral option. If we turn now to consider the procedures established higher up the episcopal hierarchy, we find a similar set of concerns.

2 *Canon law*

In *De divortio*, Hincmar gives the impression that he is selecting from a host of popes and a chorus of councils whose pronouncements make up a solid body of church law on marriage and divorce. Of this claim the modern reader should beware. We can be beguiled into thinking that the late and post-Roman Church functioned like the State as a law-making and enforcing institution. It did not. When bishops in the later Roman Empire met together in councils, discussed a matter, and agreed upon it, they kept a record of their decision; by the end of the fourth century, these decisions were regarded as 'canons'. This meant literally 'a rule', in the sense of 'a measure': the most accurate translation might be 'guideline'. The same is true for the other component of 'canon law', namely papal decretals. These were particular judgements of the bishop of Rome, issued in response to queries or petitions, subsequently held to be of more than local interest. The earliest decretals date, again, from the

[24] Nov. 117. Reynolds, *Marriage in the Western Church*, pp. 57–61. Fayer, *La familia romana, iii*, pp. 166–72.

[25] Nov. 140, *Ut matrimonium ex consensu solvi possit*; see Reynolds, *Marriage in the Western Church*, p. 60, and A. Arjava, *Women and Law in Late Antiquity* (Oxford, 1996), p. 182.

[26] R. S. Bagnall, 'Church, State and Divorce in Late Roman Egypt', in R. Somerville and K. L. Selig (eds.), *Florilegium Colombianum: Essays in Honor of Paul Oskar Kristeller* (New York, 1987), pp. 41–61.

late fourth century.[27] While the development of these guidelines speaks to the increasing confidence of the Church in the Christian Roman Empire, and while abrogation of the guidelines was anathemetized, bishops were under no illusions that their canons matched imperial law.

In the fifth, sixth, and seventh centuries, various churchmen, usually anonymous, took it upon themselves to make collections of the 'canons' of the church. One of the few we can name, Dionysius Exiguus, operating in early-sixth century Rome, was impressively comprehensive, in that he sought to include all the canons of councils in the East and West, while compiling a separate volume of papal decretals. Dionysius' collections were not, however, regarded as definitive. He himself began the work of re-editing them, a process which continued and indeed gathered pace in subsequent centuries, as we shall see below.[28]

It follows from this that our access to these early 'guidelines' is highly mediated. We are at the mercy of what the various collectors, and their later copyists chose to do with the records at their disposal. Reconstructing 'the teaching of the Church' at any given stage is problematic at best. Below we follow one instance where it is possible to trace, at least in outline, the transmission and manipulation of one canon on divorce and remarriage, as it made its way from fifth-century North Africa to ninth-century Francia.

Gaul and Spain The earliest securely dateable conciliar decrees on marriage and divorce come from Gaul. Two years after his legalization of Christianity, the Emperor Constantine called his bishops to Arles. Canon 10 of the council of Arles, like the Gospel of Matthew, addresses itself to betrayed husbands:

> Concerning those men who find that their wives are committing adultery – these being young Christian men who are forbidden to marry [*prohibentur nubere*] – it is decreed that as far as possible [*quantum possit*] they should be counseled [*consilium eis detur*] not to marry again *as long as their wives are alive, even though the latter are adulteresses*.[29]

[27] K. Zechiel-Eckes, *Die erste Dekretale. Der Brief Papst Siricius' an Bischof Himerius von Tarragona vom Jahr 385 (JK 255)*, ed. D. Jasper, MGH Studien und Texte 55 (Hannover, 2013). See further D. Jasper and H. Fuhrmann, *Papal Letters in the Early Middle Ages* (Washington, DC, 2001).

[28] See A. Firey, 'Collectio Dionysiana', at http://ccl.rch.uky.edu/dionysiana-article for a discussion and further references.

[29] *Conciles gaulois du IVe siècle*, J. Gaudemet and C. Munier (eds.), Sources Chrétiennes, 241 (Paris, 1977), pp. 52–3, and nn. 1–2; tr. Reynolds, *Marriage in the Western Church*, p. 181. Our italics.

Scholars have puzzled over the wording of this canon.[30] Again, ambivalence may have been the point. The bishops gathered at Arles thought that it was forbidden to remarry before the repudiatee's death, but they tolerated the remarriage of cuckolded young men. Under Roman law, they had little other option.

Meanwhile, from Spain, an interesting series of canons on divorce is ascribed to the council of Elvira (near Granada) supposedly held in 306. Both the early date and the unusual focus on sex has meant that this council has caught the eye of modern scholars. But the cautions expressed above about the nature of canon law collections apply in abundance here. Our first full record of 'the canons of Elvira' comes in the seventh century *Collectio Hispana*, to which we shall return. Only the first part of the Elvira collection can be dated with any confidence to the fourth century, although not before Constantine. Two canons concern us here, Elvira 8 and 9:

8: Again women who, without any preceding cause, leave their husbands and take up with other men are not to receive communion even at the end.
9: Further, a baptized woman who leaves her *adulterous* baptized husband and marries another is forbidden to marry him; if she does she shall not receive communion until the death of her former husband unless, by chance, the pressure of illness demands that it be given.[31]

A woman who leaves her innocent husband and remarries has to be excommunicated; a woman who leaves her guilty husband and remarries is excommunicated as well, but with mitigation. The husband's adultery is therefore seen as a partial justification for the wife's decision to divorce him and remarry.

Why the focus on women, not men? Pierre Nautin has argued that the bishops of Elvira saw the case of betrayed husbands as already regulated

[30] P. Nautin, 'Le canon du concile d'Arles de 314 sur le remariage après divorce', *Recherches de Science Religieuse*, 61 (1973), 353–62. Nautin suggests a plausible emendation of the text, but it is disputed. H. Crouzel, 'A propos du concile d'Arles. Faut-il mettre "non" avant "prohibentur nubere" dans le canon 11 (ou 10) du concile d'Arles de 314 sur le remariage après divorce?', *Bulletin de littérature ecclésiastique*, 75 (1974), 25–40; repr.: Crouzel, *Mariage et divorce, célibat et caractère sacerdotaux dans l'église ancienne. Études diverses* (Turin, 1982) VII does not agree with Nautin's view, and Reynolds, *Marriage in the Western Church*, p. 182 follows him. Gaudemet writes that Nautin's suggestion would solve the problem of the inconsistency, but also that no manuscript evidence supports it. See also C. Munier, 'L'échec du mariage dans l'église ancienne', *Revue de droit canonique*, 38 (1988), 26–40, at 35; and Bagnall, *Church, State and Divorce*, p. 49.

[31] *La colección canónica Hispana. iv. Concilios galos; concilios hispanos, primera parte*, G. Martinez Diez and F. Rodriguez (eds.), Monumenta Hispaniae Sacra, 4 (Madrid, 1984), pp. 244–5; tr. S. Laeuchli, *Power and Sexuality: the Emergence of Canon Law at the Synod of Elvira* (Philadelphia, PA, 1972), p. 127; our italics.

by Matthew.[32] This is suggested by other canons of Elvira, which impose on men the duty of repudiating an adulterous wife without stating that remarriage is prohibited. Nautin goes on to suggest that the bishops were swimming against the current, in a culture where women could remarry after repudiating their adulterous husbands. Spanish Christians, in other words, read Matthew's 'adultery exception' to apply both to men and to women.[33]

We shall see below that the Elvira canons, as transmitted by the *Hispana*, exercised Hincmar's attention. In the meantime, we need to turn to the most important theatre of canon law activity in the fifth century, namely North Africa.

North Africa: Augustine and the Council of Carthage, 407 From 393 onwards, almost every year, the Catholic bishops of North Africa assembled to regulate their church. They met, initially, as a minority communion, attempting to organize in the face of the larger and more confident Donatist Church. As they started (with imperial support) to gain the upper hand over the Donatists, their ambitions extended into opining on the lives of the laity. These pronouncements, it would have amazed the assembled bishops to learn, were to form the kernel of the western canon law tradition. As we have seen, 'the African council' was central to Hincmar's understanding of the 'gospel truth' about the marriage bond.

We can identify which council, indeed which canon, Hincmar had in mind, and how it reached him. At the 407 Council of Carthage, the bishops weighed into the Latin discussion of the issues raised by Matthew:

> It is resolved that, following gospel and apostolic teaching, a husband who has been dismissed by his wife, or a wife who has been dismissed by her husband, should in neither case be joined to another person, but rather should remain as they are, or be reconciled to each other. If they reject this, they should be brought to penitence. In this case the promulgation of an imperial law should be sought.[34]

[32] P. Nautin, 'Divorce et remariage dans la tradition de l'Église latine', *Recherches de Science Religieuse*, 62 (1974), 7–54, at 19–20. Cf. the witness of the Ambrosiaster for fourth-century Rome: Reynolds, *Marriage in the Western Church*, p. 183; and in general D. G. Hunter, 'The Significance of Ambrosiaster', *Journal of Early Christian Studies*, 17 (2009), 2–26.

[33] Reynolds, *Marriage in the Western Church*, p. 181, arrives independently at the same conclusion.

[34] 'Placuit ut, secundum euangelicam et apostolicam disciplinam, neque dimissus ab uxore, neque dimissa a marito, alteri coniungantur, sed ita maneant, aut sibimet reconcilientur; quod si contempserint, ad paenitentiam redigantur. In qua causa legem imperialem petendam promulgari.' Munier, *Concilia Africae*, p. 218, tr. C. Humfress, *Orthodoxy and the Courts in Late Antiquity* (Oxford, 2007), p. 208.

This is Hincmar's 'African canon'. It was indeed regionally distinctive. Taking a harder line than either their Gallic or Hispanic colleague bishops, the African bishops determined that neither a male nor a female repudiatee could remarry.

In this decision, they were doubtless swayed by Augustine, now ten years in post as bishop of Hippo. A few years previously, in his treatise *De bono coniugale*, Augustine had insisted:

> Divine scripture recommends this [conjugal] compact, on condition that a woman cast out by her husband is not permitted to marry another for as long as her husband is alive, and a husband rejected by his wife cannot take another unless the one who has left him dies.[35]

But he had gone much further. *Pace* Matthew, Augustine had argued that neither repudiator nor repudiatee could remarry. Even if they were separated, they were actually still bound together, held by 'some sacred symbol of something more profound than this feeble mortality of ours'.[36] In 405, in a letter to Bishop Exuperius of Toulouse, which it is possible had reached North Africa, Pope Innocent I had echoed Augustine in insisting that neither party involved in a divorce could remarry.[37]

This cluster of authorities – Augustine, Innocent, and the 407 remarriage canon – are often taken as evidence to show that a 'normative' prohibition on remarriage after divorce was well established in the early fifth century.[38] This is, as we have seen, what Hincmar sought to claim. We might rather stress the hesitancy and diversity of opinion, beginning with Augustine himself. His extreme position on remarriage is, as he says himself, wishful thinking: 'But who is unaware that the laws of the pagans [*iura gentilium*] rule otherwise, for when divorce separates them, both wife and husband marry whom each wants without any guilt subject to human

[35] Augustine, *De bono coniugali* 3, ed. P. G. Walsh, Oxford Early Christian Texts (Oxford, 2001), pp. 6–7, 'cuius confederationem ita diuina scriptura commendat ut nec dimissae a uiro nubere liceat alteri quamdiu uir eius uiuit, nec dimisso ab uxore liceat alteram ducere, nisi mortua fuerit quae recessit'.

[36] Augustine, *Do bono conugali* 7, ed. Walsh, p. 16: 'Quod nequaquam puto tantum ualere potuisse, nisi alicuius rei maioris [ex] hac infirma mortalitate hominum quoddam sacramentum adhiberetur, quod deserentibus hominibus atque id dissoluere cupientibus inconcussum illis maneret ad poenam, siquidem interueniente diuortio non aboletur illa confoederatio nuptialis, ita ut sibi coniuges sint etiam separati, cum illis autem adulterium committant, quibus fuerint etiam post suum repudium copulati, uel illa uiro uel ille mulieri.'

[37] Innocent I, *Ep.* 6. 6. 12, PL 20, 500–1; ed. H. Wurm, 'Decretales selectae ex antiquissimis Romanorum Pontificum epistulis decretalibus', *Apollinaris* 12 (1939), 40–93, at 51–2.

[38] Arjava, *Women and Law in Late Antiquity*, p. 180; Crouzel, *L'Église primitive*, p. 313. Reynolds, *Marriage in the Western Church*, pp. 151–2 (see also 213 and 215). See also Saar, *Ehe – Scheidung*, p. 73.

punishment?'[39] At the 407 Council of Carthage, Augustine's colleagues tacked towards Matthew's less extreme position. They recognized that there was every likelihood that repudiatees would in fact remarry, and little they could do to prevent them. The regime of 'penitence' they recommend is by definition after the event. Only a change in imperial law – which unlike Augustine they did not attempt to call 'pagan' – would make a difference.

In the post-imperial West, however, the 407 remarriage canon was to enjoy a new career: the later copyists on whom we rely for our knowledge of the canon made a concerted attempt to lend it extra force. In pre-Carolingian collections, this canon is transmitted in three places. These are, in chronological order: the early sixth-century collection of canons of Dionysius Exiguus; the *Breviatio canonum* of Ferrandus of Carthage, working in mid sixth-century North Africa; and the seventh-century *Collectio Hispana*. Both Ferrandus and the *Hispana* compiler may have had access to Dionysius' collection – which makes it all the more interesting when they deviate from him. We shall argue that it is the latest witness, the *Hispana*, which offers what seems to be the least adulterated version. In Dionysius and Ferrandus, by contrast, we see an unfolding strategy for recasting the canon.

Dionysius worked a century or so after the 407 Council of Carthage, and on the opposite shore of the Mediterranean, in Rome. The best modern guide to his reception of North African canons remains F. L. Cross, writing in the early 1960s.[40] Cross showed how Dionysius came to include a dossier of canonical material he called the *Register of Carthage*. This was a chronologically arranged record of the councils held usually at Carthage between 393 and 419. It is probably the work of a single compiler operating in North Africa around 420, although several authors may have worked at it across the fifth century.[41] At some point the *Register* came to Rome, perhaps in the hands of a Catholic refugee from the Vandal Arian regime in North Africa. When he began his work of canon gathering, however, Dionysius did not know of it. The first edition of his collection includes only one African council, from 419. The Carthage *Register* came subsequently to his attention, and he reworked his collection so as to include it.

Dionysius was not a passive editor. To incorporate the *Register*, he inserted what is most likely a fictional scene into his record of the

[39] Augustine, *De bono coniugale* 7, tr. Walsh, p. 17.

[40] F. L. Cross, 'History and Fiction in the African Canons', *Journal of Theological Studies*, 12 (1961), 227–47.

[41] C. Munier, 'La tradition littéraire des canons africains (345–525)', *Recherches Augustiniennes*, 10 (1975), 1–22, at 16.

Council of Carthage of 419. Supposedly, at that meeting the *Register* was read out loud.[42] This imagined recitation of all previous African synods since 393 serves to lend a specious unity to African canonical activity that had, in fact, been spread across nearly two decades.[43] As he had done with the canons of the Greek councils, Dionysius numbered all 138 African canons sequentially.[44] The 407 remarriage canon becomes, accordingly, No. 102 of the canons of the Church of Carthage.

Furthermore, in his second edition, as he tells us in the preface, Dionysius supplied titles for the new canons. And here we come to an editorial crux. The title he gave to the 407 remarriage canon was anything but a neutral description. It runs: 'ABOUT THOSE MEN WHO DISMISS WIVES AND THOSE WOMEN WHO DISMISS HUSBANDS, LET THEM REMAIN AS THEY ARE.'[45] This is a monstrous gloss.[46] The body of the text, as we have seen, says nothing at all about repudiators– *only those who are repudiated*. The effect of the new title, then, is to bring the canon in line with the position advanced by Augustine and Innocent in the early fifth-century.[47]

North African Augustinians responded positively to this recasting. Between 523 and 546, Ferrandus of Carthage compiled a *Breviatio canonum*, a list of Eastern and African ecclesiastical canons.[48] The format allowed Ferrandus free rein with the 407 canon, which is itemized thus: 'That those who dismiss their wives, or those women who dismiss their husbands, cannot marry another but must either remain celibate or be reconciled'.[49] We can see at once what has happened. In the Ferrandus'

[42] Cross, 'History and Fiction', p. 235

[43] Munier, *La tradition littéraire des canons africains*, p. 16. See also *Concilia Africae a. 345 – a. 525*, ed. C. Munier, Corpus Christianorum Series Latina, 259 (Turnhout, 1974), p. 173.

[44] See Fr. Glorie, 'Dionysii Exigui Praefationes', in *Scriptores 'Illyrici' Minores*, CCSL 85 (Turnhout, 1972), 41; tr. R. Somerville and B. C. Brasington, *Prefaces to Canon Law Books in Latin Christianity Selected Translations, 500–1245* (New Haven, 1998), 48.

[45] Munier, *Concilia Africae*, p. 218. 'DE HIS QVI VXORES AVT QVAE VIROS DIMITTVNT, VT SIC MANEANT.' Our translation.

[46] And an exceptional one: we can find no comparable example in the *Register of Carthage* as transmitted in the *Dionysiana*. This suggests that the title of canon 102 was a specific intervention on this topic, not simply a function of Dionysius' editorial habit. It remains conceivable that he found the title in the *Register*; it is also conceivable that this is an innocent mistake from a copyist.

[47] Dionysius does not include Innocent's *Ep.* 6 referred to above: its first appearance in canonical collections is in the Dacheriana (c. 74).

[48] P. Landau, 'Die Breviatio canonum des Ferrandus in der Geschichte des kanonischen Rechts. Zugleich nochmals zur Benutzung der Dionysiana bei Gratian', in H. Zapp, A. Weiß, and S. Korta (eds.), *Ius canonicum in Oriente et Occidente*, Adnotationes in ius canonicum, 25 (Frankfurt am Main, 2003), pp. 297–309, at 300.

[49] Fulgentius Ferrandus' *Breviatio canonum*, item 163, Munier, *Concilia Africae*, p. 301: 'Vt hi qui uxores, aut <quae> viros, dimittunt, alteri non nubant sed aut continentes maneant aut sibi reconcilientur.' Our translation. Cresconius' *Concordia canonum*,

list, Dionysius' title has taken over from the canon itself. Ferrandus manages to shift attention away entirely from the repudiatee to the repudiator (of either gender).

Further work could be done on the relationship between the 407 canon and its title as they appear in Dionysius' collection and in Ferrandus' *Breviatio canonum.*[50] Were there contemporary circumstances which prompted his elision of the contents of the 407 canon, or was this an innocent function of Ferrandus' editorial habit? Very likely we can see here the influence of Ferrandus' mentor, Fulgentius of Ruspe.[51] An admirer of the bishop of Hippo, Fulgentius had advanced Augustine's thinking on the marriage vow, to make it every bit as strong as the vow to virginity.[52] Pursuing these questions is beyond the remit of this study.

The mutation of the 407 remarriage canon in Italy and North Africa contrasts with the mode of its reception in Spain. We may turn to the *Collectio Hispana*, redacted in several successive versions in seventh-century Visigothic Spain.[53] The *Hispana* compiler had before him Dionysius' collection, but he seems also to have had access to African material not available to Dionysius, and he presents it differently.[54] While Dionysius gives the African canons a continuous numbering, the *Hispana* divides its African material into eight sections, each ascribed to a different council, seven held in Carthage, the last in Milevis.

Hispana council 8 (of Milevis) includes as canon 17 the 407 remarriage canon. The text of the canon is to all intents and purposes as we find it in Dionysius' collection.[55] But the title is as follows: 'THAT NEITHER A

whose manuscripts often contain also Ferrandus' *Breviatio* as a kind of index, does not include any version of the remarriage canon of Carthage 407.

50 According to Munier's introduction to the edition of the *Breviatio canonum*, Ferrandus drew his material from two books of African conciliar canons: one with the councils of the whole Latin North African from 345 to 427, the other with councils of the province of Byzacena between 416 and 523. Munier, *Concilia Africae*, p. 285.

51 Cooper, *Fall of the Roman Household*, p. 176.

52 See further K. Cooper, 'Marriage, Law, and Christian Rhetoric in Vandal Africa', in J. P. Conant and Susan T. Stevens (eds.), *North Africa under Byzantium and Early Islam, ca. 500–ca. 800* (Washington, DC, 2015) pp. 237–49.

53 *La colección canónica Hispana. iii. Concilios griegos y africanos*, G. Martinez Diez and F. Rodriguez (eds.), Monumenta Hispaniae Sacra, 3 (Madrid, 1982), pp. 281–454. A description of the African material in the *Collectio Hispana* is provided in *La colección canónica Hispana. i. Estudio*, G. Martinez Diez (ed.), Monumenta Hispaniae Sacra, serie canónica, 1 (Madrid, 1966), pp. 287–8.

54 L. Fowler-Magerl, *Clavis canonum: Selected Canon Law Collections Before 1140. Access with Data Processing*, MGH, Hilfsmittel, 21 (Hanover, 2005), p. 39. The *Hispana councils 1* and 2, ascribed to fourth-century Carthaginian synods, are not present in any other extant canonical collection. Munier, *Concilia Africae*, pp. XIX–XX. See also H. Hess, *The Early Development of Canon Law and the Council of Serdica* (Oxford, 2002), p. 52.

55 Munier, *Concilia Africae*, p. 366: 'Placuit quoque secundum euangelicam et apostolicam disciplinam, ut neque dimissus ab uxore, neque dimissa a marito, alteri coniungantur,

DISMISSED MAN NOR A DISMISSED WOMAN BE JOINED TO ANOTHER'.[56] While Dionysius' title effectively rewrites the canon, that in the *Hispana* accurately summarizes it, keeping the focus on repudiatees. This is not the only instance where the titles given to African canons in the Hispana are more in line with their content than the Dionysian titles.[57] Whether this reflects a more sober editorial style, or particular circumstances in Visigothic Spain is, again, beyond the reach of this study.

At this point, a summary may be in order. Christian tradition was divided on spouse repudiation and remarriage. Matthew's *dicta* left several questions unanswered, which successive teachers, councils, and canonists sought to answer in different ways.

Text	Repudiation allowed?		Repudiator may remarry?		Repudiatee may remarry?	
	Men	Women	Men	Women	Men	Women
Matthew	Yes		Yes			No (?)
Arles	Yes		No			
Elvira		Yes	No			
Augustine	Yes	Yes	No	No	No	No
Innocent	Yes	Yes	No	No	No	No
Carthage 407	Yes	Yes			No	No
Dionysian title	Yes	Yes	No	No		
Ferrandus	Yes	Yes	No	No		
Hispana	Yes	Yes			No	No

What the table shows in particular is the eccentricity of Augustine, and of Innocent I in refusing remarriage under any circumstances. They did not represent 'the norm'; even in his own backyard, Augustine's position did not carry all before it.[58] It was only a century or so after his death that the canon law of the African Church was retrospectively brought into line with his teachings – and then not everywhere. Before the eighth century, in our

sed ita maneant, aut sibimet reconcilientur; quod si contempserint, ad paenitentiam redigantur. In qua causa legem imperialem petendam promulgari.' It is not of course impossible that there were two Councils.

[56] Munier, *Concilia Africae*, p. 366: 'VT NEQUE DIMISSUS NEQVE DIMISSA ALTERI CONIVNGANTVR', Our translation.

[57] On *Hispana council 3*, Munier writes 'Sed tituli Hispanici multo pressius medullam canonum, quam tituli collectioni Remensis et ipsius Dionysii syllogarum, exprimunt'; Munier, *Concilia Africae*, pp. 326–7.

[58] See further C. Leyser, 'Augustine in the Latin West, 430-c. 900', in Mark Vessey (ed.), *A Companion to Augustine*, Blackwell Companions to the Ancient World (Oxford, 2012), pp. 450–64.

surviving manuscripts, the 407 remarriage canon appears nowhere else but the three places we have discussed: Dionysius' collection, Ferrandus' *Breviatio Canonum* and the *Collectio Hispana.*[59] All of this was to change under the Carolingians – but as we shall see, even Hincmar was not able to erase the tentative and incoherent character of the canonical tradition.

The Carolingian moment

The Carolingian Empire was a new world for bishops. In the late Roman period, bishops were, for the most part, creatures dependent on the State; in eighth-century Francia, by contrast, they were king-makers (ritually at least, through the ceremony of anointing); and they were acknowledged experts in the law. Whereas in the Roman Empire, episcopal courts and church councils were sideshows, now royal assemblies took their cue from ecclesiastical protocol. The king met with his notables to issue decrees (capitularies) for implementation across the realm.

Marriage was at the heart of the Carolingian vision of the social order.[60] It could hardly be otherwise, given that their rule depended on a constant reiteration that they, the royal family, were the sole legitimate kings of the Franks.[61] Carolingian moral literature gave to the married couple a central role in social formation: the family was the place where the values of *fides* and *castitas* had to be passed on to the next generation.[62] In this context, dissolving the bond of marriage was unthinkable: the Augustinian position on divorce and remarriage became a cornerstone of the Carolingian reforms.[63] Consensual divorce, the legitimacy of which went without saying in Roman law until the sixth century, was no longer on the table – unless the couple mutually decided upon a life of sexual

[59] The canon is present in a late branch (around 830) of the *Collectio Vetus Gallica*, which otherwise does not contain it: H. Mordek, *Kirchenrecht und Reform im Frankenreich. Die* collectio Vetus Gallica, *die älteste systematische Kanonensammlung des Fränkischen Gallien. Studien und Edition, Beiträge zur Geschichte und Quellenkunde des Mittelalters*, 1 (Berlin and New York, 1975), p. 561.

[60] P. Toubert, 'La théorie du mariage chez les moralistes Carolingiens', in *Il matrimonio nella società altomedievale*, Settimane di studio del CISAM (Spoleto, 1977), pp. 233–86 603–30, at 256–67. See now S. Joye, 'Family Order and Kingship according to Hincmar', in R. Stone and C. West (eds.), *Hincmar of Rheims: Life and Works* (Manchester, 2015) pp. 190–210.

[61] See S. Airlie, '*Semper fideles*? Loyauté envers les Carolingiens comme constituant de l'identité aristocratique', in R. Le Jan (ed.), *La royauté et les élites dans l'Europe carolingienne* (Lille, 1998), pp. 129–43; C. Leyser, 'From Maternal Kin to Jesus as Mother: Royal Genealogy and Marian Devotion in the Ninth-Century West', in C. Leyser and L. Smith (eds.), *Motherhood, Religion, and Society in Medieval Europe, 400–1400* (Farnham, 2011), pp. 21–39.

[62] K. Heene, *The Legacy of Paradise: Marriage, Motherhood and Woman in Carolingian Edifying Literature* (Frankfurt, 1997).

[63] Reynolds, *Marriage in the Western Church*, p. 215.

continence. We are in a new era, where those seeking to move from one spouse to another now had to argue that their first union was invalid.

This radical programme was implemented in the name of tradition. At the centre of the Carolingian project was a notion of *correctio* – setting to right. 'Correction' was an active process in which Carolingian intellectuals decided what tradition ought to be, and proceeded from there. They had no compunction about leaving material on the cutting room floor, or about forging it outright.[64]

All of this sets a context for Lothar, Teutberga, and Hincmar's *De divortio*. The case and the treatise arose after some three generations of high-level, highly learned discussion of the conjugal bond. That said, we should not mistake their elite culture for ours: this was a world in which trial by ordeal was readily available as a procedure for the arbitration of disputes, and in which rational men discussing marriage had reason to fear the operation of love magic.[65]

1 *Marriage and remarriage*

We may resume the story of the Carthage 407 remarriage canon, to track its assimilation into Carolingian canonical collections. In 774, Charlemagne conquered the Lombard kingdom of Italy. According to historiographical tradition, this was the occasion for the presentation to him by Pope Hadrian I of a new version of the collections of Dionysius, the so-called Dionysio-Hadriana. As Abigail Firey has shown, this is a tidy myth of origins concealing a more complex process of ongoing 'correction' of what Dionysius had done. Broadly stated, Dionysius' second edition was reworked; his collection of papal decretals was added to it, and a series of new decretals tacked onto the end.[66] We see that the Carthaginian canon has been retained, with a new numeration, but with the title that Dionysius had given it.[67]

[64] For an overview and further references, see C. Leyser, 'Late Antiquity in the Medieval West', in P. Rousseau (ed.), *A Companion to Late Antiquity*, Blackwell Companions to the Ancient World (Oxford, 2009), pp. 29–42.

[65] On the ordeal, see R. Bartlett, *Trial by Fire and Water: the Medieval Judicial Ordeal* (Oxford, 1986), and further this chapter, p. 174. On love magic, see Hincmar. *De divortio*, Resp. 15–17, pp. 205–15, and more broadly, C. Rider, *Magic and Impotence in the Middle Ages* (Oxford, 2006).

[66] A. Firey, 'Mutating Monsters: Approaches to "Living Texts" of the Carolingian Era', *Digital Proceedings of the Lawrence J. Schoenberg Symposium on Manuscript Studies in the Digital Age*, 2 (2010), 1–14.

[67] The Dionysio-Hadriana compilers unpicked Dionysius' assimilation of all the African material into one sequence. They numbered the 33 decrees of Carthage 419 separately from the canons of the *Register of Carthage*. Hence our canon, numbered 102 in Dionysius' collection, becomes canon 69 in the Dionysio-Hadriana. This is important, as it allows us to identify Hincmar's source for this canon: see this chapter, pp. 176–7.

The next stage was the reception of the remarriage canon in lay law. This we can date with confidence to 789. Charlemagne's annual assembly of that year resulted in the issuing of a monumental capitulary, the so-called *Admonitio generalis*. This collection of 82 measures for the moral and educational improvement of the kingdom drew heavily upon canon law, possibly from the Dionysio-Hadriana.[68]

To all people. Again in the same [council of Carthage], that neither a wife dismissed by her husband can take another man while her husband is alive, nor the husband can take another [wife] while the previous wife is alive.[69]

This is a new, 'corrected' wording. Carthage 407, as we have seen, considers repudiatees; Dionysius sought to shift the focus on repudiators. Here the focus is, it seems, on a couple: the husband repudiates the wife, for reasons unspecified. She cannot remarry, but neither can he. Repudiation, then, is permitted, but not remarriage.[70]

This rewording became standard.[71] It appears also in Charlemagne's *Capitulare missorum* of 802, and in later capitularies.[72] Episcopal synods decreed that it was prohibited to remarry after repudiating an adulterous partner.[73] Individual churchmen, such as Theodulf of Orleans, likewise moved to rule out remarriage after divorce.[74] At the end of the Carolingian period, when Regino of Prüm compiled his *De synodalibus causis*, the last great canonical collection of the Carolingian period, he included the 407 canon in both its original wording (without the Dionysian title) and in the reworded form of the *Admonitio generalis*.[75]

[68] Firey, 'Mutating Monsters' again sounds a sceptical note here.

[69] "Omnibus. Item in eodem [concilio Cartaginense], ut nec uxor a viro dimissa alium accipiat virum vivente virum suo, nec vir aliam accipiat vivente uxore priore". *Capitularia regum Francorum*, ed. A. Boretius, MGH Capit., I (Hannover and Leipzig, 1883), p. 56, l. 36–7.

[70] Reynolds mentions this episode in the Carolingian reception of canon 102, but he does not draw attention to the effects of the change in the wording: Reynolds, *Marriage in the Western Church*, p. 215.

[71] *Capitularia regum Francorum*, p. 103, ll. 10–11.

[72] In Ansegis' work, 827: *Die Kapitulariensammlung des Ansegis*, ed. G. Schmitz, MGH Capit., I (Hannover, 1996), p. 456, ll. 12–14. And in the *Collectio capitularium* of Benedict Levita: *Tomi primi supplementa. 2: Capitularia spuria, canones ecclesiastici, bullae pontificum*, ed. G. H. Pertz, MGH Leges, II,2 (Hannover, 1837), Bk 1, cap. 79; p. 50.

[73] The council of Cividale of 796/7 provided an 'authorized' interpretation to the problematic passages of Matthew's Gospel: *Concilia aevi Karolini*, ed. A. Werminghoff, MGH Conc. II,2 (Hannover and Leipzig, 1908), p. 207. Ca. 2 of the council of Paris, 829: Werminghoff, *Concilia aevi Karolini, 2*, pp. 670–1.

[74] Reynolds, *Marriage in the Western Church*, p. 215. However, Theodulf's text (*Capitularia II*) did not have a great diffusion in the ninth century: *Capitula episcoporum*, 2, ed. R. Pokorny and M. Stratmann, MGH Capitula Episcoporum II (Hannover, 1995), pp. 145, 162–3.

[75] W. Hartmann, *Das Sendhandbuch des Regino von Prüm*, Ausgewählte Quellen zur Deutschen Geschichte des Mittelalters Freiherr-vom-Stein-Gedächtnisausgabe, 42 (Darmstadt, 2004), p. 300, canons 103 and 105.

Here, as elsewhere, there is a relentless quality to Carolingian moralizing.

We might update the table as follows:

Text	Repudiation?		Repudiator may remarry?		Repudiatee may remarry?	
	Men	Women	Men	Women	Men	Women
D-Hadriana	Yes	Yes			No	No
Admonitio	Yes	Yes	No			No
Cividale 797	Yes	Yes	No	No	No	No
Theodulf	Yes	Yes	No	No	No	No
Paris 829	Yes	Yes	No	No	No	No

On this basis, historians of marriage can say that the Augustinian position forbidding any remarriage after divorce was well established in the Carolingian empire.[76] For contemporaries, however, this raised as many questions as it solved: were there really no exceptions? What, in particular, were the rules of the game with regard to annulment? Opinions differed. Hincmar can be found in 860 brokering the invalidation of an unconsummated union;[77] on the other hand, some of his colleagues, as the Lothar-Teutberga case went on, were prepared to argue that marrying even after an annulment was not permitted.[78] The king's Great Matter was an opportunity for specialists to work at the frontiers of legal science, although the stakes were alarmingly high.

2 *Hincmar's* De divortio

We may now return to the scene of deliberations in 860. Lothar had a plan, but it was not working. Fashionably learned as his advisers were, they had counselled that it would be difficult to make the case for remarriage after a divorce. What Lothar needed was to demonstrate that his marriage had never been valid. Accordingly, Teutberga was accused of having been sodomized by her brother, and of aborting the pregnancy that

[76] J. Imbert, 'Indissolubilité du mariage a l'époque carolingienne', *Revue de Droit Canonique*, 38 (1988), 41–56, at 44.

[77] Cf. Hincmar's solution in a parallel case: R. Bof, 'Raymund's Daughter's Divorce in the 9th Century: a Woman's Textual Role in the Breaking of an Alliance', in C. Salvaterra and B. Waaldijk (eds.), *Paths to Gender: European Historical Perspectives on Women and Men*, CLIOHRES Transversal themes (Pisa, 2009), pp. 195–207.

[78] Evidence that this idea – *ex post facto* sanctioned unfitness to marriage due to pre-marital sins – was not universally accepted amongst Frankish clergy is provided by the extremely interesting *Gutachten einiger Bischöfe* of 862: W. Hartmann, *Konzilien der Karolingischen Teilreiche 860–874*, pp. 78–86, esp. p. 84.

had followed this: the incestuous pollution would have made her unfit to serve as a bride, vitiating her subsequent union with Lothar. To repudiate Teutberga was to be rid of a counterfeit wife, so the royal argument went, and to be free to marry properly for the first time.

For several years now, and in several different ways, Lothar had sought to establish Teutberga's guilt. Most inconveniently for the king, in 858 she had been vindicated in a trial by ordeal. Her champion had been unharmed by boiling water. How could this be? Perhaps the queen had secretly confessed before her champion undertook the trial. No longer in bad faith, at least before God, she had been able to come through. Or again, maybe she had managed to hold in her mind someone else with the same name as her brother, but with whom she had not shared her bed.[79] The 860 Aachen synods were designed to expose Teutberga's subterfuges. She was found guilty, both of incest and of cheating the ordeal process, and dispatched to a convent.

Many of those present had their doubts about all this. They reached out twice to Hincmar, sending first a list of eight questions, and then, months later, a further seven. Hincmar is unlikely to have welcomed the attention, or to have been surprised by it. He had been under pressure to attend the 860 synods, or least to send a proxy, and had gone to the trouble of putting on record his reasons for not doing so.[80] Now he was going to have to go on record again.

Hincmar's treatise *De divortio* is a massive compendium, 161 pages in the superb edition of Letha Böhringer. The one surviving manuscript (Par. Lat. 2866) is a work in progress. It presents a copy of Hincmar's responses to the first set of eight questions (which became fifteen in his replies) followed by his second set of seven responses, and then a series of additional notes and revisions. The manuscript is part of a network of texts, including a record of the proceedings of the Aachen councils (transcribed in the *De divortio*); a further Rheims manuscript (dated to 870) transmits what are effectively Hincmar's notes towards the composition of his treatise (Par. Lat. 12445, also edited by Böhringer, an *Arbeitshandschrift*).[81] The *De divortio* is a witness to the discussions of Hincmar and his episcopal colleagues, held at the very centre of political affairs.

It must be said that these discussions are hard to follow.[82] Modern readers in search of the 'argument' in *De divortio* continue to scratch their

[79] Hincmar, *De divortio*, Resp 7–9, pp. 161–7.
[80] Hincmar, *De divortio*, Resp 3c, p. 130.
[81] L. Böhringer, 'Der eherecthliche Traktat im Paris. Lat. 12445, einer Arbeitshandschrift Hinkmars von Reims', *Deutsches Archiv für Erforschung des Mittelalters*, 46 (1990), 18–47.
[82] Airlie, 'Private Bodies', pp. 13–14. Böhringer, "Gewaltverzicht", p. 286, n. 110. K. Heidecker, *The Divorce of Lothar II: Christian Marriage and Political Power in the*

heads. On the one hand, Hincmar agreed that Lothar could remarry if the king's wife had in fact been found guilty of pre-marital incest. On the other, he had his doubts about the grounds on which the Aachen synods had overturned the verdict of the ordeal. A secret confession could not be set up against a public process like the ordeal.[83] Why was the matter being revisited at all?[84] What he actually thought of Teutberga remains unclear – but seeking to extract clarity from Hincmar may be to ask the wrong question. We might suggest that, politically, his main goal was to avoid tipping his hand: in early 860, it was not yet clear who was going to find vindication in the prolonged ordeal that was the whole affair. Hincmar's priority, then, was to demonstrate expertise, not to burn bridges, and to wait.

We will focus our attention on one question and answer, the fifth in the first series of responses. This is the point at which the treatise starts to move forward. The first three questions and answers set up Hincmar's understanding of what happened at Aachen. The fourth question concerns marriage: on what terms it should be entered into and sustained. Hincmar clears his throat here, by discharging some Augustinian maxims about the good of marriage, highly familiar to a literate contemporary audience.

Next Hincmar turns to face what, as we have seen, was a question with a long history.

> [And tell us] how or for what causes marriages can be separated once they have been entered into, and without which causes they must not be separated. And after a separation, whether the man or woman, whichever one is still alive, can hope for another union; and whether, sinning within marriage, they should each be judged by the same judgement.[85]

The substance of Hincmar's answer can be quickly summarized: remarriage is not allowed to either partner until the other partner is dead, for whatever reason they separated. But such a summary misses the point. As just seen, Lothar was not seeking a divorce or even a separation, but an

Carolingian World, tr. T. M. Guest, Conjunctions of Religion and Power in the Medieval Past (Ithaca, NY and London, 2010), p. 82.

83 Hincmar, *De divortio*, Resp 11, pp. 174–6. This key aspect of the case has attracted much fruitful attention. See in particular, A. Firey, *A Contrite Heart: Prosecution and Redemption in the Carolingian Empire* (Leiden, 2009); and J. van Doren, 'The Divorce of Lothar II (860), and the Resignation of Eboo of Rheims (835) compared', unpublished paper.

84 Hincmar, *De divortio*, Resp 6, p. 160.

85 Hincmar, *De divortio*, Interr. 5, p. 135: 'Qualiter vel pro quibus rebus secundum auctoritatem inita coniugia separari valeant et sine quibus separari non debeant, et si post disiunctionem vir aut femina uterque vivens ad aliam debeat copulam adspirare vel si pari iudicio quiscumque eorum in coniugio peccans debeat iudicari.'

invalidation of his union with Teutberga. In that sense, this question and the answer represent a knowingly irrelevant set piece.

Furthermore, we should note that Hincmar's apparently hard-line position on remarriage here was spliced with a repeated affirmation that bishops were not seeking to claim a monopoly of jurisdiction over marriage. At the mid-point of his reply, Hincmar tells the decades-old story of Northildis, a woman who, in 822, had petitioned Lothar's father Louis about the (unspecified) way her husband was treating her. Louis had turned the case over to the bishops; they in turn had judged it to be a matter for Louis and the lay nobility, and had sent it back without opining. Hincmar reports that the nobles were delighted by the 'discretion' shown by the bishops. This case, like that of Northildis, should be decided by the married laity.[86] Not unlike his late Roman counterparts, Hincmar' is aiming here at conflict management not doctrinal certainty.

We may turn now to the internal mechanics of Hincmar's argument in this response. To this he had given no little thought. Sections of the text of Responses Four and Five are to be found all but verbatim in the Rheims *Arbeitshandschrift*.[87] Doubtless summoning research assistance, Hincmar had not wanted to leave anything to chance in his summation of the tradition on remarriage: even throat-clearing needed rehearsal.

He opens Response Five with Augustine on Luke to assert the indissolubility of marriage even in the face of adultery; and Augustine again on the fidelity of Joseph who remained married to Mary, despite not being the father of her child.[88] Then follows a series of three canons: one from the Council of Ancyra, the remarriage canon from the 407 Council of Carthage, and Elvira 9. The Carthage canon is quoted as follows:

> And about their separation in the Council of Africa, chapter 69, it is written: 'It pleased us, that according to the Gospel and Apostolic discipline, neither a husband left by his wife nor a wife by her husband may be joined to another, but let them remain thus or be reconciled. And if they ignore this, let them be brought to repentance.'[89]

We can see at once that Hincmar here uses the same numeration as the Dionysio-Hadriana text, rather than Dionysius (because the canon is

[86] Hincmar, *De divortio*, Resp 5, p. 141.
[87] See Böhringer, 'Der eherecthliche Traktat im Paris. Lat. 12445'.
[88] Hincmar, *De divortio*, Resp 5, p. 135, citing Augustine, *Contra Iulianum* V. 12. 47f.
[89] Hincmar, *De divortio*, Resp. 5, p. 136: 'Et de eorum separatione in concilio Africano capitulo LXVIIII ita scriptum habetur: Placuit, ut secundum evangelicam et apostolicam disciplinam neque dimissus ab uxore neque dimissa a marito alteri coniungantur, sed ita maneant aut sibimet reconcilientur; quod si contempserint, ad poenitentiam redigantur.'

numbered 69 not 102),[90] but that he has excised the title, and the clause about imperial law, a point to which we return below.

He continues with Elvira 9, which, we may remember, punishes the remarriage of the woman who repudiates her adulterous husband.[91] To cover the case of the husband who divorces his adulterous wife, Hincmar uses his first decretal source, the letter written by Pope Innocent, which we met above.[92] A text by Ambrose follows, stating more explicitly that men and women are bound by the same law.

Hincmar moves next onto procedural issues, concerning the punishment of adultery: two conciliar canons provide the relevant authority (Agde 25 and Elvira 8). The central section of Response Five is dedicated to the ideal consonance of ecclesiastical norms and secular procedures of judgement. It is here that he inserts the story of Northildis at the court of Louis the Pious.[93]

Next, Hincmar resumes the massing of authorities behind the blanket prohibition of remarriage after repudiation, turning now to Augustine and Jerome.[94] He concludes with the appeal to evangelical truth from which we quoted at the outset.[95] And then, in peroration, Hincmar continues with a quotation of Paul, the first direct quotation from the New Testament on the topic of remarriage in this Response:

> Whence, if the precept was not the Lord's and so evident, so that even Paul . . . did not dare to change anything at all of it, saying 'Concerning the wife: it is not I but the Lord who commands the wife not to leave her husband, and that if she leaves, she must remain unmarried or be reconciled to her husband', or if there was such a passage in the Scripture, that authors would understand it differently, though not contrary to faith, then we would follow the decision of many and of the greatest authority, as we have it in the canons.[96]

Canons and Scripture are in harmony, Hincmar stresses, because both prohibit remarriage after repudiation.

Hincmar's summa at once affirms the solidity of tradition, and betrays its fragility. The problem was the same as that faced by late and post-Roman churchmen and canonists. The Gospel texts were vague, the synodal decrees reticent: both needed reinforcement from the more trenchant decretal or paranetic tradition. Three facets of Hincmar's *correctio*

[90] And the not Dacheriana, where the canon is numbered 75, although some copies (e.g. Cologne 122) note the Dionysio-Hadriana numeration. The spectrum of numeration possibilities is most easily established by a search for the canon on the Carolingian Canon Law database, at http://ccl.rch.uky.edu.

[91] Hincmar, *De divortio*, p. 136, ll. 9–12. [92] Hincmar, *De divortio*, p. 136, ll. 16–25.

[93] Hincmar, *De divortio*, p. 137, l.17 – p. 142, l. 6.

[94] Hincmar, *De divortio*, p. 142, l. 7 – 143, l. 24.

[95] Hincmar, *De divortio*, p. 143, ll. 8–11. [96] Hincmar, *De divortio*, p. 143, ll. 11–17.

of tradition bear emphasis here. First, he avoids a direct encounter with Matthew's adultery exception. Hincmar never quotes in full and directly either Mt 5: 27–32 or Mt 19: 3–9, the passages introducing the wife's *fornicatio* as a justification for divorce. Matthew features only indirectly, in two passages drawn from Augustine and Jerome, where the ambiguities of the Gospel have already been 'handled'.[97]

Second, the authority of Elvira is muzzled. Canons 8 and 9, it will be recalled, treat repudiation without any justification, and repudiation in the case of adultery. Both opened up juridical possibilities Hincmar sought to close down. If used in sequence, they might convey the impression that divorce was common: Hincmar's tactic was to keep the decrees firmly apart. Canon 8 is therefore used where Hincmar is generically discussing the causes of the repudiation which have to be brought before a judge. Canon 9 appears as the crucial authority in the section on indissolubility of marriage; it is also supplemented, as seen, with the decretal of Innocent, which makes indissolubility apply to both genders.

Third, there is Hincmar's treatment of 'the African Council' 407 remarriage canon. While accorded pride of place in Hincmar's peroration on 'gospel truth', its contents were less than fully edifying for Hincmar's purposes, in leaving open the possibility that repudiators might remarry. Here Hincmar takes an unexpected turn: he makes the problem worse. The retitling of the canon by Dionysius, retained in the Dionysio-Hadriana, might have allowed Hincmar to gloss the canon differently. He could, with Ferrandus, have obliterated the canon behind the title to focus purely on repudiators. Instead the title is omitted, as is the final clause about seeking an imperial law if the couple refuse to reconcile. Hincmar kept both the repudiator and the ruler out of the picture. In the context of 860, when the repudiator and the ruler were the same person, this was perhaps a prudent choice. The drift of the Response overall is not to leave room for doubt – no remarriage after repudiation – but presented with the chance to close the door here, Hincmar leaves it ajar.

'Here's what we all agree on' is the overall tone of Response Five of *De Divortio*. It is a classic move in any complex negotiating situation. Hincmar's only problem was that the tradition itself contained many different layers. More could be said about other synods, and about the use of patristic authorities, in this section of the treatise alone.[98] For now it may be asked, if the conciliar record was so complicated, why not do

[97] Hincmar, *De divortio*, pp. 142–3.

[98] For example, 'the Ambrosiaster', seen to be Ambrose in the ninth century, who explicitly supports a double standard approach to divorce: the husband can divorce his adulterous wife and remarry, while the wife can only dismiss her adulterous husband, without the possibility of remarriage. This posed a problem for Carolingian supporters of the

without it altogether? Here also, Hincmar's circumstances may have constrained him. Across the arc of the whole treatise, he needed to argue that public assembles of bishops and notables were the right venue for the adjudication of these issues. Unverifiable records of secret confessions of the sort that Lothar was attempting to deploy were not fit for purpose. Drawing himself up, Hincmar will have no part of this.

And being only a tiny little man, I do not dare to produce a definitive judgment or to join a consensus in a matter which is so great, involving such eminent persons, in which so much has been done by such important people, and about which so important and so many people have been consulted, in the absence of large-scale meeting, consultation and consensus, and before I have gone through the authorities of the Scriptures and the decrees of the Fathers.

'Transparency' is not quite a word in Hincmar's lexicon, but a commitment to it undergirds his treatise. He comes back, here and elsewhere, to this:

I think it appropriate to write the words of the great Leo to Rusticus Bishop of Narbonne: In matters, he said, which were doubtful or obscure, we thought it best to pursue whatever was neither contrary to the Gospel precepts nor to the decrees of the Holy Fathers.[99]

Given that Gospel precept and the decrees of the Holy Fathers were themselves doubtful and obscure, this left Hincmar with a remarkably free hand.

Conclusion

Universally acknowledged truths tend to accrue around men, in possession of a good fortune, who go in search of wives, or of second wives. Jane Austen reminds us that producing these truths requires room to manoeuvre, equivocation, even ironic distance. Dogma does not help. Certainly 'the Christianization of marriage' does not well describe developments in the Latin West from the fifth to the ninth centuries. There was no homogenous 'Church' in this period, institutionally or doctrinally; 'Christian tradition' was far less coherent, and more malleable than the standard account would suggest.

This may have posed a rhetorical challenge to canonists or bishops seeking clarity – but it was not in the last resort a deficiency. Traditions are

Augustinian position, among them Hincmar: see *Konzilien der karolingischen Teilreiche 860–874*, ed. W. Hartmann, MGH Conc. IV (Hannover, 1998), p. 79, ll. 34; L. Böhringer, 'Das Recht im Dienst der Machtpolitik? Anmerkungen zu einer Neuerscheinung über die Scheidungsaffäre König Lothars II', *Mitteilungen des Instituts für Österreichische Geschichtsforschung*, 119 (2011), 146–54, at 151.

[99] Hincmar, *De divortio*, Resp 3, p. 131.

supposed to be malleable; it is a sign of their depth and durability. The function of tradition so conceived is to make consensus possible, and to allow participants in the tradition to adapt or even to anticipate changing circumstance; in short to keep the peace.

Marriage, likewise, was a mechanism for *societas* as Augustine said.[100] But it could, of course, generate conflict, in which case those arbitrating had difficult choices to make. If we had to sum up 'the western Church on divorce' in this period, we would have to say that keeping the peace was more important to churchmen than asserting the sacrality of the marriage bond. In the case of Lothar, the Church did not split, none of the women or the advisers were beheaded. Hincmar, as has been observed, was no Thomas More, but he did a better job than Cardinal Wolsey as a maker and sustainer of social order.[101] Certainly the story ends better for him than it did for Wolsey.

[100] See Augustine to Ecdicia, *Ep* 262, as quoted in the Introduction, above p. 12.
[101] Böhringer, 'Gewaltverzicht, Gesichtswahrung und Befriedung durch Öffentlichkeit', p. 287.

8 The memory of Gregory the Great and the making of Latin Europe, 600–1000

Conrad Leyser

The exercise of power in the post-Roman West presents a paradox. As has long been remarked, successor states in the western provinces were weak, economically and in terms of infrastructure – but they were large in terms of territory. The kingdoms of the Visigoths, the Lombards, and the Franks covered huge areas. In part, it has been argued, there was an inversely proportional relationship between their breadth and their shallowness. And what they lacked in material resources, they made up for with ideological capital. These thin sheets of authority were held together by the memory of the expanse of Roman authority, as mediated in particular by the Church.[1] The 'ascent of Latin Europe' owes as much to ecclesiastical narrative bravura as it does to conquest of land or subjugation of the peasantry.[2]

Pope Gregory I (d. 604) is a test case for this view of the power of cultural memory to enable political authority. His reputation as a maker of early medieval societies rests on a well-known *coup de théâtre*: the decision to send monks to convert the new inhabitants of Roman Britain. Here, if ever, is a legend of power at a distance.[3]

Our focus in this essay is on the less spectacular, but apparently more solid, evidence of Gregory's *Register*. His surviving correspondence comprises over 800 letters, the most extensive documentary record of any

[1] P. Fouracre, 'Cultural Conformity and Social Conservatism in Early Medieval Europe', *History Workshop Journal*, 33 (1992), 152–61. This chapter is intended as a companion piece to my study cited at Note 49. Earlier versions were delivered to and improved by audiences in Princeton, Oxford, Sheffield, and Zurich. It was completed in the genial setting of the Seminar für mittelalterliche Geschichte at the University of Tübingen: my thanks to Steffen Patzold and his colleagues there. My thanks also to Lucia Castaldi, Kate Cooper, Bernard Gowers, Annette Grabowski, Bruno Judic, Rudolf Pokorny, Helmut Reimitz, Roger Reynolds, Herbert Schneider, and Charles West for their collegiality and correction.

[2] Cf. K. J. Leyser 'The Ascent of Latin Europe', in *id.*, *Communications and Power in the Early Middle Ages*, 2 vols., ed. T. Reuter (London, 1994), I, pp. 215–32.

[3] For the mission and its later memory, see H. Mayr-Harting, 'Two Conversions to Christianity: the Bulgarians and the Anglo-Saxons', The Stenton Lecture 1993 (Reading, 1994).

figure in the early Middle Ages, spanning the length and breadth of Europe and the Mediterranean. Early medieval readers saw here the outlines of Latin Christendom taking shape, and modern scholars, in their gratitude for such a rich early medieval archive, have tended to follow suit. One should beware, however. We do not have the original *Register*: what we have is a sample, selected by later enthusiasts for their own needs and purposes. Put at its strongest, the Latin Christendom of Gregory's *Register* is a product not of sixth-century papal administration, but of Carolingian and post-Carolingian memory and myth-making.[4]

The retrospective construction of Pope Gregory as founder of Christendom was a long-drawn out process, with two, perhaps three phases.[5] In the first, up to the mid ninth century, Gregory was conscripted to support an aggressive regnal, and then an imperial church. His texts were excerpted, reset, and used to develop a range of institutions – in particular the monastery and the episcopacy. These were fundamental to the construction of the Carolingian Empire.

Charlemagne's Empire and Gregory's Europe were to diverge, however. In what we might see as 'Phase Two', Rome took back the memory of Gregory from Frankish courts: in the 870s, a Roman biographer dubbed him 'Great', to rival the greatness of Charles.[6] Finally, in the third phase, after the splintering of Carolingian rule, the memory of Gregory acquired its own momentum. The forced emancipation from empire threw churchmen back on their own cultural resources. It became not only possible, but even necessary to draw on Gregory as a survivor of imperial collapse. He became an icon of ecclesiastical autonomy – a means to articulate a Christian Europe without the awning of an emperor's power.

Gregory's Europe

Gregory himself had no blueprint for Latin Christendom. His own landscape was that of ancient imperial Christianity. As Robert Markus emphasized several decades ago, seen in its 'proper context', Gregory's

[4] Cf. B. Judic, 'Le registre des lettres de Grégoire le Grand: une création carolingienne?' in J. Desmulliez, C. Hoët-Van-Cauwenberghe, J. Jolivet (eds.), *L'étude des correspondances dans le monde romain de l'Antiquité classique à l'Antiquité tardive: permanences et mutations* (Villeneuve d'Ascq, 2010), pp. 1–21.

[5] Blazing a trail here is B. Judic, '"*totius Europae speculator*": la fondation d'une culture médiéval europèene et la construction d'une auctoritas: la postérité de Grégoire le Grand dans la haut moyen âge latin', unpublished thesis, 2 vols., Université Lille (1999).

[6] John the Deacon, *Vita Gregorii* IV. 63, PL 75, 213C. On titular 'greatness', see P. Lehmann, 'Mittelalterliche Beinahmen und Ehrentitel', *Historisches Jahrbuch*, 49 (1929), 215–39.

Europe was 'in every way closer to the Europe of Justinian than that of Charlemagne'.[7] Furthermore, as I have argued elsewhere, Gregory did not expect any future: his most solid conviction was that the world was about to end.[8] He was thus at once a highly conventional Roman aristocrat, and a radical eschatological prophet. He either accepted the status quo, or he did without it altogether: institution building for the future did not occur to him as a relevant goal.

By birth, Gregory was a privileged Roman aristocratic insider, and his career followed a well-worn pattern.[9] He moved from secular to ecclesiastical administration, from Rome to Constantinople and back again. When in 590 Pope Pelagius II died of the plague, Gregory was the obvious choice to succeed him. What made him unusual was his profession as a monk, the first indeed to occupy the throne of St Peter. This rogue element in his *curriculum vitae* notwithstanding, Gregory was inclined to think of the Church in wholly traditional terms. The Emperor was thus his master, even if he, Gregory, was *de facto* ruler in Rome. He may have sent missionaries to Britain and cultivated links with Frankish or Lombard kings, but Gregory did not for a moment see himself as looking to establish the papacy as an autonomous power leading a confederation of Christian barbarian peoples.

Gregory's insensitivity to Latin Christendom as an entity was not a failure of the imagination: far from it. He was more than capable of envisioning a different order to the one in which he lived. He thought, in fact, on a cosmic scale. His own most certain belief was that the end of the world was at hand. Everywhere, he saw signs of the looming cataclysm. Storms came out of the blue in summer; a sinner's corpse burst from its resting place, summoned as it were early to Judgement. In the visions of dying teenagers, as in the celebration of the Mass, the nearness of the Apocalypse was palpable and eerie to Gregory, like the light at sunrise.[10] As a preacher of the Last Days, Gregory styled himself after the Old Testament prophets – in particular Ezekiel – whose task it was to announce to the people their sins. Above all he took as his model the Apostle Paul. As Paul had done, Gregory saw it to be his duty to gather in the faithful in preparation for Judgement. It was for this reason that he

[7] See R. A. Markus, 'Gregory the Great's Europe', *Transactions of the Royal Historical Society*, 5th ser. 31 (1981), 21–36, at 36.

[8] C. Leyser, *Authority and Asceticism from Augustine to Gregory the Great* (Oxford, 2000), pp. 131–88.

[9] R. A. Markus, *Gregory the Great and his World* (Cambridge, 1997) is the definitive biography.

[10] See, for example, Gregory, *Homiliae in Evangelia* II.35.1, PL 76, 1260C; Gregory, *Dialogi* II. 55 and IV. 18, A. de Vogüé and P. Antin (eds.), Sources chrétiennes 260, 182 & SC 265, 70 (Paris, 1979 and 1980).

sent monks to Britain: not as a first step towards a medieval future, but, as 'unfinished business' before the end of time.

Gregory's radical eschatology co-existed with his conservative institutional identity. He moved back and forth between the routine conduct of business and the heightened consciousness of the end times with a facility his modern readers find confusing. His literary output reflects this ease. On the one hand, we have the sermons of scriptural exegesis, in particular 35 books of dense meditation on the meaning of the book of Job. (Homilies on Ezekiel and the Gospels have also survived.) On the other hand, we have the voluminous correspondence. While we may be impressed by the scale of the *Register* as we have it, this is likely to have been a quarter of what Gregory produced, as we shall see.

Besides these torrents of exegesis and correspondence, there are two texts, the *Pastoral Rule*, a treatise on the proper conduct of authority; and the *Dialogues*, a collection of miracle stories of Italian holy men and women, cast in the classic form of ancient philosophical instruction.[11] Like any well-educated ancient person, Gregory could shift between rhetorical genres. Ultimately, however, he maintained a unified perspective. His vision of authority was a moral one. He was not interested in institutions *per se*, be they monastic or clerical. Anyone – layperson, ascetic, or holder of clerical office – could and, if suitably qualified, should assume authority in order to guide the faithful in the Last Days.

Without the eschatological frame, however, what did Gregory's body of work mean? If we trace the reception of his works, it is clear that his medieval readers supplied an institutional rationale to a set of largely pragmatic and provisional arrangements. Many modern studies have assumed that he was, in fact, following a policy and building for the future.[12] As a verdict on Gregory, this is unwarranted – but as a characterization of the priorities of Gregory's early medieval readers, it is entirely accurate.

Charlemagne's Gregory: the imperial moment

By the time Charles, king of the Franks, had been crowned Emperor of the Romans, Gregory had been remade as a usable, indeed an indispensable, resource. This was not a coincidence. The Emperor's *literati*, Alcuin of York, Theodulf of Orleans, and Paul the Deacon, were all, in ways that remain to be fully explored, advocates of Gregory's value. Their

[11] On the *Dialogues*, see now M. Dal Santo, *Debating the Saints' Cults in the Age of Gregory the Great* (Oxford, 2012).

[12] G. Jenal, *Italia Ascetica atque Monastica*, 2 vols. (Stuttgart, 1995) shows conclusively that Gregory did not pursue a monastic 'policy'.

success in 'selling' him is borne out in Carolingian library collections, such as Fleury or St Gall.[13] In the early ninth century, a 'Gregory package' consisted of the following elements: a (usually compressed) sample of his exegesis; the *Pastoral Rule*; the *Dialogues*; a biography; and an epitome of the *Register*. These elements had been assembled across the seventh and eighth centuries, in Spain, England, Lombard Italy, and Francia itself.

We may begin with the exegesis. The task of rendering Gregory's moral intensity into manageable units of institutional resource began, in fact, before his death, and with Gregory's complicity. His notary Paterius had begun a commonplace book, noting down Gregory's interpretation of verses of Scripture delivered incidentally in the course of his discourses on Job or Ezekiel.[14] Gregory insisted that these be systematically set out in the canonical order of scripture. The resulting *Liber testimoniorum* was widely diffused across early medieval libraries, and set a pattern for other excerptors in the seventh century, such as Taio of Saragossa, or the Irish monk Lathcen. In his epitome of the *Moralia*, Lathcen filleted out the lengthy disquisitions on the moral meaning of the text, to produce a lapidary series of statements about how to respond to demonic attack.[15] The net effect of these seventh-century excerptors of Gregory was to help in the diffusion of his authority, while actually draining away what was specific about his meaning. By the end of the seventh century, in the *Liber scintillarum* attributed to Defensor of Ligugé, excerpts from Gregory take their place alongside those of Augustine, Jerome, Cassian, and other Latin *patres*.[16]

In the case of his treatise on *Pastoral Rule*, Gregory's readers were able to go further, and to press Gregory's authority directly into the service of institutional authority.[17] Gregory composed the text on his accession to papal office. Dedicated to a bishop John (most likely of Ravenna), and sent to episcopal colleagues around the Mediterranean, the text is a treatise on the assumption and conduct of office. It is couched, however, in rigorously neutral terms as a tract for all rulers (*rectores*), not only

[13] See further L. Castaldi (ed.), *La trasmissione dei testi latini del Medioevo, Gregorius I Papa* (Florence, 2013).

[14] See now L. Castaldi, F. Martello, '"Tempera quasi aurum": origine, redazione e diffusione del *Liber testimoniorum* di Paterio', *Filologia Mediolatina*, 18 (2011), 23–107.

[15] Lathcen, *Egloga quam scripsit Lathcen filius Baith de Moralibus Iob quas Gregorius fecit*, ed. M. Adriaen, CCSL 145 (1969). For an overview, see R. Wasselynck, 'Les compilations des "Moralia in Job" du VIIe au XIIe siècle', *Recherches de Théologie ancienne et médiévale*, 29 (1962), 5–32.

[16] *Defensoris Liber scintillarum*, ed. H. Rochais, CCSL, 117 (Turnhout, 1957); the text awaits a full modern treatment.

[17] As finely observed in P. R. L. Brown, *The Rise of Western Christendom: Triumph and Diversity, 200–1000*, rev. edn. (Oxford, 2013).

bishops.[18] The bulk of the text is devoted to detailing what kind of corrective guidance (*admonitio*) a ruler should give to those in his charge. Different readers sought to harness it to different institutional purposes: for Isidore and Bede, it served as a blueprint for Christian kingship; for Gregory's contemporary Columbanus, it was a blueprint for abbatial authority. By the mid ninth century, however, it is fair to say that an episcopal reading had taken over. In the 860s, Hincmar of Rheims urges his nephew Hincmar of Laon to treat the work as a handbook for his conduct of office. It should be on the altar of every bishop at consecration.[19]

A similar range of interpretative possibilities attended the reception of the *Dialogues*. Some early medieval readers responded to the otherworldly immediacy of the text: across the seventh century, a number of visionary narratives amplified Gregory's sense that spiritual realms were tremblingly close.[20] Other readers took a more studied perspective: in their hands, Gregory's effort in philosophical instruction became a resource in the institutional development of Benedictine monasticism. Gregory had mentioned the *Rule of St Benedict* very briefly in his account of Benedict in the *Dialogues*, but had not promoted it as a code for monks to follow. Gregory's Benedict is a miracle-working prophet of the end times, very different from the wisdom teacher projected in the *Rule*.[21] From the mid eighth century, however, with the refoundation of Benedict's abbey of Montecassino, the opportunity to assimilate Gregory's narrative of Benedict's life with the *Rule* transmitted under his name was too good to pass up. A number of Gregory's readers in the Latin West took this opportunity. Pre-eminent among these was Paul the Deacon, monk of Montecassino, author of a *Life of Gregory*, and editor of a small selection of his letters (fifty four of them).[22] In his *History of the Lombards*, Paul gave both Benedict and Gregory central roles, as he sought to present himself to the Carolingians as a cultural broker for Italian traditions.[23]

[18] R. A. Markus, 'Gregory the Great's Rector and his Genesis', in J. Fontaine, R. Gillet, and S. Pellistrandi (eds.), *Grégoire le Grand*, Colloques internationaux du Centre National de la Recherche Scientifique, Centre culturel les Fontaines, 15–19 septembre 1982 (Paris, 1986), pp. 137–46.

[19] Hincmar of Rheims, *Opusculum LV capitulorum*, pref., ed. R. Schieffer, MGH Conc. IV Supp. II (Hannover, 2003), pp. 99–361, at 146.

[20] See further I. Moreira, *Dreams, Visions, and Spiritual Authority in Merovingian Gaul* (Ithaca, NY, 2000).

[21] Leyser, *Authority and Asceticism*, p. 182.

[22] Known as the 'P' collection: see D. Jasper and H. Fuhrmann, *Papal Letters in the Early Middle Ages* (Washington, DC, 2001), p. 72.

[23] A start on this topic has been made by C. Azzara, 'La figura di Gregorio magno nell'opera di Paolo Diacono', and M. Costambeys, 'The Monastic Environment of Paul the Deacon', both in P. Chiesa (ed.), *Paolo diacono. Uno scrittore fra tradizione longobardo e*

Just as Gregory's story of Benedict was yoked to the *Rule* in order to give the *Rule* greater prestige and institutional heft, so Gregory's own biography became a medium for the shaping of his message. Gregory, in fact, was the most 'storied' of the Latin Fathers, receiving repeated biographical treatment. Gregory's status as icon of authority takes form across the successive writings and rewritings of his life story.

The first freestanding biography is the so-called Whitby *Life*, written in England c. 700 by an ascetic (male or female) associated with the monastery of Whitby in Northumbria. It survives in one copy, but we know it was widely read and adapted, as we shall see. The main theme of the *Life* was the reach of Gregory's grace – whether in space or time. He had reeled in the far-flung English; at the end of time, the Whitby author envisages, he would lead them in to heaven. Gregory's range extends backwards in time. Through his tears, in a story 'marvellous to tell and marvellous to hear', the Emperor Trajan is redeemed from Hell. Neither barbarians at the rim of the world, nor the Romans of centuries ago, were beyond his power, inherited from St Peter, to bind and to loosen.[24]

The earliest reader of the Whitby *Life* whom we can identify is Bede. He posed the same question – how did Gregory exercise power at a distance? – but had a different answer. Less through miracles than through letters, proposed Bede. In his *Ecclesiastical History*, Bede told the story of Augustine's mission as an epistolary novel.[25] Through the sequence of letters sent by Gregory, readers can track the progress of the mission, Gregory's change of heart about the use of pagan temples, and his concern over Augustine's growing sense of his own importance. Bede is among our earliest witnesses to the availability of Gregory's letters outside Rome, and our first source for the *Libellus Responsionum*, the replies to the series of questions Augustine had asked from the missionary field.[26] Unlike other early medieval Gregorians, however, Bede's goal was not to build ecclesiastical institutions. In his view, the English Church had become overly complacent as an institutional structure, and in writing the

rinnovamento carolingio (Udine, 2000), pp. 29–38, and pp. 129–38. See also C. Leyser, 'Late Antiquity in the Medieval West', in P. Rousseau (ed.), *Blackwells Companion to Late Antiquity* (Oxford, 2009), pp. 29–42.

24 *Vita Gregorii* 29, ed. B. Colgrave, *The Earliest Life of Gregory the Great* (Cambridge, 1985), pp. 127–9. The reception of this story is traced by G. Whatley, 'The Uses of Hagiography: the Legend of Pope Gregory and the Emperor Trajan in the Middle Ages', *Viator*, 15 (1984), 25–63.

25 Bede, *Historia ecclesiastica gentis Anglorum*, ed. and tr. B. Colgrave and R. A. B. Mynors (Oxford, 1969), I. 27–32. T. Mommsen, 'Die Papstbriefe bei Beda', *Neues Archiv*, 17 (1892), 387–96 is the classic discussion.

26 See P. Meyvaert, 'Le "Libellus responsionum" à Augustin de Cantorbéry: une oeuvre authentique de Saint Grégoire le Grand', in Fontaine, Gillet, and Pellistrandi (eds.), *Grégoire le Grand*, pp. 543–50.

history of its heroic missionary past, he sought to give a moral jolt to the Church in his own day.[27]

These English characterizations of Gregory reverberated through later centuries. At some point in the late eighth or early ninth century, an unknown author spliced together Paul the Deacon's *Life of Gregory* with several of the miracle stories from the Whitby *Life*, including that concerning the Emperor Trajan. The resultant *Life of Gregory* was wildly successful, surviving in well over a hundred copies, at least as many as Paul's original composition. It seems to have circulated under his name – but its appeal, we suggest, lay in its redirection, without the English tilt, of the Whitby *Life*'s sense of the breadth and immediacy of Gregory's power.[28]

Carolingian interest in Gregory only increased as the Empire steered into crisis in the generation after Charlemagne. The tension between Charlemagne's son Louis the Pious and his own sons set up questions about the moral accountability of those in power that Gregory's texts were ideally suited to answer. Specifically, with his performance of public penance in 822, Louis inaugurated two decades of intensive discussion about how to correct the ruler when he was in error. One scholar has called the Empire of Louis 'the penitential state': it could equally have been called 'the Gregorian state', so focussed was the court on the agenda Gregory worked through in the *Pastoral Rule*.[29] As another scholar has shown, this was a critical moment in the self-consciousness of bishops in the Frankish kingdom, and their sense of themselves as delivering *admonitio* to the Emperor.[30]

Rome's Gregory: John the Deacon and the *Register*

The apotheosis of Gregory north of the Alps was to meet with a concerted response in Rome. In the early 870s, the Roman deacon John surveyed the literary scene of Gregory commemoration. There was scarcely a

[27] See further A. Thacker, 'Bede's Idea of Reform', in P. Wormald, D. Bullough, R. Collins (eds.), *Ideal and Reality in Frankish and Anglo-Saxon Society: Studies presented to J. M. Wallace-Hadrill* (Oxford, 1983), pp. 130–53.

[28] C. Leyser, 'The Memory of Pope Gregory the Great in the Ninth Century: a Redating of the Interpolator's *Vita Gregorii* (*BHL* 3640)', in F. Santo (ed.), *Gregorio magno e le origini dell' Europa, Atti del convegno internazionale, Firenze, 13–17 maggio 2006* (Florence, 2014), pp. 51–64.

[29] M. de Jong, *The Penitential State: Authority and Atonement in the Age of Louis the Pious, 814–840* (Cambridge, 2009). On the memory of Louis the Pious, see C. Booker, *Past Convictions: the Penance of Louis the Pious and the Decline of the Carolingians* (Philadelphia, PA, 2009).

[30] S. Patzold, *Episcopus. Wissen über Bischöfe im Frankenreich des späten 8. bis frühen 10. Jahrhunderts* (Ostfildern, 2008).

people of Europe who had not offered an account of Gregory, he observed: the Franks (through a brief notice in Gregory of Tours), the Anglo-Saxons, through the Whitby *Life* and Bede, and the Lombards, through Paul the Deacon. This was an irony, notes John, in that Gregory had hated the Lombards. But there was no Roman account of Rome's most famous son. In response, John produced the longest saint's life in early medieval Europe. His ambition was nothing less than a programmatic summation of Gregory commemoration, and indeed of Gregory's work itself.[31]

The bulk of John's text was composed of extracts from Gregory's *Register*. Consciously or not, John picked up on Bede's intuition that the way to tell Gregory's story was through his letters. In finding a way both to evoke and to contain the profusion of Gregory's correspondence, John shows remarkable poise – more than some of Gregory's biographers since. To appreciate this, we have to explain what happened to the letters, for which John is in fact our key source.

From the historian's point of view, the story of Gregory's *Register* is one of loss. What John tells us is that the original *Register* was kept in fourteen papyrus volumes in the papal archive: one volume for each of the fourteen years for which Gregory had been Pope (590–604).[32] These volumes have not survived: John is in fact our last witness for their existence.

In the eighth century, there is evidence that the *Register* was consulted and selectively copied by visitors to Rome. Besides Bede and Paul the Deacon, as noted above, there were two principal excerptors of the *Register*. In the early eighth century, an archbishop of Cologne organized the copying of some 200 letters from the year 595. We have no sources documenting his intentions. The Cologne collection amounts to a sample of Gregory's papacy in administrative action, and this may have been what the archbishop wanted: a practical manual, or even a formulary, for his conduct of episcopal office.[33]

The biggest and most influential selection from the *Register* was made in Rome itself by Pope Hadrian I (772–95). From the fourteen papyrus

[31] John the Deacon, *Vita Gregorii, pref.* PL 75, 61B-C. See further G. Arnaldi, 'Giovanni Immonide e la cultura a Roma al tempo di Giovanni VIII', *Bulletino dell'Instituto Storico Italiano per il Medio Evo e Archivo Muratoriano*, 68 (1956), 33–89; G. Arnaldi, '"Giovanni Immonide e la cultura a Roma al tempo di Giovanni VIII": Una *retractatio*', in G. Arnaldi and G. Cavallo (eds.), *Europa medievale e mondo Bizantino. Contatti effetive e possibilità di studi comparativi* (Rome, 1997), pp. 163–77.

[32] John the Deacon, *VG pref* and IV.71, PL 75, 62C and 223B. See further Jasper and Fuhrmann, *Papal Letters*, 70–2; L. Castaldi, 'Il *Registrum Epistularum* di Gregorio Magno', *Filologia Mediolatina*, 11 (2004), 55–97.

[33] For the Cologne collection, see L. Fowler Magerl, 'The Use of the Letters of Pope Gregory I in Northeastern France and Lorraine before 1100', in M. Ascheri, Friederch Ebel, et al. (eds.), *Festschrift für Knut Wolfgang Nörr* (Cologne, 2003), pp. 237–60.

volumes, papal scribes selected 684 letters, approximately 50 from every year of Gregory's papacy. These they put into two parchment volumes. We have no evidence for the criteria of selection or the numbers omitted. If the 200 letters from the Cologne collection are at all typical, roughly a quarter of which of which are found in Hadrian's selection for 595, then we have a multiplier of 'times four' for the original *Register*: it may have contained 2000–3000 texts.[34] Modern critical editions of the *Register*, then, amount to an assimilation of the Cologne collection (known to scholars as 'C') with the Hadrianic epitome (known as 'R'), to produce a total of some 850 letters.[35]

Hadrian's purposes in making his selection and the basis of his criteria remain an enigma. It may be that his is a random sample. An obvious point to make, though, is that the vast majority of letters selected concern Italy. This may have reflected the balance of the original *Register*. It must also reflect Hadrian's context in the wake of Carolingian conquest of Italy in 774. Commemoration of Gregory's authority in Italy is surely part of the great shift in papal loyalties in the late eighth century, moving away from Byzantium, and into closer and closer collaboration with Frankish kings. Hadrian's epitome was made at the same time as the copying of the *Codex Carolinus* – a systematic collection of correspondence between the popes and Frankish kings – from papyrus to parchment. Gregory did not imagine his official position outside of an Eastern imperial context, but Hadrian did.[36]

While its genesis may be inscrutable, its effect is clear: Hadrian's edition of the *Register* transformed the meaning of canon law in the West. Gregory's letters were a new resource; they had not featured at all strongly in earlier collections, which took Dionysius Exiguus' early sixth-century compilations as the end point of the canonical tradition. If the decretal tradition was not closed after all, reasoned Carolingian canonists, then it could be re-invented wholesale.

Such a re-invention was the work of the following generation. The 830s witnessed, in the heat of the conflict between Louis the Pious and his

[34] E. Pitz, *Papstreskripte im frühen Mittelalter. Diplomatische und rechtsgeschichtliche Studien zum Brief-Corpus Gregors den Großen* (Sigmaringen, 1990) suggests that the original *Register* may have contained 20,000 letters.

[35] P. Ewald, 'Studien zur Angabe des Registers Gregors I', *Neues Archiv*, 3 (1878), 433–625; leading to the edition, Gregory, *Registrum epistularum*, ed. P. Ewald and L. Hartmann, 2 vols., MGH Epp. I-II (1891–99). The more recent edition of D. Norberg, 2 vols., CCSL 140, 140A (1982) does not add to Ewald's discussion of the manuscripts.

[36] For a suggestive reading of Hadrian I in this context, see now S. Scholz, 'Das Papsttum, Roms wirtschaftliche Lage und die Enteignung der päpstlichen Patrimonien in der Mitte des 8. Jahrhunderts', in S. Weinfurter (ed.), *Päpstliche Herrschaft im Mittelalter. Funktionen-Strategien-Darstellunsformen* (Ostfildern, 2012), pp. 11–25.

sons, the construction of a cavernous series of canon law forgeries, the Pseudo-Isidore.[37] This extraordinary project went back to early papal history to combine the decretals the Carolingians had actually received together with those that they wished they had inherited. At the end of the Collection came a series of letters of Gregory. These came almost all from 'R', but included also the *Libellus Responsionum* transmitted by Bede. As the figure whose *Register* had re-opened the decretal tradition, Gregory in some sense legitimized the whole enterprise of the Pseudo-Isidore.[38]

In the period 800–1000, there was no other canonical resource like 'R'. Canonical extracts from it were juxtaposed with selections from the Pseudo-Isidore. From the mid ninth century, there start to proliferate large- and small-scale collections, excerpting from the Pseudo-Isidore and Gregory – while being careful to distinguish between them.[39] In the 880s, for example, a canonical collection was made for the bishop of Milan, Anselm. It was divided into twelve books, according to theme, and each book was divided into three sections: papal decretals, including the Pseudo-Isidore, extracts from 'R', and finally from Roman law.[40] While exegetical florilegia, as we have seen, smoothed over the difference between Gregory and other *patres*, canonical collections continued to 'mark' Gregory as distinctive. Eventually, in the early eleventh-century Collection of Burchard of Worms, Gregory would be folded in with the rest of the Latin tradition: for the moment, he had a distinctive, as yet unassimilated, profile.[41]

Meanwhile in Rome, an attempt was made to take control of the memory of Gregory as unleashed by 'R'. In the late eighth century, when Hadrian sponsored the making of 'R', the papal sense of ownership may have been implicit rather than explicit; from the 860s, however, Gregory and his letters were openly brandished by an expansive papacy.

[37] For an introductory discussion, see Jasper and Fuhrmann, *Papal Letters*, 137–94; and further www.pseudoisidor.mgh.de/

[38] H. Fuhrmann, *Einfluss und Verbreitung der pseudoisidorsichen Fälschungen. Von ihrem Auftauchen bis in die neuere Zeit Schriften der MGH* 12, 3 vols. (Munich, 1972–74), vol. I, pp. 189–91.

[39] The association between the Pseudo-Isidore and 'R' solidified in the following generations, and spread across the Frankish Empire. In one branch of the Pseudo-Isidore family ($A2_R$), a series of 36 letters was appended (the so-called R3 version); in another, an additional series of extracts of 46 letters was tacked on. See further Jasper and Furhmann, *Papal Letters*, pp. 75–7.

[40] P. Fournier, 'L'origine de la collection "Anselmo dedicata"', *Mélanges P. F. Girard* (Paris, 1912), pp. 478–95 remains the best introduction to the *Collectio*, which is as yet unedited. L. Kéry, *Canonical Collections of the Early Middle Ages, ca. 400–1140* (Washington, DC, 1999), pp. 124–8.

[41] See further H. Schneider, 'Die Kanonisten und Gregor der Grosse. Von der *Collectio Vetus Gallica* bis zur *Anselmo dedicata*', in Santo (ed.), *Gregorio magno e le origini dell' Europa*, pp. 551–76.

In the race with the Byzantine Patriarchate to secure the allegiance of the Bulgarians, Pope Nicholas I cast his approach to Khan Boris on the pattern of Gregory's mission to the Anglo-Saxons. His *Consulta Bulgarorum* addressed to the Khan was a self-conscious iteration of Gregory's *Libellus Responsionum* to Augustine.[42] Although (or because) the Bulgarian mission failed, the Gregorian programme gathered momentum. In the early 870s, Pope John VIII instructed his chancery to keep his correspondence on the model of Gregory's *Register.*[43] At Easter of 873, John commissioned a namesake, the Roman deacon John, to write a *Life of Gregory* – to which we may now return.

John's *Life of Gregory* is a huge, hybrid text. It is less hagiography than a canonical tract on episcopal office, which assimilates the life and teaching of Gregory to 'R'. What John sought to do, then, was to impose some kind of thematic order onto the nearly seven hundred letters selected by Hadrian's scribes. Of these, he in turn selected some two hundred for excerpting. John ostentatiously describes the fourteen papyrus volumes of the original *Register* as the documentary bedrock of his account. It is, however, no more than bluster: all of John's extracts are to be found in 'R'.[44]

John may have had done this deliberately. While this is a source of bitter frustration to the historian of the sixth century, who would like nothing more than a glimpse of the original papyri, it tells us something of John's purposes. While claiming privileged knowledge of the archive, John's goal was in fact to create a widely accessible Gregory. His readers would be able to check his selection of the letters next to 'R'. As we shall see, his readings were gratefully received by subsequent canonists. His *Life* was ten times more successful than 'R' itself (which we have in full in some 15 manuscripts), with over 150 copies surviving, including some made within a decade of the completion of the text.[45]

In a further attempt to bring order, John says he will organize his text in four books, on the pattern of Gregory's *Pastoral Rule*: what sort of man should be a ruler, how he should respond to office, what sort of admonitions he should deliver, and finally how he should return to himself.[46]

[42] Mayr-Harting, 'Two Conversions'.

[43] See D. Lohrmann, *Das Register Papst Johannes' VIII* (Tübingen, 1968).

[44] As shown by Castaldi, 'Il *Registrum*'. See John the Deacon, *VG pref.*, PL 75, 62B, and the discussion of John's context in C. Leyser, 'Charisma in the Archives: Roman Monasteries and the Memory of Gregory the Great, c. 870 – c. 940', in W. Pohl and F. de Rubeis (eds.), *Le scritture dai monasteri, II Seminario internazionale di studio 'I monasteri nell'alto medioevo* (Rome, 2003), pp. 207–26.

[45] See L. Castaldi, *Iohannes Hymmonides diaconus romanus. Vita Gregorii I papa: (B.H.L. 3641–3642)*, Vol. I, *La tradizione manoscritta* (Florence, 2004). The edition itself is in preparation.

[46] John the Deacon, *VG pref.*, PL 75, 62B.

Like Hincmar (above p. 186), John insists upon an episcopal, in fact a papal, interpretation of Gregory's text. What sort of man should be a ruler: Pope Gregory. What sort of advice should he give? The directives issued by Gregory in 'R'. Where Gregory in Book III of the Rule had outlined a series of abstract pieces of moral guidance, John's Book III is composed entirely of extracts from 'R'. Book III is indeed the centre of gravity of his text: unlike Books I, II, and IV it is unadulterated by any narrative content. John clears the decks to construct 'Gregorian policy' from the miscellany of texts in 'R'. What he offers is a sustained treatise on the acquisition and transmission of episcopal office of the sort that Gregory himself had never considered.

The episcopal Gregory: bishops and careerism

On one topic in particular, Carolingian readers were keen to extract a ruling from Gregory and his *Register*: the translation of a bishop from one see to another. Was it permissible? Much late Roman tradition held that a bishop was a servant to his flock, whom he should not abandon in pursuit of his own advancement. This apparently obscure corner of canon law has only recently begun to attract its due measure of attention.[47]

The creation of the Carolingian empire had made it possible to imagine the Church as a career. For the ambitious – both those bishops who won, and those displaced in the struggle for preferment – professional mobility now became essential. Across the ninth-century West, then, bishops debated how episcopal office was to be assumed and transmitted. Gregory was a key resource in this discussion. We can track the issue across the series of texts outlined above – 'R', the Pseudo-Isidore, John the Deacon – and, as we shall see, in the post-Carolingian excerptors of 'R'. We meet, inevitably, Formosus, bishop of Porto, pope in 891, then posthumously accused of having moved sees illegitimately.[48] The so-called Synod of the Corpse is usually wheeled out by scholars to demonstrate the decadence of the unreformed Church. Viewed with less prejudice, the trial of Formosus takes its place as an episode in the much wider story arc of Gregory the Great's commemoration.[49]

[47] See S. Scholz, *Transmigration und Translation. Studien zum Bistumswechsel der Bischöfe von der Spätantike bis zum Hohen Mittelalter* (Cologne, 1992); and M. Sommar, 'The Changing Role of the Bishop in Society: Episcopal Translation in the Middle Ages', unpublished PhD Thesis, Syracuse University (1998).

[48] See now W. Hartmann, I. Schröder, and G. Schmitz (eds.), *Die Konzilien der Karolingischen Teilreiche 875–911*, MGH Conc. V (Hannover, 2012), pp. 416–19.

[49] C. Leyser, 'Episcopal Office in the Italy of Liudprand of Cremona, c. 890-c.970', *English Historical Review*, 125 (2010), 795–817.

Gregory's ninth- and tenth-century readers honed in on the instances where he had authorized bishops to move from one see to another. The context was usually one of pastoral crisis – the destruction of sees by the invading Lombards, or simply the incapacitation through age of incumbents. Thus in 590, Bacaudus of Formia is instructed to take over the see of Minturno (*Reg.* I.8); Martin of Corsica is instructed both to move and to become visitor to another see (*Reg* I. 77; I. 79). In 592, John of Alessio is instructed to move from his see, which has been devastated, to Squillace; Gregory adds that he should watch out for stray Africans or Manichees, who might try to obtain ordination (*Reg.* II. 37). In the same year, John of Velletri is instructed both to move his see to Arenata (*Reg.* II.17) and to merge his church with that of Tres Tabernas (II. 48). Gregory was merely attempting to deal with the exigencies of his situation. Given the formulaic character of the letters, it is likely, in fact, that these letters were all composed by notaries, in accordance with standard procedure. Here we have Gregory the passive follower of convention.

As recorded in 'R' and in the hands of later canonists, however, Gregory's decisions represented an active body of law that could be set against the rulings of earlier canonical tradition. In the later Roman Empire, councils had warned against ambitious bishops seeking to move from place to place.[50] Gregory's notaries do not mention these decisions. If they knew of them, it is likely that they saw no reason to cross-reference rulings about the sees of Antioch or Constantinople with their own desperately obscure rural situations. Four centuries later, Carolingian churchmen busied themselves with exactly this task of cross-referencing, as they sought to make sense of canonical tradition.

Gregory's rulings as visible in 'R' may well have lain behind the creativity of the Pseudo-Isidore with regard to the question of translation; but his authority was most explicitly invoked in the 860s, in the case of Actard of Nantes. Actard was a bit player in episcopal politics – but his case came to involve a contest over who spoke for Gregory, and it established a 'script' for how the question of translation was to be discussed.

In brief, the situation was this.[51] Actard, an aspiring protégé of Charles the Bald, had requested a transfer from the see of Nantes, whence he claimed he had been driven by Vikings, to the see of Tours. The request was initially supported by Hincmar of Rheims, who sought Actard's help

[50] See, for example, Nicaea can. 15; Antioch (330 X 341), can. 21; Sardica (343), can. 1, as transmitted in the Dionysio-Hadriana and the Pseudo-Isidore; see Scholz, *Transmigration*, pp. 18–36, and M. Sommar, 'Pragmatic Application of Proto-Canon Law: Episcopal Translation', in L. J. Hall (ed.), *Confrontation in Late Antiquity* (Cambridge, 2003), pp. 89–101.

[51] See Fuhrmann, *Einfluss und Verbreitung*, pp. 278–80.

in negotiating the deposition of his nephew, Hincmar of Laon. Pope Hadrian II, however, managed to subvert Hincmar of Rheims' purposes by refusing to ratify the deposition of Hincmar, but willingly granting Actard his transfer. Hadrian supported his position with an appeal to the Pseudo-Isidore, and a string of citations from 'R'.[52]

Hincmar's reply to Hadrian, a letter known as *De quibus apud*, is a rhetorical masterpiece, using the majesty of Gregory the Great to belittle Actard's case for translation.[53] Hadrian had drawn on Gregory: Hincmar demonstrated a still more fluent command of Gregorian texts, drawing on the *Pastoral Rule* and the *Homilies on the Gospels* as well as 'R' (*Reg.* II. 37 on John of Squillace; *Reg.* III. 13 on Agnellus of Fondi; *Reg.* I. 8 on Bacaudus of Formia). The Gregorian criteria the pope had used to justify Actard's translation in fact condemned it. Actard was no humble refugee, driven from his see by barbarians: he was, on the contrary, a coward and a *mercenarius*, seeking only his own advancement.

Hadrian II died with Actard's situation unresolved. Who was there to answer Hincmar? Attention has usually focused on the contribution of Anastasius Bibliothecarius, who is the most likely author of a treatise on episcopal translation drawn from the Pseudo-Isidore, to which Hincmar had not referred.[54] For a text which meets Hincmar head on, however, we may turn to John the Deacon's *Life of Gregory*. John, it should be noted, mentions neither Actard nor Hincmar; he was, however, in the inner circle of Anastasius Bibliothecarius. John is also the likely author of the notice for Hadrian II in the *Liber Pontificalis*, and he will have known at least that the question of translation was in the air.

In his *Life of Gregory*, John sets out a Gregorian summa on the issue of career mobility.[55] Book III, as we saw above, is comprised entirely of extracts from 'R', focussed on episcopal office. John begins with simony and Gregory's uncompromising campaign against it (Bk III. 1–8). Episcopal office cannot be trafficked: it is a gift of the spirit. But it may be portable. John then starts to consider the circumstances in which

[52] Hadrian II, *Ep.* 34, MGH *Epp.* VI (1875), pp. 738–40.

[53] For the text, see PL 126, 210–30; for discussion, see M. Sommar, 'Hincmar of Reims and the Canon Law of Episcopal Translation', *Catholic Historical Review*, 88 (2002), 429–45.

[54] See J. Pozzi, 'Le manuscrit Tomus XVIII de la Vallicelliana et le libelle *De episcoporum transmigratione et quod non temere iudicetur regule quadraginta quattuor*', *Apollinaris*, xxxi (1958), 313–50 (including an edition of the text). This advanced a series of Pseudo-Isidorian decretals to support translation. As noted in Sommar, 'Hincmar of Reims', it is characterized by its lack of overlap with Hincmar's *De quibus apud*. It is possible that the treatise was an attempt to outflank Hincmar's Gregorian erudition.

[55] John the Deacon, *Vita Gregorii* III. 8–22 PL 75, 133–43. See further F. Bougard, 'Composition, diffusion et réception des parties tardives du "Liber pontificalis" romain (VIII-IX siècles)', in F. Bougard and M. Sot (eds.), *Liber, Gesta, histoire* (Turnhout, 2009), pp. 127–52, esp. pp. 131–4.

bishops might move: when sees were vacant, or when they themselves had been forcibly displaced (Bk III. 8–13). In two key chapters, John assembles the case law for Gregory's authorization of translation (Bk III. 14–15; the cases of Bacaudus of Formia, Martin in Corsica, John of Squillace, and John of Velletri).[56] Then comes an element of caution: there was at least one case where Gregory had stopped short of moving a bishop to a see that was in trouble (Bk III. 18). Paul of Nepi had acted as a visitor to Naples but had then returned to his own see. Gregory, John avers, was concerned lest vacant sees be regarded as sites to ransack. These cautions stated, however, the overall effect of John's presentation is to make translation seem feasible, and indeed desirable, when properly managed. Actard, who by this point seems to have been installed at Tours, might have taken this as a defence of his position – and a demonstration that Hincmar had no monopoly of the authority of Gregory.

For John, as for Hincmar then, Gregory was a giant whose pronouncements could be used to assess contemporary bishops. But while it was possible to extract from 'R' a relatively coherent account of the issue, John could not control the way his own text, with its monumental portrait of Gregory, was received or used. And he did not resolve the specific issue one way or the other. The adjudication of cases of translation remained a volatile business, as the sequel was to show.

Within four years of the papal defence of Actard, and before John had finished his *Life of Gregory*, the tables were turned on the bishop of Rome. In 876, Pope John VIII seems to have accused Formosus of aspiring to papal office.[57] Formosus, who had been Nicholas I's man in the field in Bulgaria, was guilty enough to have fled the city. John VIII repeatedly secured his formal condemnation. John the Deacon, meanwhile, may have been associated with this disgrace: his elaborate attempts to distance himself from Formosus seem to suggest as much.[58] In 882, however, John VIII was assassinated, and Formosus returned to Rome. Within ten years, he assumed papal office – only to be pursued beyond the grave for his perceived lust for power.

Debate over Formosus' legitimacy as pope, and the legitimacy of the ordinations he performed, continued deep into the tenth century, and

[56] Note that John's friend Gauderic was Bishop of Velletri. After John's death, Gauderic seems to have completed John's *Life of Clement*. See G. Orlandi (ed.), *Iohannis Hymmonidis et Gauderici Veliterni, Leonis Ostiensis, Excerpta ex Clementinis Recognitionibus a Tyrannio Rufini Translatis* (Milan, 1968).

[57] Merseburg 104, ff47v-49v for the Roman synod of June 876 and the Synod of Troyes, 878; see Hartmann et al. (eds.), *Konzilien 875–911*, pp. 29–30, and 76–148.

[58] See P. Devos, 'Le mystérieux épisode final de la *Vita Gregorii* de Jean Diacre. Formose et sa fuite de Rome', *AB* 82 (1964), 356–81; and now the brilliant piece of detective work by L. Castaldi, 'Le dediche di Giovanni Immonide', *Filologia mediolatina*, 17 (2010), 39–69.

beyond.[59] As we shall see, both Formosus' accusers and his defenders deployed material that had been cued up in the debate over Actard, and by John the Deacon. Auxilius, Formosus' champion in the early tenth century, explicitly invoked Actard's case, and he made an extravagant play for the authority of Gregory. Auxilius was prepared to go so far as to say that Gregory's authority was greater than that of all the Church councils: 'doctor suavissimus et papa beatissimus, Gregorium dico, vere Gregorium'.[60] In the course of these polemics, the figure of Gregory is in fact more substantial than the wraith of Formosus.[61]

Europe's Gregory: Church after Empire

The memory of Gregory served well the needs of ninth-century Carolingian ideologues, but in the era after empire, Gregory came into his own as a resource for episcopal authority, now freed from the role of handmaiden to earthly rule. As 'kinglets' (Regino of Prum) took the place of imperial dynasts, bishops come to the fore.[62] The realization dawned: centuries ago, the Church had survived the disintegration of an empire – why not again? Gregory had repelled the Lombards from the gates of Rome. He had found a way to sustain the Church in Italy and across the Latin West. For tenth-century bishops, Gregory's *Register* was a mirror of how to survive, and indeed to prosper in a world otherwise spinning out of control.

This was true above all in Italy. For some eighty years after the death of the Emperor Charles the Fat in 888, and before the arrival of Otto I in 962 as the new Roman Emperor, no earthly ruler held secure sway. The insecurity of successive kings of Italy worked to the advantage of those whose support they had to buy. Bishops ate up regalian rights, and showed very little scruple in trading their loyalty to the highest bidder.[63]

[59] See the texts and the discussion in A. Grabowsky, 'Streit um Formosus. Edition und Analyse der Streitschriften des Auxilius', unpublished PhD thesis, University of Tübingen (2012), which will replace E. Dümmler (ed.), *Auxilius & Vulgaris: Quellen und Forschungen zur Geschichte des Papstthums im Anfänge des Zehnten Jahrhunderts* (Leipzig, 1866). For the eleventh-century polemics, see W. K. Firminger, 'St Peter Damiani and "Auxilius"', *Journal of Theological Studies*, 26 (1924–25), 78–81; J. Ryan, 'Cardinal Humbert of Silva Candida and Auxilius: the "Anonymous Adversary of *Liber I Adversus Simoniacos*"', *Mediaeval Studies*, 13 (1951), 218–23.

[60] Auxilius, *De ordinationibus a Formoso papa factis*, ed. Dümmler, *Auxilius*, 107.

[61] John the Deacon, *VG* 100, PL 75, 241A for the wraith of Formosus; and for literature, see this chapter, Note 58.

[62] See S. Airlie, 'Sad stories of the death of kings': Narrative Patterns and Structures of Authority in Regino of Prum's *Chronicon*', in E. M. Tyler and R. Balzaretti (eds.), *Narrative and History in the Early Medieval West* (Turnhout, 2006), pp. 105–31.

[63] See, for example, C. Pivano, *Stato e chiesa da Berengario I ad Arduino, 888 – 1015* (Turin, 1908); P. Delogu, 'Vescovi, conti e sovrani nella crisi del regno italico (Ricerche sull'aristocrazia carolingia in Italia, III)', *Annali della scuola speciale per archvisti e bibliotecari*

In a world ruled by bishops, Gregory's *Register* was a treasure trove to be raided for imaginative self-justification. A brilliant generation of learned clerics conjured an Italian Church that otherwise had no existence, given the fractured nature of political authority in the peninsula. The *Register* was at once a travelogue for bishops who were forced to stay put, and a set of entitlements for those ambitiously on the move. Some of these bishops – Atto of Vercelli, Rather of Verona, Liudprand of Cremona – have imprinted the historical record with their egos.[64] Others are known to us only by name, if at all. For these men, our best evidence comes in the form of 'farraginous' canonical collections characteristic of the tenth century.[65] These assemblages, like attics, resist attempts to tidy them up, but some recurring themes are clear. Formosus haunts these collections, as does the discussion of transfer; above all, however, we find the letters and world of Gregory the Great.

Let us briefly take two codices, one from North Italy, largely ignored by scholars, and the other a much better-known codex from the South; both transmit canonical collections made (at least in part) at the turn of the tenth century. The north Italian manuscript, Merseburg 104, written c. 900, is an assemblage of loosely tessellated elements, held together by the presence of Gregory.[66] There are four sections to the codex, three of which seem to have been initially bound together, before the later addition of the fourth. At the end of the first section, Formosus makes a darting appearance: there are records of his condemnations in the mid-870s. A cluster of Pseudo-Isidore texts and extracts from the *Register* follow, centred on the question of episcopal translation. In the third section, however, the codex devolves into a series of extracts from the *Register*, spasmodically interrupted by other authors (Alcuin; the *Collectio Anselmo dedicata*). Episcopal translation remains a concern – as witnessed in an extract from Cassiodorus' *Historia Tripartita* – but the larger purpose

dell'Universita di Romà, viii (1968), 3–72. For the broader context, see C. Wickham, *Early Medieval Italy: Central Power and Local Society 400–1000* (London, 1981), pp. 168–92.

64 See I. van Renswoude, 'The Sincerity of Fiction: Rather and the Quest for Self-Knowledge', and R. Meens, 'In the Mirror of Eusebius: the Episcopal Identity of Atto of Vercelli', both in R. Corradini, M. Gillis, R. McKitterick, and I. van Renswoude (eds.), *Ego-Trouble: Authors and their Identities in the Early Middle Ages* (Vienna, 2010) pp. 227–42 and 243–8.

65 R. Reynolds, 'Tenth- and Eleventh-Century Collections in Italy', in W. Hartmann and K. Pennington (eds.), *The History of Western Canon Law to 1000* (Washington, DC, in preparation).

66 Kéry, *Canonical Collections*, pp. 190–1 for what bibliography there is on this manuscript, to which Rudolf Pokorny's contribution to Hartmann and Pennington *Western Canon Law to 1000* will add significantly. For a discussion of a comparable manuscript, Milan, Ambrosiana G 58 sup, see C. Mor, *Una piccola collezione di testi gregoriani del secolo VIII,* in *Etudes d'histoire du droit canonique dédieés à Gabriel Le Bras*, 2 vols (Paris, 1965), pp. 283–91.

of the collection is harder to parse.[67] What strikes the reader forcibly is the name GREGORIUS, which appears 'in bold', that is, inked in, on more pages than it does not. The codex is thereby riveted to his authority, and this may be enough to explain its production.[68]

From southern Italy, we have the *Collection in 452 Titles*, to be found in the much-discussed Vallicellian Tome XVIII. The manuscript itself is now dated to the early eleventh century, but a version of the *Collection in 452 Titles* must have been made earlier, as sustained use of its contents was made by Auxilius in his defence of Formosus in the early tenth century.[69] A little noticed *terminus post quem* is provided by an explicit citation, deep into the *Collection*, of John the Deacon's *Life of Gregory* ('hoc de sancti Gregorii vita quam iohannes levita descripsit ablatum est'.)[70] Overall it would be too much to claim that Gregory dominates the *Collection in 452 Titles*, which is an altogether more expansive venture than the assemblage in the Merseburg book. That said, in the first half of the *Collection*, Gregory's *Register* is a constant point of reference. In particular, the codex includes a collection of 55 *Sententiae ex codice qui appellatur regestum epistolarum sancti gregorii pape* carefully set out in chronological order;[71] and a similar epitome of the *Moralia in Job*. In the space of four pages, an epitomator has gone through Gregory's text (or another epitome) in order, selecting brief passages, sometimes no more than a sentence long.[72] Armed with these densely compressed versions of the *Register* and the *Moralia*, we may suppose, the book's readers had nothing to fear from this or other-worldly powers.

To look for pattern in the making and the use of the *Register* across the tenth century may be to ask the wrong question. The meaning of Gregory's letters may have been more talismanic than content-driven. What stands out on the manuscript pages of these compendia is Gregory's name, and the names of his addressees. These books allowed their clerical readers to conceive of a Latin Church which they hoped to build and to sustain, with or without the support of temporal power.

[67] Merseburg 104, ff. 132v-133r for the extract from Cassiodorus *Historia Tripartita* XII. 8, listing bishops who have moved sees.

[68] By the end of the tenth century, the codex was in Merseburg, where it is likely to have played a role in the debate over Giselher's attempted suppression of the see and translation to Magdeburg. For an outline of the case, see Scholz, *Transmigration*, pp. 177–87.

[69] As shown by S. Lindemans, 'Auxilius et le manuscrit Vallicellian Tomus XVIII', *Revue d'histoire ecclesiastique*, lvii (1962), 470–84.

[70] Vallicellian T. XVIII, f. 210r.

[71] For a list of the l71etters extracted, see Fowler Magerl, 'The Influence'.

[72] This epitome has never been studied, to my knowledge. It bears comparison with other tenth-century epitomes of the *Moralia*, on which see G. Braga, 'Moralia in Iob: Epitomi dei secoli VII-X e loro evoluzione', in Fontaine, Gillet, and Pellistrandi (eds.), *Grégoire le Grand*, pp. 561–8.

All of this helps us in turn to reconstruct the world that produced Rather of Verona and Liudprand of Cremona. These men were open careerists, as I have argued elsewhere.[73] Rather's attempts at self-promotion are indeed well known. Initially installed at Verona, and then displaced for treason, he made two attempts, both only temporarily successful, to reclaim his seat there; and for a brief period in the early 950s, he tried unsuccessfully to transfer north of the Alps to Liège. He protested indefatigably that each of his attempted moves was legitimate, compiling a list of precedents which resumed the discussion of episcopal translation across the past three generations. The list concludes, as we should now expect, with the illustrious presence of Gregory.[74] Rather's erudition proved futile, and he died without a see. But if he failed, the episcopal cadre to which he belonged, and the Gregorian discourse he invoked, were there to stay.

Gregory himself knew both triumph and disaster. As he had made explicit, Job's story resonated with him: 'Perhaps it was no chance that stricken as I am, I should recount the story of one stricken.'[75] Gregory's *Moralia in Iob* in turn spoke vividly to a tenth-century audience. Rather and his colleague Liudprand both drew heavily on the *Moralia* as they sought to broadcast their own sense of injustice and victimization.[76] But desperation was not the end of Job's story: having proved impervious to the ordeals to which he was subjected, Job's patience was duly rewarded by the Lord. The concluding sections of the *Moralia* concern the moral problems not of suffering, but of success. In his *Antapodosis*, Liudprand, having begun his text in spite and in exile, found that he was concluding it as occupant of the see of Cremona. Like Gregory's Job, then, Liudprand meditates at length on prosperity, failure, and just deserts.[77]

The *Antapodosis* has long been taken as a text which heralds the rise of a Christian Latin Europe, both in its cosmopolitanism, and in its prejudices.[78] Its precocity should not obscure its appeal, in its very framing, back to Gregory. The *Antapodosis* was dedicated to a Spanish bishop, Reccared, whom Liudprand had met at Constantinople. Gregory's *Moralia* were begun in Constantinople and dedicated to a Spanish bishop,

[73] Leyser, 'Episcopal Office'.
[74] Rather of Verona, *Conclusio deliberativa* xl, ed. P. Reid, *Opera minora Ratherius Veronensis*, Corpus Christianorum Continuatio Mediaevalis, 46 (Turnhout, 1976), p. 6.
[75] Gregory, *Moralia in Iob, Epistola ad Leandrum* I, ed. M. Adriaen, CCSL, 143 (Turnhout, 1979), pp. 1–2
[76] See H. Jessen, *Die Wirkungen der augustinischen Geschichtsphilosophie auf die Weltanschauung und Geschichtsschreibung Liudprands von Cremona* (Bamberg, 1921).
[77] Liudprand, *Antapodosis* VI. 10.
[78] See K. J. Leyser, 'Ends and Means in Liudprand of Cremona', in *Communications and Power*, I, 125–42.

Leander of Seville. There is a perfect overlay between Liudprand's literary geography and Gregory's – of which Liudprand cannot have been unaware. In this sense, his performance as a narrator throughout follows in tracks he perceived Gregory to have laid centuries ago.

Liudprand's narrative seems a world away from the obscure legal collections of Merseburg. Indeed, one writer has seen in Italy in this period a divergence between the airily high culture of theocratic narrative, and the more grounded world of the law.[79] This is not a necessary contrast, as a parallel example may demonstrate. In 1973, Richard Southern argued that 'English History' as a narrative genre developed after the Norman Conquest as a determined effort of documentation provoked by a 'land grab'.[80] Monasteries after 1066 fought with all the means at their disposal to defend their property rights against the rapacious invader. From their determination to protect their land, Southern argued, developed the archive of the Anglo-Saxon past, whether authentic or forged.

My suggestion is that churchmen in the Latin West after the Carolingians used the memory, and specifically the *Register*, of Gregory the Great in an analogous way. The *Register* allowed them to access a past in which the Church had heroically survived the collapse of an Empire, emerging with a clear moral title to rule. At the same time, it provided an explicit mandate to develop a flexible and orderly career structure, allowing churchmen to stand free of imperial power and its vicissitudes. The *libertas ecclesiae*, around which zealots were to rally after the first millennium, became imaginatively possible in the tenth century, which we can no longer condemn as an era of 'corruption'.

For all that he was central to this effort, Gregory himself, we might remember, would have found it misdirected: no amount of institution-building on earth could compare to the community of believers to be gathered in by the justice of God at the end of time.

[79] C. J. Wickham, 'Lawyers' Time: History and Memory in Tenth and Eleventh-Century Italy', in H. Mayr-Harting and R. I. Moore (eds.), *Studies in Medieval History presented to R. H. C. Davies* (London, 1985), 53–72.

[80] R. W. Southern, 'The Sense of the Past', *Transactions of the Royal Historical Society* 5th ser. 23 (1973), 243–63.

9 The weight of opinion: religion and the people of Europe from the tenth to the twelfth century[1]

R. I. Moore

The last and longest of the miracles of Our Lady of Rocamadour collected in 1172–3 is entitled 'A woman saved from the fire'.[2] It tells how Lombarda was accused of sorcery by her neighbours in St Sever in Gascony, conjuring an epidemic which caused many deaths in the town. She was saved by the intercession of the Virgin of Rocamadour, to whose church she had made pilgrimage two years before and upon whose compassion she now threw herself, confessing all her sins and praying devoutly for mercy. The story is meant to convey the impression of a lawless crowd of enraged peasants hurling the hapless victim to her death in the flames: 'having made up their minds that the innocent woman was to be burned alive [the people] ... were gathering wood ... fetching torches and bringing sulphur, pitch and wax, and whatever else might make the fire burn, to throw onto the pyre'. But there are some inconsistencies. As she was dragged to the fire 'Lombarda wept copiously and called out in a loud voice to the blessed Virgin of Rocamadour ... She made the sign of the holy cross, and confidently called out the name of the Lady of Rocamadour. She then submitted herself to the dangers of the pyre, passing over it without being burned at all, and even more remarkably, without feeling any heat from the fire.' In other words, this was not a spontaneous execution or lynching, but an ordeal in one of its standard forms, which involved walking barefoot through or over burning brands. That is why it was preceded by an interval of three days, during which Lombarda was imprisoned, which the text represents simply as the time necessary to gather sufficient materials for a satisfactory incineration, and why despite several references to the people's intention that Lombarda should die in the flames it does not actually say that she had been condemned to death. Indeed, 'they condemned her [as a sorceress] without

[1] An earlier version of this paper was written for the California Medieval History Seminar at the Huntington Library, 29 May 2004. I am grateful to its participants and to the editors and contributors of the present volume for their comment and criticism.

[2] M. Bull, *The Miracles of our Lady of Rocamadour* (Woodbridge, 1999), iii. 24, 198–201.

any proper judgement and any formal pronouncement of the death penalty; she was not properly convicted, nor had she made a confession'.

As those words illustrate, trial by ordeal was by the later part of the twelfth century under vigorous attack from the literate as a primitive and superstitious travesty of justice. Nevertheless, we see in this story its workings as they were uncovered in Peter Brown's classic analysis.[3] It was a device to enable the community to arrive at a conclusion in a case that was not readily susceptible to resolution by direct evidence. Here it was a sorcery accusation of a kind very familiar in small communities the world and the centuries over. It might as easily have involved heresy, or sexual misconduct, or injury to children, animals, or crops, as the epidemic which Lombarda was accused of causing. The interval of three days during which the trial was prepared afforded time for the matter to be thoroughly threshed out; the 'judgement of God' would allow those whose view had not prevailed to give way gracefully. Initially opinion in St Sever had been sharply divided: 'a crowd of more than twenty thousand people, men and women, had flocked from all directions to witness the spectacle: some of them praying for the woman, some hurling abuse at her'. 'And it was the abuse which was the louder' our author adds, discreetly indicating the crux of the miracle, for when Lombarda emerged unscathed 'all present, both those hostile towards the woman and those who were her friends, joined in singing a hymn and glorified the lord'. Similar unanimity, in the opposite direction, had been described by Guibert of Nogent some sixty years earlier, when suspected heretics had been put to the ordeal by water at Soissons, and 'thrown into the vat of water Clement floated like a straw. Seeing this the whole assembly went rapturous with joy'.[4]

The scribes at Rocamadour were anxious not so much to conceal what had really been going on – for it seems unlikely that any contemporary audience would have failed to see immediately what I have spelled out so laboriously – as to minimize its structured and deliberative character. Their reason for presenting it as merely a primitive and barbarous affair whose outcome was predetermined (saving a miracle) by the superstitious vengefulness of the peasants was also identified by Brown. Although trial by ordeal apparently originated as a mechanism of royal justice[5] it had

[3] P. Brown, 'Society and the Supernatural: a Medieval Change', *Daedalus*, 104 (1975), 133–51, reprinted in *Society and the Holy in Late Antiquity* (Chicago, 1981); see also P. Hyams, 'Trial by Ordeal: the Key to Proof in Early Common Law', in M. S. Arnold (ed.), *On the Laws and Customs of England* (Chapel Hill, 1981), pp. 90–126.

[4] *De vita sua* iii. 17, trans. P. J. Archambault, *A Monk's Confession: the Memoirs of Guibert of Nogent* (University Park, PA, 1996), p. 198.

[5] R. Bartlett, *Trial by Fire and Water: the Medieval Judicial Ordeal* (Oxford, 1986), but on its wider argument see the review by S. D. White, *Speculum*, 64/2 (1989), 385–8.

become in the tenth and eleventh centuries a means by which communities acting on their own account dealt with a variety of disputes. It tested not so much the weight of the evidence as the standing of the accused in the community, and the acceptability of his or her behaviour not only in the particular case at issue but more generally. As such it was directly opposed to the rational principles that underlay the revival of both civil and ecclesiastical justice throughout twelfth-century Europe (rational, that is, in the language of their champions), and therefore repugnant to the source of that justice, the authority of royal and ecclesiastical judges. Brown illustrated the implications of this opposition with the story of how an Anglo-Saxon jury declared free of injury the hands of a number of peasants who had been made to carry the hot iron after being accused by William Rufus of poaching in his New Forest. 'Is God a just judge?' the king burst out. 'Damn whoever thinks it. You shall be judged by my just judgement, and not by God's!'

That was precisely the end towards which royal and papal clerks alike worked throughout the twelfth century, taking countless cases that would formerly have been tried in the community into their own courts, under their own procedures, and building up a vigorous barrage of anecdote and propaganda against ordeal as irrational, arbitrary, and superstitious. This presentation of Lombarda's case is an example. Ordeal was effectively abolished at last by the Fourth Lateran Council in 1215, by prohibiting priests from performing the rituals by which, as 'the judgement of God', it must of necessity be accompanied. In 1114 Guibert of Nogent had applauded the reaction of 'the faithful people' when the Bishop of Soissons decided to submit to an ecclesiastical council the fate of the 'heretics' so plainly condemned by their ordeal: 'fearing the spread of this cancer, [they] took the matter of justice into their own zealous hands' by breaking open the prison and burning them alive. But Guibert was already, and uncharacteristically, behind the times. There are a handful of other cases, at Liège in 1145 and Cologne in 1147, for instance, in which a verdict by ordeal unfavourable to suspected heretics was followed by lynching, allegedly despite clerical resistance.[6] But at Trier c. 1120 and at Vézelay in 1165 the ordeal acquitted people accused of heresy, and c. 1160 Albero, parish priest of Mercke near Cologne, but an educated man, declared himself willing to submit to it when he was accused of heresy by his bishop.[7] As Rufus had commented, traditional procedures offered all too fragile a guarantee that the outcome of a criminal proceeding would

[6] R. I. Moore, 'Popular Heresy and Popular Violence, 1022–1179', in W. J. Sheils (ed.), *Toleration and Persecution*, Studies in Church History, 21 (Oxford, 1984), pp. 43–50.

[7] R. I. Moore, *The War on Heresy: Faith and Power in Medieval Europe* (London, 2012), pp. 165–6.

be the one that was desired by the authorities, whether secular or ecclesiastical. And the habit of communal self-assertion might be deeply entrenched. Some forty years after Lombarda's ordeal the town of St Sever showed itself a hotbed of anticlerical sentiment when it conducted a vigorous and imaginative revolt against its lord the abbot – and, more remarkably on the very eve of the Albigensian crusade, got away with it.[8]

By attributing her escape to the intervention of the Virgin rather than the outcome of the ordeal, Lombarda's miracle vividly illustrates one of the ways in which during the twelfth century manipulation of the supernatural was removed from the uses of the community and subjected to the control of the clerks. It does so also in a second. *The Book of Miracles* in which it is recorded was compiled in 1172–3. We owe the precision of that knowledge to the fact that the cult at Rocamadour, today (according to its custodians) the second most visited religious site in France, was developed very rapidly from around 1165, under the patronage of Henry II as Duke of Aquitaine. The reasons, which as far as I know have yet to be fully elucidated,[9] are not germane here, except to underline that neither the fact nor the manner of the recording of Lombarda's story was accidental. She arrived at the shrine accompanied by a large party of noble women with whom she had set out to give thanks immediately after her acquittal. Her interrogation and that of her companions, and the decisions about how to put them on record, were of course the work of the custodians of the shrine, constructed according to a common pattern.[10] There is no mention, as there typically would have been in an equivalent eleventh-century story, that anyone at St Sever suggested at the time that a miracle had taken place, though it would be surprising if nobody actually did so: that was for the servants of Our Lady to determine, at Rocamadour itself, and to preserve for posterity in the way that they saw fit.

Compare this with the explanation given to a northern visitor about a hundred and fifty years earlier by the abbot of Ste Foy at Conques, some thirty miles to the southeast of Rocamadour, of why his monks allowed the calm and dignity of their services to be interrupted by the unseemly songs and cries of the peasants, who being illiterate could not

[8] B. Cursent, 'Excursus. Une affaire du non-hérésie en Gascogne en l'année 1208', in M. Zerner (ed.), *Inventer l'hérésie? Discours polémiques et pouvoirs avant l'inquisition* (Nice, 1998), pp. 257–62. St Sever is c. 100 km south of Bordeaux, 150 km west of Toulouse.

[9] See, however, Bull, *Miracles*, pp. 74–90; Emma Mason, 'Rocamadour in Quercy above all other churches': the Healing of Henry II', in W. J. Sheils (ed.), *The Church and Healing*, Studies in Church History, 19 (Oxford, 1982), pp. 39–54; B. Ward, *Miracles and the Medieval Mind* (London, 1982), pp. 45–50. J. Rocacher, *Rocamadour et son pèlerinage. Étude historique et archéologique* (Toulouse, 1979) is more archaeological than historical.

[10] Cf. the helpful observations of Bull, *Miracles*, pp. 35–6.

join properly in the chanting of the psalms.[11] Once, in his youth, the abbot said, the monks had decided to forbid 'the unsuitable commotion made by the wild outcries of the peasants and their unruly singing'. Finding that they were unable to enforce silence during services they ordered the doors of the church to be closed at night, and the swarms of peasants to be refused admission to the vigils, until one night an unusually large crowd of pilgrims appeared 'shouting and demanding that they should be allowed to come inside the walls of the monastery'. Then, 'suddenly while we were sleeping the bars of the doors were spontaneously unfastened' and 'when we rose in the middle of the night for matins we found the church so full of people keeping the vigil that each one of us had difficulty forcing his way forward to his own station'. Some of the monks suggested that perhaps the opening of the doors had been a miracle. On reflection the others saw the strength of their case. As the then abbot put it, 'If I reassess my own attitude carefully in the light of what you have told me I am satisfied that on account of the simplicity of these people an innocent little song, even a peasant song, can be tolerated somehow. For it may be that if this custom were abolished the crowds that frequent the sanctuary would also disappear. Nevertheless, we should not believe that God rejoices over a little song; it is the hardship of keeping vigil and the good will of simple people that please Him.'

In acknowledging, albeit somewhat hesitantly, the voice of the people as the voice of God the abbot had, whether he knew it or not, no less an authority than Odo of Cluny. In his *Life* of Count Gerald of Aurillac, who died in 909, Odo had found himself compelled to investigate the miracles popularly alleged to have been performed by Gerald both *in vita* and at his tomb. He put some of them on record, but he was far from comfortable about it. Indeed his anxious insistence that Gerald's claim to sanctity was established not by these marvels, 'which are often performed even by the reprobate',[12] but by his religious life, strongly suggests that Odo's object in writing this very influential *Life* was not to establish a cult but to legitimize and even sanitize one that already existed.[13] Throughout the tenth and eleventh centuries, and well into the twelfth, popular

[11] *The Book of Ste. Foy*, 2.12, trans. P. Sheingorn (Philadelphia, PA, 1995), pp. 137–8; R. I. Moore, *The First European Revolution, c. 970 – 1215* (Oxford, 2000), p. 26.

[12] *Vita Geraldi*, PL 133 cols. 641–704, at col. 667.

[13] D. Barthélemy, *Chevaliers et miracles. La violence et la sacré dans la société féodale* (Paris, 2004), pp. 45–65, whose views are discussed at length below, rejects this reading on the ground that Odo's object in this *life* was to depict Gerald according to the Cluniac model of the monastic life rather than as the old-fashioned Aquitanian lord he had actually been. Yet Odo's desire to downplay such cults remains evident, and if indeed there was none in this case it is hard to see why he should have conceded that they were sometimes inspired 'even by the reprobate'.

acclamation of miracles performed by living holy men was commonplace. These miracles were quite different in character from those that were recorded at the shrines.[14] They involved not only – or indeed, most often – curing the ailments of disciples and supplicants, but feeding them in time of hunger, sheltering them from the elements, and securing retribution from and visiting vengeance upon their oppressors. In short, miracles *in vita* demonstrated the powers of lordship, supernaturally exercised – which is to say, in effect, popularly acclaimed. The proud and haughty count who was foolhardy enough to scorn Romuald of Ravenna's command to return the cow stolen from a *muliercula* (the same epithet that is used of Lombarda) and choked on its meat, or the owner of the fishpond which dried up when he refused to pay the tithe to which Abbot Pontius considered his house of St André at Avignon entitled, were left in no doubt of the consequences of disobedience.

It may have looked as though the shoe was on the other foot when, to protest against the invasion of their cloister and damage to some of their houses by the men of the terrible Count Fulk Nerra, the canons of Tours laid the bodies of their saints on the floor of St Martin's, fenced them and Martin's tomb around with thorns, and closed the church to the local people, admitting only pilgrims. But Fulk came barefoot through the streets to make amends and promise that the injury would not be repeated.[15] This 'humiliation' of the relics, like the widely and very variously used gestures of ritual supplication themselves (the *clamor*),[16] was another way in which the religious could rally public opinion to their support by dramatizing their helplessness in the face of worldly power and pride. And very effective it might be – provided, of course, that public opinion was indeed prepared to acknowledge and acclaim their holiness, which is to say, their freedom from the pollutions of the world. Holy power, in other words, was power exercised from below, dependent not on appointment, consecration, or ordination, but on popular reputation and the ability to command and exploit it. That is why it was distrusted by bishops and others in positions of authority, as Odo of Cluny distrusted

[14] In this I differ (as Barthélemy apparently does not) from P. A. Sigal, *L'homme et le miracle dans la France médiévale* (Paris, 1985), pp. 17–35; see Moore, 'Between Sanctity and Superstition: Saints and their Miracles in the Age of Revolution', in M. Rubin (ed.), *The Work of Jacques le Goff and the Challenges of Medieval History* (Woodbridge, 1997), pp. 55–67.

[15] P. Geary, 'L'humiliation des saints', *Annales*, 34 (1979), 27–42 and *Living with the Dead in the Middle Ages*, pp. 10–76. The episode is also discussed by L. K. Little, *Benedictine Maledictions: Liturgical Cursing in Romanesque France* (Ithaca, NY and London, 1993), pp. 131–2.

[16] See G. Koziol, *Begging Pardon and Favor: Ritual and Political Order in Early Medieval France* (Ithaca, NY and London, 1992).

the miracles of Gerald of Aurillac – and why it is so remarkable to find even Odo's mighty successors from the middle of the tenth to the beginning of the twelfth century relying on it, not because they preferred it to the formal authority conferred by their ecclesiastical titles but because it worked better.[17]

This is a momentous contrast. Ninth-century western Francia is presented to us, until quite near its end, as ruled by strong and energetic emperors casting the mantle of their protection over the poor and the religious, through the confident agency of counts for the most part loyal and effective, and bishops for the most part secure in their authority. It was followed, according to the traditional account, by two centuries of great social and political instability. The 'breakdown of public order' which accompanied the gradual disintegration first of the empire of Charlemagne, and then of his governmental legacy, undermined authority with consequences both negative and positive, but in either case frequently involving the destruction of old communities and old subordinations, and the construction of new ones. Social anomie was even more disruptive. Many were driven from their land as estates were consolidated, and many more fled to escape the servitude which that same consolidation brought in its trail, making their way to the towns that were appearing everywhere. The anxieties and discontents that accompanied these catastrophes affected far more than those who were directly touched by them, so people began to band together in self-defence against the forces of anarchy and depredation.[18]

That, in brief, was the late-twentieth-century orthodoxy upon which Dominique Barthélemy has conducted a sustained and comprehensive assault.[19] What he denies, in the first place, is not that such things happened, but that there was anything new about them. For him, as for Fichtenau more than half a century ago,[20] the order maintained by the Carolingian state, with its superficially impressive insistence on protection for *miserabiles personae* against the greed of the mighty, was merely the inflated rhetoric of barbarian kings flattered by their clerical

[17] Moore, 'Sanctity and Superstition'.

[18] For the classic statements of this perspective, G. Duby, *The Chivalrous Society* (London, 1977); J. P. Poly and E. Bournazel, *La mutation de l'an mil* (Paris, 1980), translated as *The Feudal Transformation, 900 – 1200* (New York, 1991); P. Bonnassie, *From Slavery to Feudalism in South-Western Europe* (Cambridge, 1991); T. N. Bisson, 'The Feudal Revolution', *Past & Present*, 142 (1994), 6–42.

[19] D. Barthélemy, 'La mutation de l'an mil, a-t-elle eu lieu?' *Annales. Economies, Sociétés, Civilisations*, 47 (1992), 767–77; *La mutation de l'an mil, a-t-elle eu lieu? Servage et chevalerie dans la France des Xe et XIe siècle*s (Paris, 1997), translated as *The Serf, the Knight and the Historian* (Ithaca, NY and London, 2009).

[20] H. Fichtenau, *Das Karolingische Imperium* (Zurich, 1949), translated as *The Carolingian Empire* (Oxford, 1957), esp. ch. 7.

advisers into repackaging themselves as Roman Emperors. In the real world the long, slow changes which issued in the crystallization of the familiar 'medieval' order towards the end of the twelfth century – there is no argument about that – proceeded on their tortuous and infinitely varied paths marked by no dramatic acceleration or change of course in the decades around the millennium. Until that crystallization was complete, it has not been the least of Barthélemy's contributions to insist (with Patrick Geary, Stephen White, and others)[21] we must understand the maintenance of order and assess its condition in terms not of an essentially rhetorical antithesis between government and anarchy, but (as Max Gluckman would have recommended) of feud and its resolution, of the customary mechanisms which 'restrain the conflicts from destroying the wider social order'.[22]

For Barthélemy the familiar story of the decline of public authority after the ninth century, and the dramatic assertion in the eleventh of a new social order growing out of the consequent anarchy represents in its religious as in its secular dimensions a change of rhetoric more than of substance.[23] Tenth- and eleventh-century sources describe a world in which church and poor, deprived of royal protection, huddle together helpless against the ravages of a brutal and lawless aristocracy, with no weapon to defend themselves except the power of public opinion rallied and sanctified by religious leadership. The archetypal image is that of Aquitaine in the 990s, when in response to calls from the bishops and abbots of the region great crowds of people flocked to meeting places, where they swore on the relics of the saints carried there in procession to support the churches and each other against the depredations of the warring aristocracy.[24] This, for Georges Duby and the generation that was beguiled by his vision, was the beginning of the Peace of God movement, carried over much of western and southern Francia in the next forty years to prepare the ground both for the reform of the church and the

[21] Geary, *Living with the Dead in the Middle Ages* (Ithaca, NY, 1994); White's main contributions to this debate are collected in S. D. White, *Feuding and Peace-Making in Eleventh-Century France* (Aldershot, 2005). See further this volume.

[22] M. Gluckman, *Custom and Conflict in Africa* (Oxford, 1956), p. 2. The '*société faidale*' of Barthélemy's *Chevaliers et miracles* (see esp. pp. 11–22) is directly equivalent to Gluckman's 'feuding' – as opposed to feudal – society; Gluckman's 'The Peace in the Feud', *Past & Present*, 8 (1955), 1–14 is cited at p. 4.

[23] Barthélemy, 'The Peace of God in the Days of the Millennium' in *The Serf*, pp. 245–301; Duby, *L'an mil et la paix de Dieu* (Paris, 1999).

[24] For a good introduction to the historiography and history, inclined on the whole to accept the sources more or less at face value, T. Head and R. Landes (eds.), *The Peace of God: Social Violence and Religious Response in Aquitaine around the Year 1000* (Ithaca, NY and London, 1992).

reanimation of secular authority, which from the later eleventh century onwards 'made the middle ages'.[25]

The problem with that, though it can certainly continue to be abundantly documented, as it has been for some generations now, is that it begs the question so sharply posed by Barthélemy, of how much these stirring scenes owed to the interests and presentational skills of their chroniclers. His lengthy analysis concludes that we cannot disentangle 'popular' devotion either from that of the clerics through whose record alone it is accessible or from the nature and function of the record itself. Brutally to caricature, for the sake of brevity and clarity, arguments of great erudition and power, the miracles associated with the relics appear in this light as the currency of the competition in which each hagiographer was engaged for the glory of his particular saint; the crowds that are so vividly depicted as flocking to these councils as the stock characters of ecclesiastical rhetoric.[26] The popular enthusiasm which the narrative sources associate with the Peace of God is and can be known to us only as, and so far as, it has a role in the drama produced and directed by the monks: '"the people" had no autonomous religious expression'.[27]

It is the great strength of Barthélemy's case against a social 'mutation' in the decades around 1000 that it is massively consistent. But that is also a potential weakness. Wherever he looks, whether at the imposition of serfdom, the proliferation of castles, the emergence of knighthood, or the articulation of opposition to the secularization of ecclesiastical services and offices – and he has examined each of these in great detail and in many aspects – Barthélemy finds that the dramatic – or melodramatic – crises and turning points described in the narrative sources are not reflected in the gradual and piecemeal changes that can be traced on the ground. It is always a central element of the argument that his predecessors have read their texts with too eager an anticipation of what is to be found in them, and have consequently attached more clear cut and uni-directional significance to variations in vocabulary and phraseology than untidy reality will bear. He is quite entitled to argue that the same weaknesses that he has detected in so many readings of the secular evidence vitiate those of the religious. But conversely, it would follow that to the extent that a case can be made for reading the religious sources as describing some reality beyond a mere reflection of the pretensions of their authors they are capable also of supporting a wider argument for changes in reality as well as in rhetoric.

[25] See especially G. Duby, *L'an mil*, 2nd edn. (Paris, 1980).
[26] D. Barthélemy, *L'an mil et la paix de Dieu. La France chrétienne et féodale* (Paris, 1999), pp. 269–329, esp. p. 312.
[27] Barthélemy, *L'an mil*, p. 329.

Even if we leave aside the most radical possibility, that the crowds that are said to have appeared on these occasions were entirely imaginary, or so insignificant as to be unremarkable, Barthélemy undeniably points to an uncomfortable circularity in the case for sudden and dramatic change. It is by no means clear – and in the nature of things, since we hear directly only one side of the story, it never can be – whether on any particular occasion, and therefore in general, religious leaders were able to exercise power because they had the backing of popular opinion (whatever, exactly, that may mean), or whether, conversely, the anger or enthusiasm of 'the people' was invested by the endorsement of prestigious religious leaders with a moral force that it would otherwise not have possessed. Since (and in this I agree with Barthélemy) the circularity from which the dilemma arises is inherent in the texts, it cannot be resolved merely by scrutiny of them. The question amounts to this. Historians have naturally and properly described and explained the momentous changes that took place in eleventh- and twelfth-century Western Europe and their consequences, repercussions, and spin-offs, in terms of the actions, interests, and mentalities of those who held and contended for land and office, secular and ecclesiastical. Neither their sources nor their theory encourage them to do otherwise. But were these really the only sources of power, or was there another term in the equation?[28] Did 'the people' constitute an independent factor in that equation, or were they only part of the armoury, either physical or rhetorical, of those who exercised real power? If the former, who were 'the people'? What was the source of their power, and why was it, at least on the face of it, so much more apparent at some times than at others?

For Barthélemy too there was a moment, extending to one or two generations, when popular power was real and decisive. 'For thirty years popes and their legates and supporters accepted, or even sought, "popular" or rather societal support against bad clerks and even against the princes who supported them.' This was a crucial point in the 'true social mutation' of the year 1100, an expression which Barthélemy 'employs in general for a period of about sixty years, between 1060 and 1120'.[29] What

[28] Cf. Barthélemy: 'to my mind the various manifestations of the Peace of God should be viewed more as illustrations that the *rustici* possessed a certain structural weight ('un certain poids structurel': *La Mutation*, p. 329) than as occasions on which they entered history'. *The Serf*, p. 273.

[29] Barthélemy, *Chevaliers et miracles*, pp. 226–8, and more fully 'La mutation de l'an 1100', *Journal des savants*, 1 (2005), 3–28. I do not dwell on the anomalies of Barthélemy's chronology: no one has shown more cogently the impossibility of assigning precise chronological limits to changes which are nevertheless real, and which can be closely examined only when pinned down, however artificially. But it is worth noticing that in its most generous formulation his 'mutation' lasted for much the same time as that of Duby and Bonnassie, and began barely a generation after theirs was completed.

makes it so is social transformation, urbanization arising from a marked increase of artisanship and of commerce, 'and still more of the schools', the ambition of seigneurial officials (*ministeriales*) strategically placed to profit both materially and politically from that development, and rapidly growing in wealth and power, to all intents and purposes independently of their lords. The demands for a commune heard in these decades, leading to insurrections like as those at Cambrai in 1077 and Laon in 1111–12, were in effect trials of strength between men like these and their former patrons and masters. In those struggles, which interacted with the conflict over investiture, as well as in the pursuit of that conflict in Italy, the popular role was crucial. But 'suddenly in 1100 the climate changes, and a new generation of better educated clerks takes the reins, tending to restore clerical unity by indulgence and compromise, and to exclude the people, including the nobles, from what it sees as the business of the church'. Hence the emergence of 'a new elite, let us say a bourgeoisie, which rivals, or complements, the knights', and gradually replaces them in the towns (except where there is a princely court), sharing power with a clerical elite of literate canons, judges, and masters.

This striking reformulation of what Barthélemy modestly presents as a return to an older view obscured for half a century by the 'false mutation' of 1000 necessarily raises the same questions about continuity and change as did that mutation itself. As to the twelfth century it is perhaps a little dramatic in its expression. The story of Lombarda with which we began is a sufficient reminder of how slowly the exclusion of the laity from 'ecclesiastical' concerns was achieved. Even at the highest level of heresy accusations and trials it was not until after the Council of Rheims in 1148 that the participation of the laity was decisively excluded. Up to that point the essentially and openly political implications of heresy accusations not only permitted but required the involvement of the privileged laity in hearing them, and provided at least a walk-on role for the rest.[30] More broadly, Thomas Bisson has recently reminded us in great detail how gradual and precarious was the assertion of public authority in secular affairs during a very long twelfth century, which (even though Bisson's focus is on princely authority and the manner in which it was conceived) must surely be understood, at least in part, as both assisting the social 'mutation', if that is what it was, and assisted by it.[31] Meanwhile the force of public opinion remained, however fitfully, at

[30] R. I. Moore, 'Heresy as Politics and the Politics of Heresy, 1022–1180', in R. Mazo Karras, J. Kaye, and E. A. Matter (eds.), *Law and the Illicit in Medieval Europe* (Philadelphia, PA, 2008), pp. 33–46.

[31] T. N. Bisson, *The Crisis of the Twelfth Century: Power, Lordship and the Origins of European Government* (Princeton, NJ, 2009).

least an occasional check on even the most over-weening power. In spite of the thoroughness and brutality of the Norman conquest of England, for example, and the absoluteness of the conquerors' material power, many of the most eminent and powerful individuals in the Norman regime (including both Ranulf Flambard, bishop of Durham 1099–1198, and under William Rufus *totius regni procurator*, and [Steven's] Queen Matilda) felt the need of the legitimacy which could be conferred by association with the acknowledged leaders of the Old English community, as it was represented by the hermits who flourished so conspicuously at that time.[32] The traditional preoccupation of historiography with centralizing institutions and perspectives has allowed such influences to be persistently overlooked. Consider, for example, the determination of so many medievalists to explain the presence and persistence of 'heresy' in the countryside of late twelfth-century Languedoc by elaborating inquisitorial fantasies about the missionaries of obscure Balkan sects, while neglecting to consider what indigenous religious leadership there may have been, or how and by whom it was exercised.[33] It does not require any great imagination to consider how a Godric of Finchale, a Christina of Markyate, or a Wulfric of Haselbury might have resisted more overtly demands for submission to new superiors and the imposition of new customs, or how easily, if they had done so, their austerities and eccentricities might have been represented as manifestations of extreme asceticism carried to the point of heresy – indeed, of dualist heresy, gnostically inspired. Nor, conversely, does it take a great deal more to envisage circumstances in which the *boni homines* of Laurac or Albi might have secured a spiritual reputation to equal the monks of Grandmont, whose austerity impressed

[32] H. Mayr-Harting, 'Functions of a Twelfth-Century Recluse', *History*, 60 (1975), 337–52; R. I. Moore, 'Ranulf Flambard and Christina of Markyate', in R. Gameson and H. Leyser (eds.), *Belief and Culture in the Middle Ages: Studies Presented to Henry Mayr-Harting* (Oxford, 2001), pp. 231–5. *Totius regni procurator* is William of Malmesbury's description of Flambard, *De gestis pontificum anglorum*, ed. N. E. S. A. Hamilton, Rolls Series (London, 1870), p. 254.

[33] There is, as always, an element of excuse in the fact that we know very little about this, as we do about every other aspect of life in the countryside, and that such attempts as there have been to elucidate it in respect of the Languedoc have too often been associated with a gamut of intellectually disreputable causes running most of the way from the fate of the Grail to neo-nazism and back again. I am not about to add my name to that lugubrious list by attempting to supply from the resources of an overstocked imagination the details of beliefs and cults which have been hidden from us by a millennium-long ecclesiastical conspiracy of silence. That there was no such conspiracy should not need saying, but probably does. For a scholarly and invigorating statement of the case for scepticism in respect of most aspects of the traditional account of 'Catharism' in the Languedoc, see M. Pegg, *The Corruption of Angels: The Great Inquisition of 1245 – 6* (Princeton, NJ, 2001), and of its political construction and progressive demonization J. L. Biget, *Hérésie et inquisition dans le midi de la France* (Paris, 2007) and Moore, *War on Heresy*.

Henry II so much that he wanted to be buried among them, and who are habitually referred to as *boni homines* by his closest chronicler.[34] That is why, as Barthélemy emphasizes, the drive to remove holy power from the disposition of 'the people' and place it securely in clerical hands was one of the most consistent endeavours of reformers in the twelfth century.[35] It was achieved not only by bringing under control the recognition of miracles, the making of saints, even the burial of popular preachers, by getting rid of trial by ordeal and so on, but also, and more fundamentally, through the reorganization of the parish and its services, which now became everywhere the frame and focus of country life, and the mechanism through which all its social arrangements were controlled. Hence, the sacraments of infant baptism, church marriage, extreme unction, and burial in the churchyard, as well as annual confession before Easter communion, were insisted upon with renewed determination, and those who resisted them, or doubted their necessity, were denounced as heretics.

With regard to the eleventh century the question is more substantial, and more difficult. Barthélemy cites as an example of the reality of popular power in the crucial middle decades Colin Morris' discussion of the use of ordeals in the disputes between reformers and 'simoniacs' in Italy, adding that the archives of Angevin monasteries show a marked increase in use of the ordeal around the same time.[36] His view is in harmony, therefore, with my own attempt to describe 'the appearance of the crowd on the stage of public events' at this time, and even with my youthfully impetuous characterization of it as 'one of the most obvious novelties of the eleventh century', which arose from a similar though (it need hardly be said) much less refined view of social change.[37] Yet it is precisely the novelty of popular action in and after the 1050s that seems to me to be thrown into question by Barthélemy's analysis of the miracles of the tenth and earlier eleventh centuries and his conclusion as to the extent

[34] *Gesta Regis Henrici Secundi*, ed. W. Stubbs, Rolls Series (London 1867), I, p. 198; see further R. I. Moore, 'Les albigeois d'après les chroniques angevines', *La croisade albigeoise. Colloque de Carcassonne CEC octobre 2002* (Carcassonne, 2004), pp. 81–90.

[35] See esp. B. Stock, *The Implications of Literacy: Written Language and Models of Interpretation in the Eleventh and Twelfth Centuries* (Princeton, NJ, 1983). Even so, however, the continuing persistence and ingenuity of unprivileged lay people in using the frameworks of piety provided by the church to articulate their own social needs and aspirations remains impressive: see the pioneering study of Simon Yarrow, *Saints and their Communities* (Oxford, 2006).

[36] Barthélemy, *Chevaliers et miracles*, p. 228; C. Morris, '*Judicium Dei:* the Social and Political Significance of the Ordeal in the Eleventh Century', in D. Baker (ed.), *Church Society and Politics*, Studies in Church History, 12 (Oxford, 1973), pp. 95–111.

[37] R.I. Moore, 'Family, Community and Cult on the Eve of the Gregorian Reform', *Transactions of the Royal Historical Society* 5th ser., no. 30 (1980), 49–79.

to which they can be regarded as vehicles of popular participation in public events. If the crowds who attended the ordeals of the mid-eleventh century and made effective the assault on the 'simoniac' clergy were the same as the 'people' who had formerly acclaimed miracles (and continued to do so for most of the twelfth century), had they somehow acquired power that they had not previously possessed? If they were not the same, what was the difference, and how and why did the one give way to the other?

Like all students of popular religious movements I owed a great deal to the inspiration of Norman Cohn.[38] But the crowd that I described in 1980 as 'changing the course of events' in the middle of the eleventh century 'by making the force of popular indignation available to those who knew how to raise it' was not drawn from Cohn's 'disoriented poor' in pursuit of the millennium. It resembled rather the model of the pre-industrial crowd more recently described by George Rudé and E. P. Thompson and brilliantly analysed in its religious manifestations by Natalie Zemon Davis.[39] It was largely composed, that is to say, not of the poorest of the poor but of people with a settled place and at least a modest stake in society, merchants and shop-keepers, craftsmen and artisans, often including officials or priests, and drew its force from them, seeing itself as upholding community values imperilled by corrupt or incompetent magistrates or clerks in whose stead it acted. This characterization rested in the first place on Cinzio Violante's examination of the Patarenes of Milan,[40] and is at least consistent with the famous though usually less specific accounts of popular unrest in the decades around 1100, of Sigebert of Gembloux, Guibert of Nogent, Galbert of Bruges, and so many others. By implication it is reiterated, and greatly clarified, in Barthélemy's description, quoted above, of the new bourgeoisie which was emerging at that time. We may agree, therefore, granted all the obvious reservations in respect both of the quality of the evidence and the uniformity, continuity, and universality of its appearance and

[38] N. Cohn, *The Pursuit of the Millennium*, 3rd edn. (London 1970), pp. 53–70.

[39] The foundation texts of an immense literature were G. Rudé, 'The Gordon Riots: a Study of the Rioters and their Victims', *Transactions of the Royal Historical Society*, 5th ser., no. 6 (1956), 93–114, E. P. Thompson, 'The Moral Economy of the English Crowd in the 18th Century', *Past & Present*, 50 (1971), 76–136, and N. Zemon Davis, 'The Rites of Violence in Sixteenth-century France', *Past & Present*, 59 (1973), 59–91, reprinted in Zemon Davis, *Society and Culture in Early Modern France* (Stanford, CA, 1975), pp. 152–88.

[40] C. Violante, 'I laici nell movimento patarino', *I laici nella 'societas christiana' dei secoli xi e xii*, Pubblicazioni dell'Universitá cattolica dell Sacro Cuore, Miscellanea del Centro di studi medievali V (Milan, 1968), pp. 597–687. For a similar description of the urban populations of Flanders at this time, and one notably anti-mutationist in its implications, A. Verhulst, *The Rise of Cities in North-West Europe* (Cambridge, 1999), pp. 119–22.

development, that this was the crowd of the urban future. The question that remains is how, if at all, it related to 'the people' of the rural past – whether its appearance was evolutionary or revolutionary, whether it had any meaningful continuity with what are almost invariably represented in religious contexts as the spontaneous, unordered popular gatherings of the tenth and eleventh centuries. And not only the past, for just such gatherings notoriously continued to be described in the early decades of the twelfth century, most obviously around the hermit preachers who were especially active and influential in just those regions of the west of France that have figured most prominently in Barthélemy's discussion.[41] That may suggest that the question of continuity with which we are concerned is not only between kinds of human groups, but also, more familiarly, between town and country.

To state the question is to see that absolute though those oppositions may be in principle, and clear as they may become in practice over the long term, they are by no means necessarily so at any particular time or place, and certainly not at the times and places of the present discussion. The understanding of the ordeal and its working which is agreed on all sides presupposes a structured community, capable of arriving at and proclaiming a collective decision that proceeded from a shared understanding not only of what would constitute a just outcome, but of the weight that should be attached to particular considerations and circumstances, to local conditions and customs, to the influence of particular individuals in the debate, and so on. In this connection it is worth noting that the influence of the English hermits mentioned above derived not only from their reputations for personal holiness but also, and not at all coincidentally, through their often distinguished Old English blood and their networks of connection among the conquered majority.[42] What we accept for ordeals we can hardly reject in accounting for the acclamation of miracles, or for the resort to the *clamor* or the humiliation of relics. However it might have suited the convenience or ideology of monastic writers to present such events, whether positively or negatively, as the spontaneous eruption of untutored emotion – to deny the actors the power, in Barthélemy's phrase, of autonomous religious expression – none of these actions could have had meaning otherwise.

[41] For example, in the rediscovered portion of Andreas' *Life* of Robert of Arbrissel, describing the struggles for possession of his body after his death at Orsan (Berry) and the letters of reprimand to Robert of Marbod of Rennes and Geoffrey of Vendôme, conveniently collected and translated by B. Venarde, *Robert of Arbrissel: a Medieval Religious Life* (Washington, DC, 2003).

[42] Cf. R. Fleming, 'Rural Elites and Urban Communities in Late Saxon England', *Past & Present*, 141 (1993), 3–37.

The phrase itself, it must be added, harbours a certain ambiguity. It was obviously and always the case that the sentiments expressed in reported collective action were not autonomous in that they were recorded only because, and only as, chroniclers and scribes chose, or were instructed, to record them. They are known to us because they were seen to embody, or being presented as embodying, the values and causes that those writers endorsed. The sustained and imaginative rigour that Barthélemy has brought to the application of this truth, scarcely in itself a novel one, to the feuds of the tenth and eleventh centuries in western France, and especially to the events associated with the Peace of God, is a salutary corrective to the insufficiently discriminating enthusiasm of some recent accounts, including my own.[43] It does not follow, however, that the actions themselves were always orchestrated, or even initiated, by the monks. On their way to the Council of Charroux in 989 with the relics of St Junian the monks of Nouaillé stopped at Ruffec, near Poitiers. The villagers erected a cross at the spot where the bones had rested and made a fence round it. 'Many days later' a wild bull attacked the fence and fell dead. The nearby stream was dammed to make a pool, at which people came to wash, including a woman who by doing so was cured of leprosy. Letaldus of Micy was happy to record these triumphs of his patron in the appropriate light and language,[44] but the very fact that he does not describe similar events at other places where Junian had paused on the journey suggests that the initiatives to create the enclosure and to dam the stream had not come from the monks. They were decisions of the villagers of Ruffec. So were the designation of the death of the bull and the cure of the woman as miracles – for that is how Letaldus describes their actions, though he does not endorse them by using the word. Further, in making these decisions the villagers not only acted collectively but in the process became a more cohesive community, and one more aware of itself. In doing so they displayed, in miniature as it were, the same interaction between religious expression and the assertion of communal identity that in Flanders and northern Italy would make the cause of religious reform a dynamic of the emerging commune in Barthélemy's 'true mutation' of 1060–1120. They may even have illustrated the mechanics, as it were, of the link suggested by Vermeesch between the Peace of God and the earliest communes.[45]

[43] Moore, *First European Revolution*, pp. 7–10.

[44] *Delatio corporis s. Juniani in synodum Karrofensem*, PL 137, cols. 825–6; T. Head, *Hagiography and the Cult of Saints: the Diocese of Orléans 800 – 1200* (Cambridge, 1990), pp. 175–6.

[45] A. Vermeesch, *Essai sur les origines et la signification de la commune dans le Nord de la France (xie. et xiie. siècles)* (Heule, 1966).

The power of the people, we may conclude, was always present, and always potentially more dynamic than 'a certain structural weight' suggests. Ultimately, its source lay in the notorious inefficiency of unadulterated coercion to harness labour and secure its profits.[46] However unequal the balance of brute power between 'the people' and their lords, a measure of consent, secured less through ideological manipulation than ingrained socialization, was necessary to a stable, productive social order. The famous depiction in John of Worcester's chronicle of the nightmare of Henry I, in which the terrified king found his bed surrounded by peasants wielding forks and scythes, testifies to awareness of that truth on the part of even – perhaps especially – the ablest and most ruthless of lords.[47] Consent implies legitimacy, and legitimacy was affirmed, or challenged, in part by the voice of the people. For a good deal of the time that voice could, with skill and persistence, be successfully orchestrated – even persuaded to forgo its autonomy – but sometimes it had to be accommodated, if only to prevent it from being directed by the wrong hands, until it could be marginalized again. Which was the case at any particular moment depended on the cohesiveness of the elite, and therefore on the state of the forces by which it was divided.

For their respective proponents the essence of both our mutations lay not in the religious demonstrations that symbolized and energized them, but in the emergence of new social groups, which challenged and for a time appeared seriously to threaten the cohesiveness of the dominant elite in its current form. Dominique Barthélemy has shown conclusively that neither the emergence of castellan lordship nor the unfolding of what Duby, Bonnassie, and others described as its consequences was by any means so abrupt or universal in reality as the logic of the numerous antitheses from which their analyses had proceeded seemed to require. Whether the classic antithesis between town and village, or town and country, upon which his own 'mutation of 1100' seems to rest is susceptible to a similar demystification – whether for example, the more specialized division of labour and the inability to feed itself that in principle distinguish the city from the village demands in practice a point at which it abruptly becomes inescapable, or whether the one state of affairs might merge almost imperceptibly into the other – is a question too large to pursue here, though the well-known persistence of agriculture and horticulture within city walls seems to tell against absoluteness. But in its

46 Without entering the ancient question of the nature and relationship of slavery and serfdom in our period (to which Barthélemy's contribution is of the first importance) I note that the otherwise somewhat abstruse work of P. Dockès, *Medieval Slavery and Liberation* (Chicago, 1982) contains interesting reflections on this point.

47 Oxford, Corpus Christ College MS 157, 382.

religious aspects his account implies too sharp a break on either side. On the one hand, popular power in religious guise had a more continuous history and deeper roots than he concedes. On the other, squeezing it back to the margin was a longer and more laborious business than he suggests. As Barthélemy has taught us so well, the metaphor of mutation is more useful for shaping questions than answers.

Nevertheless, Barthélemy's more general conclusion is unquestionably correct. The twelfth century remains a decisive turning point.[48] In this field as in so many others, we see by 1180 or so that the lineaments of a new world have settled into place, more complex and more ordered than its predecessor. The alternation between periods when bishops could afford to denounce popularly acclaimed holy men, and those when they must at least pretend to admire or even emulate them, was over. The power of the people to proclaim the presence of the holy was never again (in the middle ages) so visible or so pervasive as it had been in the heady days when it sustained the abbots of St Martin against the ferocity of the Counts of Anjou and turned the world upside down for Gregory VII. We need not necessarily regret it. It is easy to sentimentalize the little community, to forget that small tyrannies may be quite as tyrannous over those subject to their power as large ones. In acknowledging the price that was paid for the large community that the clerks of the twelfth century established, which we call Europe, we need not follow Oscar Wilde's cynic by denying its value. But the religion of the people of medieval Europe has been marginalized not only by its contemporaries but by historians, who have largely acquiesced in its removal from the record. That we should regret unequivocally. There is too much that we will not understand until it is restored.

[48] Cf. A. Vauchez, *Sainthood in the Later Middle Ages* (Cambridge, 2005), p. 6: 'the remarkable increase in the number of recent saints who were venerated by the faithful in some regions, the presence of a public opinion which was very receptive to "modern" forms of sanctity and gave rise to a large number of intercessors . . . marks a turning point in the history of western Christendom'.

10 'The peace in the feud' revisited: feuds in the peace in medieval European feuds

Stephen D. White

'Did you want to kill him, Buck?'
'Well, I bet I did.'
'What did he do to you?'
'Him? He never did nothing to me.'
'Well, then, what did you want to kill him for?'
'Why nothing – only it's on account of the feud.'

Mark Twain, Huckleberry Finn, *ch. 18.*

I believe it would be profitable to apply these analyses to those periods of European history when the feud was still apparently the main instrument for the redress of injury.

Max Gluckman, 'The Peace in the Feud'.

The feud

According to a well-informed ethnographer of the mid-nineteenth-century Mississippi Valley, the following definition of feud was proposed by a boy called Buck Grangerford, whose family of Southern aristocrats had been trading vengeance killings with their peers, the Shepherdsons, since before Buck was born:

A feud is this way. A man has a quarrel with another man, and kills him; then that other man's brother kills *him*; the other brothers, on both sides, goes for one another; then the *cousins* chip in—and by and by everybody's killed off, and there ain't no more feud. But it's kind of slow, and takes a long time.[1]

How had the Grangerford's feud with the Shepherdsons started? About thirty years before, Buck said, 'There was trouble 'bout something, and then a lawsuit to settle it; and the suit went agin one of the men, and so he up and shot the man that won the suit – which he would naturally do, of course. Anybody would.' Buck didn't rightly know 'what the row was

[1] M. Twain, *Adventures of Huckleberry Finn (Tom Sawyer's Comrade)*, ed. V. Fischer and L. Salamo, The Mark Twain Project of The Bancroft Library (Berkeley, CA, 2010), ch.18 (pp. 142–55), at p. 146.

about in the first place' and he had no idea which side had lost the lawsuit and started the killing.[2] Nevertheless, Buck, who had already lost two brothers in the feud, feuded with his family's enemies enthusiastically and was angry at himself when he just missed killing an older boy from the Shepherdson family. Shortly after Buck had explained what a feud was to a bewildered Huckleberry Finn, he and four other Grangerfords were ambushed by a band of Shepherdsons, who lost a few men but killed Buck's father and two of his brothers. Buck and his nineteen-year-old cousin Jim tried to get away. Nevertheless, with Huck watching from the tree he'd climbed to escape the feud, the surviving Grangerfords hunted Buck and Jim down and shot them dead. Huck came down from the tree and covered Buck's face and Jim's. Then he slipped away, leaving the surviving Grangerfords and Shepherdsons to kill each other off. Which they would naturally do, of course. *Anybody* would.

Huckleberry Finn is not often cited in scholarly work on feuding in early European societies. However, if one leaves aside Buck Grangerford's proto-functionalist theory that in the very, very long run feuds produce a kind of peace, namely the peace of the dead, the pseudo-folk-model of feuding among Southern gentlefolk that Mark Twain consciously deployed for satirical purposes in 1885, closely resembles the academic model of feuding that medievalists down to the present day have often built into their writings on this subject. Feuding was identified by Julius Goebel with 'an antiphony of incessant violence', by C. W. Prévité-Orton with 'a state of incessant private warfare', and by Marc Bloch with 'interminable quarrels'.[3] When a man was killed, according to Bloch, his death had to be avenged; 'the family group went into action and the feud [*faide*] came into being ... No moral obligation was more sacred than this .... The whole kindred [*lignage*] took up arms to punish the murder of one of its members or merely a wrong that he had suffered. But vengeance was not directed solely against the death of the wrongdoer himself, for active solidarity [among the victim's kin] was matched by passive solidarity equally strong' among the slayer's kin, who were ready to attack the victim's kin when it was their turn to take blood vengeance. In Marc Bloch's feudal society, 'Blood thus called for blood', just as it did in Mark Twain's nineteenth-century Mississippi Valley.[4]

[2] Twain, *Adventures of Huckleberry Finn*, p. 146.

[3] J. Goebel, *Felony and Misdeameanor: a Study in the History of English Criminal Law* (New York, 1937), p. 85; C. W. Prévité-Orton, *The Shorter Cambridge Medieval History*, 2 vols., 1st edn. (Cambridge, 1952), vol. 1, pp. 128–9; M. Bloch, *Feudal Society*, trans. L. A. Manyon (London, 1961), p. 7.

[4] Bloch, *Feudal Society*, pp. 126, 127.

Among the elements that Marc Bloch's model of feud shares with Mark Twain's, four assumptions are particularly important. First, the only purpose of a feud is to take vengeance on members of the opposing kin group. Second, a homicide or other injury automatically triggers the impulse in the victim's kin to take vengeance, without any of them needing to justify the feud (except by invoking a crude version of the *lex talionis*) or persuade fellow kinsmen to join in it.[5] Acting on identical impulses, the slayer's kinsmen respond to every act of retaliation by the homicide victim's kin by taking vengeance on them. Third, since neither side feels an impulse to make peace and there are no mechanisms for establishing it, conflicts of this kind are interminable. Fourth, the feud and the acts of revenge that constitute it are thus the politically irrational, socially dysfunctional, and psychologically pathological practice of a primitive society or subculture.

The peace in the feud

It was the third and fourth assumptions – that feuds were interminable and that feuding and revenge were irrational and barbaric – that Max Gluckman contested both in his famous essay on 'The Peace in the Feud', which appeared in *Past & Present* in 1955, and in the version of the essay that he published in the same year as the first chapter of *Custom and Conflict in Africa*, where he fully explained the broader implications of his argument about feuding.[6] In both versions, Gluckman contended that, contrary to the popular view of feuding – which anthropologists had long since abandoned but many medievalists still entertained – feuds did *not* produce endless private warfare in societies where 'private vengeance and self-help are the main overt sanctions against injury by others, and where this exercise of self-help is likely to lead to the waging of feuds'.[7] Instead, Gluckman maintained, feuds broke out less frequently than was generally supposed and often ended with settlements. Relying on E. E. Evans-Pritchard's analysis of feuding among the Nuer, Gluckman explained that in this tribe of pastoralists without rulers, if a member of an agnatic kinship group is killed, other group members '*must* exact vengeance for him against the killer or one of the killer's vengeance group, or [else] they *must* obtain blood-cattle in compensation for the

[5] On the law of the talion, see W. I. Miller, *Eye for an Eye* (New York, 2006).

[6] M. Gluckman, 'The Peace in the Feud', *Past & Present*, 8 (1955), 1–14; Gluckman, 'The Peace in the Feud', in Gluckman, *Custom and Conflict in Africa* (Oxford, 1955), ch. 1 (pp. 1–26). See also Gluckman, *Politics, Law and Ritual in Tribal Society* (Chicago, 1965), esp. ch. 3, 'Stateless Societies and the Maintenance of Order' (pp. 81–122).

[7] Gluckman, 'Peace in the Feud', pp. 2, 13; *Custom and Conflict*, pp. 3, 22.

death from this vengeance group'.[8] However, because custom demanded revenge – and feud – and thus provided both a sanction and a deterrent to the very acts that would provoke a feud, these conflicts took place much less often than the Twain/Bloch Model would have suggested. Moreover, because 'each vengeance group of agnatic kinsmen is divided by the different maternal and conjugal and local attachments of individual members', Gluckman continued, 'some members of each warring group have an interest in bringing about a settlement of quarrels'. As a result, there is bound to be 'pressure . . . to try to compromise the affair', rather than continue a chain of vengeance killings indefinitely.[9] Nevertheless, he emphasized, he was not suggesting that 'divided loyalties and interests will always prevent a dispute from arising, or prevent social dislocation and change', but rather that they tended 'to inhibit quarrelling . . . provided that there is a general need for peace, and recognition of a moral order in which this can flourish'.[10] Thus, 'There is only pressure towards the establishing of peaceful relations – or, rather, the re-establishing of peaceful relations after a breach.'[11]

In *Custom and Conflict in Africa*, Gluckman took his argument about the peace in the feud a step further by maintaining that it illustrated the workings of what I shall call the Invisible Hand of Custom, not just in African tribes without rulers such as the Nuer, but also in the mid-twentieth-century South African state and in other societies as well.[12] He thus claimed broad applicability to a wide range of societies for two statements in 'The Peace in the Feud'. First, 'where custom divides in one set of relationships, it produces cohesion, through the settlement of quarrels, in a wider range of social life'.[13] Second, 'custom appears to exacerbate [conflicts]; but in doing so custom also restrains [them] from destroying the wider social order'.[14] To substantiate *Custom and Conflict*'s 'central argument' that 'conflicts in one set of relationships leads to the establishment of cohesion in a wider set of relationships', the book considered not only feuding, but rebellion, 'estrangement within the

[8] Gluckman, 'Peace in the Feud', p. 6; *Custom and Conflict*, p. 11; italics added. Gluckman said ('Peace in the Feud', p. 1 n. 1; *Custom and Conflict*, p. 166) that his discussion was 'based' on E. E. Evans-Pritchard, *The Nuer: a Description of the Modes of Livelihood and Political Institutions of a Nilotic People* (Oxford, 1940), which discusses feud at pp. 140–52; and Evans-Pritchard, *Kinship and Marriage among the Nuer* (Oxford, 1951). Gluckman also cited, *inter alia*, E. Colson, 'Social Control in Plateau Tonga Society', *Africa*, 23 (1953), 199–212; and S. F. Nadel, *The Nuba* (London, 1948).

[9] Gluckman, 'Peace in the Feud', pp. 6, 12; *Custom and Conflict*, pp. 12, 20.

[10] *Custom and Conflict*, p. 25.

[11] 'Peace in the Feud', p. 11; *Custom and Conflict*, p. 19.

[12] *Custom and Conflict*, pp. 1–3, 23–6.

[13] 'Peace in the Feud', p. 8; *Custom and Conflict*, p. 14.

[14] 'Peace in the Feud', p. 1; *Custom and Conflict*, p. 2.

elementary family', witchcraft, and ritual in 'tribal societies'; it also examined industrial strikes and the 'colour bar' in South Africa, though Gluckman worried that his theory no longer applied to racial conflict there.[15]

Since the theory held that the Invisible Hand of Custom ultimately produced social cohesion in societies ranging from the stateless to the state-run, Gluckman thought 'it would be profitable to apply it to those long-distant periods in European history where the feud was still apparently the main instrument for redress of injury'.[16] What he meant by this became clear when he criticized medieval historians for failing to consider how the structure of vengeance groups and local groups would have generated pressure for settling feuds. He therefore questioned the statement in Sir Frederick Pollock and Frederic William Maitland's *History of English Law* that 'personal injury was in the first place a cause of feud, or private war'.[17] Since, according to Gluckman, the Anglo-Saxon vengeance group called the *sib* consisted of an entire kindred traced 'through males and females, up to sixth cousins' and must therefore have been a 'widely scattered grouping which could not mobilize', he concluded that 'in a long-settled district, where there had been much intermarrying, almost everyone would have been a member of everyone else's sib. Hence where vengeance had to be taken, or redress enforced, some people would have been members of both plaintiff and defendant sibs. They would surely have exerted pressure for just settlement.'[18]

Ten years later, Gluckman made the same point at greater length in *Politics, Law and Ritual in Tribal Society*, where he criticized Marc Bloch for exaggerating the prevalence of feuding in feudal society, and for claiming that medieval feuds led to 'interminable quarrels' and for 'overlooking the pressures of countervailing relationships' to settle feuds.[19] Since Gluckman did not first ascertain that the pressures for peace that he saw in 'stateless' societies truly existed in medieval European ones before criticizing Bloch for overlooking them in the latter,[20] he evidently

[15] *Custom and Conflict*, pp. 2, 164.

[16] 'Peace in the Feud', p. 2; *Custom and Conflict*, p. 4; see also *Politics, Law and Ritual*, p. 113.

[17] Sir F. Pollock and F. W. Maitland, *The History of English Law before the Time of Edward I*, 2nd edn. (1898; rpt. Cambridge, 1968), p. 46.

[18] 'Peace in the Feud', p. 13; *Custom and Conflict*, pp. 21–2.

[19] *Politics, Law, and Ritual*, p. 114; at p. 112, Gluckman also faulted Bloch for failing to make 'sufficient allowance for what is unlikely to be recorded or remembered, as against what passes into folk history, or allow enough for the form in which events entered that history. The vendetta that results from unsuccessful compromise is more likely to be remembered than disputes which are settled.'

[20] Convinced that feuding groups consisted of cognatic kindreds, not just in Anglo-Saxon England, but in continental Europe, Gluckman overlooked Bloch's identification of French feuding groups as '*lignages*'.

believed, as the following passage shows, that the Invisible Hand of Custom was at work in virtually all early European societies, even if they differed radically from 'stateless' societies in Africa:

> The study of stateless societies may thus give a model for interpreting the surviving fragments of evidence about our own historical past. This study also focuses attention onto principles which operate in all forms of groups, ranging from modern states to business organizations, schools, universities, and recreational societies. The more members of these groups are associated with one another through a variety of ties, linking different sets of persons, the less can factional dispute and intrigue destroy the general consensus of major group membership.[21]

Applying the peace in the feud

Given how frequently medieval historians have cited 'The Peace in the Feud' over the last half-century, they have obviously considered it relevant to the study of feuding, disputing, and violence.[22] Yet whether they truly applied Gluckman's theory of feuding is a matter of debate.[23] On the

[21] *Politics, Law, and Ritual*, p. 115. Here, Gluckman acknowledges the possibility that cross-cutting ties might be too weak and too few to prevent disputes from undermining 'the general consensus', but seems to have overlooked it except when studying modern South Africa.

[22] On the relevance of Gluckman's 'Peace in the Feud' to the study of the late Roman church, see D. Natal and J. Wood, 'Playing with Fire: Conflicting Bishops in Late Roman Spain and Gaul', in this volume. Other recent references to the article by medievalists include; W. Brown, *Violence in Medieval Europe* (Edinburgh, 2011), pp. 16–18; J. G. H. Hudson, 'Feud, Vengeance and Violence in England from the Tenth to the Twelfth Centuries', in B. S. Tuten and T. L. Billado (eds.), *Feud, Violence and Practice: Essays in Medieval Studies in Honor of Stephen D. White* (Farnham, 2010), pp. 29–53, at p. 52 n. 113; T. Roche, 'The Way Vengeance Comes: Rancorous Deeds and Words in the World of Orderic Vitalis', in S. A. Throop and P. R. Hyams (eds.), *Vengeance in the Middle Ages: Emotion, Religion and Feud* (Farnham, 2010), pp. 115–36, at p. 117; T. B. Lambert, 'Introduction: Some Approaches to Peace and Protection in the Middle Ages', in T. B. Lambert and D. Rollason (eds.), *Peace and Protection in the Middle Ages*, Durham Medieval and Renaissance Monographs and Essays, 1 (Durham, 2009), pp. 1–16, at pp. 6–7; J. B. Netterstrøm, 'Introduction: The Study of Feud in Medieval and Early Modern History', in Netterstrøm and B. Poulson (eds.), *Feud in Medieval and Early Modern Europe* (Aarhus, 2007), pp. 9–67, at 9–10; P. Haidu, *The Subject Medieval/Modern: Text and Governance in the Middle Ages* (Stanford, CA, 2004), p. 20; Hyams, *Rancor and Reconciliation in Medieval England* (Ithaca, NY, 2003), pp. 14–16; S. Carroll, 'The Peace in the Feud in Sixteenth- and Seventeenth-Century France', *Past & Present*, 178 (2003), 74–114; J. R. Ruff, *Violence in Early Modern Europe, 1500–1800* (Cambridge, 2001), p. 82; T. Dean, *Crime in Medieval Europe, 1200–1500* (Edinburgh, 2001), pp. 99–102; J. M. Hill, *The Cultural World in Beowulf* (Toronto, 1995), pp. 30–1.

[23] For a different assessment of Gluckman's influence on medievalists, see Barbara H. Rosenwein, 'Les émotions de la vengeance', in D. Barthélemy, F. Bougard, and R. Le Jan (eds.), *La vengeance, 400–1000*, Collection de l'école française de Rome, 357 (Rome, 2006), pp. 237–57, at pp. 238–9.

one hand, those who take a jaundiced view of the influence of anthropology on the study of medieval history have suggested that by slavishly adopting the theory, medievalists have concealed the violence and irrationality of feuding, mischaracterized it as an effective legal sanction against wrongdoing, and naïvely assumed that when a feud broke out, mediators associated with both parties could easily settle it and restore law, order, and social equilibrium. According to Daniel Lord Smail, the anthropological theory that

> the feud and its attendant institutions of peacemaking comprised a legal system that offered a basis for political order [was] not slow to cross from anthropology to history. A major conduit was [Gluckman's] 'The Peace in the Feud', which developed Evans-Pritchard's argument that the feud, as it expanded through the grades of kinship, inevitably compromised people with a foot in both camps; these people were then activated to quell the discord.[24]

Elsewhere, Smail claimed that 'by the early 1960s, European social historians had been won over by [the] appeal' of the anthropological theory that 'vengeance [was] both rational and effective when practised by members of stateless societies' and that feuding was 'a kind of legal system' and 'a system of order'.[25] When, in 1992 Thomas Head and Richard Landes cited Renato Rosaldo's complaint about 'the "extraordinary optimism" of the functionalist approach' to feuding and wrote that no 'easy peace' could be found in the Capetian kingdom during the years around 1000, they implied that 'The Peace in the Feud', not the study of charter-evidence, was the main basis for attacks on the theory that a violent feudal revolution at the turn of the millennium was associated with endless feuding and incessant violence.[26] In 1998 Thomas N. Bisson made a similar point about the baleful influence of 'The Peace in the Feud' on so-called dispute-resolutionists (including the present author). In their work on feuding and peace-making among nobles, Bisson implied, these scholars had overlooked or cavalierly ignored the violence inflicted on the powerless, because they had adopted what he ironically called 'the approved model of a stateless society' – a model that could only have been the one articulated in Gluckman's 'Peace in the Feud' and

[24] D. L. Smail, 'Common Violence: Vengeance and Inquisition in Fourteenth-Century Marseille', *Past & Present*, 151 (1996), 28–59, at 29–30.

[25] Smail, 'Factions and Vengeance in Renaissance Italy. A *Review Article*', *Comparative Studies in Society and History*, 38 (1996), 781–9.

[26] T. Head and R. Landes, 'Introduction', in Head and Landes (eds.), *The Peace of God: Social Violence and Religious Response in France around the Year 1000* (Ithaca, NY, 1992), pp. 1–20, at p. 16 and n. 42, citing R. Rosaldo, *Ilongot Headhunting, 1883–1974: a Study in Society and History* (Stanford, CA, 1980), p. 273. See this chapter at Note 84.

Evans-Pritchard's book on *The Nuer*.[27] In a historiographical essay on the study of medieval and early modern feuding, Jeppe Büchert Netterstrøm recently asserted that Gluckman's argument that 'Feud violence was not the outcome of anarchy but rather a structuring, ordering principle in "stateless" tribal societies' had been accepted by medievalists since the 1950s and that 'the tendency to functionalise, rationalize, legalise/legitimize feuding is still today a major drive in feud research'.[28]

However, even if Gluckman's 'Peace in the Feud' had clearly articulated the optimistic, hyper-functionalist theory of feuding that was routinely imputed to him by those searching for functionalists under the bed of medieval historiography, very few of the medievalists who cited the article ever suggested that feuding necessarily deterred feuding, or ultimately created social cohesion and political order, or constituted a legal system, or provided a basis for political order, or was just another way of making peace.[29] Nor did they ignore the impact of upper-class feuding on the powerless or imply that methods of dispute-processing used by nobles were available to peasants.[30] Instead, they simply challenged, as Gluckman had done, two assumptions built into the Twain/Bloch Model: first, that feuds were interminable, because the vengeance that the feuding parties took or sought to take in them was unlimited; and, second, that no mechanisms for controlling, limiting or settling feuds existed. To contest these assumptions, they did not rely on a model of feuding in stateless societies; instead, they examined the specific forms of violence used in particular feuds and other feud-like conflicts, analysed the specific goals achieved by waging feuds, and deconstructed the

27 T. N. Bisson, *Tormented Voices: Power, Crisis, and Humanity in Rural Catalonia, 1140–1200* (Cambridge, MA, 1998), pp. 145–6 and n. 9; see also p. 144 and n. 8. Subsequently, Bisson charged the same historians with adopting 'the model of feud constructed by legal anthropologists' such as Gluckman: T. N. Bisson, *The Crisis of the Twelfth Century: Power, Lordship, and the Origins of European Governance* (Princeton, NJ, 2009), p. 20 and n. 43; see also p. 21 and n. 44.

28 Netterstrøm, 'Introduction', pp. 10, 11. For a brilliant critique of the influence of functionalist anthropology on the study of medieval European rituals, see P. Buc, *The Dangers of Ritual: Between Early Medieval Texts and Social Scientific Theory* (Princeton, NJ, 2001).

29 On Gluckman's work and its relationship to British structuralist-functionalism, see, for example, J. Vincent, *Anthropology and Politics: Visions, Traditions, and Trends* (Tucson, AZ, 1990), esp. pp. 276–84, 375–81; R. P. Werbner, 'The Manchester School in South-Central Africa', *Annual Review of Anthropology*, 13 (1984), 157–85. For a valuable critique of functionalist studies of 'dispute-settlement' in Africa, see M. Chanock, *Law, Custom and Social Order: The Colonial Experience in Malawi and Zambia* (Portsmouth, NH, 1998), pp. 3–47.

30 *Pace* W. Brown and P. Górecki, 'Where Conflict Leads: On the Present and Future of Medieval Conflict Studies in the United States', in Brown and Górecki (eds.), *Conflict in Medieval Europe: Changing Perspectives on Society and Culture* (Aldershot, 2003), pp. 265–85, at pp. 282–3.

formulaic discourses in terms of which disputants routinely represented themselves as victims and their enemies as victimizers. They also showed that there were established mechanisms for settling these conflicts – mechanisms were sometimes used effectively to make peace between parties to feuds, even when courts lacked the power to judge disputes and enforce their judgements.[31] Nevertheless, although none of these findings depended on arguments advanced by Gluckman in 'The Peace in the Feud', it would be wrong to conclude that his article has been unimportant for the study of medieval societies, since, as we shall see, it continues to be a useful weapon for combatting updated versions of the Twain/Bloch Model of feud as an endless process of wild, unlimited, anarchic, pathologically irrational violence.

Evidently, the first historian to cite 'The Peace in the Feud' in a study of medieval feuding was J. M. Wallace-Hadrill, whose essay of 1959 on 'The Bloodfeud of the Franks' serves as an instructively ambiguous case-study of the application of Gluckman's argument to earlier European history.[32] Although the essay, Wallace-Hadrill wrote, 'owed much' to Gluckman's *Custom and Conflict in Africa*, just how much it owed is difficult to say. To be sure, Gluckman's peace can be seen in Wallace-Hadrill's Merovingian feud, when the latter writes that 'Feuding in the sense of incessant private warfare is a myth'.[33] There is also at least a hint of the Invisible Hand of Custom in Wallace-Hadrill's statement that there are 'natural pulls inherent in feud-society towards settlement and composition'. In fact, Wallace-Hadrill explicitly acknowledged his debt to Gluckman, when he identified in Merovingian Francia 'the situation [that Gluckman had] envisaged in another context ... where the mere elaboration and interdependence of kin groups may ensure a kind of immobility. Common blood and propinquity will always make for settlement.'[34] Here and in the passage just quoted about 'natural pulls ... towards settlement', one can hear echoes of Gluckman's statement that 'some members of each warring group [in a feud] have an interest in bringing

[31] For a pioneering essay presenting a similar argument, see F. L. Cheyette, '*Suum Cuique Tribuere*', *French Historical Studies*, 6 (1970), 287–99.

[32] J. M. Wallace-Hadrill, 'The Bloodfeud of the Franks', *Bulletin of the John Rylands Library, Manchester*, 41 (1958–9), 459–87; rpt. in Wallace-Hadrill, *The Long-Haired Kings and Other Studies in Frankish History* (London, 1962), pp. 121–47, at p. 123 n. 1; see also pp. 125–6. Although Ian Wood acknowledges that 'Wallace-Hadrill did learn something from Gluckman' and that some of their 'underlying concerns' are similar, he cites 'other and earlier influences [on Wallace-Hadrill's work] which modern historians have tended to forget'; he therefore warns them against 'get[ting] too carried away by connections between Wallace-Hadrill and Gluckman': I. Wood, '"The Bloodfeud of the Franks": a Historiographical Legend', *Early Medieval Europe*, 14 (2006), 489–504, at 489, 490, and 493.

[33] Wallace-Hadrill, 'Bloodfeud', p. 147. [34] 'Bloodfeud', pp. 125–6.

about a settlement of quarrels' and of his dictum that 'where custom divides in one set of relationships, it produces cohesion, through the settlement of quarrels, in a wider range of social life'.[35] Finally, Wallace-Hadrill certainly built peace into his influential 'working definition of feud', which differs significantly, not just from the one built into the Twain/Bloch Model, but from the one implicit in Dorothy Whitelock's valuable discussion of feud in early medieval England. Although Whitelock, writing several years before Gluckman published 'The Peace in the Feud', noted that a homicide victim's kinsmen could accept compensation 'without loss of honour', she never stated or implied that they might be pressured to do so and make peace with their adversaries.[36] Wallace-Hadrill, by contrast, treated peace-making as an integral part of feuding when he wrote: 'We may call [feud], first, the threat of hostility between kins; then, the state of hostility between them; and, finally, the satisfaction of their differences and a settlement on terms acceptable to both.'[37]

Nevertheless, Wallace-Hadrill's conclusions about the Merovingian feud were 'the reverse of clear-cut', as were his ways of applying 'The Peace in the Feud' to it. Instead of emphasizing the power of the 'natural pulls inherent in feud-society towards settlement and composition' or citing the workings of the Invisible Hand of Custom, Wallace-Hadrill sounded less like Max Gluckman than he did like Pierre Bourdieu or William Ian Miller when he wrote, 'Always it is touch-and-go what will happen; it will depend on what the kins think, how extensively they or their followings are mobilizable, how rich they are or how ready to pay or to receive payment, how much the bishop or the king feels disposed to intervene.'[38] Wallace-Hadrill implied that micro-political strategizing – and not the Invisible Hand of Custom – determined how any given feud would proceed, when he wrote: 'Except generally where honour was obviously involved, kins and families would find reasons and excuses to look to composition first, whether of their own making or under the protection of the courts. Their efforts might break down, and often did; and so might the efforts of the courts.'[39] Moreover, as his references to kings, courts, and bishops show, Wallace-Hadrill did not treat common blood and propinquity as the only sources of pressure for settling Merovingian feuds. There was also a state, if not The State. There was also the Frankish church. Finally, Wallace-Hadrill pluralized the Merovingian bloodfeud and presented it as his own analytical construct,

[35] Gluckman, *Custom and Conflict*, p. 14.
[36] D. Whitelock, *The Beginnings of English Society* (Harmondsworth, 1952), p. 40.
[37] Wallace-Hadrill, 'Bloodfeud', 122. [38] 'Bloodfeud', p. 146.
[39] 'Bloodfeud', p. 147.

not as an indigenous model, by blurring the distinctions between bloodfeud and feud and between feud and conflict. Noting that 'homicide was but one of many kinds of injuries from which a feud might spring', he believed that while Merovingian feuds took many different forms, they differed significantly from Carolingian feuds. Since 'feud remains undefined by those who have resort to it', moreover, 'We must search for our feuds . . . in a maze of terms that can mislead: the Frankish *faithu*, latinized as *faidus*, may mean what we are after, or it may mean something different; feud may lurk behind [Latin words for 'enemy' or 'vengeance'], or it may not.'[40] If the Merovingian bloodfeud was so hard to identify, was it an objectively defined subject of historical inquiry or an analytical construct of Wallace-Hadrill's own invention that others could deconstruct or construct differently?

Because Gluckman's own argument about the peace in the feud was less than clear-cut and Wallace-Hadrill's partial application of it even less so, the medieval historians who cited 'The Peace in the Feud' from the 1960s onwards were free to apply it in different ways – or not to apply it at all. How or whether they did one or the other seems to have depended partly on what region of Europe and what sub-period of the Middle Ages they studied. No one ever suggested that feuding in Merovingian Francia, early and late Anglo-Saxon England, Scandinavia and Iceland, Catalonia, late medieval Austria and Germany, Lombard Italy, Carolingian Francia, and post-Carolingian Francia could be reduced to the same model, much less to a legal system. At the same time, what medievalists did or did not make of Gluckman's article also depended partly on whether they were influenced by anthropological studies of feuding and disputing that contested or by-passed Gluckman's, but that critics of his malign influence on medieval history have consistently ignored. As a result, anyone wishing to identify anthropological influences on the study of medieval feuding should give less attention to Gluckman and Evans-Pitchard than to the writings of such scholars as Fredrik Barth, Sally F. Moore, Jacob Black-Michaud, Christopher Boehm, Renato Rosaldo, Michelle Rosaldo, Klaus Koch, F.G. Bailey, and, above all, Pierre Bourdieu.[41]

[40] 'Bloodfeud', pp. 122–3.

[41] Among the anthropological studies of feud and revenge cited in S. D. White, 'Feuding and Peace-Making in the Touraine around the Year 1100', *Traditio*, 42 (1986), 195–263; rpt. in White, *Feuding and Peace-Making in Eleventh-Century France*, Variorum Collected Studies (Aldershot, 2005), ch. 1 at p. 203 n. 37 are: F. Barth, *Political Leadership among Swat Pathans*, London School of Economics Monographs on Social Anthropology, 19, corrected edn. (London, 1965), pp. 81–6; E. L. Peters, 'Some Structural Aspects of the Feud among the Camel-Herding Bedouin of Cyrenaica', *Africa*, 37 (1967), 261–82; S. F. Moore, 'Legal Liability and Evolutionary Interpretation: Some Aspects of Strict

Furthermore, the importance of Gluckman's article to historians of medieval feuding also depended on whether they were influenced by other historians whose perspective on feuding had something in common with his. One of these was Georges Duby, who, in the late 1940s, had emphasized the role of social networks in limiting violence in the eleventh-century Mâconnais.[42] The other was Otto Brunner, who, in 1939, had characterized the 'noble' feud as the keystone of the medieval legal and political order.[43] Although Brunner, like Gluckman, contested the conventional view that vengeance and feud were 'prior to law and society' by arguing that they were sanctioned by custom and law and regulated by them, and although Duby identified pressures for settling feuds very similar to the ones that Gluckman later described, the feuds that both of these historians studied seemed to differ so radically from the ones analysed by Gluckman that the possibility of applying the latter's ideas to them seemed remote. Not only were they carried on in highly stratified societies ruled, in the case of Brunner's feuds, by powerful lords; they were waged primarily if not exclusively by nobles, whom Brunner represented as seeking 'retribution and vengeance in order to restore the broken order of Right', but whose methods of waging feuds of this kind were interpreted very differently, as we shall see, by other scholars.[44]

Liability, Self-Help and Collective Responsibility', in M. Gluckman (ed.), *The Allocation of Responsibility* (Manchester, 1972), pp. 51–107; J. Black-Michaud, *Cohesive Force* (Oxford, 1975); C. Boehm, *Blood Revenge: the Anthropology of Feuding in Montenegro and Other Tribal Societies* (Lawrence, KS, 1984). For overlapping lists of anthropological studies of feud, see Miller, *Bloodtaking and Peacemaking: Feud, Law, and Society in Saga Iceland* (Chicago, IL, 1990), p. 349 n. 2; and Hyams, *Rancor and Reconciliation*, p. 8 n. 10. For critiques of structuralist history, see White, 'Tenth-Century Courts at Mâcon and the Perils of Structuralist History: re-Reading Burgundian Judicial Institutions', in Brown and Górecki, *Conflict in Medieval Europe*, pp. 37–68, rpt. in White, *Feuding and Peace-Making*, ch. 9 at pp. 61–2. On the influence of anthropological studies of disputing on studies of medieval Scandinavia, see K. Esmark and H. J. Orning, 'General Introduction', in K. Esmark, L. Hermanson, H. J. Orning, and H. Vogt (eds.), *Disputing Strategies in Medieval Scandinavia* (Leiden, 2013), pp. 1–28, at pp. 27–8.

42 See this chapter at Note 86.

43 O. Brunner, *Land und Herrschaft: Grundfragen der territorialen Verfassungsgeschichte Östereichs im Mittelalter*, 6th edn. (Vienna, 1973), trans. as *Land and Lordship: Structures of Governance in Medieval Austria* by H. Kaminsky and J. V. H. Melton (Philadelphia, PA, 1992). Brunner's views on feud are restated and developed in H. Kaminsky, 'The Noble Feud in the Later Middle Ages', *Past & Present*, 177 (2002), 55–83. According to Hyams, *Rancor and Reconciliation*, p. 14 n. 31, Brunner's arguments provide as much 'encouragement' to re-think conventional views of medieval feud as do Gluckman's 'Peace in the Feud.'

44 Brunner, *Land and Lordship*, pp. 16, 28. On Brunner's influence on the study of feud in Germany, see Netterstrøm, 'Introduction', pp. 20–8, which underestimates the force of the critique of Brunner's theory of feud in G. Algazi, *Herrengewalt und Gewalt der Herren im späten Mittelalter. Herrschaft Gegenseitigkeit und Sprachgebrauch* (Frankfurt, 1992) and in other works of Algazi's cited in Notes 52 and 54.

Indeed, there was little agreement about what a 'feud' was.[45] Guy Halsall argued vehemently for defining it in a way that ruled out the possibility of there being any peace in it.[46] Others avoided the subject and wrote only of vengeance.[47] Still others defined 'feud' very loosely or simply listed its main characteristics in particular regions of Europe during specific sub-periods of the Middle Ages. For them, the question of whether there were pressures for peace in any particular feuding culture was a matter for empirical investigation. William Ian Miller broadened and deepened Wallace-Hadrill's working definition of feud in three ways: first, by identifying nine characteristics of medieval Icelandic feuds, including the existence of 'culturally acceptable means for making temporary or permanent settlements' in them; second, by arguing that 'The bloodfeud is frequently moral, often juridical, and always political'; and, finally, that 'The feud was more than the series of overt actions that made it up' and included 'the relationship between the parties [and] the state of the participants' minds.'[48] Paul Hyams took a different position. Arguing that 'Feud starts with an effort to avenge injury, generally violent injury, and often a killing', he identified eight other characteristics of feud, including the stipulation that 'Emotions both fuel the response [to injury] and determine its quantum and nature.'[49] In identifying the main characteristics of feuds in medieval France, the present author treated the decision to avenge a homicide or other injury, mainly as the product of strategic choice, rather than obedience to a binding legal obligation or powerful emotional urges. He also noted how frequently feuds were associated with long-term political conflicts; considered the possibility

[45] For the debate, see Netterstrøm, 'Introduction', pp. 37–64; Brown, *Violence in Medieval Europe*, pp. 15–16.

[46] G. Halsall, 'Violence and Society in the Early Medieval West: an Introductory Survey', in Halsall (ed.), *Violence and Society in the Early Medieval West* (Woodbridge, 1998), pp. 1–45; see also M. Bennett, 'Violence in Eleventh-Century Normandy: Feud, Warfare and Politics', in Halsall, *Violence and Society*, pp. 108–25. For opposing viewpoints see, for example, D. Barthélemy, 'Feudal War in Tenth-Century France', in Throop and Hyams (eds.), *Vengeance in the Middle Ages*, pp. 105–13, at p.107; Hyams, 'Was There Really Such a Thing as Feud in the High Middle Ages', in Throop and Hyams (eds.), *Vengeance in the Middle Ages*, pp. 131–75; White, 'Un imaginaire faidal. La représentation de la guerre dans quelques chansons de geste', in Barthélemy, F. Bougard, and R. Le Jan (eds.), *La vengeance, 400–1000*, Collection de l'école française de Rome, 357 (Rome, 2006), pp. 175–98.

[47] See, for example, Brown, *Violence in Medieval Europe*, p. 16.

[48] Miller, *Bloodtaking and Peacemaking*, pp. 180–1; and Miller, 'Choosing the Avenger: Some Aspects of the Bloodfeud in Medieval Iceland and England', *Law and History Review*, 1 (1983), 159–204. Eighteen characteristics of feud are listed in J. Byock, 'Defining Feud: Talking Points and Iceland's Saga Women', in Netterstrøm and Poulsen, *Feud in Medieval and Early Modern Europe*, pp. 95–112 at pp. 96–9. For other lists, see Boehm, *Blood Revenge*, pp. 218–19; and Netterstrøm, 'Introduction', pp. 49–59.

[49] Hyams, *Rancor and Reconciliation*, pp. 8–9 lists nine features of feud.

that feuding was sometimes a pretext for plundering; suggested that feuding could be seen as a genre of political action; and toyed with the idea that a feud could not be waged without there being a story about it.[50]

The problem of determining just how much of Gluckman's peace historians found in medieval feuds was further complicated by subsidiary debates about four interrelated issues: first, whether so-called noble feuds waged by lords over land claims should be distinguished from 'vendettas' carried on by members of all classes seeking to avenge homicides;[51] second, whether a single dimension of feud – the legal, the emotional, the economic, the political, or the violent – should be privileged over all the others or whether feuds should be understood, in Gadi Algazi's wonderfully mysterious phrase, 'as multi-layered practices with multiple social uses and unexpected hidden edges';[52] third, whether 'literary' as opposed to 'historical' accounts had any place in the study of medieval feuds;[53] and, finally, whether the physical force used in prosecuting 'noble' feuds amounted to mere 'violence' or whether it could be fully understood only by considering its legal, moral, political, and economic dimensions from the perspectives of victims, perpetrators, and third-party observers.[54] Given how complicated the historiography of

[50] White, 'Feuding and Peace-Making', pp. 246–57; see also White, 'Un imaginaire faidal'.

[51] The case for doing so was presented by Brunner and re-stated by Kaminsky in writings cited in this chapter in Note 54. On homicide and vengeance for homicide in 'noble feuds', see White, 'Feuding and Peace-Making' and 'Un imaginaire faidal'.

[52] G. Algazi, 'Pruning Peasants: Private War and Maintaining the Lord's Peace in Late Medieval Germany', in E. Cohen and M. de Jong (eds.), *Medieval Transformations: Texts, Power and Gifts in Context* (Leiden 2000), pp. 245–74, at p. 259. See also White, 'Un imaginaire faidal'.

[53] On the use of sagas for the study of Icelandic feuding, see W. I. Miller, *Bloodtaking and Peacemaking*, pp. 43–76; and V. W. Turner, 'An Anthropological Approach to the Icelandic Saga', in *The Translation of Culture: Essays to E.E. Evans-Pritchard* (London, 1971), pp. 349–74. On the use of *chansons de geste* for similar purposes, see White, 'Un imaginaire faidal'. On the dangers of using literary narratives to study feuds, see, for example, P. Sawyer, 'The Bloodfeud in Fact and Fiction', *Acta Jutlandica: Skrifter fra Aarhus Universitet*, 63 (1987), 27–38. For a critique of recent efforts to use medieval French literary texts to study vengeance, see White, 'The Feelings in the Feud: The Emotional Turn in the Study of Vengeance', in K. Esmark, L. Hermanson, H. J. Orning, and H. Vogt (eds.), *Disputing Strategies in Medieval Scandinavia* (Leiden, 2013), pp. 281–311.

[54] For the first approach, see Bisson, *Tormented Voices; Crisis of the Twelfth Century*; and 'The Feudal Revolution', *Past and Present*, 142 (1994), 6–42. For the second, see the work of Brunner cited in Note 55. For the third approach, see White, 'Feuding and Peace-Making'; White, 'Re-penser la violence: De 2000 à 1000', *Médiévales*, 37 (1999), 205–23; rpt. in White, *Feuding and Peace-Making*, ch. 3; White, 'The "Feudal Revolution": Comment', *Past and Present*, 152 (1996), 205–23; rpt. in White, *Feuding and Peace-Making*, ch. 2; W. I. Miller, 'Getting a Fix on Violence', in Miller, *Humiliation and Other Essays on Honor, Social Discomfort, and Violence* (Ithaca, NY, 1993), pp. 53–92; G. Algazi, 'The Social Uses of Private War: Some Late Medieval Views Reviewed', *Tel Aviver Jahrbuch fur deutsche Geshichte*, 22 (1993), 253–73; Algazi, 'Pruning Peasants'.

medieval feuding became, disagreements inevitably arose about whether conflicts in this or that region of medieval Europe really counted as feuds[55] and, if they did, whether there was even a hint of a peace in them. Whatever positions historians took in debates over the anthropologizing of medieval feuds, it was impossible to cite anyone who was not a card-carrying medievalist without running the risk of being charged with embracing functionalism, 'optimistic' American functionalism, intellectual eclecticism, or, simply, anthropology.

For these reasons, the reception of Gluckman's 'Peace' into the study of medieval feuding was not a mechanical process of applying an anthropological theory to medieval evidence. To be sure, one historian lauded 'The Peace in the Feud' for demonstrating that 'the blood-feud [was] an instrument of cohesion'.[56] Another suggested that Carolingian feuds led to the restoration of peace.[57] A third maintained that feuds 'were often intended to establish a balance ... and thus to restore an equilibrium of honor'.[58] However, the usual way of using Gluckman's 'Peace in the Feud' was to by-pass his broader argument about cohesion arising out of conflict, to invoke his attack on the view that feuds were interminable, and to explore the hypothesis advanced by Gluckman and other anthropologists that under certain very specific conditions there might be a kind of peace in certain kinds of feuds. Even though Joel T. Rosenthal cited the article along with Evans-Pritchard's discussion of feud in *The Nuer* when characterizing early medieval feuding as 'a method whereby a society without strong central (or non-kinship linked) government sought to achieve a balance between its centrifugal and its centripetal elements', he also observed that 'The divisive aspects of the feud constantly threatened to disrupt any social ties which sought to transcend family groupings'.[59] John M. Hill valued Gluckman's 'idea of pressure for settlement short of violence or at least of runaway violence) between feuding

[55] See, for example, Bennett, 'Violence in Eleventh-Century Normandy'; Hudson, 'Feud, Vengeance and Violence'.

[56] K. Thomas, 'History and Anthropology', *Past & Present*, 24 (1963), 3–24, at 20 n. 34.

[57] R. Le Jan, *Famille et pouvoir dans le monde franc (viie-xe siècle). Essai d'anthropologie sociale* (Paris, 1995), p. 90. For a critique of certain approaches to the study of medieval 'dispute-settlement', see White, 'The Study of Disputes in Medieval France', in White, *Feuding and Peace-Making*, ch. 8, pp. 1–14, esp. 10–14.

[58] P. J. Geary, 'Living with Conflicts in Stateless France: a Typology of Conflict Management Mechanisms, 1050–1200', in Geary, *Living with the Dead in the Middle Ages* (New York, 1994), pp. 125–62, at p. 146; other feuds, he continues, were 'waged to achieve a temporary advantage and force the enemy into negotiating the deeper underlying issues' (p. 146). 'The ultimate purpose of negotiation', Geary concludes, 'was to establish a *pax* or *amicitia* between the parties, that is, to create a positive relationship to replace the state of war' (p. 150).

[59] J. T. Rosenthal, 'Marriage and the Blood Feud in "Heroic" Europe', *British Journal of Sociology*, 17 (1966), 133–44, at 136–7, 138.

people', but thought he was 'more hopeful than absolutely right about the peace in the feud in most societies where feuds occur'.[60] The present author argued that although cross-cutting ties probably created pressure to settle feuds in the Lower Touraine c.1100, these conflicts 'may have been more common and more difficult to stop than [Gluckman's] theory would suggest' and concluded that if there was a peace in the medieval feud, there was certainly 'a feud in the medieval peace' as well.[61] While noting Gluckman's contributions to an understanding of dispute-processing in the years around 1000, Richard Barton warned against substituting 'a world of peaceful harmony for one of brutal anarchy'.[62] Hyams acknowledged the 'power' of the theory of Evans-Pritchard and Gluckman that 'feuding could function as an instrument of routine social control'; but he significantly qualified the theory, just as Gluckman had done in 'The Peace in the Feud', by arguing that feud could generate peace only in the right circumstances.[63] Miller argued that in medieval Iceland, there were culturally acceptable methods of settling feuds. But by identifying the feud as a means of gaining and holding power in medieval Iceland, he ruled out the possibility of there being a stable peace in it; he also maintained that there was no peace at all when feud 'exceeded the limits of its own rules'.[64] When in 2001 Trevor Dean asked, 'Was there peace in the medieval European feud?', he was on solid ground when he answered, 'Numerous historians doubt it.'[65]

Feuding with the peace in the feud

As we have just seen, writers on medieval European feuds took note of Gluckman's 'Peace in the Feud', while questioning its full applicability to medieval feuds and, in particular, to the feud-like conflicts called 'wars'

60 Hill, Cultural World in Beowulf, pp. 30, 32.

61 White, 'Feuding and Peace-Making', 258–9, 263; see also White, 'Clotild's Revenge: Politics, Kinship and Ideology in the Merovingian Blood Feud', in S. K. Cohn and S. A. Epstein (eds.), *Portraits in Medieval and Renaissance Living: Essays in Memory of David Herlihy* (Ann Arbor, MI, 1996), pp. 107–30; rpt. in White, *Re-Thinking Kinship and Feudalism in Early Medieval Europe* (Aldershot, 2005), ch. 3, which criticizes structuralist-functionalist models of feuding, such as Gluckman's, and juridical models, such as Brunner's, as well at pp. 112–14.

62 R. E. Barton, *Lordship in the County of Maine, c. 890–1160* (Woodbridge, 2004), p. 187.

63 Hyams, *Rancor and Reconciliation*, p. 10; see the entire discussion at pp. 3–33. See also Hyams, 'Feud in Medieval England', *Haskins Society Journal*, 3 (1992), 1–21; Hyams, 'Feud and the State in Late Anglo-Saxon England', *Journal of British Studies*, 40 (2001), 1–43.

64 Miller, *Bloodtaking and Peacemaking*, ch. 6; 'Choosing the Avenger', p. 160.

65 Dean, *Crime in Medieval Europe*, p. 100. According to Brown, *Violence in Medieval Europe*, p. 17, 'The "peace in the feud" model... poses some problems for medieval historians.'

(*werrae*) that nobles waged in many regions of Europe during much of the middle ages. In certain cases, they also challenged several assumptions about feuding that Gluckman's analysis, as previously noted, shared with the Twain/Bloch Model:[66] first, that vengeance against an enemy was the sole purpose of feuding; second, that feuding groups were made up of the principal parties' male kin; and, third, that these groups spontaneously assembled themselves to take vengeance against their enemies. The first of these assumptions was impossible to reconcile with the finding that the main way of waging a feud in the highly stratified societies of medieval Europe was, as Brunner put it, 'to "distress" [a rival lord] by pillage and devastation, "plundering and burning"',[67] not for the purpose of taking vengeance on him, but 'to compel [him] either to accept the challenger's version of Right, or to seek arbitration, or to lodge a judicial complaint, or, in certain conditions, to offer battle'.[68] However, by challenging Brunner's view that noble feuding was simply a legal process, Gadi Algazi not only provided another way of contesting the assumption that the sole purpose of feuding was the irrational one of taking uncontrolled vengeance; his work also brought out with particular clarity further differences between medieval European feuding and the feuds studied by anthropologists such as Gluckman. By emphasizing that it was not the challenger's opponent, but rather his opponent's peasants whom the challenger and his men pillaged and plundered,[69] Algazi showed, *inter alia*, that there were strong economic incentives for feuding.

Previously, Georges Duby had emphasized the same dimension of noble feuds in France, where waging war, he said, was so intimately associated with pillaging and plundering an enemy's lands and peasants that it 'fulfilled a primordial economic function at least as important as that of productive labor'.[70] Robert Fossier believed that the real objective in noble feuds was 'to take by force what one could neither buy nor receive [as a gift]', while Pierre Bonnassie saw 'the quest for booty' as the motivating force behind conflicts of this kind in eleventh-century

[66] According to Kaminsky, 'Noble Feud', nobles waged similar feuds in later medieval England.

[67] Brunner, *Land and Lordship*, pp. 67, 69. For similar inventories of 'violent' acts, see White, 'The "Feudal Revolution": a Comment', p. 210.

[68] Brunner, *Land and Lordship*, p. 69.

[69] G. Algazi, 'Pruning Peasants'; see also White, 'Feuding and Peace-Making', p. 202.

[70] G. Duby, *Le dimanche de Bouvines* (Paris, 1973), p. 77. Among 'les vrais moteurs' of these conflicts, Duby cited 'des rancoeurs et des convoitises de chefs de bande, des emportements personnels, des affaires de famille, de répudiation, d'adultère, des affronts mal digérés, des promesses non tenues, des amitiés trahies, la soif de prendre, de surpasser les autres, de mettre un rival à ses pieds pour la satisfaction de le relever d'un air bonasse' (p. 44).

Catalonia.[71] Looking more deeply into the latent functions of feuding by plundering in societies sharply divided between lords and peasants, Algazi concluded, 'By participating in private wars against each other, lords were [unwittingly] engaged in the uncoordinated production of the need [of peasants] for protection'; he also suggested that for the men who engaged in it, the 'pruning' of peasants – as it was sometimes called in late medieval sources – was a significant element in the inculcation of class values and the re-production of an aristocratic *habitus.*[72] In making these arguments, Algazi also undercut the presupposition of older writers that feuding was a totally irrational process. The same presupposition was further undermined by finding that these conflicts generally arose out of disputes over landed property, rather than homicides, and could serve as vehicles for territorial aggrandizement.[73] In analysing feuds in medieval Iceland, Miller broadened this argument when he described the feud as 'one of the key structures in which the competition for power, the struggle for dominance, is played out'.[74]

Re-thinking the methods, the goals, and the long-term and short-term effects of medieval feuding while regarding feuds as rational political processes led to a clearer understanding of who participated in them and what their participation entailed. Gluckman took it for granted, as Marc Bloch and Mark Twain both did, that feuding groups consisted of kinsmen whose participation in a feud was determined by custom, if not by a strong sense of moral obligation and by an irrepressible impulse to take vengeance. However, in the wars studied by Brunner and Algazi, Duby and his followers, and by Barthélemy and the present author, the groups that engaged in plundering the lands and peasants of a lord's enemy were largely made up of the lord's clients. Though their participation in their lord's feuds might well have been represented as a matter of political, legal, or moral obligation, it was also determined by economic incentives in the form of opportunities to take plunder and the hope of further rewards – opportunities that the lord was expected to provide them with. Although there are good grounds for thinking that rival clienteles in noble wars were linked by cross-cutting ties, whatever pressures for peace these relationships may have generated were unlikely to have been as compelling as the ones whose existence Gluckman posited in 'The Peace in the Feud'.[75]

[71] R. Fossier, *Enfance de l'Europe, Xè-XIIè siècles. Aspects économiques et sociaux*, 2 vols. (Paris, 1982), 1, pp. 424–5; P. Bonnassie, 'From the Rhône to Galicia: Origins and Modalities of the Feudal Order', in Bonnassie, *From Slavery to Feudalism in South Western-Europe* (Cambridge, 1991), pp. 104–131, at pp. 109, 120.

[72] Algazi, 'Pruning Peasants'; see also White, 'Feuding and Peace-Making'.

[73] See White, 'Un imaginaire faidal'. [74] Miller, *Bloodtaking and Peacemaking*, p. 181.

[75] For one way of playing out this argument, see White, 'Feuding and Peace-Making'.

Whether noble feuds were interpreted in the manner of Brunner, Duby and his followers, or Algazi, the present author and others, Gluckman's arguments for a peace in the feud hardly applied to them. When revenge for a wrong or, rather, for an act that could be plausibly represented as a wrong took the form of plundering a lord's peasants, rather than taking blood vengeance on him or on his supporters, the fear of provoking a feud could not have been a powerful deterrent to wrong-doing, particularly since he and his men retained the option of plundering his enemy's peasants in return. Indeed, it is difficult to tell whether plundering peasants was a way of feuding or whether feuding was an occasion or pretext for plundering. Furthermore, since, contrary to what Gluckman supposed, the supporters of each opposing lord in a noble war were rarely, if ever, recruited exclusively from among his patrilineal kinsmen, the opposing groups in the conflict would not necessarily have been linked, as he assumed they would have been, by 'cross-cutting' ties based primarily on cognatic kinship. If, instead, feuding groups of this kind were largely made up of a lord's clients and friends, plus some of his kin, and if group members were all associated with the same castle or castles that the lord controlled, then pressures for peace in feuds would have been weaker than Gluckman predicted and settlements of feuds would not necessarily have been arranged in the ways he described..[76]

The revenge of the peace in the feud

As Gluckman's 'Peace' came to be seen as largely inapplicable to medieval European feuding, one might have expected it to become a mere reference point in the historiography of medieval dispute-processing. But this would be to underestimate its value as an analytical and rhetorical tool for dispelling the myths about vengeance and violence that still have a hold on the history of medieval Europe.[77] Whether historians identify feuding with incessant quarrelling, unlimited violence, or an emotional compulsion to take vengeance, 'The Peace in the Feud' has had something to offer to their critics. In 1963 one historian praised it for exposing 'the fallacy, common among medievalists, that the feud led to incessant private warfare'.[78] Later, Gluckman's article played a different role in

[76] See Kaminsky, 'Noble Feud', pp. 55–6, which distinguishes 'noble' feuds waged over property rights from bloodfeuds or vendettas, whereas White, 'Feuding and Peace-Making' argues for conflating the two kinds of feuds, at least for certain purposes.

[77] Besides, one should not rule out the possibility that the article's catchy title alone is so offensive and anxiety-provoking to those who believe that only the state can bring social peace that they cannot help but exaggerate its influence.

[78] K. Thomas, 'History and Anthropology', *Past & Present*, 24 (1963), 3–24, at 20, n. 34. According to J. Wormald, 'Bloodfeud, Kindred and Government in Early Modern

critiques of the theory that a 'feudal revolution' in the years around 1000 unleashed 'unlimited violence' and 'anarchy' in West Francia and possibly elsewhere. Currently, at a time when an 'emotional turn' in the study of medieval feuding seems to be leading historians to revive Sir Francis Bacon's view of revenge as 'wild justice', 'The Peace in the Feud' makes it easier to understand this tendency as a challenge to all efforts to treat feuding as a rational process.

One of the main effects of the arguments for a feudal revolution in the years around 1000 was to inscribe a new version of this model into medieval historiography, as historians translated alarming images of violence and vengeance from monastic sources into the claim that a collapse of public authority led to a sudden upsurge in violence perpetrated by petty nobles and knights. The violence included interminable feuds driven by 'inter-family hatred, [with] each aggression leading to vengeance, each vengeance to a new vengeance';[79] and veritable 'atrocities', such as 'arson, murders, mutilations, etc.'[80] This method of dramatizing violence is illustrated in a book on the so-called feudal mutation in a single village, which, in a mere eleven pages, referred to 'the increase in violence', 'a general increase in violence', 'mounting anarchy', 'threatening violence', 'social turmoil', the 'sudden flare-up of violence', 'a veritable social tempest', 'the social storm', a 'region... convulsed from top to bottom', 'anarchy', 'disorder and violence', 'violence... unleashed', 'tumult', 'the spiral of social crisis', 'the pillaging of warriors out of control', and local nobles who 'plunged society into anarchy' by 'unleashing violence'.[81]

In this historiographical context, 'The Peace in the Feud' became a tool for undercutting the unsubstantiated, over-dramatized claims of the *mutationnistes* about endless feuding, incessant violence, warriors out of control, and anarchy.[82] Since there was no evidence that 'public authority' had collapsed at this time or that its collapse triggered incessant

Scotland', *Past & Present*, 87 (1980), 54–97, at 55, 'Feud can no longer be regarded as a matter of rival groups slogging it out to the death of themselves and their descendants, until time, exhaustion or a more powerful authority brought it to an end.'

79 Bonnassie, 'From the Rhône to Galicia', p. 120.

80 Bonnassie, 'From the Rhône to Galicia', p. 120. For the debate on the feudal revolution, see the literature cited in White, 'Tenth-Century Courts at Mâcon', p. 37, n. 3.

81 G. Bois, *The Transformation of the Year 1000: the Village of Lournand from Antiquity to Feudalism*, trans. J. Birrell (Manchester, 1992), pp. 135, 136, 137, 138, 139, 145, 148, 149, 150, 152, 153. For 'warrior violence', 'aristocratic violence', 'lawlessness and violence', 'open violence', 'acts of violence', 'rising violence', 'the disorders of the day', and 'the usurpations of a warrior aristocracy', see C. Lauranson-Rosaz, 'Peace from the Mountains: the Auvergnat Origins of the Peace of God', in Head and Landes, pp. 104–34 at pp. 106, 107, 109, 115, 117, 132.

82 Along with other works of his cited in notes 46 and 85, see Barthêlemy, *The Serf, the Knight, and the Historian*, trans. Graham Robert Edwards (Ithaca, NY, 2009), esp. pp. 1–11, 302–13.

feuding and endless violence, it was all too obvious that these claims depended heavily on the assumption debunked in Gluckman's article that 'societies which have no governmental institutions' are virtually certain to break up in 'lawlessness'.[83] Cheyette could therefore criticize the *mutationnistes* for presupposing that 'without constraint from above society will fall into anarchy . . . the strong will do what they wish and the weak will suffer what they must'.[84] When Barthélemy cited Gluckman's work and that of other Africanist anthropologists in attacking '*mutationnisme*', he did not deny that wars between lords injured peasants or that seigneurial régimes were ultimately based on the use of force; instead, he contested the myth of unlimited feudal violence by showing that there were limits on it and by documenting the existence of forms of peacemaking that historians of the feudal revolution had ignored.[85] Even though, in medieval Europe, the 'cross-cutting' ties determined by kinship that Gluckman had discussed in 'The Peace in the Feud' did not generate the kind of pressure for peace he had imagined, social networks and social networking undoubtedly facilitated peace-making – as Duby and Cheyette had previously suggested[86] – in eleventh-century France, where there were 'customary mechanisms', as Gluckman called them, that 'restrain[ed] conflicts from destroying the wider social order'.[87]

More recently, the reaction against so-called anthropological approaches to medieval feuding on the spurious grounds that they 'functionalize, rationalize, legalize/legitimize feuding' and the replacement of

[83] Gluckman, 'Peace in the Feud', p. 1; *Custom and Conflict*, pp. 2–3.

[84] F. L. Cheyette, 'Some Reflections on Violence, Reconciliation, and the "Feudal Revolution"', in W. Brown and P. Górecki (eds.), *Conflict in Medieval Europe: Changing Perspectives on Society and Culture* (Aldershot, 2003), pp. 243–64, at p. 248.

[85] Barthélemy, *L'an mil et la paix de dieu: la France chrétienne et féodale* (Paris, 1999), pp. 20–2; Barthélemy, *La société dans le comté de Vendôme: de l'an mil au xive siècle* (Paris, 1993), pp. 13–15, 350–1; Barthélemy, 'La vengeance, le jugement et le compromis', in *Le règlement des conflits au moyen âge*, XXXIe Congrès de la S. H. M. E. S. (Angers, juin, 2000), Société des Historiens Médiévistes de l'Enseignement Supérieur Public (Paris, 2001), pp. 11–20, at pp. 14–17.

[86] Duby, 'Recherches sur l'évolution des institutions judiciaries pendant le Xe et le XIe siècle dans le sud de la Bouirgogne', *Le Moyen Âge*, 52 (1946), 149–94; 53 (1947), 15–35; trans. as 'The Evolution of Judicial Institutions: Burgundy in the Tenth and Eleventh Centuries', in Duby, *The Chivalrous Society*, trans. C. Postan (Berkeley, CA, 1980), pp. 115–58, at p. 158 ('Moral obligations and the persuasion of their peers were all that could impose a limit to their violence and greed.'); Duby, *La société aux XI et XIIe siècles dans la region mâconnaise* (Paris, 1971), p. 165 ('Seules, des considerations morales contiennent la turbulence des riches; la foi et le serment sons les soutiens de la paix.') and p. 170 ('l'aristocratie ne connaît d'autres contraintes que des pressions morales, à l'ordre dans les hautes classes de la société laïques et maintenues avant tout par la foi.').

[87] Gluckman, *Custom and Conflict*, p. 2. The '*société faidale*' of Barthélemy's *Chevaliers et miracles* (see esp. pp. 4, 11–22) closely resembles Gluckman's 'feuding society': see Gluckman 'The Peace in the Feud'.

these approaches with ones that emphasize 'dysfunctional and irrational behavior' in feuds[88] and draw on neuroscience and evolutionary psychology can be associated with the very old belief that vengeance is driven by uncontrolled emotion.[89] According to the evolutionary psychologist Steven Pinker, vengeance is 'an easily pushed button in everyone's brain [that] is, quite literally, an urge'; in fact, he tells us, the desire for vengeance resembles the craving for 'nicotine, cocaine, or chocolate'.[90] Without endorsing this particular theory of vengeance, Paul R. Hyams advocates the assimilation of the best of 'evolutionary psychology' into the study of medieval vengeance,[91] while Daniel Lord Smail's work on the relationship between emotions and political action draws on neuropsychology and neurophysiology.[92] Where is this emotional turn in the study of vengeance and feuding taking us?[93] If we combine Hyams' statements that the 'urge to avenge wrongs was well-nigh universal [in medieval Europe] and irresistible to all save the very saintly'; that 'people who see themselves as having been wronged feel an almost insuperable urge to return the favour, if possible with added interest',[94] and that in feuding, 'Emotions both fuel the response [to injury] and determine its quantum and nature',[95] we seem to be moving both forward and backward to a view of feuding that differs radically from Gluckman's, because

[88] Netterstrøm, 'Introduction', p. 11.

[89] For one view of the reaction against anthropological approaches, see Netterstrøm, 'Introduction'; for another, see White, 'The Feelings in the Feud', pp. 281–311. On the failure of functionalist studies of feuding to examine emotions at all, see Rosenwein, 'Les émotions', pp. 237–9.

[90] S. Pinker, *The Better Angels of Our Nature: Why Violence has Declined* (New York, 2011), pp. 530–1, 532. On the value of incorporating the findings of evolutionary psychology about vengeance and violence into historical studies, see J. C. Wood, 'The Limits of Culture? Society, Evolutionary Psychology and the History of Violence', *Cultural and Social History*, 4 (2007), 95–114; Wood, 'Evolution, Civilization and History: a Response to Wiener and Rosenwein', *Cultural and Social History*, 4 (2007), 559–65; G. Hanlon, 'Review-Article: The Decline of Violence in the West: From Cultural to Post-Cultural History', *English Historical Review*, 128 (2013), 367–400. For a critique of 'the turn to affect' in the humanities and criticisms of the scientific studies on which the turn depends, see R. Leys, 'The Turn to Affect: a Critique', *Critical Inquiry*, 37 (2011), 434–72; Leys, 'How Did Fear Become a Scientific Object and What Kind of Object is It?', *Representations*, 110 (2010), 66–104. See also M. Sahlins, *The Use and Abuse of Biology: an Anthropological Critique of Sociobiology* (Ann Arbor, MI, 1976); and Sahlins, *The Western Illusion of Nature* (Chicago, 2008).

[91] Hyams, 'Afterword', in S. A. Throop and P. R. Hyams (eds.), *Vengeance in the Middle Ages: Emotion, Religion and Feud* (Farnham, 2010), pp. 203–20, at pp. 217–18.

[92] Smail, *On Deep History and the Brain* (Berkeley, CA, 2008), pp. 113–14; see also p. 118. See also works in 'Feelings'.

[93] For a fuller discussion, see White, 'Feelings in the Feud'.

[94] Hyams, 'Was There Really Such a Thing as Feud in the High Middle Ages?', in S.A. Throop and Hyams (eds.), *Vengeance in the Middle Ages: Emotion, Religion and Feud* (Farnham, 2010), pp. 151–75 at p. 170.

[95] Hyams, *Rancor and Reconciliation*, pp. 8–9 lists nine features of feud.

it entails what William Ian Miller calls a 'notion of revenge that trivializes it' by portraying it as 'crazed, uncontrolled, admitting no reason, no rule of limitation'. If so, Miller continues, vengeance serves, along with feud itself, as 'a stand-in for anarchy'.[96] The emotional turn in the study of medieval feuding takes us in this direction by reducing the feud to a potentially endless series of individual acts of vengeance, which are mediated by the emotional impulses of individuals to take vengeance, not by rational deliberation by groups and individuals about why or whether to take vengeance, and which are undertaken only to achieve a kind of emotional satisfaction that has a physiological basis.[97] Because evolutionary psychologists and those who follow them postulate that the impulse to take vengeance and the satisfaction achieved by taking it are hard-wired into everyone's brain, they have ruled out the option of maintaining that vengeance is the expression of a 'primitive' mentality. Still, Pinker, at least, treats the feud as the mark of a primitive or, at least, pre-modern society when he takes a position categorically rejected in 'The Peace in the Feud' that 'Feuding and anarchy go together.'[98]

Pinker's views about feuding thus have a certain affinity with the ones expressed in the overblown, under-researched, yet surprisingly influential book by René Girard, *Violence and the Sacred* (*La violence et le sacré*), which unabashedly endorses a version of the Twain/Bloch Model of feuding. More than fifteen years after the 'The Peace in the Feud' appeared, Girard confidently espoused views that the article had directly contested:

> Vengeance is an interminable, infinitely repetitive process. Every time it turns up in some part of the community, it threatens to involve the whole social body. There is the risk that the act of vengeance will initiate a chain reaction whose consequences will quickly prove fatal to any society of modest size. The multiplication of reprisals instantaneously puts the very existence of a society in jeopardy.[99]

Since the 'violence' of 'interfamily vendettas or blood feuds', Girard continued, 'is virtually nonexistent in our own culture, perhaps it is here that we should look for the fundamental difference between primitive societies and our own'.[100]

[96] Miller, 'In Defense of Revenge', pp. 73–4.
[97] According to Miller, 'In Defense of Revenge', p. 77, 'The psychology of revenge was a rather complex affair and it would misrepresent that complexity to situate it within any particular vengeance taker.'
[98] Pinker, *Better Angels*, p. 538.
[99] R. Girard, *Violence and the Sacred*, trans. P. Gregory (French ed., 1972; Baltimore, MD, 1977), pp. 14–15. Girard also called vengeance 'a vicious circle' (p. 15) and 'an unending process' (p. 17).
[100] Girard, *Violence and the Sacred*, pp. 14–15.

Among the writers on feuding considered here, Girard stands alone in all but calling it a 'primitive' practice and thereby ignoring every issue that Gluckman raised in 'The Peace in the Feud'. Still, more than a hint of Girard's attitude is conveyed by the imagery deployed by historians who identify medieval feuding with 'an antiphony of incessant violence', 'incessant private warfare', 'interminable quarrels', and 'anarchy' and now with uncontrollable emotional urges and irresistible impulses to take blood vengeance. For this reason, it might be a law of historiographical development that the more historians ignore the practices that were used to bring medieval feuds to a halt, or the limits on the violence of feuding, or the rational dimensions of feuding or the rationality of the people who feuded, the more influence 'The Peace in the Feud' will have on their critics. When Gluckman wrote 'The Peace in the Feud', the belief that feuds were interminable was well embedded in the field of medieval history. In writings on the 'feudal revolution' during the 1970s and 1980s, the same belief took on new force, as the violence and vengeance of lay nobles and knights were repeatedly represented as uncontrollable. Subsequently, when writers on medieval vengeance attacked what they disparaged as 'functionalist' analyses of it, they bolstered their claims that the desire for vengeance and the practice of it were innate to humans by invoking the theories of evolutionary psychologists and neuroscientists. In the particular historiographical contexts under discussion, Gluckman's 'Peace and the Feud' proved its value, though not because it presented a theory of feuding that was readily applicable to conflicts of any kind in eleventh-century France. It was valuable as a weapon against received ideas about feuding and anarchy, whether they came in the form of the Twain/Bloch model of feuding, the economistic version of it that the *mutationnistes* embraced, the moralized one that fitted neatly into liberal historiography in the United States, or the view of vengeance as being an emotional impulse hard-wired into the human brain. Because medieval historians themselves are often unable to control their own urges and impulses to recycle elements of the Twain/Bloch Model of feuding by characterizing feuds as interminable, the violence of feuding as unlimited, vengeance as irrational, and the people who practised it as crazed if not crazy, and because new uses for the othering of the Other's vengeance and violence can always be found, Gluckman's 'Peace in the Feud' may never go completely out of style.

Bibliography

Abbreviations

CCSL	*Corpus Christianorum, Series Latina*
CSEL	*Corpus Scriptorum Ecclesiasticorum Latinorum*
MGH	*Monumenta Germaniae Historica*
MGH AA	*MGH Auctores Antiquissimi*
MGH Capit.	*MGH Capitularia Regum Francorum*, ed. A. Boretius and V. Krause, 2 vols. (Hannover, 1883, 1897)
MGH Epp.	*MGH Epistolae*
MGH SRL	*MGH Scriptores Rerum Langobardicarum et Italicarum*
MGH SS	*MGH Scriptores (in folio)*
MGH SRG	*MGH Scriptores Rerum Germanicarum*
MGH SRM	*MGH Scriptores Rerum Merovingicarum*
PL	*Patrologia Latina*

Manuscripts

Cologne, Erzbischöfliche Diözesan und Dombibliothek cod. 212

Merseburg 104

Milan, Ambrosiana G 58 sup.

Oxford, Corpus Christ College MS 157.

Vallicelliana T. XVIII

Primary

Acta Concilii Taurinensium 1, CCSL 148 (Turnhout, 1963).

Acts of the Scillitan Martyrs, in H. Musurillo (ed.), *The Acts of the Christian Martyrs* (Oxford, 1972), pp. 86–9.

Ambrose, Epistulae et acta, ed. H. J. Vogels, CSEL 82.1–3 (Vienna 1968, 1990, 1982).

Annales Mettenses Priores, ed. B. von Simson, MGH SRG (Hannover and Leipzig, 1905), tr. with commentary P. Fouracre and R. Gerberding, *Late Merovingian France: History and Hagiography* 640–720 (Manchester, 1996), pp. 350–70.

Annals of St Bertin, tr. J. Nelson, *Ninth-Century Histories: the Annals of St Bertin* (Manchester, 1991).

Ansegis, *Die Kapitulariensammlung des Ansegis*, ed. G. Schmitz, MGH Capit., I (Hannover, 1996).

Augustine, *De bono coniugali*, ed. P. G. Walsh, *Oxford Early Christian Texts* (Oxford, 2001).

Auxilius, *De ordinationibus a Formoso papa factis*, ed. E. Dümmler, *Auxilius & Vulgaris: Quellen und Forschungen zur Geschichte des Papstthums im Anfänge des zehnten Jahrhunderts* (Leipzig, 1866).

Æthelwulf, De abbatibus, ed. A. Campbell (Oxford, 1967).

Bede, *De eo quod ait Isaias* PL 94, 702–10. *De Tabernaculo*, ed. D. Hurst, CCSL 119a (Turnhout, 1969); *On the Tabernacle*, tr. A. Holder, Translated Texts for Historians 18 (Liverpool, 1994).

De Templo, ed. D. Hurst CCSL 119a (Turnhout, 1969) *On the Temple*, tr. S. Connolly, Translated Texts for Historians 21 (Liverpool: Liverpool University Press, 1995).

Historia ecclesiastica gentis Anglorum, ed. and tr. B. Colgrave and R. A. B. Mynors (Oxford, 1969).

Homiliarum euangelii libri ii, ed. D. Hurst, CCSL 122 (Turnhout, 1955); *Homilies on the Gospels: Book One, Advent to Lent, Book Two, Lent to the Dedication of the Church*, tr. L. T. Martin and D. Hurst, Cistercian Studies 110 (Kalamazoo, MI, 1991).

In epistolas VII catholicas, ed. D. Hurst, CCSL 121 (Turnhout, 1983);

Commentary on the Seven Catholic Epistles, tr. D. Hurst, Cistercian Studies, 82 (Kalamazoo, 1985).

In Ezram et Neemiam libri III, ed. D. Hurst, CCSL, 199a (Brepols, 1969); *On Ezra and Nehemiah*, tr. S. DeGregorio, Translated Texts for Historians 47 (Liverpool, 2006). *In Cantica Canticorum*, ed. D. Hurst, CCSL 119B (Turnhout, 1983); *On the Song of Songs and Other Selected Writings*, tr. A. Holder (New York, 2011).

In Habacuc, ed. J. E. Hudson, CCSL 119B (Turnhout, 1972); *On Tobit and the Canticle of Habakkuk*, tr. S. Connolly (Dublin, 1997).

In Lucae evangelium expositio, ed. D. Hurst, CCSL 120 (Turnhout, 1960).

In Marci euangelium expositio, ed. D. Hurst, CCSL 120 (Turnhout, 1960).

In primam partem Samuhelis libri III, ed. D. Hurst, CCSL 119 (Turnhout, 1962).

In principium Genesim, ed. C. W. Jones, CCSL 118a (Turnhout, 1967); *On Genesis*, tr. C. B. Kendall, Translated Texts for Historians 48 (Liverpool, 2008).

In prouerbia Salomonis, ed. D. Hurst, CCSL 119B (Turnhout, 1983).

In Regum librum xxx quaestiones, ed. D. Hurst, CCSL 119 (Turnhout, 1962).

Retractatio in Actus Apostolorum, ed. M. L. W. Laistner, CCSL 121 (Turnhout, 1960).

Vita Cuthberti, ed. and tr. B. Colgrave, Two Lives of Saint Cuthbert (Cambridge, 1940).

Benedictus Levita, *Tomi primi supplementa. 2: Capitularia spuria, canones ecclesiastici, bullae pontificum*, ed. G. H. Pertz, MGH Leges II,2 (Hannover, 1837).

Boniface, *Epistolae*, PL 20.

The Book of Ste Foy, tr. P. Sheingorn (Philadelphia, PA, 1995).

Le carte più antiche di S. Antonino di Piacenza, ed. E. Falconi (Parma, 1959).

Le carte private della cattedrale di Piacenza, ed. P. Galetti (Parma, 1978).

Chartae Latinae antiquiores: Facsimile-Edition of the Latin Charters, 2nd Series, Ninth Century, ed. G. Cavallo and G. Nicolaj (Zurich, 1997-)

Chronicle of 754, ed. E. López, *Cronica mozarabe de 754. Edición critica y traduccíon* (Zaragoza, 1980).

Chronicorum Caesaraugustanorum Reliquiae, ed. T. Mommsen, MGH AA XI, *Chronica Minora* 2 (Berlin, 1894).

Chronicon Gallica a CCCCLII a DXI, ed. T. Mommsen, MGH AA IX, *Chronica Minora* 1 (Berlin, 1892), pp.646–62; *Gallic Chronicle of 452*, in R. Burgess (ed. and tr.) 'The Gallic Chronicle of 452: a New Critical Edition with a Brief Introduction', in R. Mathisen and D. Shanzer (eds.), *Society and Culture in Late Antique Gaul: Revisiting the Sources* (Aldershot, 2001), pp. 52–84.

Clotharii Edictum, ed. A. Boretius, *Capitularia Regum Francorum* I, MGH Legum, sectio II, i (Hannover, 1883), pp. 20–3.

Codex Carolinus, in P. D. King (tr.), *Charlemagne: Translated Sources* (Lambrigg, 1987), pp. 269–307.

Codex diplomaticus Amiatinus. Urkundenbuch der Abtei S. Salvatore am Montamiata. Von den Anfängen bis zum Regierungsantritt Papst Innozenz III. (736–1198), 4 vols. (Tübingen, 1974–2004).

Codex Diplomaticus Langobardiae, ed. G. Porro Lambertenghi, *Historiae Patriae Monumenta*, 13 (Turin, 1873); vol. II, ed. L. Schiaparelli (Rome, 1933); vol. V, ed. H. Zielinski (Rome, 1986); vol. IV/1, ed. C. Brühl (Rome, 1981).

La colección canónica Hispana. i. Estudio, ed. G. Martinez Diez, Monumenta Hispaniae Sacra, serie canónica, 1 (Madrid, 1966); *iii. Concilios griegos y africanos*, ed. G. Martinez Diez and F. Rodriguez (Madrid, 1982); *iv. Concilios galos; concilios hispanos, primera parte*, ed. G. Martinez Diez and F. Rodriguez (Madrid, 1984).

Conciles gaulois du IVe siècle, ed. J. Gaudemet and C. Munier, Sources Chretiennes, 241 (Paris, 1977).

Concilia aevi Karolini. 2, ed. A. Werminghoff, MGH Conc. II,2 (Hannover and Leipzig, 1908); Hartmann, W. (ed.), *Die Konzilien der karolingischen Teilreiche 860–874*, MGH Conc. IV (Hannover, 1998); Hartmann, W., I. Schröder, and G. Schmitz (eds.), *Die Konzilien der karolingischen Teilreiche 875–911*, MGH Conc. V (Hannover, 2012).

Concilia Africae a. 345 – a. 525, ed. C. Munier, CCSL 259 (Turnhout, 1974).

Concilios Visigóticos e Hispano-Romanos, ed. José Vives (Barcelona and Madrid, 1963).

Constitutio Saluberrima (17 April 418), MGH Epp. 3.13 (Berlin, 1894).

Cyprian, *De lapsis and ecclesiae catholicae unitate*, ed. and tr. Maurice Bévenot (Oxford, 1971).

De episcoporum transmigratione et quod non temere iudicetur regule quadraginta quattuor, in J. Pozzi, 'Le manuscrit Tomus XVIII de la Vallicelliana et le libelle *De episcoporum transmigratione et quod non temere iudicetur regule quadraginta quattuor*', *Apollinaris*, xxxi (1958), 313–50.

Defensoris Liber scintillarum, ed. H. Rochais, CCSL 117 (Turnhout, 1957).

Delatio corporis s. Juniani in synodum Karrofensem, PL 137, cols. 825–6.

Digesta, ed. T. Mommsen, *Corpus Iuris Civilis*, vol. 1, 16th edn (Berlin, 1954).

Ecgberht of York, *Succinctus dialogus ecclesiasticae institutionis*, ed. A. W. Haddan and W. Stubbs, *Councils and Ecclesiastical Documents Relating to Great Britain and Ireland*, 3 vols (Oxford, 1869–71) III (1871), pp. 403–13.

Episulae Austrasicae, ed. W. Gundlach, MGH Epp. 3 (Hanover 1892); Italian tr. E. Malaspina, *Il Liber epistolarum della cancelleria austrasica (saec. V-VI)* (Rome, 2001).

Evans Grubbs, J. (ed.), *Women and Law in the Roman Empire: a Sourcebook on Marriage, Divorce and Widowhood* (London and New York, 2002).

The Formularies of Angers and Marculf: Two Merovingian Legal Handbooks, tr. A. Rio (Liverpool, 2008).

Fredegar, *Chronicon*, ed. B. Krusch, MGH SRM II (Hanover, 1888, repr. 1984); *The Fourth Book of the Chronicle of Fredegar with its Continuations*, ed. and tr. J. M. Wallace-Hadrill (London, 1960).

Fowler-Magerl, L. *Clavis canonum: Selected Canon Law Collections Before 1140. Access with Data Processing*, MGH, Hilfsmittel, 21 (Hanover, 2005).

Die Gesetze der Angelsachsen, ed. F. Liebermann, 3 vols (Halle a.S., 1903–1916), I (1903).

Gesta Regis Henrici Secundi, ed. W. Stubbs, Rolls Series (London 1867).

Gildas, *De Excidio et Conquestu Britanniae*, tr. M. Winterbottom, *Gildas, the Ruin of Britain* (London and Chichester, 1978).

Gregory of Catino, *Regestum Farfense*, ed. I. Giorgi and U. Balzani, *Il Regesto di Farfa*, 5 vols. (Rome, 1879–1914).

Gregory of Tours, *Decem libri historiarum*, ed. B. Krusch and W. Levison, MGH SRM I,1 (Hannover, 1951); tr. Lewis Thorpe, *The History of the Franks* (London, 1974).

Gregory the Great, *Dialogi*, ed. A. de Vogüé and P. Antin, Sources chrétiennes 260 and 265 (Paris, 1979 and 1980).

Homiliae in Evangelia, PL 76.

Moralia in Iob, ed. M. Adriaen, CCSL 143, 143A, 143B (Turnhout, 1979).

Registrum epistularum, eds. P. Ewald and L. Hartmann, 2 vols., MGH Epp. I–II (1891–99); ed. D. Norberg, 2 vols., CCSL 140, 140A (Turnhout, 1982)

Regula Pastoralis, PL 77, cols. 13–128.

Guibert of Nogent, *Monodiae*, tr. P. J. Archambault, *A Monk's Confession: the Memoirs of Guibert of Nogent* (University Park, PA, 1996).

Gunthramni regis Edictum, ed. A. Boretius, MGH Capit. I (Hanover, 1883; repr. 1984).

Hincmar of Rheims, *De divortio Lotharii regis et Theutbergae reginae*, ed. L. Böhringer, MGH Conc. IV Suppl. I (Hannover, 1992).

De quibus apud, PL 126, cols. 210–30.

Opusculum LV capitulorum. ed. R. Schieffer, MGH Conc. IV Supp. II (Hannover, 2003), pp. 99–361.

Hydatius, *Chronicon*, in R. W. Burgess (ed. and tr.), *The Chronicle of Hydatius and the Consularia Constantinopolitana* (Oxford, 1993).

I placiti del regnum Italiae, ed. C. Manaresi, 3 vols. (Rome, 1955–60).

John of Biclaro, *Chronica Minora II*, ed. T. Mommsen, MGH AA XI (Berlin, 1894).

John the Deacon, *Vita Gregorii*, PL 75, cols. 59–240.

Iohannis Hymmonidis et Gauderici Veliterni, Leonis Ostiensis, Excerpta ex Clementinis Recognitionibus a Tyrannio Rufini Translatis, ed. G. Orlandi (Milan, 1968).
Julian of Toledo, *The Story of Wamba: Julian of Toledo's 'Historia Wambae Regis'*, tr. J Martinez Pizarro (Washington, DC, 2005).
Lactantius, *De Mortibus Persecutorum*, ed. J. L. Creed (Oxford, 1984).
Lathcen, *Egloga quam scripsit Lathcen filius Baith de Moralibus Iob quas Gregorius fecit*, ed. M. Adriaen, CCSL, 145 (1969).
Leges Langobardorum (643–866), ed. F. Beyerle, *Die Gesetze der Langobarden*, Germanenrechte Neue Folge, Westgermanisches Recht, 2nd edn. (Witzenhausen, 1962).
Lex Ribuaria, ed. F. Beyerle and R. Buchner, MGH Legum sectio I, vol. 3 pt. I (Hannover, 1954).
Lives of the Fathers of Merida, tr. A. Fear, *Lives of the Visigothic Fathers* (Liverpool, 1997), pp. 46–105.
The Miracles of our Lady of Rocamadour, ed. and tr. M. Bull (Woodbridge, 1999).
Miracula sancti Columbani, ed. H. Bresslau, MGH SS XXX/2 (Hannover, 1934), pp. 993–1015.
Pactus Legis Salicae, ed. K. Eckhard, MGH Legum, sectio I, vol. IV (Hannover, 1926).
Passio Leudegarii, tr. with commentary, P. Fouracre and R. Gerberding, *Late Merovingian France: History and Hagiography 640–720* (Manchester, 1996), pp.193–253.
Paul the Deacon, *Historia Langobardorum*, ed. G. Waitz, MGH SRL (Hannover, 1878).
Priscillian, *Tractate*, ed. G. Schepss, CSEL 18 (Vienna, 1889).
Prosper Tironis, *Chronicon* (a. 412), ed. T. Mommsen, MGH SS AA IX (Berlin, 1892), 385–485.
Ranulf Flambard, *De gestis pontificum anglorum*, ed. N. E. S. A Hamilton, Rolls Series (London, 1870).
Rather of Verona, *Conclusio deliberativa*, ed. P. Reid, *Opera minora Ratherius Veronensis*, Corpus Christianorum Continuatio Mediaevalis, 46 (Turnhout, 1976).
Regino of Prüm, *De synodalibus causis*, in W. Hartmann (ed.), *Das Sendhandbuch des Regino von Prüm*, Ausgewählte Quellen zur Deutschen Geschichte des Mittelalters Freiherr-vom-Stein-Gedächtnisausgabe, 42 (Darmstadt, 2004).
Revised Royal Frankish Annals, Lorsch Annals, St Nazarius Annals, tr. P. D. King, *Charlemagne: Translated Sources* (Lambrigg, 1987); *Royal Frankish Annals*, tr. W. Scholz, *Carolingian Chronicles* (Ann Arbor, MI, 1972), pp. 37–125.
Robert of Arbrissel: a Medieval Religious Life, ed. and tr. B. Venarde (Washington, DC, 2003).
Sulpicius Severus, Chronicle, ed. Ghislaine de Senneville-Grave, *Sulpice Severe, Chroniques*, Sources chrétiennes, 441 (Paris, 1999).
The Theodosian Code, tr. C. Pharr, *The Theodosian Code and Sirmondian Constitutions* (Princeton, NJ, 1952).
Theodulf of Orleans, *Capitula Episcoporum, 2*, ed. R. Pokorny and M. Stratmann, MGH Capit. Episcoporum II (Hannover, 1995).

Twain, M. *Adventures of Huckleberry Finn (Tom Sawyer's Comrade)*, ed. V. Fischer and L. Salamo, The Mark Twain Project of The Bancroft Library (Berkeley, CA, 2010).

Die Urkunden der Merovinger, ed. T. Kölzer, MGH. Diplomata regum Francorum e stirpe Merovingica, 2 vols. (Hannover, 2001).

Die Urkunden Pippins, Karlmanns und Karls des Großen, ed. E. Mühlbacher, MGH, Diplomata Karolinorum, I (Hanover, 1906).

Vita Caesarii, ed. B. Krusch, MGH SRM III (Hannover, 1896).

Vita Geraldi, PL 133, cols. 641–704.

Vita Germani Gandivallensis, ed. B. Krusch, MGH, SRM V (Hannover, 1910), pp. 33–40.

Vita Gregorii, ed. B. Colgrave, *The Earliest Life of Gregory the Great* (Cambridge, 1985).

Vita Melania, ed. D. Gorce, *Vie de Sainte Mélanie*, Sources Chrétiennes, 90 (Paris, 1962); English tr. E. A. Clark, *Gerontius, The Life of Melania the Younger: Introduction, Translation, and Commentary* (Lewiston, Lampeter, and Queenston, 1984).

Volpini, R. 'Placiti del "Regnum Italiae" (secc. IX-XI). Primi contributi per un nuovo censimento', in P. Zerbi (ed.), *Contributi dell'Istituto di storia medioevale*, III (Milan, 1975), pp.245–520.

Zechiel-Eckes, K. (ed.), *Die erste Dekretale. Der Brief Papst Siricius' an Bischof Himerius von Tarragona vom Jahr 385 (JK 255)*, ed. D. Jasper, MGH Studien und Texte, 55 (Hannover, 2013).

Zosimus, *Epistolae*, ed. W. Grundlach, MGH Epp. III (Berlin, 1892).

Secondary

Airlie, S. 'Private Bodies and the Body Politic in the Divorce Case of Lothar II', *Past & Present*, 161 (1998), 3–38.

'Sad stories of the death of kings: Narrative Patterns and Structures of Authority in Regino of Prum's *Chronicon*', in E. M. Tyler and R. Balzaretti (eds.), *Narrative and History in the Early Medieval West* (Turnhout, 2006), pp. 105–31.

'*Semper fideles*? Loyauté envers les Carolingiens comme constituant de l'identité aristocratique', in R. Le Jan (ed.), *La royauté et les élites dans l'Europe carolingienne* (Lille, 1998), pp. 129–43.

Algazi, G. *Herrengewalt und Gewalt der Herren im späten Mittelalter. Herrschaft Gegenseitigkeit und Sprachgebrauch* (Frankfurt, 1992).

'Pruning Peasants: Private War and Maintaining the Lord's Peace in Late Medieval Germany', in E. Cohen and M. de Jong (eds.), *Medieval Transformations: Texts, Power and Gifts in Context* (Leiden 2000), pp. 245–74.

'The Social Uses of Private War: Some Late Medieval Views Reviewed', *Tel Aviver Jahrbuch fur deutsche Geshichte*, 22 (1993), 253–73.

Amselle, J.-L. *Mestizo Logics: Anthropology of Identity in Africa and Elsewhere* (Stanford, CA, 1998).

Arjava, A. *Women and Law in Late Antiquity* (Oxford, 1996).

Arlinghaus, F.-J. 'From "Improvised Theater" to Scripted Roles: Literacy and Changes in Communication in North Italian Law Courts (Twelfth-

Thirteenth Centuries)', in K. Heidecker (ed.), *Charters and the Use of the Written Word in Medieval Society* (Turnhout, 2000), pp. 215–37.

Arnaldi, G. 'Giovanni Immonide e la cultura a Roma al tempo di Giovanni VIII', *Bulletino dell'Instituto Storico Italiano per il Medio Evo e Archivo Muratoriano*, 68 (1956), 33–89.

'"Giovanni Immonide e la cultura a Roma al tempo di Giovanni VIII": Una retractatio' in G. Arnaldi and G. Cavallo (eds.), *Europa medievale e mondo Bizantino. Contatti effetive e possibilità di studi comparativi* (Rome, 1997), pp. 163–77.

Azzara, C. 'La figura di Gregorio magno nell'opera di Paolo Diacono', in P. Chiesa (ed.), *Paolo diacono. Uno scrittore fra tradizione longobardo e rinnovamento carolingio* (Udine, 2000), pp. 29–38.

Babut, C. É. *Le concile de Turin: essai sur l'histoire des églises provençales au Ve siècle et sur les origines de la monarchie ecclésiastique romaine (417–450)* (París, 1904).

Bagnall, R. S. 'Church, State and Divorce in Late Roman Egypt', in R. Somerville and K. L. Selig (eds.), *Florilegium Colombianum: Essays in Honor of Paul Oskar Kristeller* (New York, 1987), pp.41–61.

Balzaretti, R. 'The Monastery of Sant'Ambrogio and Dispute Settlement in Early Medieval Milan', *Early Medieval Europe*, 3 (1994), 1–18.

Barbero, A. and M. I. Loring, 'The Catholic Visigothic Kingdom', in P. Fouracre (ed.), *New Cambridge Medieval History*, I, pp. 346–70.

'The Formation of the Sueve and Visigothic Kingdoms in Spain', in Fouracre (ed.), *New Cambridge Medieval History*, I, pp. 162–92.

Barnes, T. D. *Constantine: Dynasty, Religion and Power in the Later Roman Empire* (Oxford, 2011).

Early Christian Hagiography and Roman History (Tübingen, 2010).

Barth, F. *Political Leadership among Swat Pathans*, London School of Economics Monographs on Social Anthropology, 19, corrected edn. (London, 1965), pp. 81–6.

Barthélemy, D. *L'an mil et la paix de dieu: la France chrétienne et féodale* (Paris, 1999).

Chevaliers et miracles. La violence et la sacré dans la société féodale (Paris, 2004).

'Une crise de l'écrit? Observations sur des actes de St-Aubin d'Angers (XIe siècle)', *Bibliotheque de l'Ecole des Chartes*, 155/1 (1997), 95–117.

'Feudal War in Tenth-Century France', in S. A Throop and P. R. Hyams, *Vengeance in the Middle Ages: Emotion, Religion and Feud* (Farnham, 2010), pp. 105–13.

'La mutation de l'an mil, a-t-elle eu lieu?' *Annales. Economies, Sociétés, Civilisations*, 47 (1992), 767–77.

La mutation de l'an mil, a-t-elle eu lieu? Servage et chevalerie dans la France des Xe et XIe siècles (Paris, 1997), tr. as *The Serf, the Knight and the Historian* (Ithaca, NY and London, 2009).

'La mutation de l'an 1100', *Journal des savants*, 1 (2005), 3–28.

'The Peace of God in the Days of the Millennium', in *The Serf, the Knight and the Historian* (Ithaca, NY, and London, 2009), pp. 245–301.

La société dans le comté de Vendôme: de l'an mil au xive siècle (Paris, 1993).

'La vengeance, le jugement et le compromis', in *Le règlement des conflits au moyen âge*, XXXIe Congrès de la S. H. M. E. S. (Angers, juin, 2000), Société des Historiens Médiévistes de l'Enseignement Supérieur Public (Paris, 2001), pp. 11–20.

Bartlett, R. *Trial by Fire and Water: the Medieval Judicial Ordeal* (Oxford, 1986).

Barton, R. E. *Lordship in the County of Maine, c. 890–1160* (Woodbridge, 2004).

Bell, C. *Ritual Theory, Ritual Practice* (Oxford, 1992).

Bennett, M. 'Violence in Eleventh-Century Normandy: Feud, Warfare and Politics', in *Halsall, Violence and Society in the Early Medieval West* (Woodbridge, 1998), pp. 108–25.

Bickerman, E. J. 'Review: A. M. H. Jones, *Later Roman Empire 284–602*', *American Historical Review*, 70/3 (1965), 750–1.

Biget, J. L. *Hérésie et inquisition dans le midi de la France* (Paris, 2007).

Birley, A. R. 'Magnus Maximus and the Persecution of Heresy', *Bulletin of the John Rylands Library of Manchester*, 66/1 (1983), 13–43.

Bisson, T. N. *The Crisis of the Twelfth Century: Power, Lordship and the Origins of European Government* (Princeton, NJ, 2009).

'The Feudal Revolution', *Past & Present*, 142 (1994), 6–42.

Tormented Voices: Power, Crisis, and Humanity in Rural Catalonia, 1140–1200 (Cambridge, MA, 1998).

Blackburn, M. '"Productive Sites" and the Pattern of Coin Loss in England, 600–1180', in T. Pestell and K. Ulmschneider (eds.), *Markets in Medieval Europe: Trading and Productive Sites, 650–850* (Macclesfield, 2003), pp. 20–36.

Black-Michaud, J. *Cohesive Force* (Oxford, 1975).

Blair, J. *The Church in Anglo-Saxon Society* (Oxford, 2005)

Bloch, M. *Feudal Society*, tr. L. A. Manyon (London, 1961).

Boehm, C. *Blood Revenge: the Anthropology of Feuding in Montenegro and Other Tribal Societies* (Lawrence, KS, 1984).

Bof, R. 'Raymund's Daughter's Divorce in the 9th Century: a Woman's Textual Role in the Breaking of an Alliance', in C. Salvaterra and B. Waaldijk (eds.), *Paths to Gender: European Historical Perspectives on Women and Men*, CLIOHRES Transversal themes (Pisa, 2009), pp. 195–207.

Böhringer, L. 'Der eherecthliche Traktat im Paris. Lat. 12445, einer Arbeitshandschrift Hinkmars von Reims', *Deutsches Archiv für Erforschung des Mittelalters*, 46 (1990), 18–47.

'Gewaltverzicht, Gesichtswahrung und Befriedung durch Öffentlichkeit. Beobachtungen zur Entstehung des kirchlichen Eherechts im 9. Jahrhundert am Beispiel Hinkmars von Reims', in S. Esders (ed.), *Rechtsverständnis und Konfliktbewältigung. Gerichtliche und außergerichtliche Strategien im Mittelalter* (Cologne, Weimar, and Vienna, 2007), pp. 255–90.

'Das Recht im Dienst der Machtpolitik? Anmerkungen zu einer Neuerscheinung über die Scheidungsaffäre König Lothars II', *Mitteilungen des Instituts für Österreichische Geschichtsforschung*, 119 (2011), 146–54.

Bois, G. *The Transformation of the Year 1000: the Village of Lournand from Antiquity to Feudalism*, tr. J. Birrell (Manchester, 1992).

Bonnassie, P. 'From the Rhône to Galicia: Origins and Modalities of the Feudal Order', in *From Slavery to Feudalism in South-Western Europe* (Cambridge, 1991).

Bonnet, M. *Le latin de Grégoire de Tours* (Paris, 1890).

Booker, C. *Past Convictions: the Penance of Louis the Pious and the Decline of the Carolingians* (Philadelphia, PA, 2009).

Booth, P. *Crisis of Empire: Doctrine and Dissent at the End of Late Antiquity* (Berkeley, CA, 2014).

Bougard, F. 'Composition, diffusion et réception des parties tardives du "Liber pontificalis" romain (VIII–IX siècles)', in F. Bougard, M. Sot (eds.), *Liber, Gesta, histoire* (Turnhout, 2009), pp. 127–152.

'Écrire le procès. Le compte rendu judiciaire entre VIIIe et XIe siècle', *Médiévales*, 56 (2009), 23–40.

'Entre Gandolfingi et Obertenghi. Les comtes de Plaisance aux Xe et XIe siècles', *Mélanges de l'École Française de Rome. Moyen Âge*, 101/1 (1989), 11–66.

'"Falsum falsorum judicum consilium". L'écrit et la justice en Italie centro-septentrionale au XIe siècle', *Bibliothèque de l'école des chartes*, 155/1 (1997), 299–314.

La justice dans le royaume d'Italie de la fin du VIIIe siècle au début du XIe siècle, Bibliothèque des Écoles Françaises d'Athènes et de Rome, 291 (Rome, 1995).

'Pierre de Niviano, dit le Spolétin, sculdassius, et le gouvernement du comté de Plaisance à l'époque carolingienne', *Journal des savants, juillet-décembre* (1996), 291–337.

'La relique au procès. Autour des miracles de saint Colomban', in *Le règlement des conflits au Moyen Âge*, Actes du XXXIe congrès de la Société des historiens médiévistes de l'enseignement supérieur public (Paris, 2000), pp. 35–66.

Bowes, K. 'Early Christian Archaeology: a State of the Field', *Religion Compass*, 2 (2008), 575–615.

'Personal Devotions and Private Chapels', in Virginia Burrus (ed.), *A People's History of Christianity. Volume 2: Late Ancient Christianity* (Minneapolis, MN, 2005), pp. 188–210.

Private Worship, Public Values, and Religious Change in Late Antiquity (Cambridge, 2008).

Boyle, L. E. 'Diplomatics', in J. M. Powell (ed.), *Medieval Studies: an Introduction*, 2nd edn. (Syracuse, NY, 1992), pp. 82–113.

Bradshaw, P. F. *The Search for the Origins of Christian Worship: Sources and Methods for the Study of Early Liturgy*, 2nd edn. (London, 2002).

Braga, G. 'Moralia in Iob: Epitomi dei secoli VII–X e loro evoluzione', in J. Fontaine, R. Gillet, and S. Pellistrandi (eds.) *Grégoire le Grand*, Colloques internationaux du Centre National de la Recherche Scientifique, Centre culturel les Fontaines, 15–19 septembre 1982 (Paris, 1986), pp. 561–8.

Brakke, D. *Athanasius and the Politics of Asceticism* (Oxford, 1995).

Brooks, N. *The Early History of the Church of Canterbury* (Leicester, 1984).

Brown, G. H. 'Bede's Neglected Commentary on Samuel', in S. DeGregorio (ed.), *Innovation and Tradition in the Writings of the Venerable Bede* (Morgantown, WV, 2006), pp. 121–42.

'Bede's Style in his Commentary On 1 Samuel', in J. Roberts and A. Minnis (eds.), *Text, Image, Interpretation: Studies in Anglo-Saxon Literature in Honour of Eamonn Ó'Carragáin* (Turnhout, 2007), pp. 233–51.

'Le Commentaire problématique de Bède sur le premier Livre de Samuel', in S. Lebecq, M. Perrin, and O. Szerwiniack (eds.), *Bède le Vénérable entre Tradition et Postérité*, Histoire de l'Europe de Nord-Ouest 34 (Villeneuve d'Ascq, 2005), pp. 87–96.

Brown, P. R. L. *The Cult of Saints: Its Rise and Function in Late Antiquity* (London, 1982).

'Gregory of Tours. Introduction', in K. Mitchell and I. N. Wood (eds.), *The World of Gregory of Tours* (Leiden, 2002).

The Ransom of the Soul: Wealth and the Afterlife from Late Antiquity to the Early Middle Ages (Cambridge, MA, 2015).

Religion and Society in the Age of St Augustine (London, 1972).

'The Rise and Function of the Holy Man in Late Antiquity', *Journal of Roman Studies*, 61 (1971), 80–101.

'The Rise and Function of the Holy Man in Late Antiquity, 1971–1997', *Journal of Early Christian Studies*, 6.3 (1998), 353–76.

The Rise of Western Christendom: Triumph and Diversity, 200–1000 (2nd edn. Oxford, 2002; rev. edn 2013).

'Society and the Supernatural: a Medieval Change', *Daedalus*, 104 (1975), 133–51, reprinted in *Society and the Holy in Late Antiquity* (Chicago, 1981).

Through the Eye of a Needle: Wealth, the Fall of Rome and the Making of Christianity in the West, 350–550 AD (Princeton, NJ, 2012).

Brown, W. *Unjust Seizure: Conflict, Interest and Authority in an Early Medieval Society* (Ithaca, NY, 2001).

Violence in Medieval Europe (Harlow, 2011).

Brown, W., M. Costambeys, M. Innes, and A. Kosto (eds.), *Documentary Culture and the Laity in the Early Middle Ages* (Cambridge, 2012).

Brown, W. and P. Górecki (eds.), *Conflict in Medieval Europe: Changing Perspectives on Society and Culture* (Aldershot, 2003), pp. 1–35.

Brühl, C. 'Die Entwicklung der diplomatischen Methode im Zusammenhang mit dem Erkennen von Fälschungen', in *Fälschungen im Mittelalter. Internationaler Kongreß der Monumenta Germaniae Historica München, 16.-19. September 1986*, vol. III (Hannover, 1988), pp. 11–27.

Brunner, O. *Land und Herrschaft: Grundfragen der territorialen Verfassungsgeschichte Östereichs im Mittelalter*, 6th edn. (Vienna, 1973), tr. as *Land and Lordship: Structures of Governance in Medieval Austria* by H. Kaminsky and J. V. H. Melton (Philadelphia, PA, 1992).

Brunsch, S. H. 'The Authority of Documents in Early Medieval Italian Pleas', in B. Bolton and C. Meek (eds.), *Aspects of Power and Authority in the Middle Ages* (Turnhout, 2007), pp. 277–88.

Buc, P. *The Dangers of Ritual: Between Early Medieval Texts and Social Scientific Theory* (Princeton, NJ, 2001).

Burgess, R. and M. Kulikowski, *Mosaics of Time: the Latin Chronicle Tradition from the First Century BC to the Sixth Century AD* (Turnhout, 2013).

Burrus, V. *The Making of a Heretic: Gender, Authority, and the Priscillianist Controversy* (Berkeley, CA, 1995).

Byock, J. 'Defining Feud: Talking Points and Iceland's Saga Women', in J. B. Netterstrøm and B. Poulson (eds.), *Feud in Medieval and Early Modern Europe* (Aarhus, 2007), pp. 95–112.

Cameron, A. 'Agathias on the Early Merovingians', *Annali della Scuola Normale Superiore di Pisa. Classe di lettere e filosofia* ser. 2, 37 (1968), pp. 95–140.

Cameron, A. 'Enforcing Orthodoxy in Byzantium', in K. Cooper and J. Gregory (eds.), *Discipline and Diversity* (Woodbridge, 2007), pp. 1–24.

'The "Long" Late Antiquity: a Late Twentieth-Century Model', in T. P. Wiseman (ed.), *Classics in Progress: Essays on Ancient Greece and Rome* (Oxford, 2002), pp. 165–91.

Campbell, J. 'The Church in Anglo-Saxon Towns', in J. Campbell, *Essays in Anglo-Saxon History* (London, 1986), pp. 139–54.

'Elements in the Background to the Life of St Cuthberht and his Early Cult', in J. Campbell, *The Anglo-Saxon State* (London, 2000), pp. 85–106.

'Questioning Bede', in M. Henig and N. Ramsay (eds.), *Intersections: the Archaeology and History of Christianity in England, 400–1200. Papers in Honour of Martin Biddle and Birthe Kjølbye-Biddle*, BAR British Series 505 (Oxford, 2010), pp. 119–27.

Carrié, J.-M. 'Developments in Provincial and Local Administration', in A. Bowman, A. Cameron, and P. Garnsey (eds.), *The Cambridge Ancient History, Volume 12: The Crisis of Empire, AD 193–337*, 2nd edn. (Cambridge, 2005), pp. 269–312.

Carroll, M. T. A. *The Venerable Bede: His Spiritual Teachings* (Washington, DC, 1946).

Carroll, S. 'The Peace in the Feud in Sixteenth- and Seventeenth-Century France', *Past & Present*, 178 (2003), 74–114.

Carsten, J. *After Kinship* (Cambridge, 2004).

Castaldi, L. 'Le dediche di Giovanni Immonide', *Filologia mediolatina*, 17 (2010), 39–69.

Iohannes Hymmonides diaconus romanus. Vita Gregorii I papa: (B.H.L. 3641–3642), Vol. I, La tradizione manoscritta (Florence, 2004*).*

'Il Registrum Epistularum di Gregorio Magno', *Filologia Mediolatina*, 11 (2004), 55–97.

(ed.), *La trasmissione dei testi latini del Medioevo, Gregorius I Papa* (Florence, 2013).

and F. Martello, '"Tempera quasi aurum": origine, redazione e diffusione del *Liber testimoniorum* di Paterio', *Filologia Mediolatina*, 18 (2011), 23–107.

Castellanos, S. '*Tributa and Historiae*: Scale and Power at a Turning Point in Post-Roman Spain', in J. Escalona and A. Reynolds (eds.), *Scale and Scale Change in the Early Middle Ages: Exploring Landscape, Local Society, and the World Beyond* (Turnhout, 2011), pp. 187–214.

Castellanos, S. and I. Martin Viso, 'The Local Articulation of Central Power in the North of the Iberian Peninsula (500–1000), *Early Medieval Europe*, 13 (2005), 1–41.

Castagnetti, A. *Arimanni in 'Langobardia' e in 'Romania' dall'età carolingia all'età communale* (Verona, 1996).

Chadwick, H. *Priscillian of Avila: the Occult and the Charismatic in the Early Church* (Oxford, 1976).

Chanock, M. *Law, Custom and Social Order: The Colonial Experience in Malawi and Zambia* (Portsmouth, NH, 1998).

Chaume, M. *Les origins du duché de Bourgogne* (Dijon, 1926).

Cheyette, F. L. 'Georges Duby's *Mâconnais* after Fifty Years: Reading it then and now', *Journal of Medieval History*, 28 (2002), 291–317.

'Suum Cuique Tribuere', *French Historical Studies*, 6 (1970), 287–99.

Clark, E. A. 'Constraining the Body, Expanding the Text: the Exegesis of Divorce in the Later Latin Fathers', in W. E. Klingshirn and M. Vessey (eds.), *The Limits of Ancient Christianity* (Ann Arbor, MI, 1999), pp. 153–71.

Cohn, N. *The Pursuit of the Millennium*, 3rd edn. (London 1970).

Colson, E. 'The Contentiousness of Disputes', in P. Caplan (ed.), *Understanding Disputes: the Politics of Argument* (Oxford, 1995), pp. 65–82.

'Social Control in Plateau Tonga Society', *Africa*, 23 (1953), 199–212.

Cooper, K. 'Approaching the Holy Household', *Journal of Early Christian Studies*, 15 (2007), 131–42.

'Christianity, Private Power, and the Law from Decius to Constantine: the Minimalist View', *Journal of Early Christian Studies*, 19/3 (2011), 327–43.

'Closely Watched Households: Visibility, Exposure and Private Power in the Roman *Domus*', *Past & Present*, 197 (2007), 3–33.

The Fall of the Roman Household (Cambridge, 2007).

'Gender and the Fall of Rome', in P. Rousseau and J. Raithel (eds.), *A Companion to Late Antiquity* (Oxford, 2009), pp. 187–200.

'The Household as a Venue for Religious Conversion', in B. Rawson (ed.), *A Companion to Families in the Greek and Roman Worlds* (Oxford, 2010), pp. 183–97.

'Insinuations of Womanly Influence: An Aspect of the Christianization of the Roman Aristocracy', *Journal of Roman Studies*, 82 (1990), 150–64.

'Marriage, Law, and Christian Rhetoric in Vandal Africa', in J. P. Conant and Susan T. Stevens (eds.), *North Africa under Byzantium and Early Islam, ca. 500–ca. 800* (Washington, D.C., 2015) pp. 237–49.

'Martyrdom, Memory, and the "Media Event": Visionary Writing and Christian Apology in Second-century Christianity', in D. Janes and A. Houen (eds.), *Terrorism and Martyrdom: British Perspectives in Global Context* (Oxford, 2014), pp. 23–39.

'Ventriloquism and the Miraculous: Conversion, Preaching, and the Martyr Exemplum in Late Antiquity', in K. Cooper and J. Gregory (eds.), *Signs, Wonders, and Miracles*, Studies in Church History, 41 (Woodbridge, 2005), pp. 22–45.

Corke-Webster, J. 'Author and Authority: Literary Representations of Moral Authority in Eusebius of Caesarea's The Martyrs of Palestine', in P. Gemeinhardt and J. Leemans (eds.), *Christian Martyrdom in Late Antiquity: History and Discourse, Tradition and Religious Identity*, Arbeiten zur Kirchengeschichte 116 (Berlin/New York, 2012), pp. 51–78.

'Trouble in Pontus: the Pliny-Trajan Correspondence on the Christians Reconsidered' (unpublished manuscript).

'Violence and Authority in Eusebius of Caesarea's *Ecclesiastical History*', PhD thesis, University of Manchester (2013).
Costambeys, M. 'Disputes and Courts in Lombard and Carolingian Central Italy', *Early Medieval Europe*, 15 (2007), 265–89.
'The Monastic Environment of Paul the Deacon', in P. Chiesa (ed.), *Paolo diacono. Uno scrittore fra tradizione longobardo e rinnovamento carolingio* (Udine, 2000), pp. 129–38.
Croke, B. *Count Marcellinus and His Chronicle* (Oxford, 2001).
Cross, F. L. 'History and Fiction in the African Canons', *Journal of Theological Studies*, 12 (1961), 227–47.
Crouzel, H. *L'Église primitive face au divorce*, Theologie historique, 13 (Paris, 1971).
'A propos du concile d'Arles. Faut-il mettre "non" avant "prohibentur nubere" dans le canon 11 (ou 10) du concile d'Arles de 314 sur le remariage après divorce?', *Bulletin de littérature ecclésiastique*, 75 (1974), 25–40; repr.: Crouzel, *Mariage et divorce, célibat et caractère sacerdotaux dans l'église ancienne. Études diverses* (Turin, 1982).
Cursent, B. 'Excursus. Une affaire du non-hérésie en Gascogne en l'année 1208', in M. Zerner (ed.), *Inventer l'hérésie? Discours polémiques et pouvoirs avant l'inquisition* (Nice, 1998), pp. 257–62.
Dagron, G. 'Les moines et la ville: Le monachisme à Constantinople', *Travaux et mémoires*, 4 (1970), 229–76.
Dal Santo, M. *Debating the Saints' Cults in the Age of Gregory the Great* (Oxford, 2012).
Darby, P. *Bede and the End of Time* (Farnham, 2012).
Daudet, P. *Études sur l'histoire de la jurisdiction matrimoniale. Les origines carolingiennes de la compétence exclusive de l'Église (France et Germanie)* (Paris, 1933).
Davies, W. and P. Fouracre (eds.), *The Languages of Gift in the Early Middle Ages* (Cambridge, 2010).
Property and Power in Early Medieval Europe (Cambridge, 1996).
The Settlement of Disputes in Early Medieval Europe (Cambridge, 1986).
Dean, J. M. 'The World Grown Old and Genesis in Middle English Historical Writings', *Speculum*, 57 (1982), 548–68.
Dean, T. *Crime in Medieval Europe, 1200–1500* (Edinburgh, 2001).
Declercq, G. 'Originals and Cartularies: the Organization of Archival Memory (Ninth-Eleventh Centuries)', in K. Heidecker (ed.), *Charters and the Use of the Written Word in Medieval Society* (Turnhout, 2000), pp. 147–70.
DeGregorio, S. 'Bede's *In Ezram et Neemiam* and the Reform of the Northumbrian Church', *Speculum*, 79 (2004), 1–25.
'Footsteps of His Own: Bede's Commentary on Ezra and Nehemiah', in Gregorio (ed.), *Innovation and Traditionin the Writings of the Venerable Bede* (Morgantown, WV, 2006), pp. 143–68.
'Nostrorum socordiam temporum: the Reforming Impulse of Bede's Later Exegesis', *Early Medieval Europe*, 11 (2002), 107–122.
'The Venerable Bede and Gregory the Great: Exegetical Connections, Spiritual Departures', *Early Medieval Europe* 18 (2010), 43–60.
de Jong, M. B. *The Penitential State: Authority and Atonement in the Age of Louis the Pious, 814–840* (Cambridge, 2009).

'The State of the Church: Ecclesia and Early Medieval State Formation', in W. Pohl and V. Wieser (eds.), *Der frühmittelalterliche Staat – europäische Perspektiven* (Vienna, 2009), pp. 241–54.
Delogu, P. *An Introduction to Medieval History* (London, 2002).
'Vescovi, conti e sovrani nella crisi del regno italico (Ricerche sull'aristocrazia carolingia in Italia, III)', *Annali della scuola speciale per archvisti e bibliotecari del'Universita di Romà*, viii (1968), 3–72.
Delumeau, J.-P. 'Sociétés, cadres de pouvoir et règlement des conflits en Italie du Xe siècle à l'émergence des juridictions communales', *Actes des congrès de la Société des historiens médiévistes de l'enseignement supérieur public. 31e congrès* (Angers, 2000), pp. 169–88.
Devos, P. 'Le mystérieux épisode final de la *Vita Gregorii* de Jean Diacre. Formose et sa fuite de Rome', *AB* 82 (1964) 356–81.
Dhondt, J. 'Henri Pirenne: historien des institutions urbaines', *Annali della fondazione italiana per la storia amministrativa*, 3 (1966), pp. 81–129.
Dockès, P. *Medieval Slavery and Liberation* (Chicago, 1982).
Dodwell, C. R. *Anglo-Saxon Art: a New Perspective* (Manchester, 1982).
Dresch, P. and H. Skoda (eds.), *Legalism:Anthropology and History* (Oxford, 2012).
Drinkwater, J. F. 'The Bacaudae of Fifth-Century Gaul', in J. Drinkwater and H. Elton (eds.), *Fifth-Century Gaul: a Crisis of Identity?* (Cambridge, 1992), pp. 208–17.
'The Usurpers: Constantine III (407–411) and Jovinus (411–13)', *Britannia*, 29 (1998), 269–98.
Duby, G. *L'an mil*, 2nd edn. (Paris, 1980).
L'an mil et la paix de Dieu (Paris, 1999).
Le chevalier, la femme et le prêtre. Le mariage dans la France féodale, La force des Idées (Paris, 1981); tr. C. Postan, *The Chivalrous Society* (London, 1977).
Le dimanche de Bouvines (Paris, 1973).
'Recherches sur l'évolution des institutions judiciaries pendant le Xe et le XIe siècle dans le sud de la Bourgogne', *Le Moyen Âge*, 52 (1946), 149–94; 53 (1947), 15–35; tr. as 'The Evolution of Judicial Institutiopns: Burgundy in the Tenth and Eleventh Centuries', in Duby, *The Chivalrous Society*, tr. C. Postan (Berkeley, CA, 1980), pp. 115–58.
La société aux XIe et XIIe siècles dans la region mâconnaise (Paris, 1953).
Duchesne, L. *Fastes Episcopaux de l'Ancienne Gaul*, vol. I (Paris, 1894).
Histoire ancienne de l'Église, vol. III (Paris, 1910).
Dumézil, B. *Les racines chrétiennes de l'Europe: Conversion et liberté dans les royaumes barbares Ve – VIIIe siècle* (Paris, 2005).
Dunn, M. *The Christianization of the Anglo-Saxons c. 597-c.700: Discourses of Life, Death, and Afterlife* (London, 2009).
Esders, S. 'Avenger of all perjury" in Constantinople, Ravenna, and Merovingian Metz. St Polyeuctus, Sigibert I, and the division of Charibert's Kingdom in 568', in A. Fischer (ed.), *Cultural Transfers in the Mediterranean, 5th – 9th Centuries* (Bangor, 2014), pp. 17–40.
'Der Reinigungseid mit Helfern. Individuelle und kollektive Rechtsvorstellungen in der Wahrnehmung und Darstellung frühmittelalterlicher Konflikte', in Esders (ed.), *Rechtsverständnis und Konfliktbewältigung: Gerichtliche und*

außergerichtliche Strategien im Mittelalter (Cologne, Weimar, and Vienna, 2007), pp. 55–77.

Römische Rechtstradition und merowingisches Königtum. Zum Rechtscharakter politischer Herrschaft in Burgund im 6. und 7. Jahrhundert, Veröffentlichungen des Max-Planck-Instituts für Geschichte, 134 (Göttingen, 1997).

Escalona, J. 'The Early Middle Ages: a Scale-based Approach', in J. Escalona and A. Reynolds (eds.), *Scale and Scale Change in the Early Middle Ages: Exploring Landscape, Local Society, and the World Beyond* (Turnhout, 2011), pp. 9–30.

Escribano Paño, M. V. 'Heresy and Orthodoxy in Fourth-Century Hispania: Arianism and Priscillianism', in K. Bowes and M. Kulikowski, eds., *Hispania in late antiquity: current perspectives* (Leiden, 2005), 121–50.

Esmark, K. and H. J. Orning, 'General Introduction', in K. Esmark, L. Hermanson, H. J. Orning, and H. Vogt (eds.), *Disputing Strategies in Medieval Scandinavia* (Leiden, 2013), pp. 1–28.

Evans-Pritchard, E. E. *The Nuer: a Description of the Modes of Livelihood and Political Institutions of a Nilotic People* (Oxford, 1940).

Everett, N. 'Literacy and the Law in Lombard Government', *Early Medieval Europe*, 9 (2000), 93–127.

Ewald, P. 'Studien zur Angabe des Registers Gregors I', *Neues Archiv*, 3 (1878), 433–625.

Ewig, E. 'Die fränkischen Teilungen und Teilreiche (511–613)', in *Ewig Spätantikes und Fränkisches Gallien*, 1 (Munich, 1976), pp. 114–71.

Fayer, C. *La familia romana. iii. Concubinato, divorzio, adulterio*, Problemi e ricerche di storia antica, 22 (Rome, 2005).

Feller, L., A. Gramain, and F. Weber, *La fortune de Karol. Marché de la terre et liens personnels dans les Abruzzes au haut moyen âge*, Collection de l'École française de Rome, 347 (Rome, 2005).

Fichtenau, H. *Das Karolingische Imperium* (Zurich, 1949), translated as *The Carolingian Empire* (Oxford, 1957).

Ficker, J. *Forschungen zur Reichs- und Rechtsgeschichte Italiens*, I (Innsbruck, 1868; repr. Aalen, 1961).

Filson, F. 'The Significance of the Early House Churches', *Journal of Biblical Literature*, 58 (1939), 105–12.

Firey, A. *A Contrite Heart: Prosecution and Redemption in the Carolingian Empire* (Leiden, 2009).

'Mutating Monsters: Approaches to "Living Texts" of the Carolingian Era', *Digital Proceedings of the Lawrence J. Schoenberg Symposium on Manuscript Studies in the Digital Age*, 2 (2010), 1–14.

Firminger, W. K. 'St Peter Damiani and "Auxilius"', *Journal of Theological Studies*, 26 (1924–25), 78–81.

Fleming, R. *Britain after Rome: the Fall and Rise, 400–1070* (London, 2010).

'Rural Elites and Urban Communities in Late Saxon England', *Past & Present*, 141/1 (1993), 3–37.

Foley, W. T. and N. J. Higham, 'Bede and the Britons', *Early Medieval Europe*, 17 (2009), 154–85.

Fontaine, J. 'Education and Learning', in P. Fouracre (ed.), *The New Cambridge Medieval History*, I (Cambridge, 2005), pp. 735–59.

Foot, S. *Monastic Life in Anglo-Saxon England, c. 600 – 900* (Cambridge, 2006).

Fortes, M. and E. E. Evans Pritchard (eds.), *African Political Systems* (Oxford, 1940).

Fossier, R. *Enfance de l'Europe, Xè-XIIè siècles. Aspects économiques et sociaux*, 2 vols. (Paris, 1982), 1.

Fouracre, P. *The Age of Charles Martel* (Harlow, 2000).

'Attitudes Towards Violence in Seventh– and Eighth-Century Francia', in G. Halsall (ed.), *Violence and Society in the Early Medieval West* (Woodbridge, 1998), pp. 59–75.

'Carolingian Justice: the Rhetoric of Improvement and Contexts of Abuse', in *La giustizia nel altomedioevo (secoli V–VIII)*, Settimane di studio del CISAM, 42 (Spoleto, 1995), pp. 771–803.

'Conflict, Power and Legitimation in Francia in the Late Seventh and Eighth Centuries', in I. Alfonso, H. Kennedy, and J. Escalona (eds.), *Building Legitimacy: Political Discourses and Forms of Legitimation in Medieval Societies* (Leiden, 2004), pp. 3–26.

'Cultural Conformity and Social Conservatism in Early Medieval Europe', *History Workshop Journal*, 33 (1992), 152–60.

'Francia and the History of Early Medieval Europe', *Journal of the Haskins Society*, 23 (2011), 1–21.

'Marmoutier and its Serfs in the Eleventh Century', *Transactions of the Royal Historical Society*, 6th ser., no. 15 (2005), 29–49.

'Merovingian History and Merovingian Hagiography', *Past & Present*, 127 (1990), 3–38.

'The Nature of Frankish Political Institutions in the Seventh Century', in I. Wood (ed.), *Franks and Alemanni in the Merovingian Period: an Ethnographic Perspective* (Woodbridge, 1998), pp. 285–316.

'Space, Culture and Kingdoms', in P. Linehan and J. L. Nelson (eds.), *The Medieval World* (London, 2001), pp. 366–80.

Fournier, P. 'L'origine de la collection "Anselmo dedicata"', *Mélanges P. F. Girard* (Paris, 1912), 478–95.

Fowden, G. *Before and After Mohammed: The First Millennium Refocussed* (Princeton, NJ, 2014).

Fowler Magerl, L. 'The Use of the Letters of Pope Gregory I in Northeastern France and Lorraine before 1100', in M. Ascheri, Friederch Ebel, et al. (eds.), *Festschrift für Knut Wolfgang Nörr* (Cologne, 2003), pp. 237–60.

Fox, R. *Kinship and Marriage: an Anthropological Perspective* (Cambridge, 1967).

Frye, D. 'Bishops as Pawns in Early Fifth-Century Gaul', *Journal of Ecclesiastical History*, 42/3 (1991), 349–61.

Fuhrmann, H. *Einfluss und Verbreitung der pseudoisidorsichen Fälschungen: von ihrem Auftauchen bis in die neuere Zeit Schriften der MGH 12*, 3 vols. (Munich, 1972–74), vol. I, pp. 189–91.

Gaddis, M. *There is No Crime for Those Who Have Christ: Religious Violence in the Christian Roman Empire* (Berkeley and Los Angeles, CA, 2005).

Geary, P. J. *Aristocracy in Provence: the Rhône Basin at the Dawn of the Carolingian Age* (Stuttgart, 1985).

'Ethnic Identity as a Situational Construct in the Early Middle Ages', *Mitteilungen der anthropologischen Gesellschaft in Wien*, 113 (1983), pp. 15–26.

'Extra-Judicial Means of Conflict Resolution', in *La giustizia nel altomedioevo (secoli V-VIII)*, Settimane di studio del CISAM, 42 (Spoleto, 1995), pp. 569–602.

'Gift Exchange and Social Science Modelling: the Limitations of a Construct', in G. Algazi, V. Groebner, and B. Jussen (eds.), *Negotiating the Gift: Pre-modern Figurations of Exchange* (Göttingen, 1991), pp. 129–40.

'L'humiliation des saints', *Annales*, 34 (1979), 27–42.

'Living with Conflicts in Stateless France: a Typology of Conflict Management Mechanisms, 1050–1200', in *Geary, Living with the Dead in the Middle Ages* (Ithaca, NY, 1994), pp. 125–62 (a revised translation of 'Vivre en conflit dans une France sans état. Typologie des méchanismes de règlement des conflits, 1050–1200', *Annales ESC*, 41 [1986], 1107–33).

Giardina, A. 'Esplosione di tardoantico', *Studi Storici*, 40 (1999), 157–80.

Girard, R. *Violence and the Sacred*, tr. P. Gregory (French edn., 1972; Baltimore, MD, 1977).

Gluckman, M. *Custom and Conflict in Africa* (Oxford, 1955).

'Interhierarchical Roles: Professional and Party Ethics in Tribal Areas in South and Central Africa', in M. J. Swartz (ed.), *Local-level Politics: Social and Cultural Perspectives* (London, 1969), pp. 69–94.

'The Peace in the Feud', *Past & Present*, 8 (1955), 1–14.

Politics, Law and Ritual in Tribal Society (Chicago, 1965).

'Social Anthropology in Central Africa', *Rhodes-Livingstone Journal*, 20 (1956), pp. 1–27.

'Tribalism in Modern British Central Africa', *Cahiers d'Études Africaines*, 1/1 (1960), 55–70.

'Tribalism, Ruralism and Urbanism in South and Central Africa', in V. W. Turner (ed.), *Colonialism in Africa 1870–1960. Part III: Profiles of Change* (Cambridge, 1971), 127–66.

Gluckman, M., J. C. Mitchell, and J. A. Barnes, 'The Village Headman in British Central Africa', *Africa: Journal of the International African Institute*, 19/2 (1949), 89–106.

Godelier, M. *The Enigma of the Gift*, tr. N. Scott (Chicago, IL, 1999).

Goebel, J. *Felony and Misdemeanor: a Study in the History of English Criminal Law* (New York, 1937).

Goetz, H.-W., J. Jarnut, and W. Pohl (eds.), *Regna and Gentes: the Relationship between Late Antique and Early Medieval Peoples and Kingdoms in the Transformation of the Roman World* (Leiden, 2003).

Goffart, W. 'From *Historiae* to Historia Francorum and Back Again: Aspects of the Textual History of Gregory of Tours', in Th. F. X. Noble and J. J. Contreni (eds.), *Religion, Culture and Society in the Early Middle Ages: Studies in Honour of Richard Sullivan* (Kalamazoo, MI, 1987), pp. 55–76.

The Narrators of Barbarian History: Jordanes, Gregory of Tours, Bede and Paul the Deacon (Princeton, NJ, 1988).
Rome's Fall and After (London, 1989).
Goody, J. *The Development of Family and Marriage in Europe* (Oxford, 1983).
The Expansive Moment: the Rise of Social Anthropology in Britain and Africa, 1918–1970 (Cambridge, 1995).
Grabowsky, A. 'Streit um Formosus. Edition und Analyse der Streitschriften des Auxilius', unpublished PhD thesis, University of Tübingen (2012).
Grafton, A. and M. Williams, *Christianity and the Transformation of the Book: Origen, Eusebius and the library of Caesarea* (Cambridge, MA, 2006).
Griffe, É. *La Gaule chrétienne à l'époque romaine*, vol. II (Paris, 1957).
Guerreau-Jalabert, A. 'La Parenté dans l'Europe médiévale et moderne: à propos d'une synthèse récente', *L'Homme*, 29 (1989), 69–93.
Guyotjeannin, O. '*Penuria scriptorum.* Le mythe de l'anarchie documentaire dans la France du Nord (Xe-première moitié du XIe siècle)', *Bibliothèque de l'École des Chartes*, 155 (1997), 11–44.
Haidu, P. *The Subject Medieval/Modern: Text and Governance in the Middle Ages* (Stanford, CA, 2004).
Haines-Eitzen, K. *Guardians of Letters: Literacy, Power and the Transmitters of Early Christian Literature* (Oxford, 2000).
'The Social History of Early Christian Scribes', in B. D. Ehrman and M. Holmes (eds.), *The Text of the New Testament in Contemporary Research: Essays on the Status Quaestionis* (Leiden, 2013), pp. 479–95.
Halsall, G. *Barbarian Migrations and the Roman West 376–568* (Cambridge, 2007).
'Childeric's Grave, Clovis' Succession and the Origins of the Merovingian Kingdoms', in R. Mathison and D. Schanzer (eds.), *Society and Culture in Late Roman Gaul* (Aldershot, 2001), pp. 116–33.
'Nero and Herod? The Death of Chilperic and Gregory's Writing of the Histories', in K. Mitchell and I. Wood (eds.), *The World of Gregory of Tours* (Leiden, 2002), pp. 337–50.
'The Preface to Book V of Gregory of Tours' Histories: Its Form, Context and Significance', *The English Historical Review*, 122 (2007), 297–317.
'Violence and Society in the Early Medieval West: an Introductory Survey', in G. Halsall (ed.), *Violence and Society in the Early Medieval West* (Woodbridge, 1998), pp. 1–45.
Hamerow, H. *Early Medieval Settlements: the Archaeology of Rural Communities in North-West Europe, 400–900* (Oxford, 2002).
Hanlon, G. 'Review-Article: The Decline of Violence in the West: From Cultural to Post-Cultural History', *English Historical Review*, 128 (2013), 367–400.
Hardh, B. and L. Larsson (eds.), *Central Places in the Migration and Merovingian Periods* (Lund, 2002).
Harries, J. D. 'Constructing the Judge: Judicial Accountability and the Culture of Criticism in Late Antiquity', in R. Miles (ed.), *Constructing Identities in Late Antiquity* (London, 1999), pp. 214–33.
'Courts and the Judicial System', in C. Heszer (ed.), *The Oxford Handbook of Jewish Daily Life in Roman Palestine* (Oxford, 2010), pp. 85–101.

'Creating Legal Space: Settling Disputes in the Roman Empire', in C. Heszer (ed.), *Rabbinic Law in its Roman and Near Eastern Context* (Tübingen, 2003), pp. 63–81.

Law and Empire in Late Antiquity (Cambridge, 2004).

'Resolving Disputes: the Frontiers of Law in Late Antiquity', in R. E. Mathisen (ed.), *Law, Society and Authority in Late Antiquity* (Oxford, 2001), pp. 68–82.

Harrington, D. J. 'The Reception of Walter Bauer's "Orthodoxy and Heresy in Earliest Christianity" during the Last Decade', *Harvard Theological Review*, 73 (1980), 289–98.

Head, T. *Hagiography and the Cult of Saints: the Diocese of Orléans 800 – 1200* (Cambridge, 1990).

Head, T. and R. Landes (eds.), *The Peace of God: Social Violence and Religious Response in Aquitaine around the Year 1000* (Ithaca, NY, and London, 1992).

Heather, P. *The Fall of Rome: a New History of Rome and the Barbarians* (London, 2005).

Heidecker, K. *The Divorce of Lothar II: Christian Marriage and Political Power in the Carolingian World*, tr. T. M. Guest, Conjunctions of Religion and Power in the Medieval Past (Ithaca, NY, and London, 2010).

Heinzelmann, M. *Bischofsherrschaft in Gallien, Zur Kontinuität römischer Führungsschichten vom 4. bis zum 7. Jahrhundert. Soziale, prosopographische und bildungsgeschichtliche Aspekte*, Beihefte der Francia, 5 (Munich, 1976).

'Grégoire de Tours 'père de l'histoire de France'?' in Y.-M. Bercé and Ph. Contamine (eds.), *Histoire de France, historiens de France* (Paris, 1994), pp. 19–45.

Gregor von Tours (538–594) 'Zehn Bücher Geschichte'. Historiographie und Gesellschaftskonzept im 6 Jahrhundert (Darmstadt, 1994). (Eng. tr. *Gregory of Tours: History and Society in the Sixth Century*, tr. C. Caroll (Cambridge, 2001).)

'La réécriture hagiographique dans l'œuvre de Grégoire de Tours', in Heinzelmann and M. Goullet (eds.), *La réécriture hagiographique dans l' occident médieval: transformations formelles et idéologiques*, Beihefte der Francia, 58 (Sigmaringen, 2003), pp. 15–70.

Hermanowicz, E. T. 'Catholic Bishops and Appeals to the Imperial Court: a Legal Study of the Calama Riots in 408', *Journal of Early Christian Studies*, 12/4 (2004), 483–523.

Hesse, H. *The Early Development of Canon Law and the Council of Serdica* (Oxford, 2002).

Higham, N. J. *The Kingdom of Northumbria: AD 350–1100* (Stroud, 1993).

(Re-) Reading Bede: the Ecclesiastical History in Context (London, 2006).

Ecgfrith: High-king of Britain (Donington, forthcoming).

Higham, N. J. and M. J. Ryan, *The Anglo-Saxon World* (London, 2013).

Hilchenbach, K. *Das vierte Buch der Historien von Gregor von Tours: Edition mit sprachwissenschaftlich-textkritischem und historischem Kommentar*, 2 vols. (Bern et al., 2009).

Hill, J. M. *The Cultural World in Beowulf* (Toronto, 1995).

Hillner, J. 'Clerics, Property, and Patronage: the Case of the Roman Titular Churches', in *Antiquité tardive*, 14 (2006), 59–68.

'Monastic Imprisonment in Justinian's Novels', *Journal of Early Christian Studies*, 15 (2007), 205–37.

Hodges, R. *The Anglo-Saxon Achievement* (London, 1989).

Hofmann, J. 'The Men Who Would be Kings: Challenges to Royal Authority in the Frankish Regna, c. 500–700', unpublished PhD thesis, Queen's College, University of Oxford (2008).

Hudson, J. G. H. 'Court Cases and Legal Arguments in England, c.1066–1166', *Transactions of the Royal Historical Society* 6th ser., no. 10 (2000), 91–115.

'Feud, Vengeance and Violence in England from the Tenth to the Twelfth Centuries', in B. S. Tuten and T. L. Billado (eds.), *Feud, Violence and Practice: Essays in Medieval Studies in Honor of Stephen D. White* (Farnham, 2010), pp. 29–53.

Humfress, C. 'Bishops and Lawcourts in Late Antiquity: How (Not) to Make Sense of the Legal Evidence', *Journal of Early Christian Studies*, 19/3 (2011), 375–400.

Orthodoxy and the Courts in Late Antiquity (Oxford, 2007).

Hunter, D. G. 'The Significance of Ambrosiaster', *Journal of Early Christian Studies*, 17 (2009), 2–26.

Huntley, F. L. 'Macbeth and the Background of Jesuitical Equivocation', *Proceedings of the Modern Languages Association of America*, 79 (1964), 390–400.

Hyams, P. R. 'Afterword', in S. A. Throop and P. R. Hyams (eds.), *Vengeance in the Middle Ages: Emotion, Religion and Feud* (Farnham, 2010), pp. 203–20.

'Feud and the State in Late Anglo-Saxon England', *Journal of British Studies*, 40 (2001), 1–43.

'Feud in Medieval England', *Haskins Society Journal*, 3 (1992), 1–21.

Rancor and Reconciliation in Medieval England (Ithaca, NY, 2003).

'Trial by Ordeal: the Key to Proof in Early Common Law', in M. S. Arnold (ed.), *On the Laws and Customs of England* (Chapel Hill, 1981), pp. 90–126.

'Was There Really Such a Thing as Feud in the High Middle Ages', in S. A. Throop and Hyams, *Vengeance in the Middle Ages: Emotion, Religion and Feud* (Farnham, 2010), pp. 151–75.

Imbert, J. 'Indissolubilité du mariage a l'époque carolingienne', *Revue de Droit Canonique*, 38 (1988), 41–56.

Innes, M. *State and Society in the Early Middle Ages: the Middle Rhine Valley, 400–1000* (Cambridge, 2000).

Jacobs, A. S. 'The Disorder of Books: Priscillian's Canonical Defense of Apocrypha', *The Harvard Theological Review*, 93/2 (2000), 135–59.

James, E. *The Origins of France: From Clovis to the Capetians, 500–1000* (London, 1982).

Jarnut, J. 'Gregor von Tours, Frankengeschichte II, 12: Franci Egidium sibi regem adiscunt: Faktum oder Sage', in K. Brunner and B. Merta (eds,), *Ethnogenese und Überlieferung. Angewandte Methoden der Frühmittelalterforschung*, Veröffentlichungen des Instituts für Österreichische Geschichtsforschung, 31 (Vienna, 1994), pp. 129–34.

Jasper, D. and H. Fuhrmann, *Papal Letters in the Early Middle Ages* (Washington, DC, 2001).

Jenal, G. *Italia Ascetica atque Monastica*, 2 vols. (Stuttgart, 1995).

Jenkins, T. *The Life of Property: House, Family, and Inheritance in Béarn, South-West France* (New York, 2010).

Jessen, H. *Die Wirkungen der augustinischen Geschichtsphilosophie auf die Weltanschauung und Geschichtsschreibung Liudprands von Cremona* (Bamberg, 1921).

John, E., *Land Tenure in Early England: A Discussion of Some Problems* (Leicester, 1960)

Johnson, A. P. and J. Schott (eds.), *Eusebius of Caesarea: Traditions and Innovations* (Cambridge, MA, 2013).

Jones, A. H. M. *Later Roman Empire 284–602: a Social, Economic and Administrative Survey* (Oxford, 1973).

Jorge, A. M. C. M. 'The Lusitanian Episcopate in the 4th Century: Priscilian of Ávila and the Tensions Between Bishops', *e-journal of Portuguese History* 4/2 (2006), available online at: brown.edu/Departments/Portuguese_Brazilian_Studies.

Joye, S. 'Family Order and Kingship according to Hincmar', in R. Stone and C. West (eds.), *Hincmar of Rheims: Life and Works* (Manchester, 2015), pp. 190–221.

Judic, B. 'Le registre des lettres de Grégoire le Grand: une création carolingienne?' in J. Desmulliez, C. Hoët-Van-Cauwenberghe, J. Jolivet (eds.), *L'étude des correspondances dans le monde romain de l'Antiquité classique à l'Antiquité tardive: permanences et mutations* (Villeneuve d'Ascq, 2010), pp. 1–21.

'"*totius Europae speculator*": la fondation d'une culture médiéval européene et la construction d'une auctoritas: la postérité de Grégoire le Grand dans la haut moyen âge latin', unpublished PhD thesis, 2 vols., Université Lille (1999).

Jussen, B. *Patenschaft und Adoption im frühen Mittelalter*, Veröffentlichungen des Max Planck Instituts für Geschichte, 98 (Göttingen 1991), pp. 177–98.

Kaminsky, H. 'The Noble Feud in the Later Middle Ages', *Past & Present*, 177 (2002), 55–83.

Karras, R. 'The History of Marriage and the Myth of Friedelehe', *Early Medieval Europe* 14 (2006), 119–51.

Kasten, B. *Königssöhne und Königsherrschaft: Untersuchungen zur Teilhabe am Reich in der Merowinger– und Karolingerzeit*, MGH Schriften 44 (Hannover, 1997).

Keefer, S. L. '*Đonne se cirlisca man ordales weddigeð*: the Anglo-Saxon Lay Ordeal', in S. Baxter et al. (eds.), *Early Medieval Studies in Memory of Patrick Wormald* (Farnham, 2009), pp. 353–68.

Kershaw, P. J. E. *Peaceful Kings: Peace, Power and the Early Medieval Political Imagination* (Oxford, 2011).

Kéry, L. *Canonical Collections of the Early Middle Ages, ca. 400–1140* (Washington, DC, 1999).

Kosto, A. J. 'The Convenientia in the Early Middle Ages', *Medieval Studies*, 60 (1998), 1–54.

Koziol, G. *Begging Pardon and Favor: Ritual and Political Order in Early Medieval France* (Ithaca, NY, and London, 1992).

'Review Article: the Dangers of Polemic: Is Ritual Still an Interesting Topic of Historical Study?' *Early Medieval Europe*, 11/4 (2002), 367–88.

Krautheimer, R. 'The Beginnings of Early Christian Architecture', *Review of Religion*, 3 (1939), 127–48, reprinted in R. Krautheimer, *Studies in Early Christian, Medieval, and Renaissance Art*, ed. James S. Ackerman et al. (New York, 1969).

Three Christian Capitals: Topography and Politics (Berkeley, CA, 1983).

Krutzler, G. 'Die Wahrnehmung der nichtfränkischen Völker in der fränkischen Historiographie', in W. Pohl and G. Heydemann (eds.), *Post-Roman Transitions: Christians and Barbarian Identities in the Early Medieval West* (Turnhout, 2013), pp. 487–547.

Kuefler, M. 'The Marriage Revolution in Late Antiquity: the Theodosian Code and Later Roman Marriage Law', *Journal of Family History*, 32 (2007), 343–70.

Kulikowski, M. 'Barbarians in Gaul, Usurpers in Britain', *Britannia*, 31 (2000), 325–45.

'Two Councils of Turin', *Journal of Theological Studies*, 47/1 (1996), 159–68.

'Fronto, the Bishops, and the Crowd: Episcopal Justice and Communal Violence in Fifth-Century Tarraconensis', *Early Medieval Europe*, 11/4 (2002), 295–320.

Kuper, A. *Anthropology and Anthropologists: The Modern British School* (London, 1973; 3rd edn., 1996).

'Gluckman's Village Headman', *American Anthropologist*, 72/2 (1970), 355–8.

The Invention of Primitive Society: Transformations of an Illusion (London, 1988).

Kurze, W. 'Lo storico e i fondi diplomatici medievali. Problemi di metodo – Analisi storiche', in W. Kurze, *Monasteri e nobiltà nel senese e nella Toscana medievale. Studi diplomatici, archeologici, genealogici, giuridici e sociali* (Siena, 1989), pp. 1–22.

Laeuchli, S. *Power and Sexuality: the Emergence of Canon Law at the Synod of Elvira* (Philadelphia, PA, 1972).

Lambert, T. B. 'The Evolution of Sanctuary in Medieval England', in P. Dresch and H. Skoda (eds.), *Legalism: Anthropology and History* (Oxford, 2012), pp. 115–44.

'Introduction: Some Approaches to Peace and Protection in the Middle Ages', in T. B. Lambert and D. Rollason (eds.), *Peace and Protection in the Middle Ages, Durham Medieval and Renaissance Monographs and Essays*, 1 (Durham, 2009), pp. 1–16.

Landau, P. 'Die Breviatio canonum des Ferrandus in der Geschichte des kanonischen Rechts. Zugleich nochmals zur Benutzung der Dionysiana bei Gratian', in H. Zapp, A. Weiß, and S. Korta (eds.), *Ius canonicum in Oriente et Occidente*, Adnotationes in ius canonicum, 25 (Frankfurt am Main, 2003), pp. 297–309.

Lauranson-Rosaz, C. 'Peace from the Mountains: the Auvergnat Origins of the Peace of God', in Head and Landes (eds.), *The Peace of God: Social Violence and Religious Response in France around the Year 1000* (Ithaca, NY, 1992), pp. 104–34.

Le Goff, J. *L'Imaginaire medieval* (Paris, 1985).

Lehmann, P. 'Mittelalterliche Beinahmen und Ehrentitel', *Historisches Jahrbuch*, 49 (1929), 215–39.

Le Jan, R. *Famille et pouvoir dans le monde franc (viie-xe siècle). Essai d'anthropologie sociale* (Paris, 1995).

'Introduction', in *Les transferts patrimoniaux en Europe occidentale, VIIIe-Xe siècle, I, Mélanges de l'École Française de Rome. Moyen Âge*, 111/2 (1999), 489–97.

Lévi-Strauss, C. *Les structures élémentaires de la parenté* (Paris, 1949), Eng. tr. 1969.

Leys, R. 'How Did Fear Become a Scientific Object and What Kind of Object is It?', *Representations*, 110 (2010), 66–104. See also M. Sahlins, *The Use and Abuse of Biology: an Anthropological Critique of Sociobiology* (Ann Arbor, MI, 1976).

'The Turn to Affect: a Critique', *Critical Inquiry*, 37 (2011), 434–72.

Leyser, C. 'Augustine in the Latin West, 430-c. 900', in Mark Vessey (ed.), *A Companion to Augustine*, Blackwell Companions to the Ancient World (Oxford, 2012), pp. 450–64.

Authority and Asceticism from Augustine to Gregory the Great (Oxford, 2000).

'Charisma in the Archives: Roman Monasteries and the Memory of Gregory the Great, c. 870 – c. 940', in W. Pohl and F. de Rubeis (eds.), *Le scritture dai monasteri, II Seminario internazionale di studio 'I monasteri nell'alto medioevo* (Rome, 2003), pp. 207–26.

'"A church in the house of the saints": Property and Power in the Passion of John and Paul', in K. Cooper and J. Hillner (eds.), *Religion, Dynasty, and Patronage in Early Christian Rome, 300–900* (Cambridge, 2007), pp. 140–62.

'Divine power flowed from this book: Ascetic Language and Episcopal Authority in Gregory of Tours' *Life of the Fathers*', in K. Mitchell and I. N. Wood (eds.), *The World of Gregory of Tours* (Leiden, 2002), pp. 281–94.

'Episcopal Office in the Italy of Liudprand of Cremona, c. 890-c.970', *English Historical Review*, 125 (2010), 795–817.

'From Maternal Kin to Jesus as Mother: Royal Genealogy and Marian Devotion in the Ninth-Century West', in C. Leyser and L. Smith (eds.), *Motherhood, Religion, and Society in Medieval Europe, 400–1400* (Farnham, 2011), pp. 21–39.

'Late Antiquity in the Medieval West', in P. Rousseau (ed.), *A Companion to Late Antiquity, Blackwell Companions to the Ancient World* (Oxford, 2009), pp. 29–42.

'The Memory of Pope Gregory the Great in the Ninth Century: a Redating of the Interpolator's *Vita Gregorii* (*BHL* 3640)', in F. Santo (ed.), *Gregorio magno e le origini dell' Europa, Atti del convegno internazionale, Firenze, 13–17 maggio 2006* (Florence, 2014), pp. 51–64.

Leyser, K. J. 'The Ascent of Latin Europe' in K. J. Leyser, *Communications and Power in the Early Middle Ages*, 2 vols., ed. T. Reuter (London, 1994), I, pp. 215–32.

'Ends and Means in Liudprand of Cremona', in Leyser, *Communications and Power* I, pp. 125–42.

Rule and Conflict in an Early Medieval Society: Ottonian Saxony (London, 1979).

Liebeschuetz, W. 'The Birth of Late Antiquity', *Antiquitè Tardive*, 12 (2004), 253–61.

Lindemans, S. 'Auxilius et le manuscrit Vallicellian Tomus XVIII', *Revue d'histoire écclesiastique*, lvii (1962), 470–84.

Little, L. K. *Benedictine Maledictions: Liturgical Cursing in Romanesque France* (Ithaca, NY, and London, 1993).

Lohrmann, D., *Das Register Papst Johannes' VIII* (Tübingen, 1968).

Loseby, S. 'Marseille: A late antique success story', *Journal of Roman Studies* 82 (1992), 165–85

Luijendijk, A. *Greetings in the Lord: Early Christians and the Oxyrhynchus Papyri* (Cambridge, MA, 2008).

MacDonald, M. Y. *Early Christian Women and Pagan Opinion: the Power of the Hysterical Woman* (Cambridge, 1996).

McKitterick, R. 'Perceptions of Justice in Western Europe in the Ninth and Tenth Centuries', in *La giustizia nell'alto medioevo (secoli IX-XI)*, Settimane di studio del CISAM 44 (Spoleto, 1997), pp. 1075–102.

MacMullen, R. *Corruption and the Decline of Rome* (New Haven, CT, 1988).

Macy, G. *The Hidden History of Women's Ordination* (Oxford, 2008).

Madigan, K. and C. Osiek (eds.), *Ordained Women in the Early Church: a Documentary History* (Baltimore, MD, 2005).

Magnou-Nortier, E. 'Note sur l'expression "iustitiam facere" dans les capitulaires carolingiens', in C. Lepelley et al. (eds.), *Haut moyen age: culture, éducation et société. Études offerts à Pierre Riché* (Paris, 1990), pp. 249–64.

Manaresi, C. 'Della non esistenza di processi apparenti nel territorio del Regno', *Rivista di storia del diritto italiano*, 23 (1950), 179–217; 24 (1951), 7–45.

Markus, R. A. *Bede and the Traditions of Ecclesiastical History* (Jarrow, 1975).

Gregory the Great and his World (Cambridge, 1997).

'Gregory the Great's Europe', *Transactions of the Royal Historical Society*, 5th ser. 31 (1981), 21–36.

'Gregory the Great's Rector and his Genesis', in J. Fontaine, R. Gillet, and S. Pellistrandi (eds.), *Grégoire le Grand*, Colloques internationaux du Centre National de la Recherche Scientifique, Centre culturel les Fontaines, 15–19 septembre 1982 (Paris, 1986), pp. 137–46.

'The Problem of Self-Definition: From Sect to Church', in E. P. Sanders (ed.), *Jewish and Christian Self-Definition. Vol. 1: The Shaping of Christianity in the Second and Third Centuries* (Philadelphia, PA, 1980), pp. 1–15.

Marrocchi, M. 'Scritture documentarie e librarie per la storia di S. Salvatore al Monte Amiata (secc. XI-XIII)', *Quellen und Forschungen aus Italienischen Archiven und Bibliotheken*, 88 (2008), 34–60.

Mason, E. 'Rocamadour in Quercy above all other churches': the Healing of Henry II', in W. J. Sheils (ed.), *The Church and Healing*, Studies in Church History, 19 (Oxford, 1982), pp. 39–54.

Mathisen, R. W. *Ecclesiastical Factionalism and Religious Controversy in Fifth-Century Gaul* (Washington, DC, 1989).

Matthews, J. *Western Aristocracies and Imperial Court, 360–425* (Oxford, 1975).

Mayr-Harting, H. M. R. E 'Functions of a Twelfth-Century Recluse', *History*, 60 (1975), 337–52.

'Two Conversions to Christianity: the Bulgarians and the Anglo-Saxons', *The Stenton Lecture 1993* (Reading, 1994).

McClure, J. 'Bede's Old Testament Kings', in P. Wormald with D. Bullough and R. Collins (eds.), *Ideal and Reality in Frankish and Anglo-Saxon Society: Studies Presented to J. M. Wallace-Hadrill* (Oxford, 1983), pp. 76–98.

McLynn, N. B. *Ambrose of Milan: Church and Court in a Christian Capital* (Berkeley and Los Angeles, CA, 1994).

Meens, R. 'In the Mirror of Eusebius: the Episcopal Identity of Atto of Vercelli', both in R. Corradini, M. Gillis, R. McKitterick, and I. van Renswoude (eds.), *Ego-Trouble: Authors and their Identities in the Early Middle Ages* (Vienna, 2010), pp. 243–48.

Mengozzi, G. *Ricerche sull'attività della scuola di Pavia nell'alto Medio Evo* (Pavia, 1924).

Merdinger, J. E. *Rome and the African Church in the Time of Augustine* (London, 1997).

Metzger, B. M. *The Canon of the New Testament: Its Origin, Development, and Significance* (Oxford, 1997).

Meyvaert, P. 'Le "Libellus responsionum" à Augustin de Cantorbéry: une oeuvre authentique de Saint Grégoire le Grand', in J. Fontaine, R. Gillet, and S. Pellistrandi (eds.), *Grégoire le Grand*, Colloques internationaux du Centre National de la Recherche Scientifique, Centre culturel les Fontaines, 15–19 septembre 1982 (Paris, 1986), pp. 543–50.

Millar, F. *The Emperor in the Roman World (31 BC-AD 337)* (London, 1977).

Miller, W. I. *Bloodtaking and Peacemaking: Feud, Law, and Society in Saga Iceland* (Chicago, IL, 1990).

'Choosing the Avenger: Some Aspects of the Bloodfeud in Medieval Iceland and England', *Law and History Review*, 1 (1983), 159–204.

Eye for an Eye (New York, 2006).

'Getting a Fix on Violence', in *Miller (ed.),* Humiliation and Other Essays on Honor, Social Discomfort, and Violence (Ithaca, NY, 1993), pp. 53–92.

Momigliano, A. 'Christianity and the Decline of Empire', in Momigliano (ed.), *The Conflict between Paganism and Christianity in the Fourth Century* (Oxford, 1963), pp. 1–16.

Mommsen, T. 'Die Papstbriefe bei Beda', *Neues Archiv*, 17 (1892), 387–96.

Mordek, H. *Kirchenrecht und Reform im Frankenreich.* Die collectio Vetus Gallica, *die älteste systematische Kanonensammlung des Fränkischen Gallien. Studien und Edition*, Beiträge zur Geschichte und Quellenkunde des Mittelalters, 1 (Berlin and New York, 1975).

Moore, R.I. 'Les albigeois d'après les chroniques angevines', *La croisade albigeoise. Colloque de Carcassonne CEC octobre 2002* (Carcassonne, 2004), pp. 81–90.

'Family, Community and Cult on the Eve of the Gregorian Reform', *Transactions of the Royal Historical Society*, 5th ser., no. 30 (1980), 49–79.

The First European Revolution, c. 970 – 1215 (Oxford, 2000).

'Heresy as Politics and the Politics of Heresy, 1022–1180', in R. Mazo Karras, J. Kaye, and E. A. Matter (eds.), *Law and the Illicit in Medieval Europe* (Philadelphia, PA, 2008), pp. 33–46.

'Medieval Europe in World History', in C. Lansing and E. English (eds.), *A Companion to the Medieval World* (Chichester, 2009), pp. 563–80.

'Popular Heresy and Popular Violence, 1022–1179', in W. J. Sheils (ed.), *Toleration and Persecution, Studies in Church History*, 21 (Oxford, 1984), pp. 43–50.

'Ranulf Flambard and Christina of Markyate', in R. Gameson and H. Leyser (eds.), *Belief and Culture in the Middle Ages: Studies presented to Henry Mayr-Harting* (Oxford, 2001), pp. 231–5.

The War on Heresy: Faith and Power in Medieval Europe (London, 2012).

Moore, S. F. 'Legal Liability and Evolutionary Interpretation: Some Aspects of Strict Liability, Self-Help and Collective Responsibility', in M. Gluckman (ed.), *The Allocation of Responsibility* (Manchester, 1972), pp. 51–107.

Mor, C. *Una piccola collezione di testi gregoriani del secolo VIII, in Etudes d'histoire du droit canonique dédieés à Gabriel Le Bras*, 2 vols (Paris 1965), pp. 283–91.

Moreira, I. *Dreams, Visions, and Spiritual Authority in Merovingian Gaul* (Ithaca, NY, 2000).

Morris, C. 'Judicium Dei: the Social and Political Significance of the Ordeal in the Eleventh Century', in D. Baker (ed.), *Church Society and Politics*, Studies in Church History, 12 (Oxford, 1973), pp. 95–111.

Mostert, M. 'Forgery and Trust', in P. Schulta et al. (eds.), *Strategies of Writing* (Turnhout, 2008), pp. 35–59.

Mottahedeh, R. *Loyalty and Leadership in an Early Islamic Society*, rev. edn. (London, 2001).

Mousourakis, G. *The Historical and Institutional Context of Roman Law* (Aldershot, 2003).

Muir, E. *Ritual in Early Modern Europe*, 2nd edn. (Cambridge, 2005).

Munier, C. 'L'échec du mariage dans l'église ancienne', *Revue de droit canonique*, 38 (1988), 26–40.

'La tradition littéraire des canons africains (345–525)', *Recherches Augustiniennes*, 10 (1975), 1–22.

Murray, A. C. 'Chronology and Composition of the Histories of Gregory of Tours', *Journal of Late Antiquity*, 1 (2008), 157–74.

(ed.) *Companion to Gregory of Tours* (Leiden, forthcoming).

Nadel, S. F. *The Nuba* (London, 1948).

Nader, L. *Harmony Ideology: Justice and Control in a Zapotec Mountain Village* (Stanford, CA, 1990).

Nathan, G. S. *The Family in Late Antiquity: the Rise of Christianity and the Endurance of Tradition* (London and New York, 2000).

Nautin, P. 'Le canon du concile d'Arles de 314 sur le remariage après divorce', *Recherches de Science Religieuse*, 61 (1973), 353–62.

'Divorce et remariage dans la tradition de l'Église latine', *Recherches de Science Religieuse*, 62 (1974), 7–54.

Nelson, B. A. 'Complexity, Hierarchy, and Scale: a Controlled Comparison between Chaco Canyon, New Mexico, and la Quemada, Zacatecas', *American Antiquity*, 60/ 4 (1995), 597–618.

Nelson, J. L. 'Dispute Settlement in Carolingian West Francia', in W. Davies and P. Fouracre (eds.), *The Settlement of Disputes in Early Medieval Europe* (Cambridge, 1986), pp. 45–64.

'Introduction', in W. Davies, W. and P. Fouracre (eds.), *The Languages of Gift in the Early Middle Ages* (Cambridge, 2010), pp. 1–17.

Review of *The Peace of God*, ed. T. Head, R. Landes (1992), *Speculum*, 60 (1994), 163–9.

Netterstrøm, J. B. and B. Poulson (eds.), *Feud in Medieval and Early Modern Europe* (Aarhus, 2007), pp. 9–67.

Nicolaj, G. 'Formulari e nuovo formalismo nei processi del Regnum Italiae', in *La giustizia nell'alto medioevo (secoli IX-XI)*, Settimane di studio del CISAM XLIV (Spoleto, 1997), pp. 347–79.

Olsen, G. 'Bede as Historian: The Evidence from his Observations on the Life of the First Christian Community at Jerusalem', *Journal of Ecclesiastical History*, 33 (1982), 519–30.

Oosthuizen, S. 'Medieval Field Systems and Settlement Nucleation: Common or Separate Origins?' both in N. J. Higham and M. J. Ryan (eds.), *The Landscape Archaeology of Anglo-Saxon England* (Woodbridge, 2010), pp. 107–31.

Pagels, E. *The Gnostic Gospels* (New York, 1979).

Palanque, J. R. 'Les dissensions des Églises des Gaules à la fin du IVe siècle et la date du concile du Turin', *Revue d'Histoire de l'Église*, 21 (1934), 481–501.

Patzold, S. *Episcopus. Wissen über Bischöfe im Frankenreich des späten 8. bis frühen 10. Jahrhunderts* (Ostfildern, 2008).

'Zur Sozialstruktur des Episkopats und zur Ausbildung bischöflicher Herrschaft in Gallien zwischen Spätantike und Frühmittelalter', in M. Becher and S. Dick (eds.), *Völker, Reiche und Namen im frühen Mittelalter, Festschrift für Jörg Jarnut* (München, 2010), pp. 121–40.

Pegg, M. *The Corruption of Angels: The Great Inquisition of 1245–6* (Princeton, NJ, 2001).

Pestell, T. and K. Ulmschneider (eds.), *Markets in Medieval Europe: Trading and Productive Sites, 650–850* (Macclesfield, 2003).

Peters, L. E. 'Some Structural Aspects of the Feud among the Camel-Herding Bedouin of Cyrenaica', *Africa*, 37 (1967), 261–82.

Petracco Sicardi, G. (ed.), 'Indicazioni etniche germaniche nelle carte altomedievali piacentine', *Archivio storico per le provincie parmensi*, 4a ser., 27 (1975), 139–74.

Pietri, L. 'Évergétisme chrétien et fondations privées dans l'italie de l'antiquité tardive', in J.-M. Carrié and R. Lizzi Testa (eds.), *"Humana sapit": Études d'antiquité tardive offertes à Lellia Cracco Ruggini* (Turnhout, 2002), pp.253–63.

Pinker, S. *The Better Angels of Our Nature: Why Violence has Declined* (New York, 2011).

Pirenne, H. *Medieval Cities: Their Origins and the Revival of Trade*, tr. F. D. Halsey (Princeton, 1925).

Mohammed and Charlemagne, tr. B. Miall (New York, 1939).
Pitz, E. *Papstreskripte im frühen Mittelalter: Diplomatische und rechtsgeschichtliche Studien zum Brief-Corpus Gregors den Großen* (Sigmaringen, 1990).
Pivano, C. *Stato e chiesa da Berengario I ad Arduino, 888 – 1015* (Turin, 1908).
Pohl, W. 'Gregory of Tours and Contemporary Perceptions of Lombard Italy', in I. N. Wood and K. Mitchell (eds.), *The World of Gregory of Tours* (Leiden, Boston and Köln, 2002), pp. 131–44.
'Introduction. Strategies of Identification. A Methodological 'Profile', in Pohl and G. Heydemann (eds.), *Strategies of identification. Ethnicity and Religion in Early Medieval Europe* (Turnhout, 2013), pp. 1–64.
'Staat und Herrschaft im Frühmittelalter: Überlegungen zum Forschungstand', in S. Airlie, W. Pohl, and H. Reimitz (eds.), *Staat im frühen Mittelalter* (Vienna, 2006), pp. 9–38.
Pollock, Sir F. and F. W. Maitland, *The History of English Law Before the Time of Edward I*, 2nd edn. (1898; rpt. Cambridge, 1968).
Poly, J. P. and E. Bournazel, *La mutation de l'an mil* (Paris, 1980), tr. C. Higgett, *The Feudal Transformation, 900 – 1200* (New York, 1991).
Prévité-Orton, C. W. *The Shorter Cambridge Medieval History*, 2 vols., 1st edn. (Cambridge, 1952).
Raine, J. (ed.), *The Priory of Durham* 2 vols (London, 1864).
Rayner, J. D. *Jewish Religious Law: a Progressive Perspective*, Progressive Judaism Today, 3 (New York and Oxford, 1998).
Reimitz, H. 'Contradictory Stereotypes: "Barbarian" and "Roman" Rulers and the Shaping of Merovingian Kingship', in N. Panou and H. Schadee (eds.), *Evil Lords: Theory and Representations from Antiquity to the Renaissance* (Oxford, forthcoming).
'Cultural Brokers of a Common Past: History, Identity and Ethnicity in the Merovingian Kingdoms', in W. Pohl and G. Heydemann (eds.), *Strategies of Identification: Early Medieval Perspectives* (Turnhout, 2013), pp. 257–302.
History, Frankish Identity and the Framing of Western Ethnicity, AD 550–850 (Cambridge, 2015).
'*Omnes Franci* und *viri inlustres*. Zur Gestaltung der feinen Unterschiede in den diplomatischen und historiographischen Quellen der frühen Karolingerzeit', in C. Egger and A. Schwarcz (eds.), *Urkunden – Schriften – Lebensordnungen. Neue Beiträge zur Mediävistik. Festschrift zum 100. Geburtstag von Heinrich Fichtenau* (forthcoming).
'The Providential Past: Visions of Frankish Identity in the Transmission of Gregory of Tours' Historiae', in W. Pohl, C. Gantner, and Richard Payne (eds.), *Visions of Community: Ethnicity, Religion and Power in the Early Medieval West, Byzantium and the Islamic World* (Farnham, 2012), pp. 109–36.
Renard, É. 'Le *Pactus legis Salicae*, reglement militaire romain ou code de lois compilé sous Clovis?', *Bibliothèque de l'École des chartes*, 167 (2009), pp. 321–52.
Reuter, T. 'Debate: The "Feudal Revolution"', *Past & Present*, 155 (1997), 176–95.
Reynolds, A. *Anglo-Saxon Deviant Burial Customs* (Oxford, 2009).

Reynolds, P. L. *Marriage in the Western Church: the Christianization of Marriage during the Patristic and Early Medieval Periods*, Supplements to Vigiliae Christianae. Texts and Studies of Early Christian Life and Language, 24 (Leyden, New York, and Cologne, 1994).

Reynolds, R. 'Tenth- and Eleventh-Century Collections in Italy', in W. Hartmann and K. Pennington (eds.), *The History of Western Canon Law to 1000* (Washington, DC, in preparation).

Reynolds, S. *Kingdoms and Communities in Western Europe, 900–1300* (Oxford, 1984).

Rider, C. *Magic and Impotence in the Middle Ages* (Oxford, 2006).

Rippon, S. 'Landscape Change during the "Long Eighth Century" in Southern England', in N. J. Higham and M. J. Ryan (eds.), *The Landscape Archaeology of Anglo-Saxon England* (Woodbridge, 2010), pp. 39–64.

The Life of Bishop Wilfrid by Eddius Stephanus, ed. and tr. B. Colgrave (Cambridge, 1927).

Rives, J. B. 'Magic in Roman Law: the Reconstruction of a Crime', *Classical Antiquity*, 22/2 (2003), 313–39.

Roberts, S. *Order and Dispute: an Introduction to Legal Anthropology* (Harmondsworth, 1979).

'The Study of Dispute: Anthropological Perspectives', in J. Bossy (ed.), *Disputes and Settlements: Law and Human Relations in the West* (Cambridge, 1983), pp. 1–24.

Robinson, T. A. *'The Bauer Thesis Examined: the Geography of Heresy in the Early Christian Church* (Lewiston, NY, 1988).

Rocacher, J. *Rocamadour et son pèlerinage. Étude historique et archéologique* (Toulouse, 1979).

Roche, T. 'The Way Vengeance Comes: Rancorous Deeds and Words in the World of Orderic Vitalis', in S. A. Throop and P. R. Hyams (eds.), *Vengeance in the Middle Ages: Emotion, Religion and Feud* (Farnham, 2010), pp. 115–36.

Rollason, D. *Northumbria, 500–1100: Creation and Destruction of a Kingdom* (Cambridge, 2003).

Rosaldo, R. *Ilongot Headhunting, 1883–1974: a Study in Society and History* (Stanford, CA, 1980).

Rosenthal, J. T. 'Marriage and the Blood Feud in "Heroic" Europe', *British Journal of Sociology*, 17 (1966), 133–44.

Rosenwein, B. H. 'Les émotions de la vengeance', in D. Barthélemy, F. Bougard, and R. Le Jan (eds.), *La vengeance, 400–1000*, Collection de l'école française de Rome, 357 (Rome, 2006), pp. 237–57.

'Francia and Polynesia: Rethinking Anthropological Approaches', in G. Algazi, V. Groebner, and B. Jussen (eds.), *Negotiating the Gift: Pre-modern Figurations of Exchange* (Göttingen, 1991), pp. 361–79.

Rouche, M. *L'Aquitaine des Wisigoths aux Arabes, 418–781. Naissance d'une region* (Paris, 1979).

Rousseau, P. *Pachomius: the Making of a Community in Fourth-Century Egypt* (Berkeley and Los Angeles, CA, 1985), 3–6.

Rowlands, M. J. 'Centre and Periphery: a Review of a Concept', in M. Rowlands, M. Larsen, and K. Kristiansen (eds.), *Centre and Periphery in the Ancient World* (Cambridge, 1987), pp. 219–42.
Rubin, M. (ed.), *The Work of Jacques le Goff and the Challenges of Medieval History* (Woodbridge, 1997).
Rudé, G. 'The Gordon Riots: a Study of the Rioters and their Victims', *Transactions of the Royal Historical Society*, 5th ser., no. 6 (1956), 93–114.
Ruff, J. R. *Violence in Early Modern Europe, 1500–1800* (Cambridge, 2001).
Ryan, J. 'Cardinal Humbert of Silva Candida and Auxilius: the 'Anonymous Adversary of Liber I Adversus Simoniacos', *Mediaeval Studies*, 13 (1951), 218–23.
Ryan, M. J. 'Archbishop Ecgberht and his Dialogus', in A. Rumble (ed.), *Leaders of the Anglo-Saxon Church from Bede to Stigand*, Pubns. of the Manchester Centre for Anglo-Saxon Studies (Woodbridge, 2012), pp. 41–60.
Saar, S. C. *Ehe – Scheidung – Wiederheirat*, Ius vivens: Abt. B, rechtsgeschichtliche Abhandlungen, 6 (Münster u.a., 2002).
Sabean, D. W., S. Teuscher, J. Mathieu (eds.), *Kinship in Europe: Approaches to Long-Term Development (1300–1900)* (New York, 2007).
Sawyer, P. (ed.), *English Medieval Settlement* (London, 1979)
'The Bloodfeud in Fact and Fiction', *Acta Jutlandica: Skrifter fra Aarhus Universitet*, 63 (1987), 27–38.
Scheibelreiter, G. *Die barbarische Gesellschaft. Mentalitätsgeschichte der europäischen Achsenzeit, 5. – 8. Jahrhundert* (Darmstadt, 1999).
Scheil, A. *The Footsteps of Israel: Understanding Jews in Anglo-Saxon England* (Ann Arbor, MI, 2004).
Schneider, H. 'Die Kanonisten und Gregor der Grosse. Von der Collectio Vetus Gallica bis zur Anselmo dedicata', in F. Santo (ed.), *Gregorio magno e le origini dell' Europa, Atti del convegno internazionale, Firenze, 13–17 maggio 2006* (Florence, 2014), pp. 551–76.
Scholz, S. 'Das Papsttum, Roms wirtschaftliche Lage und die Enteignung der päpstlichen Patrimonien in der Mitte des 8. Jahrhunderts', in S. Weinfurter (ed.), *Päpstliche Herrschaft im Mittelalter. Funktionen-Strategien-Darstellunsformen* (Ostfildern, 2012), pp. 11–25.
Transmigration und Translation: Studien zum Bistumswechsel der Bischöfe von der Spätantike bis zum Hohen Mittelalter (Cologne, 1992).
Schumaker, L. *Africanizing Anthropology: Fieldwork, Networks, and the Making of Cultural Knowledge in Central Africa* (Durham, NC, 2001).
Sennis, A. The Power of Time. Looking at the Past in Medieval Monasteries', in A. Müller and K. Stöber (eds), *Self-Representation of Medieval Religious Communities. The British Isles in context* (Berlin, 2009), pp. 307–325.
'"Omnia tollit aetas et cuncta tollit oblivio". Ricordi smarriti e memorie costruite nei monasteri altomedievali', *Bullettino dell 'Instituto Storico Italiano per il Medio Evo*, 106 (2004), 93–135.
Sessa, K. 'Domus Ecclesiae: Rethinking a Category Of Ante-Pacem Christian Space', *Journal of Theological Studies*, N.S. 60 (2009), 90–108.
Sigal, P. A. *L'homme et le miracle dans la France médiévale* (Paris, 1985).

Simmel, G. 'The Sociology of Conflict: I', *American Journal of Sociology*, 9 (1903), 490–515.

Sinatti d'Amico, F. 'L'applicazione dell'Edictum in Tuscia', *Atti del V°Congresso internazionale di studi sull'alto medioevo* (Spoleto, 1973), pp.745–81.

Smail, D. L. 'Common Violence: Vengeance and Inquisition in Fourteenth-Century Marseille', *Past & Present*, 151 (1996), 28–59.

'Factions and Vengeance in Renaissance Italy. A Review Article', *Comparative Studies in Society and History*, 38 (1996), 781–9.

On Deep History and the Brain (Berkeley, CA, 2008).

Smith, J. *Europe After Rome: A New Cultural History, 500–1000* (Oxford, 2005).

Snyder, G. F. *Ante Pacem: Archaeological Evidence of Church Life Before Constantine* (Macon, GA, 2003).

Sommar, M. 'The Changing Role of the Bishop in Society: Episcopal Translation in the Middle Ages', unpublished PhD thesis, Syracuse University (1998).

'Pragmatic Application of Proto-Canon Law: Episcopal Translation', in L. J. Hall (ed.), *Confrontation in Late Antiquity* (Cambridge, 2003), pp. 89–101.

Southern, R. W. 'The Sense of the Past', *Transactions of the Royal Historical Society*, 5th ser. 23 (1973), 243–63.

'The Shape and Substance of Academic History: An Inaugural Lecture delivered before the University of Oxford, 2 November 1961', in R. Bartlett (ed.), *History and Historians: the Selected Papers of R. W. Southern* (Oxford, 2004), pp. 87–119.

Spiegel, G. 'Review: P. Buc, The Dangers of Ritual' (Princeton, NJ, 2001), *American Historical Review*, 108/1 (2003), 148–9.

Stancliffe, C. *Bede and the Britons* (Whithorn, 2007).

'Oswald "most holy and most victorious king of the Northumbrians"', in C. Stancliffe and E. Cambridge (eds.), *Oswald: Northern King to European Saint* (Stamford, 1995), pp. 33–83.

Stansbury, M. 'Source-marks in Bede's Biblical Commentaries', in J. Hawkes and S. Mills (eds.), *Northumbria's Golden Age* (Stroud, 1999), pp. 383–9.

Stark, R. *The Rise of Christianity: a Sociologist Re-considers History* (Princeton, NJ, 1996).

Stock, B. *The Implications of Literacy: Written Language and Models of Interpretation in the Eleventh and Twelfth Centuries* (Princeton, NJ, 1983).

Stoops, Jr., R. F. 'If I Suffer … Epistolary Authority in Ignatius of Antioch', *Harvard Theological Review*, 80 (1987), 161–78.

Strathern, M. *Reproducing the Future: Essays on Anthropology, Kinship, and the New Reproductive Technologies* (Manchester, 1992).

Szerwiniack, O. 'L'Histoire ecclésiastique ou le rêve d'un retour au temps de l'innocence', in S. Lebecq, M. Perrin, and O. Szerwiniack (eds.), *Bède le Vénérable entre Tradition et Postérité*, Histoire de l'Europe de Nord-Ouest 34 (Villeneuve d'Ascq, 2005), pp. 159–76.

Thacker, A. 'Bede's Idea of Reform', in P. Wormald, D. Bullough, and R. Collins (eds.), *Ideal and Reality in Frankish and Anglo-Saxon Society: Studies presented to J. M. Wallace-Hadrill* (Oxford, 1983), pp. 130–53.

'Bede, the Britons and the Book of Samuel', in S. Baxter et al. (eds.), *Early Medieval Studies in Memory of Patrick Wormald* (Farnham, 2009), pp. 129–47.

Thomas, K. 'History and Anthropology', *Past & Present*, 24 (1963), 3–24.

Thomas, Y. 'Fathers as Citizens of Rome, Rome as a City of Fathers (second century BC – second century AD)', in A. Burguière et al. (eds.); English tr., *A History of the Family, Pt 1: Distant Worlds, Ancient Worlds* (Cambridge, MA, 1996), pp. 228–69.

Thompson, C. *Making Parents: the Ontological Choreography of Reproductive Technologies* (Cambridge, MA, 2005).

Thompson, E. P. 'The Moral Economy of the English Crowd in the 18th Century', *Past & Present*, 50 (1971), 76–136.

Toubert, P. 'La théorie du mariage chez les moralistes Carolingiens', in *Il matrimonio nella società altomedievale*, Settimane di studio del CISAM (Spoleto, 1977), pp. 233–86.

Treggiari, S. *Roman Marriage: Iusti Coniuges from the Time of Cicero to the Time of Ulpian* (Oxford, 1991).

Turner, V. W. 'An Anthropological Approach to the Icelandic Saga', in *The Translation of Culture: Essays to E.E. Evans-Pritchard* (London, 1971), pp. 349–74.

Ubl, K. *Inzestverbot und Gesetzgebung: Die Konstruktion eines Verbrechens (300–1100)* (Berlin, 2008).

'L'origine contestée de la loi salique: une mise au point', *Revue de l' Institut français d'histoire en Allemagne*, 1 (2009), pp. 208–34.

Uhalde, K. *Expectations of Justice in the Age of Augustine* (Philadelphia, 2007).

Van Binsbergen, W. M. J. 'The Unit of Study and the Interpretation of Ethnicity', *Journal of Southern African Studies*, 8/1 (1981), 51–81.

van Doren, J. 'The Divorce of Lothar II (860), and the Resignation of Eboo of Rheims (835) compared', unpublished paper.

Van Dam, R. *Remembering Constantine at the Milvian Bridge* (Cambridge, 2011).

van Renswoude, I. 'The Sincerity of Fiction: Rather and the Quest for Self-Knowledge', in R. Corradini, M. Gillis, R. McKitterick, and I. van Renswoude (eds.), *Ego-Trouble: Authors and their Identities in the Early Middle Ages* (Vienna, 2010), pp. 227–42.

Vauchez, A. *Sainthood in the Later Middle Ages* (Cambridge, 2005).

Verhulst, A. *The Rise of Cities in North-West Europe* (Cambridge, 1999).

Vermeesch, A. *Essai sur les origines et la signification de la commune dans le Nord de la France (xie. et xiie. siècles)* (Heule, 1966).

Vessey, M. 'The Demise of the Christian Writer and the Remaking of "Late Antiquity": From H.-I. Marrou's St Augustine (1938) to Peter Brown's Holy Man (1983)', *Journal of Early Christian Studies*, 6 (1998), 377–41.

Vincent, J. *Anthropology and Politics: Visions, Traditions, and Trends* (Tucson, AZ, 1990).

Violante, C. 'I laici nell movimento patarino', *I laici nella 'societas christiana' dei secoli xi e xii*, Pubblicazioni dell'Universitá cattolica dell Sacro Cuore, Miscellanea del Centro di studi medievali V (Milan, 1968), pp. 597–687.

Vollrath-Reichelt, H. *Königsgedanke und Königtum bei den Angelsachsen* (Köln, 1971).

Bede's Ecclesiastical History of the English People: a Historical Commentary (Oxford, 1988).

'The Bloodfeud of the Franks', *Bulletin of the John Rylands Library of Manchester*, 41 (1959), 459–87; rpt. in Wallace-Hadrill, *The Long-Haired Kings and Other Studies in Frankish History* (London, 1962), pp. 121–47.

Wallace-Hadrill, J. M. *Early Germanic Kingship in England and on the Continent* (Oxford, 1971).

Ward, B. *Miracles and the Medieval Mind* (London, 1982).

Ward-Perkins, B. 'The Decline and Fall Industry', *Standpoint*, September 2009.

The Fall of Rome, and the End of Civilization (Oxford, 2005).

Wasselynck, R. 'Les compilations des "Moralia in Job" du VIIe au XIIe siècle', *Recherches de Théologie ancienne et médiévale*, 29 (1962), 5–32.

Watts, E. J. *Riot in Alexandria: Tradition and Group Dynamics in Late Antique Pagan and Christian Communities* (Berkeley and Los Angeles, CA, 2010).

Weidemann, M. 'Zur Chronologie der Merowinger im 6. Jahrhundert', *Francia*, 10 (1982), 471–513.

Weiner, A. *Inalienable Possessions: the Paradox of Keeping-While-Giving* (Berkeley, CA, 1992).

Werbner, R. P. 'The Manchester School in South-Central Africa', *Annual Review of Anthropology*, 13 (1984), 157–85.

West, C. *Reframing the Feudal Revolution: Political and Social Transformation Between Marne and Moselle, c.800-c.1100* (Cambridge, 2013).

Westguard, J. A. 'Bede and the Continent in the Carolingian Age and Beyond', in S. DeGregorio (ed.), *The Cambridge Companion to Bede* (Cambridge, 2010), pp.201–15.

Whatley, G. 'The Uses of Hagiography. The Legend of Pope Gregory and the Emperor Trajan in the Middle Ages', *Viator*, 15 (1984), 25–63.

White, S. D. 'Clotild's Revenge: Politics, Kinship and Ideology in the Merovingian Blood Feud', in S. K. Cohn and S. A. Epstein (eds.), *Portraits in Medieval and Renaissance Living: Essays in Memory of David Herlihy* (Ann Arbor, MI, 1996), pp. 107–30; rpt. in White, *Re-Thinking Kinship and Feudalism in Early Medieval Europe* (Aldershot, 2005), ch. 3.

'The Feelings in the Feud: The Emotional Turn in the Study of Vengeance', in K. Esmark, L. Hermanson, H. J. Orning, and H. Vogt (eds.), *Disputing Strategies in Medieval Scandinavia* (Leiden, 2013), pp. 281–311.

'The "Feudal Revolution": a Comment', *Past & Present*, 152 (1996), 205–23; rpt. in White, *Feuding and Peace-Making in Eleventh-Century France*, Variorum Collected Studies (Aldershot, 2005), ch. 2.

Feuding and Peace-Making in Eleventh-Century France, Variorum Collected Studies (Aldershot, 2005).

'Feuding and Peace-Making in the Touraine around the Year 1100', *Traditio*, 42 (1986), 195–263; rpt. in White, *Feuding and Peace-Making in Eleventh-Century France*, Variorum Collected Studies (Aldershot, 2005), ch. 1.

'From Peace to Power: the Study of Disputes in Medieval France', in E. Cohen and M. B. de Jong (eds.), *Medieval Transformations: Texts, Power, and Gifts in Context* (Leiden, 2001), pp. 203–18; rpt. in White, *Feuding and Peace-Making in Eleventh-Century France*, Variorum Collected Studies (Aldershot, 2005), ch. 8, pp. 1–14.

'Un imaginaire faidal. La représentation de la guerre dans quelques chansons de geste', in Barthélemy, F. Bougard, and R. Le Jan (eds.), *La vengeance, 400–1000*, Collection de l'école française de Rome, 357 (Rome, 2006), pp. 175–98.

'"Pactum … legem vincit et amor judicium": the Settlement of Disputes by Compromise in Eleventh-Century Western France', *American Journal of Legal History*, 22 (1978), 281–308.

'Re-penser la violence: De 2000 à 1000', *Médiévales*, 37 (1999), 205–23; rpt. in White, *Feuding and Peace-Making*, ch. 3; White, 'The "Feudal Revolution": Comment', *Past and Present*, 152 (1996), 205–223; rpt. in White, *Feuding and Peace-Making in Eleventh-Century France*, Variorum Collected Studies (Aldershot, 2005), ch. 2.

'Review: R. Bartlett, Trial by Fire and Water: the Medieval Judicial Ordeal (Oxford, 1986), Speculum, 64/2 (1989), 385–8.

'Tenth-Century Courts at Mâcon and the Perils of Structuralist History: re-Reading Burgundian Judicial Institutions', in W. C. Brown and P. Górecki (eds.), *Conflict in Medieval Europe: Changing Perspectives on Society and Culture* (Aldershot, 2003), pp. 37–68, rpt. in White, *Feuding and Peace-Making in Eleventh-Century France*, Variorum Collected Studies (Aldershot, 2005), ch. 9.

Wickham, C. 'Compulsory Gift Exchange in Lombard Italy 650–1150', in W. Davies and P. Fouracre (eds.), *The Languages of Gift in the Early Middle Ages* (Cambridge, 2010), pp. 193–216.

Courts and Conflict in Twelfth-Century Tuscany (Oxford, 2003).

Early Medieval Italy: Central Power and Local Society 400–1000 (London, 1981).

Framing the Early Middle Ages: Europe and the Mediterranean, 400–800 (Oxford, 2005).

The Inheritance of Rome: a New History of Europe 400–1000 (London, 2009).

'Justice in the Kingdom of Italy in the Eleventh Century', in *La giustizia nell'alto medioevo (secoli IX-XI)*, Settimane di studio del CISAM XLIV (Spoleto, 1997), pp. 179–255.

'Land Disputes and their Social Framework in Lombard and Carolingian Italy', in W. Davies and P. Fouracre (eds.), *The Settlement of Disputes in Early Medieval Europe* (Cambridge, 1986), pp. 105–24, repr. with additions in C. Wickham, *Land and Power: Studies in Italian and European Social History* (London, 1994), pp. 229–56.

'The Other Transition: From the Ancient World to Feudalism', *Past & Present*, 103 (1984), 3–36.

'Problems of Comparing Rural Societies in Early Medieval Western Europe', *Transactions of the Royal Historical Society*, 6th ser., no. 2 (1992), 221–46.

Wisse, F. "The Use of Early Christian Literature as Evidence for Inner Diversity and Conflict," in C. Hedrick and R Hodgson, Jr., *Nag Hammadi, Gnosticism, and Early Christianity* (Peabody, MA, 1988), pp. 177–90.

Wolfram, H. *Intitulatio I. Lateinische Königs– und Fürstentitel bis zum Ende des 8. Jahrhunderts*, Mitteilungen des Instituts für Österreichische Geschichtsforschung, suppl. vol. 21 (Graz, Vienna and Cologne, 1967).

''Das römische Königtum der Germanen', in W. Pohl and V. Wieser (eds.), *Der Frühmittelalterliche Staat – Europäische Perspektiven*, Forschungen zur Geschichte des Mittelalters, 16 (Vienna, 2009), pp. 3–10.

Woll, I. *Untersuchungen zur Überlieferung und Eigenart der merowingischen Kapitularien*, Freiburger Beiträge zur mittelalterlichen Geschichte, 6 (Frankfurt am Main, 1995).

Wood, I. '"The Bloodfeud of the Franks": a Historiographical Legend', *Early Medieval Europe*, 14 (2006), 489–504.

'The "chain of chronicles" in London BL 16974', in Richard Corradini and Maximilian Diesenberger (eds.), *Zwischen Niederschrift und Wiederschrift: Historiographie und Hagiographie im Spannungsfeld von Edition und Kompendienüberlieferung*, Forschungen zur Geschichte des Mittelalters, 15 (Vienna, 2010), pp. 67–78.

'The Foundation of Bede's Wearmouth-Jarrow', in S. DeGregorio (ed.), *The Cambridge Companion to Bede* (Cambridge, 2010), pp. 84–96.

'The Gifts of Wearmouth and Jarrow', in P. Fouracre and W. Davies (eds.), *The Languages of Gift in the Early Middle Ages* (Cambridge, 2010), pp. 89–115.

Gregory of Tours (Bangor, 1994).

'Gregory of Tours and Clovis', *Revue belge de philologie et d'histoire* 63 (1985), 249–72.

The Merovingian Kingdoms, 450–751 (Harlow, 1994).

The Modern Origins of the Early Middle Ages (Oxford, 2013).

Wood, J. C. 'Evolution, Civilization and History: a Response to Wiener and Rosenwein', *Cultural and Social History*, 4 (2007), 559–65.

'The Limits of Culture? Society, Evolutionary Psychology and the History of Violence', *Cultural and Social History*, 4 (2007), 95–114.

Wormald, J. 'Bloodfeud, Kindred and Government in Early Modern Scotland', *Past & Present*, 87 (1980), 54–97.

Wormald, P. 'Bede, Beowulf, and the Conversion of the Anglo-Saxon Aristocracy', in R. T. Farrell (ed.), *Bede and Anglo-Saxon England: Papers in Honour of the 1300th Anniversary of the Birth of Bede, Given at Cornell University in 1973 and 1974*, BAR 46 (Oxford, 1978), pp. 32–95.

Review of J. Matthews, *Western Aristocracies and Imperial Court, 360–425* (Oxford, 1975), *Journal of Roman Studies*, 66 (1976), 217–26.

Wu, J. and Y. Qi, 'Dealing with Scale in Landscape Analysis: an Overview', *Geographic Information Sciences*, 6/1 (2000), 1–5.

Yarrow, S. *Saints and their Communities* (Oxford, 2006).

Zemon Davis, N. 'The Rites of Violence in Sixteenth-century France', *Past & Present*, 59 (1973), 59–91, repr. in Zemon Davis, *Society and Culture in Early Modern France* (Stanford, CA, 1975), pp. 152–88.

Index